The Metaverse Dilemma

The Metaverse Dilemma: Challenges and Opportunities for Business and Society

EDITED BY

CHITRA KRISHNAN
Symbiosis Center for Management Studies Noida, Symbiosis International Deemed University, Pune, India

ABHISHEK BEHL
Keele University, UK

SNIGDHA DASH
Galgotias University, India

AND

PRASHANT DEV YADAV
Symbiosis Center for Management Studies Noida, Symbiosis International Deemed University, Pune, India

emerald PUBLISHING

United Kingdom – North America – Japan – India – Malaysia – China

Emerald Publishing Limited
Emerald Publishing, Floor 5, Northspring, 21-23 Wellington Street, Leeds LS1 4DL.

First edition 2025

Editorial matter and selection © 2025 Chitra Krishnan, Abhishek Behl, Snigdha Dash, and Prashant Dev Yadav.

Individual chapters © 2025 The authors.
Published under exclusive licence by Emerald Publishing Limited.

Reprints and permissions service
Contact: www.copyright.com

No part of this book may be reproduced, stored in a retrieval system, transmitted in any form or by any means electronic, mechanical, photocopying, recording or otherwise without either the prior written permission of the publisher or a licence permitting restricted copying issued in the UK by The Copyright Licensing Agency and in the USA by The Copyright Clearance Center. Any opinions expressed in the chapters are those of the authors. Whilst Emerald makes every effort to ensure the quality and accuracy of its content, Emerald makes no representation implied or otherwise, as to the chapters' suitability and application and disclaims any warranties, express or implied, to their use.

British Library Cataloguing in Publication Data
A catalogue record for this book is available from the British Library

ISBN: 978-1-83797-525-9 (Print)
ISBN: 978-1-83797-524-2 (Online)
ISBN: 978-1-83797-526-6 (Epub)

Printed and bound by CPI Group (UK) Ltd, Croydon, CR0 4YY

INVESTOR IN PEOPLE

Contents

About the Editors	*ix*
About the Contributors	*xi*
Foreword	*xxi*
Preface	*xxiii*

Part A Introduction to Metaverse

Chapter 1 Introduction of Metaverse in Business
Udgam Mishra and Nirma Sadamali Jayawardena — *3*

Chapter 2 The Impact of Metaverse on Businesses
Sridharan A. and Sunita Kumar — *13*

Part B Technologies Driving the Metaverse

Chapter 3 Augmented Reality: Shaping the Metaverse
Ganesan Muruganantham and B. Dinesh Kumar — *33*

Chapter 4 Artificial Intelligence and the Metaverse
K. K. Shihab, Anil Vashisht, Arif Hasan and Astha Joshi — *53*

Chapter 5 Metaverse and Internet of Things: A Way to Smart Cities
Anubha Anubha, Govind Nath Srivastava and Daviender Narang — *69*

Chapter 6 Unleashing Digital Frontiers: Bridging Realities of Augmented Reality, Virtual Reality, and the Metaverse
Arjun J. Nair, Sridhar Manohar, Amit Mittal and Rishi Chaudhry — *85*

Chapter 7 Non-Fungible Tokens and Blockchain: Foundations for a Sustainable Metaverse Economy
Rim Gafsi   *113*

Part C How Can Metaverse Contribute to Sustainability?

Chapter 8 Sustainability in the Metaverse: Challenges, Implications, and Potential Solutions
Poornima Jirli and Anuja Shukla   *133*

Chapter 9 Metaverse and ESG Governance: Addressing Social and Environmental Challenges in the Virtual World
Supriya Lamba Sahdev, Ahdi Hassan, Chitra Krishnan, Jasmine Mariappan and Ivan Salazar Chang   *149*

Chapter 10 Metaverse: Transformative Pathways for Skilling, Reskilling, and Upskilling in the Digital Age
Snigdha Dash, Prashant Dev Yadav, Rishi Manrai and Aditya Kumar Gupta   *163*

Part D Potential Present and Future of Metaverse Technology

Chapter 11 Metaverse and Wellness Tourism: An Investigation on Mixed Reality (MR) Health Care Approaches in the Tourism Industry
Saranya Thaloor   *183*

Chapter 12 Metaverse: A Game Changer for Reshaping the Fashion Industry
Reema Varshney and Nimisha Rana Chaudhary   *205*

Chapter 13 Metaverse in Education: Pioneering Virtual World for Cutting Edge Hybrid Learning Experiences
Seema Garg, Namrata Pancholi, Anamica Singh and Anchal Luthra   *223*

Chapter 14 Creative Synergy: Unleashing the Potential of Artificial Intelligence and the Metaverse
Jasmine Mariappan, Supriya Lamba Sahdev, Chitra Krishnan, Firdous Ahmad Malik and Astha Gupta   *235*

Chapter 15 Good Governance and Implementation
Gaurav Duggal, Manoj Garg and Achint Nigam 249

Chapter 16 Dark Side of the Metaverse and User Protection
Gaurav Duggal, Manoj Garg and Achint Nigam 269

About the Editors

Dr Chitra Krishnan serves as an Associate Professor of HR & OB at Symbiosis Centre for Management Studies Noida, affiliated with Symbiosis International University in Pune, India. She holds a Ph.D. and is a Certified HR Analyst from IIM Rohtak. With over 17 years of combined national and international teaching experience, Dr Krishnan is highly regarded for her teaching and research abilities. Before her academic career, she held various managerial roles in the industry. Dr Krishnan is deeply committed to advancing professional education and has actively pursued rigorous academic endeavors aimed at enhancing learners' holistic development. She has authored several publications in renowned national and international journals and has presented her research at numerous conferences. Dr Krishnan's passion for writing is evident in her six published books with international publishers. She also serves as a member of the review committee for reputable conferences and journals. Her research interests encompass a wide array of topics, including Human Resource Management, Organizational Behavior, Talent Management, Diversity Management, Employee Satisfaction, Knowledge Management, Artificial Intelligence, ChatGPT, and Emotional Intelligence.

Dr Abhishek Behl is a Senior Lecturer at Keele Business School, Keele University, UK. He has earned his second Ph.D. from Indian Institute of Technology, Bombay, where his research is in the area of crowdfunding and gamification. He is a winner of the prestigious "Naik and Rastogi Award for excellence in Ph.D." from IIT Bombay. He holds a rich experience of teaching, research, and consultancy. He has taught subjects like Marketing Analytics, Gamification for Business, Marketing Research, and Qualitative Data Analytics. He has also served as a Senior Manager – Research at Centre for Innovation Incubation and Entrepreneurship, IIM Ahmedabad. His research is in the area of gamification, stakeholder engagement, sustainability, and e-commerce start-ups. He is an incoming president of Special Interest Group (SIG) – GAME of AIS. He is an Associate Editor of the *Journal of Global Information Management*; *Journal of Global Marketing*; *International Journal of Manpower*; *International Studies of Management and Organization*; *South Asia Journal of Business Studies*; *Journal of Cases on Information Technology*; Assistant Editor of *Technology Forecasting and Social Change* and is an Area Editor (South Asia) of the *International Journal of Emergency Services*. He features on the editorial board of many journals like *International Journal of Information Management*; *Journal of Electronic Commerce in Organization*; *Journal of Promotion Management*; *Young Consumer*; *Management Decision*; and *Society* *and Business Review*. He has edited three books. He has published in journals like *Industrial Marketing Management*; *International Journal of Information Management*; *IEEE Transactions on Engineering Management*; *Production Planning and Control*; *Annals of Operations Research*; *Journal of Business Research*; *Technology Forecasting and Social Change*; *Journal of Knowledge Management*; *Computers in Human Behaviour*; *Internet Research*; *International Marketing Review*; *Journal of Enterprise Information Systems*; and *Industrial Management and Data Systems*.

Dr Snigdha Dash has earned her MBA from Utkal University, Bhubaneswar, Odisha, India, and earned a Ph.D. in Management from the University of Mysore, Mysuru. She is presently associated as Professor with the School of Business, Galgotias University, Greater Noida. Her research interests include leadership, organizational citizenship behavior, organizational change, and technology adoption.

Prashant Dev Yadav holds a Ph.D. in Management from MLSU, Rajasthan. He is presently an Assistant Professor at Symbiosis Centre for Management Studies, Noida, Symbiosis International (Deemed University), Pune, India. His areas of interest are the role of technology in improving lives, technology adoption, and the decision-making style of individuals.

About the Contributors

Dr Sridharan A. is a Professor at the School of Business and Management at Christ University, India. He has done his Ph.D. in Marketing. After serving the industry for 30 years, he joined academia in 2009. During the last 14 years, he has published research papers in national and international journals and was twice awarded for best paper at two international conferences. He has published one case study in an internationally renowned journal, "Emerald Publishing," and has three Scopus-indexed papers to his credit. He has also published three papers in UGC Care and ABDC Journals. ORCID: 0000-0002-0753-3585

Anubha Anubha is a Professor of Marketing at Jaipuria Institute of Management, Ghaziabad, India. Her research interests include social media marketing, Islamic marketing, electronic word of mouth, advertising, and consumer behavior. She has published many scholarly "ABS 3 level," "ABDC," and Scopus-indexed research papers in various journals of Wiley, Emerald, Taylor & Francis, and Sage publications, including *Psychology and Marketing, Journal of Islamic Marketing, Journal of Internet Commerce, Global Knowledge,* and *Memory & Communication*. She has been an active reviewer of journals from Elsevier and Emerald. She has presented papers at various national and international conferences at MDI Murshidabad, IIM Indore, IIT Delhi, XLRI Jamshedpur, and Curtin University. Recently her edited book, *Data-Driven Approaches for Effective Managerial Decision Making*, indexed in Scopus, was published by IGI Global. ORCID: 0000-0002-2719-7697

Ivan Salazar Chang obtained a Ph.D. in Psychology. He is an expert in Economic Psychology and Sports Psychology and is a Manager at International Relations of the Chair of Sport of the Polytechnic University of Valencia. He is also CEO Manager at The Next Generation Sports and a Director of the Master's Degree in Coaching and Leadership (University of Valencia).

Nimisha Rana Chaudhary is an Academician and Research Scholar at Dayalbagh Educational Institute, Agra. She has more than five years of teaching and research experience. She has completed her Graduation from Lady Irwin College, University of Delhi, and her Postgraduate from Banasthali Vidyapith and is currently pursuing her Ph.D. in Textiles. She has been awarded a Gold Medal from Banasthali Vidyapith in her Postgraduate work. She has authored three books, published five research papers in national and international journals, and presented six research papers in national and international conferences and seminars. She has one patent in the field of Plasma Treatment of Textiles under the Department of Industrial Policy & Promotion, Ministry of Commerce and Industry. She has authored the book *Innovation and Recent Advancement in Fashion and Textiles* (South India Book Trader, 2023) in the field of Metaverse.

Rishi Chaudhry holds a Ph.D. in Management focusing on HSIDC and Industrial Development of Haryana from IMSAR, MDU, Rohtak, Haryana. Complementing his doctoral degree, he obtained an MBA in Finance & Marketing and an LL.B. from IMSAR and the Department of Law, MDU, respectively. With a rich academic background, Professor Chaudhry has served as both an Associate Professor and an Assistant Professor at IMSAR, MDU, Rohtak, Haryana. His expertise spans various domains of finance, including Corporate Finance, Financial Investment, Behavioral Finance, Micro Finance, Banking, and Insurance and Accounting. He is renowned for his adept teaching in subjects such as Financial Management, Cost and Management Accounting, Indian Financial System, and Business Statistics. In addition to his teaching responsibilities, he has actively contributed to university administration. He has held key positions including Dean of the Faculty of Management Sciences & Commerce, MDU, and Dean of the Centre for International Academic Affairs, MDU. He has been a pivotal figure as a member of the Court of University, MDU, and various other administrative bodies such as UGBOS & PGBOS, Faculty of Management Sciences & Commerce, MDU. His roles also extend to chairing significant committees including the Academic and Administrative Audit Committee, as well as the Investment Committee, at MDU. With a robust academic portfolio and administrative acumen, Professor Chaudhry continues to shape the academic and administrative landscape of MDU.

Gaurav Duggal has nearly two decades of experience and is currently EVP in Jio Platforms Limited. He is an accomplished leader, a passionate problem solver, and a lifelong student. He has written numerous papers in journals that are well-known around the world and possesses close to two dozen patents. He has spoken at numerous conferences, including ODSC, Oracle World, Agile Conferences, and others.

Rim Gafsi is a Doctor in Management Sciences from the University of Sousse in Tunisia. Her research focuses on entrepreneurship, corporate strategy, family business, business management, and innovation.

Manoj Garg is working as a Senior Innovation Lead in Jio Platforms Limited. He has experience of around 12 years in technology and management. He worked for major technology giants like Samsung. He holds a Master's degree in Electronics and Communication. He has multiple international and national grants and published patents and research papers in various technologies. Along with innovation management, he has worked on multiple industry projects.

Dr Seema Garg is an Associate Professor in Amity International Business School, Amity University, Noida, India. She has obtained her Ph.D. degree from Jamia Millia Islamia University, Delhi, India. Previously, she has done her MPhil and

MSc degrees in Operational Research from the University of Delhi, Delhi, India. She has significantly contributed to enhancing scientific understanding by participating in several national and international conferences by participating and chairing technical sessions. Her publications are in the areas of data envelopment analysis, supply chain management, modeling, and efficiency optimization in banking using data envelopment analysis application of DEA in various journals. She is a actively involved in curriculum development and maintaining the quality of assignments. She is a Merit certificate holder from CBSE and a recipient of a National Scholarship for academic performance. She has also received the Best Teacher award from MLA of Delhi.

Dr Aditya Kumar Gupta is an Associate Professor at Amity University, Noida, India. He was a certified case trainer from Harvard Business School and IIM-Ahmedabad and a marketing research teacher at IIM-Lucknow. He has two decades of teaching experience in marketing and international business domains to undergraduate students, postgraduate students, and research scholars. He had been associated with the Open University, United Kingdom, as a visiting faculty. He is an editor of *Amity Case Research Journal*, the Wiley book series, and many journals of repute. He had presented research papers at various international conference levels at IITs and IIM. He had been part of the reviewer board of many journals of international repute. He has international teaching experience with Anglia Ruskin University, Singapore Campus. He was invited to train at Delhi University and BIMTECH in neuro marketing and literature review of software applications. He has been actively involved in training programs, workshops, and FDPs for industry, academia, and scholars.

Astha Gupta, MBA, Ph.D., NET Qualified having over 20 years of experience in industry and academia. Currently working with Amity University since 2010, she is a passionate researcher in the fields of Consumer Behavior, Artificial Intelligence, Machine Learning, and Human Intelligence. She has been session chair and featured speaker at international conferences of repute. She has four books on HR to her credit and has published research work in Scopus-indexed journals. She has experience organizing Springer and IEEE Conferences in Singapore and India. She carries extensive experience in internationalization and organizing conferences in the U.S.A., Singapore, and Australia.

Dr Arif Hasan Ph.D., M.Phil., PGDBM, MBA, UGC-NET is working as an Associate Professor at Amity University Madhya Pradesh. He has over 12 years of academic, research, and industry experience. He was the awardee of the UGC Fellowship for the Doctoral Research program. His area of specialization is marketing management, research methodology, consumer behavior, and retail marketing. ORCID: 0000-0002-2716-7332

Ahdi Hassan is a Researcher at Global Institute for Research Education & Scholarship, Amsterdam, Netherlands, and IGI Commissioning Editor. From 2013 to present, he has been Associate or Consulting Editor of many publications and on editorial review boards. His articles and research papers span many fields. He has been invited as a keynote speaker over 50 times to international conferences. He used modern and scientific methods to study the relationship between the written and spoken formats of various Asian/European languages, developed artificial languages that are compatible with modern English, and scientifically analyzed ancient written material to determine its origin. He teaches English for Young Learners, English for Academic Purposes, English for Science, Technology, and Engineering, English for Business and Entrepreneurship, Business Intensive Course, Applied Linguistics, interpersonal, verbal, and nonverbal communication, cross cultural competence, language and humor, intercultural communication, culture and humor, language acquisition, and language use.

Dr Nirma Sadamali Jayawardena is an Assistant Professor in Marketing at University of Bradford, United Kingdom. She completed a Ph.D. in Marketing and Graduate Diploma of Business Research from Griffith University, Australia. She pursued a BSc in Business Management with a first-class honours from NSBM Green University, Sri Lanka and MBA in International Business from University of Colombo, Sri Lanka. She has published her work in prestigious journals and has been the recipient of several national and international awards, grants, and scholarships.

Dr Poornima Jirli is a seasoned Information Technology professional with over 15 years of experience in the industry and holds a Doctorate of Business Administration (DBA) in Strategic Innovation from SSBM Geneva. She has spent her career focused on driving technological advancements and strategic initiatives within various organizations.

Dr Astha Joshi is currently working as an Associate Professor at Amity University, Madhya Pradesh. She has 12 years of extensive teaching and research expertise in the field of management. She has been awarded a Ph.D. and presented research papers at various international and national conferences and seminars. She has also published papers in various reputed journals. ORCID: 0000-0002-2572-7252

B. Dinesh Kumar is a Research Scholar in the Department of Management Studies at the National Institute of Technology Tiruchirappalli. His research interests include Brand Management, Customer Engagement, Augmented Reality Marketing, and Consumer Behavior.

Dr Sunita Kumar is an Associate Professor in the School of Business and Management at CHRIST University, India. Her doctoral thesis was on brand strategies in retail marketing. She has published articles in various international and national refereed journals. Her areas of research interest include social media marketing, branding, advertising, and neuromarketing. ORCID: 0000-0002-0628-1873

About the Contributors xv

Dr Anchal Luthra is an Assistant Professor, at AIBS, Amity University, Noida, India. She has done a Ph.D., MBA in HR, M.Phil., and M.Ed. She carries a rich 12 years of experience in industry, research, and academia. Her area of specialization is human resource management, data analytics, and research methodology. She has presented her research work at various national and international conferences and won two best paper awards along with the Best Teacher Award and Excellence in Research award. She has published research papers in Scopus and ABDC-listed journals and successfully delivered two industry consultation projects in the area of HR and is also engaged in academic consultation.

Dr Firdous Ahmad Malik is an Assistant Professor (Economics) at the University of People in Pasadena, California. He formerly worked as a research fellow at the National Institute of Public Finance and Policy and a senior research associate at the Jindal Centre for the Global South, O.P. Jindal Global University, Sonipat–Haryana. Dr Firdous earned his Ph.D. and M.Phil. in Economics from Lucknow's Babasaheb Bhimrao Ambedkar University. He earned a post-grad in economics from Kashmir University. His research interests include microfinance, financial inclusion, and financial literacy. His national and international publications in Springer, Elsevier, Taylor & Francis, and Scopus-indexed journals have helped the academic world. Dr Firdous has published six books in addition to research articles. The titles are *Financial Inclusion Schemes in India* – Springer Publications, *Financial Behaviour of Urban Dwellings* – Notion Press, *Asymmetry of Information and Lending Risk Street Vendor Behaviour in India* – Books Clinic, and *Health System in Jammu and Kashmir: Challenges and Opportunities* – Shineeks. His sixth Springer book is *Repatriation Management and Competency Transfer in a Culturally Dynamic World*. His work *Economics of Financial Inclusion* will be released by Routledge soon. Dr Firdous is affiliated with the Young Scholars Initiative to promote research among young people. He continues to promote research by presenting, chairing, and reviewing panels at national and international conferences. He received two best paper presentations from the Jindal Centre for Global South and a best reviewer award from AIBPM Malaysian conference organizers in June 2023 for his relentless promotion of young academics.

Sridhar Manohar currently works at the Doctoral Research Center of Chitkara Business School, Chitkara University, Rajpura, Punjab. They completed their Doctorate in the area of services marketing from VIT Business School, VIT University, and hold a Bachelor's degree in Technology and dual Master's degrees in Business Administration and Organizational Psychology. The author is also certified with FDP at IIM-A and possesses expertise in service marketing, innovation and entrepreneurship, scale development process, and multivariate analytics. Their interests lie in teaching business analytics, innovation and entrepreneurship, research methodology, and marketing management. The author has published around 20 research papers that include Scopus-listed and ABDC-ranked international journals such as *Society and Business Review, Benchmarking: An International Journal, Electronics Market, Corporate Reputation Review, International Journal of Services*

xvi   *About the Contributors*

and *Operations Management,* and *International Journal of Business Excellence.* They have also presented papers and ideas at numerous international conferences.

Dr Rishi Manrai is a Mechanical Engineer with an MBA and Ph.D. in Finance. Prof Rishi has authored several research papers in double-blind peer-reviewed journals of international and national repute. He also has about 40 papers published by various national and international conferences to his credit. Recently, he won the prestigious EMERALD LITERATI AWARD 2020 for his research article "Factors Influencing Adoption of Payments Banks by Indian Customers: Extending UTAUT with Perceived Credibility" published in the *Journal of Asia Business Studies.*

Jasmine Mariappan is a dedicated educator currently serving as a Lecturer in the Department of Business Studies at the esteemed University of Technology and Applied Sciences, Ibra. With a rich academic background, she holds an M.Phil. in General Management, as well as a Master of Commerce (M.Com) and Bachelor of Commerce (B.Com) degrees. She has an experience of more than 17 years in the field of teaching. Her specialization lies in the dynamic field of Marketing, where she has honed her skills and contributed significantly to the academic community. Her passion for continuous learning and research is evident in her diverse range of interests. She is particularly focused on areas such as marketing, E-marketing, and blended learning, where she seeks to explore innovative strategies and emerging trends. Her commitment to academic excellence is further underscored by her impressive publication record. Ms Mariappan has authored numerous articles and papers, which have been featured in leading journals and presented at international conferences.

Udgam Mishra is an Assistant Professor at Tribhuvan University, where he has established himself as a leading expert in consumer behavior. With over a decade of professional experience, Udgam has made significant contributions both in academia and in administrative roles. As an accomplished researcher, he has published numerous papers in prestigious international journals and contributed to book series, enriching the global discourse on consumer behavior and management. Throughout his career, he has demonstrated exceptional leadership and mentorship, guiding various projects to fruition. His ability to blend theoretical knowledge with practical applications has made him a sought-after mentor and collaborator. Udgam's administrative expertise has also been pivotal in shaping institutional strategies and fostering an environment of academic excellence.

Amit Mittal has over two decades of domestic and international experience in academic leadership, teaching, research, consulting, training, and mentorship. His current mandate is to manage the Ph.D. programs offered at Chitkara University. Sixteen scholars have been awarded Ph.D. degrees under his guidance, and he has published over 60 Scopus/SSCI-indexed papers with a number of these included in the ABDC/ABS journal list. He was the recipient of the Chitkara University Excellence Award 2021 (February) for the highest cited author and publications with the highest H-index (Business School category). His areas of research and consulting expertise are International Marketing and Emerging Market Studies, Consumer

Behavior, Brand Management, Shopping Behavior, and Business Research Methods. He is an active resource person for FDPs, MDPs and Corporate Training. He is a member of the thesis review board of several universities. He presently reviews for reputable journals such as *Technological Forecasting and Social Change* (Elsevier), *Public Health* (Elsevier) *Benchmarking* (Emerald), *Technology Analysis and Strategic Management* (Taylor and Francis), *International Journal of Consumer Studies* (Wiley), *Journal of Public Affairs* (Wiley), *Routledge Studies in Global Student Mobility, International Journal of Emerging Markets* (Emerald), *Sustainability* (MDPI), *Management Decision* (Emerald), and *IIM KSMR* (Sage).

Dr Ganesan Muruganantham is working as a Professor in Management Studies at the National Institute of Technology, Tiruchirappalli, Tamil Nadu. He has the corporate experience in Cipla Ltd., and Dabur India Ltd. His areas of interest in teaching, research, and consultancy include branding, consumer insights, and quality management. He has received the best paper award for presenting his research paper in the USA, London, Australia, and India. His research works are available in Emerald, Inderscience, and Taylor and Francis publications.

Arjun J. Nair is working as a Professor with St. Lawrance College, Ontario, Canada as well as affiliated to Chitkara Business School, Chitkara University, Punjab, India. He has completed a Master of Science degree in Hospitality and Tourism Management from Madurai Kamaraj University, an MBA in Human Resources and Finance Management from the National Institute of Business Management in India, a Bachelor's Degree in Hotel Management, and a Diploma in Hospitality Management from the American Hotel and Lodging Association in the United States. He holds professional memberships in several organizations, including the International Management Research and Technology Consortium in New York, the International Association of Innovation Professionals, the American Management Association, the National Human Resources Association, and the Institute of Research Engineers and Doctors (Senior Member of the Universal Association of Arts and Management Professionals). With over 15 years of practical work experience in a variety of industries, such as education, exporting, hotel food and beverage, restaurant management, and management training, he offers expertise in curriculum development, project management, lecturing, tutoring, general management, business administration, business development, staff management, and public relations. He is a strategic thinker who has made significant contributions to training and facilitation, business development, and the operations and management aspects of various organizations.

Daviender Narang is working as a Professor and Director in Jaipuria Institute of Management, Ghaziabad. He has worked on a World Bank-supported project on capacity building in Ethiopia for two years. He has published several research papers in various journals of repute. He is also associated with business firms as a corporate trainer on various financial modules. He has presented several research papers at various national and international conferences.

xviii   *About the Contributors*

Prof Achint Nigam holds a Ph.D. in Marketing from the Indian Institute of Management, Lucknow and is Distinguished Professor in BITS Pilani. His areas of research interest are Metaverse, business (marketing) applications of Big Data, Blockchain, and Artificial Intelligence; Gamification; Sports Marketing, Digital Marketing; Pricing and Promotions. He has published in various journals of repute, like the *Journal of Business Research, Journal of Strategic Marketing*, and *Industrial Management and Data Systems*, among others.

Dr Namrata Pancholi is an Assistant Professor of Strategy, and International Business, at Amity University Uttar Pradesh, Noida, India. She completed her Doctorate in 2007 from M.L.S. University, Udaipur. She has over 20 years of teaching experience in Management. She has taught in several institutions, the most prominent among them is Birla Institute of Technology and Science, Pilani (Raj). She has presented papers at over 25 national and international conferences including Scopus-indexed and IEEE conferences. She has published 25 research papers, case studies, and book chapters in Scopus indexed, ABDC, UGC indexed journals, Scopus indexed books, case centers. She is also a member of the editorial board and reviewing panel of a few journals.

Dr Supriya Lamba Sahdev, Associate Professor, Alliance University, Bengaluru, Karnataka, India, is a certified academician, researcher, and coach with 12+ years of experience in marketing and international business. She had worked at Amity University, Uttar Pradesh for 10+ years. She earned two bachelors and two masters in commerce and education. She earned a Ph.D. in Management on Open Innovation in Indian Food Processing SMEs. Peer-reviewed publications in international and national journals, book chapters, and conference presentations in top management journals improve your research portfolio. She has over 50 UGC and SCOPUS research papers in reputable national and international journals and hundreds of research involvement in international/national conferences. She serves on several conference and journal review/editor committees. As Co-Convener, she has led over four international conferences. She chaired special sessions at over 6 international conferences. She is the Lead Editor for 10 journals. She has given invited presentations and workshops at national and international platforms. She published three patents, two of which were granted, and edited one book as the first author. Head of International Programs, Dr Supriya Lamba Sahdev has shown excellent leadership and a global view in forging international connections. Her academic expertise spans Research Methodology, Digital Marketing, Service Marketing, Marketing Analytics, Gamification in Marketing, International Marketing, Open Innovation, International Business, Trade Analytics, International Documentation and Logistics, International Trade, Big Data Analytics, and Artificial Intelligence in International Business and Marketing. Dr Supriya has championed technical advances in academia throughout her career. She is a leading expert in her field, contributing to research, teaching, and worldwide collaboration.

K. K. Shihab is an innovative and accomplished professional with over 14 years of experience, specializing in Artificial Intelligence, Machine Learning, and Data

Analytics. Throughout his career, Shihab has demonstrated a strong aptitude for orchestrating teams in the end-to-end deployment of AI and ML algorithms. His dedication to driving organizational excellence is evident through his collaborative efforts with leadership teams, leading to the generation of significant revenue for the organizations he has worked with, including major MNCs like First Advantage, Harman Connected Services (A Samsung Company), and Tata Consultancy Services (TCS), catering to different industries spread across geographies. With a Ph.D. in progress, an MBA, and a Bachelor's degree in Mathematics, Shihab brings a unique blend of academic rigor and business acumen to his endeavors. He is passionate about leveraging his expertise to drive transformative initiatives and achieve business success in senior leadership roles. ORCID: 0009-0004-8202-7270

Dr Anuja Shukla is working as an Associate Professor at Jaipuria Institute of Management, Noida. She has more than 12 years of teaching experience with over 24 paper publications. Her research articles have been published in the *International Journal of Information Management* (A*), *Psychology and Marketing* (A), *VISION* (C), and *FIIB* (ABS 1). She has also won best research paper awards at FMS, Symbiosis, and Amity. Her areas of research interest include eWOM, Consumer Behavior, m-Commerce, AR/VR, and emerging technologies.

Dr Anamica Singh has a Ph.D. in Management from the Birla Institute of Technology, Mesra. Before her Ph.D., her academic qualifications included a Master of Business Administration (MBA) from the Indian Institute of Information Technology & Management (IIITM), Gwalior, and a Bachelor of Technology (B.Tech) in Information Technology from J.S.S. Academy of Technical Education, Noida. She comes with a rich industry experience of more than 10 years. She has academic experience and her areas of expertise include various domains of Information Technology and management. She is currently serving Amity University, Noida as an Assistant Professor in AIBS. She has presented various research papers at both national and international conferences. She has a commendable track record of publishing papers in prestigious journals indexed in SCOPUS and SCI (Science Citation Index). Her publications in these esteemed journals underscore the high quality and relevance of her research contributions to the academic community.

Dr Govind Nath Srivastava has more than 19 years of corporate and academic experience. He started his academic career with the Institute of Chartered Financial Analysts of India and served various reputed organizations in different capacities. He is extensively engaged in research and consultancy and has published more than 20 research papers in various reputed conferences and national and international journals, including numerous Scopus-indexed journals listed in ABDC. He primarily works in consumer psychology, neuromarketing, sensory marketing, and public transportation. He is a member of the Centre for Management of Urban Affairs (CMUA) and working on the project "Public Transportation in Smart Cities."

Dr Saranya Thaloor holds a Ph.D. in Mass Communication, and an M.A. in Public Administration, as well as a NET/JRF qualification in Mass Communication.

Her primary areas of expertise in the media industry are mass media research and development communication. She has worked as a professional journalist and is an avid researcher. In both national and international journals, she has published and presented numerous research articles in the fields of media and many other subjects. Additionally, news processing, editing, and strategic communications are her areas of interest. Previously she has published chapters on feminism in entertainment media concerning digital media. ORCID: 0000-0002-4568-2987

Dr Reema Varshney, Professor and Director at Vidya Institute of Fashion Technology, Meerut has been leading the institute for the past 11 years. She is a multi-disciplinary individual with 25 years of teaching and research experience. She has several national and international publications to her credit. She has one patent in the field of Plasma Treatment of Textiles under the Department of Industrial Policy & Promotion, Ministry of Commerce and Industry. She is a convener for the Fashion Design curriculum at Dr APJ Abdul Kalam University, Lucknow. She is also a counselor in IGNOU for an MBA course.

Dr Anil Vashisht is the Offg. Vice Chancellor Amity University, Madhya Pradesh, and Director – Amity Business School. Dr Vashisht has worked with leading business Groups in India, like Reliance Industries Ltd. and Trident Group. He is actively involved in various corporate training and consultancy assignments both at the industry and institution levels. He has traveled across some of the best universities and business schools in the world such as Wharton University, Columbia University, MIT Sloan, Harvard Business School, NYU Stern, and Kellogg's Business School to name a few, and has incorporated some of the best practices in academics and administrative fields. ORCID: 0009-0002-9712-2460

Foreword

The metaverse is a concept for a future digital economy where a virtual world overlaps with our physical reality. Imagine using AI and XR technology to work, shop, and socialize in immersive virtual spaces. Blockchain and potentially quantum computing will underpin this world, allowing users to trade virtual goods and services using cryptocurrencies. Although there is a huge excitement and hope for the metaverse, there are potential downsides. It is critical to emphasize the need for a human-centered approach to metaverse development, focusing on user well-being and ethical considerations. Responsible regulations will also be crucial to creating a sustainable and positive metaverse experience for everyone.

This book, *The Metaverse Dilemma: Challenges and Opportunities for Business and Society*, is an invaluable compass for navigating this uncharted territory and understanding the diverse facets of the metaverse's potential impact. For businesses, the metaverse represents a paradigm shift. It opens new windows for the opportunity of a future digital economy and alternative opportunities for enhancing learning and training through immersive simulations. This book delves into these possibilities and explores the strategies businesses must adopt to thrive in this new environment.

This book also explores the critical synergy among key technologies such as AI, AR/VR/XR in the context of Metaverse. For example, imagine AI-powered virtual assistants catering to our needs within these digital spaces. Also imagine AI-powered AR (augmented reality) solutions bringing new experiences that blur the lines between reality and virtual, creating a truly "Phygital" experience. Despite the positive prediction of the impact of the metaverse on our society, however, the metaverse is not without its shadows. The book tackles the concept of ESG (Environmental, Social, and Governance) within the metaverse, examining how we can build a sustainable and equitable virtual world. Furthermore, the book addresses the challenges and opportunities around NFTs and blockchain technology, exploring their potential as the foundation of a robust metaverse economy. Crucially, the book deals with the question of governance and explores the need for robust frameworks to ensure responsible development and use of the metaverse. In addition, the book confronts the dark side head-on, exploring potential issues around user protection and addiction. It delves into the ethical considerations necessary to ensure a safe and inclusive virtual environment.

Finally, the book presents exciting, specific use cases of the metaverse such as (1) how wellness tourism can be revolutionized by mixed reality healthcare approaches, (2) the potential of the metaverse as a game-changer, reshaping the fashion industry, and (3) the dawn of a new era in education, with virtual worlds creating cutting-edge hybrid learning experiences. As one of the academics who has been genuinely interested in XR and Metaverse and conducted academic-industry collaborative research projects for the past decade, I believe that this book will be a useful guide as well as a good resource for researchers, businesses, and governments who want to explore the Metaverse.

Professor Timothy Jung
Chair Professor of XR, Manchester Metropolitan University, UK
President of IAITI (International Association of Immersive Technology Innovation)
Conference Chair, Annual International XR-Metaverse Conference

Preface

The Metaverse Dilemma: Challenges and Opportunities for Business and Society is a masterpiece book that desires to provide its reader with a complete scope of understanding on the new type of metaverse that is developing at a faster pace. As the chasms amid the virtual and physical lands continue to get narrow, it is urging that we move through the complex universe with innovation and considerate power.

This book has the following objectives:

1. The book seeks to explore the early conceptualization and realization of the metaverse to the current status and future status of the metaverse.
2. The book offers guidelines for actions to key concerned groups in varied sectors, including policy, business, learning, and technology. The book realization level of analysis provides the action strategy at the macro level, while the learning implications from other contemporary technologies give action at the micro level.
3. The book also calls for responsible innovation within the metaverse so that precautions are taken and one feels safe while in the metaverse.

The Metaverse Dilemma is, therefore, a foundational book on the metaverse issue that offers its readers a guide that will grant them a comprehensive scope and wisdom to navigate and exploit technology. We are excited to take you through the book.

Chapter 1: Introduction of Metaverse in Business. This chapter provides readers with the necessary information to comprehend the origin and development of the metaverse. The chapter provides a detailed explanation of the uses and possibilities of metaverse-based virtual and augmented reality technologies in the future. Brands can now engage with customers at a completely new level of interaction through Metaverse, which can't be achieved within current marketing channels. Immersive XR environments may require decision-makers to re-examine customer journeys, demographic characteristics, and customer personas.

Chapter 2: The Impact of Metaverse on Businesses. This chapter examines the impact of the metaverse on the business environment, providing valuable insights into operations, consumer interaction, and broader industry patterns. This chapter demonstrates the suitability of the metaverse in business by presenting case studies and examples of how firms and businesses are adopting metaverse solutions to stay up to date with digital transformation trends. Readers currently acquire knowledge through online stores and engaging marketing efforts that provide an immersive experience. This highlights the significant impact of incorporating the metaverse into corporate operations.

Chapter 3: Augmented Reality: Shaping the Metaverse. This chapter considers augmented reality and its critical role in actualizing a digital experience within the metaverse. Here, readers understand the practical applications of AR technologies in driving digital engagement and the power it holds across industries such as retail, healthcare, and entertainment. This chapter identifies the new level of interaction and user engagement in virtual spaces using case studies and use case scenarios.

Chapter 4: Artificial Intelligence and the Metaverse. This chapter presents the evolution of the metaverse accompanied by artificial intelligence technologies. The presented solutions may assist in creating individual recommendations and dynamic content and enhance the metaverse's immeasurability and responsiveness. This chapter may further be based on the metaverse and touch upon the moral side of AI, like data privacy, the issues of bias, and algorithmic transparency.

Chapter 5: Metaverse and Internet of Things: A Way to Smart Cities. The chapter reveals the application of the Internet of Things into the metaverse and its possible application to the Internet of Things to build a sustainable and smart city network in the future. Occupied with sensors and IoT devices, smart cities utilize the technology to monitor and act in real-time on the data on infrastructure, transportation, and other areas. This section can focus on the benefits and downsides of the IoT application to the metaverse that goes further into daily life and can be interpreted differently.

Chapter 6: Unleashing Digital Frontiers: Bridging Realities of Augmented Reality, Virtual Reality, and the Metaverse. It combines augmented reality, virtual reality, and the metaverse, constructing an image of how such developments run together to impact modern digital reality. The chapter makes it possible to understand how these concepts can coexist and enhance each other more innovatively and creatively.

Chapter 7: Non-Fungible Tokens and Blockchain: Foundations for a Sustainable Metaverse Economy. This part of the book underlines the more in-depth aspects of the non-fungible tokens and blockchain role in the foundation of the metaverse sustainable economy; by employing NFTs developed around a blockchain ledger accounting approach, unique digital assets can safely be sold and traded. The chapter outlines the NFT paradigm and examines how it transforms digital possession and monetization in digital space, particularly in the metaverse, from digital artwork and collectibles to virtual real estate and game objects.

Chapter 8: Sustainability in the Metaverse: Challenges, Implications, and Potential Solutions. The book identified that the environment of the metaverse might be an immensely significant issue; hence, this chapter directly analyzes that topic. Furthermore, it looks at the environmental, social, and economic perspectives of digital consumption and virtual correspondence. The chapter defines the ecological circumstances of the digital world, including the environmental costs of wind or data center possession and workers' servers, to create a better awareness of what an environmentally sustainable metaverse demands. Solutions and suggestions for using the metaverse and the best usage are given.

Chapter 9: Metaverse and ESG Governance: Addressing Social and Environmental Challenges in the Virtual World. In the following analysis, we will explore the relationship between the concept of metaverse and ESG (Environmental, Social and Governance). This examination will also clarify how virtual interaction can affect the social responsibility and conservation efforts of businesses and service providers. We will also discuss how the principles of metaverse can be utilized to encourage socially responsible behavior and conservationism. Furthermore, the analysis will elaborate on how rational and market principles, as well as regulatory mechanisms, can influence ethics and accountability.

Chapter 10: Metaverse: Transformative Pathways for Skilling, Reskilling, and Upskilling in the Digital Age. This chapter covers the metaverse's transformative possibilities in meeting the digital age's various skilling demands and needs. Hence, learning and training in virtuous environments, readers can explore the various virtual exposure and learning experiences that can be employed to gather the necessary skills. It requires creativity, collaborative spirit, and continuous learning exposure linked to individual distinctive learning needs.

Chapter 11: Metaverse and Wellness Tourism: An Investigation on Mixed Reality (MR) Health Care Approaches in the Tourism Industry. The chapter introduces the metaverse concept and how it is closely linked to wellness tourism in the hospitality sector. Hotels and healthcare providers can also use mixed reality for healthcare. Doing so would enable the delivery of personalized experiences and provide health services to individuals while being miles in the sky in an aircraft. The chapter gives insight into the possible advantages and disadvantages of the use of MR in the wellness tourism and hospitality industry.

Chapter 12: Metaverse: A Game Changer for Reshaping Fashion Industry. It analyses the disruptive nature of the metaverse in the fashion sector. Virtual reality has dramatically changed how fashion brands interact with their customers. It has allowed the audience to try out –outfits to determine what suits them.

xxvi Preface

Additionally, people can now attend fashion events in digital rooms. The paper highlights the potential pros and cons if the fashion industry integrates the SR into its operations.

Chapter 13: Metaverse in Education: Pioneering Virtual World for Cutting Edge Hybrid Learning Experiences. This chapter evaluates how the metaverse as a partial learning platform has been tested and found helpful in cutting-edge learning. The chapter explains that people are no longer compelled to arrive in class physically. Furthermore, students would play classroom games and "result in field trips" without having to be physically present in the classroom. The chapter elaborates on the pros and cons of Metaverse integration into the hospitality industry.

Chapter 14. Creative Synergy: Unleashing the Potential of Artificial Intelligence and the Metaverse. This chapter highlights the "creative synergy" between the metaverse and artificial intelligence. In other words, the authors focus on how AI-powered tools and algorithms can assist with content creation, curation, and collaboration within virtual reality. Most notably, AI-generated content and virtual assistants are instrumental in helping creators and developers work faster and push the boundaries of creative liberty. Automated concierges and personalized experiences, as well as automated content moderation and generation and recommendation systems, are among the examples described by the authors regarding the applications of AI in the metaverse.

Chapter 15: Good Governance and Implementation. This chapter provides an approach to good governance and implementation arrangements for adequately developing and using the metaverse. Through different examples and relevant regulatory frameworks, you will learn the approaches governments, agencies, or groups can take to enforce ethical integrity conduct, responsiveness, and reporting on the virtual setup. The chapter also describes the relevance of industry norms and self-regulated systems at the beginning of the metaverse and future aspects, especially content regulation, individual protection, data protection, and information security.

Chapter 16: The Dark Side of the Metaverse and User Protection. The final chapter considers the dark side of the metaverse, which includes various potential risks and threats for a person spending time in this virtual space. Cyberbullying, digital identity theft, and the severe spread of digital dependencies give a complete picture of why user-focused policy and cybersecurity, in general, are so important. At the same time, the part includes several likely actions and steps that can help people and organizations protect themselves from threats and adversaries presented in the metaverse. They include encryption, multi-factor authentication, digital hygiene and self-care, safety rules, and education.

The Metaverse Dilemma is a book that provides a comprehensive definition and editorial analysis of the metaverse era, including its historical beginnings, profound influence on our lives, and innovative approaches that have shaped it.

The concept of the metaverse encompasses the utilization of augmented reality and virtual reality, allowing individuals to navigate digital spaces instead of physically traversing conventional rivers and engaging in face-to-face meetings. This book provides comprehensive information on blockchain technology, including blockchain-based non-fungible coins, globalization, and the ethical challenges associated with online work. The company also recognizes the potential of the metaverse to have a good impact on inclusivity, particularly in the domains of education, health, tourism, and fashion, where they excel. It is necessary to establish a governance framework and implement user protection measures in virtual spaces. This book is well-suited for individuals who aspire to behave responsibly and exhibit inventive thinking in the realm of digital technology in the future.

Chitra Krishnan
Abhishek Behl
Snigdha Dash
Prashant Dev Yadav

Part A

Introduction to Metaverse

Chapter 1

Introduction of Metaverse in Business

Udgam Mishra[a] and Nirma Sadamali Jayawardena[b]

[a]Tribhuvan University, Nepal
[b]University of Bradford, United Kingdom

Abstract

It has become obvious to companies that the metaverse may help maximize profits. The purpose of this chapter is to describe the uses and possibilities of metaverse-based virtual and augmented reality technologies in the future. Brands can now engage with customers at a completely new level of interaction through Metaverse, which cannot be achieved within current marketing channels. Immersive XR environments may require decision makers to reexamine customer journeys, demographic characteristics, and customer personas. The main purpose of this chapter is to present an overview of metaverse applications. Further this section reveals the ways in which the business and education industry can benefit through metaverse applications. Additionally, this section reveals the real-world applications of technology in metaverse for avatar, gaming, and prospects. Finally, this chapter sheds light on the academics and practitioners by showing how metaverse elements can contribute for business processes.

Keywords: Metaverse; luxury; business; advertising; education; avatar; gaming elements

1. Introduction

The first section of this chapter presents the overview of metaverse applications. The second section of this book chapter reveals the ways in which the business and education industry can benefit through metaverse applications. The third section reveals the real-world applications of technology in metaverse for avatar, gaming, and prospects. Finally, this chapter sheds light on the academics and practitioners by showing the summary findings of the recent research studies on how metaverse elements can contribute for business following the conclusion of the chapter. "Metaverse" refers to a collaborative, decentralized digital, three-dimensional (3D) environment that offers more immersive experiences. Put it, it can be considered a cosmos existing outside the real world (Carrión, 2024). The acronym "Metaverse" combines Meta, meaning beyond, with the universe, meaning a theoretical environment connected to the physical world, and is considered the next technological big bang after the internet (Turjya et al., 2024). Soon, the metaverse will become an integral part of people's daily lives, surpassing the limitations of existing communication networks (Besson & Gauttier, 2024). Metaverse is unique because users interact virtually through a digitalized, cognitive being called an avatar. It represents the user's digital self and is interconnected as they would in the real world, but with fewer physical limitations (Park & Kim, 2024). Today, we can catch many giant business houses using Metaverse, and a few: Baidu launched the Metaverse app "XiRang" (Dwivedi et al., 2022), while Gucci Beauty introduced Drest's beauty mode (Gao et al., 2024).

The metaverse is an emerging area in virtual reality (VR) where people can engage in a shared virtual environment, such as VR, augmented reality (AR), and the Internet (Carrión, 2024). According to Dwivedi et al. (2022), the concept of metaverse can be classified into two distinct categories: metaverse as a functional tool, which encompasses applications in office work, social interactions, education, and healthcare; and metaverse as a target, which finds utility in domains such as gaming, business, role-playing, and real estate and the integration of metaverse into various aspects of our lives continues to grow, increasing businesses are adopting metaverse offices to facilitate telework and remote work (Dwivedi et al., 2022).

In this chapter, we examine the potential for Metaverse in business and other fields, examine its potential advantages, and examine contemporary trends and future prospects. The metaverse will revolutionize business by providing customers and companies with the ability to interact with digital avatars and extend their real-life experiences. It is important to note, however, that despite the possible drawbacks, the advantages of the Metaverse are substantial and warrant further investigation.

2. Metaverse: Uses and Possibilities for Future

This section will demonstrate the uses and possibilities for future using metaverse-based VR and AR technologies.

2.1. Metaverse and Business

The scholarly discourse about the advancement of metaverses primarily centers on fundamental ideas, which is fascinating. For example, it is worth noting that the gaming industry has made significant financial commitments toward developing and implementing the metaverse (Behl, Jayawardena, Pereira, et al., 2023a; Behl, Jayawardena, Bhardwaj, et al., 2024a). However, it is essential to highlight that users cannot transition seamlessly and swiftly between different virtual worlds within the metaverse (Jacobson, 2011). With each instance of movement, users begin their experience afresh, establishing a distinct realm with its unique currency (Guan et al., 2024). In addition to the potential for metaverse governance, businesses also analyze the prospect of improving their existing business models.

Several multinational corporations, such as Sony, Nissan, Amazon, Toyota, Adidas, American Apparel, Disney, and IBM, were attracted to Metaverse due to its increasing popularity (Soni et al., 2022). Nissan created its Metaverse dealership to provide residents complimentary copies of the Sentra (Jacobson, 2011). In addition, American Apparel, Disney, and Amazon established virtual stores within the Metaverse platform (Chung, 2022). Reuters established a virtual news bureau in Metaverse almost two decades ago, intending to report and write financial and cultural stories. This initiative was part of the London-based company's effort to engage new audiences via cutting-edge digital technology. Given that this tendency has already manifested, it is not surprising that corporations such as Gucci, Warner Music, JP Morgan, Atari, and Ubisoft are involved. The idea of the metaverse has become very popular in many parts of the retail industry due to the rapid development of technology. There is much potential that the metaverse, with a significantly higher market value by 2024, would drastically alter the retail scene (Yoo et al., 2023). Engagement between consumers and vendors and among consumers can be achieved within the metaverse. It enables virtual product presentations, facilitates collaborative shopping experiences, and allows for the generation of user-generated content, among other creative features (Soni et al., 2022; Yoo et al., 2023).

2.2. Metaverse and Education Sector

It is necessary to note that, metaverse is one of the most implying areas in the field of internet technology which has the potential to revolutinize the education sector (Allam et al., 2022). For example, the most important technological advancements provided and used through Metaverse are adequate to change the future of education sector (Behl, Jayawardena, Bhardwaj, et al., 2024; Behl, Jayawardena, Pereira, et al., 2023). In universities and in secondary schools even, teaching materials can be improved by adding interactive information using VR diagrams, charts and AR based in-classroom tours (Zhang, 2023). This also provides a solution to the previously described problem in education sector as metaverse can enhance the levels of student engagement. In order to expand the scope of physical education, virtual and augmented technologies may be used to seamlessly integrate physical education with virtual learning (Behl, Jayawardena, Bhardwaj, et al., 2024; Behl, Jayawardena, Pereira, et al., 2023). The adoption of the metaverse in education raises important issues regarding privacy, security, digital citizenship, and the ethical use of the metaverse. To be able to navigate the metaverse responsibly and ethically, educators and policymakers need to equip learners with digital literacy skills and the ability to think critically in order to do so (Cui et al., 2023). There are many opportunities for experiential learning within the metaverse, where students can apply theoretical knowledge to practical scenarios and solve problems with the help of immersive simulations and virtual experiences. Through the use of avatars and virtual classrooms, educational institutions will be able to create virtual classrooms within the metaverse, where students and instructors will be able to interact in real time (Jayawardena et al., 2023; Luik & Taimalu, 2021). Virtual classrooms can be set up to mimic a physical classroom environment, with whiteboards, presentation screens, and seating arrangements that are similar to those of a physical classroom. As an example, students are able to simulate chemical reactions, physics experiments, and biological processes in virtual labs, for example (Jayawardena et al., 2023).

3. The Real-World Applications of Technology in Metaverse for Avatar, Gaming, and Prospects

This section demonstrates real world applications of technology in metaverse for avatar, gaming, and prospects.

3.1. Metaverse and Avatar

When considering the metaverse avatars, it demonstrates users based on their physical appearance and have symbolic meanings with regard to the business aspects. Avatars are most of the times the digital representations of users, allowing users to represent themselves in artistic, optimistic, or particularly focused ways (Onu et al., 2023). One such example is "Second Life" which is a virtual environment created by Linden Lab in 2003 is widely regarded as an accurate representation of the Metaverse, allowing users to create avatars, build luxurious homes, and attend conferences. In Second Life (SL), users can create an alternative persona that can be a faithful representation of their real-life self, an improved version, or an entirely new identity. SL users had no limitations when creating their self-representation, unlike other virtual worlds (Richter & Richter, 2023). People perceive and interact with each other in virtual worlds through avatars, which are essential for facilitating the virtual experience (Kim et al., 2023; Turjya et al., 2024). Avatars are depictable digital representations of people or objects that facilitate communication and interaction in the metaverse environment. If VR and the metaverse progress as predicted by the developers, our digital identities will be avatars. For example, it is necessary to understand that, through well-designed avatars, users can express their identities, preferences, and sometimes their life goals, which facilitates self-representation (Behl, Jayawardena, Shankar, et al., 2024; Behl, Pereira, Jayawardena, et al., 2023). When considering virtual events, where forming social bonds and interacting with others are crucial, the high level of user interaction makes metaverse based applications a unique feature.

3.2. Metaverse and Gaming

A metaverse is also known as a shared online community where customers from all over the world gather to socialize and interact with one another (Behl, Jayawardena, Shankar, et al., 2024). It is anticipated that companies who wish to invest in the Metaverse for gaming will be able to develop cutting-edge Metaverse gaming applications, such as those utilizing blockchain technology, 3D reconstruction, AR, the Internet of Things, and artificial intelligence (Behl, Pereira, Jayawardena, et al., 2023). Metaverse games differ from traditional video games by providing extensive player interaction inside an ever-evolving universe, where the distinction between the real and virtual worlds becomes indistinct (Carrión, 2024). The Metaverse game market is projected to experience a compound annual growth rate (CAGR) of 42.33% between 2023 and 2030. The market is projected to reach approximately US$168.4 billion by 2030. The significant expansion of these platforms indicates a shift in how individuals engage with digital entertainment and establish connections with one another. Studying user engagement, particularly continuation intention, becomes highly significant (Jo et al., 2024). Games like the Sandbox, Axie Infinity, Horizon World, SL, Decentraland, and My Neighbour Alice incorporate elements of Metaverse gaming (Bau & Power, 2024).

Metaverse is also known as a shared online community where customers worldwide congregate to interact and socialize (Barta et al., 2024). Companies looking to invest in the Metaverse for gaming can create cutting-edge Metaverse gaming applications, such as those utilizing blockchain, 3D reconstruction, AR, the Internet of Things, and artificial intelligence (Bau & Power, 2024). Individuals can be charmed by the Metaverse because it gives them the impression that they are actually in the world they have visited. They can interact intricately with their surroundings in a 3D environment or setting. Furthermore, the Metaverse offers a lively and extraordinary environment where users can learn, interact socially, work, make money, and increasingly virtually attend meetings and events (Barta et al., 2024).

3.3. Metaverse and Prospect

The Metaverse will ultimately construct a realm encompassing physical and digital domains with a fully operational economy. The Metaverse can accommodate digital assets, virtual content, intellectual property (IP), and digital currencies (Barta et al., 2024). Additionally, it can be completely self-sustaining and capable of continuous improvement. The rapid evolution of technology, including advancements like 5G, AR, VR, MR, and other technologies and devices, has the potential to transform the concept of the internet. This transformation, known as the Metaverse, could create a new form of internet that offers multi-interface capabilities and fully immersive human-computer interaction. The Metaverse can potentially exceed people's expectations and become a reality (Barta et al., 2024).

Various industries, such as healthcare, medicine, education, agriculture, electronics, and other engineering and scientific fields, necessitate innovative automation to handle substantial volumes of data while upholding sustainability. The metaverse is a futuristic technology that surpasses the boundaries of our current environment (Kim, 2021). Leading IT businesses have already acted to capitalize on the Metaverse trend, and consumer brands are also creating plans for Metaverse platforms. Recently, Nvidia CEO Jensen Huang suggested that the Metaverse will be far more significant than the physical world (Kim, 2021). A community-based experience will be created in the Metaverse through platforms that allow users to connect with live virtual events, concerts, and even real-life avatars. Soon, the Metaverse may employ AR, allowing us to view "holograms" of the Metaverse and see the real world's background through AR glasses. The Metaverse will eventually be connected, allowing four avatars to move from one platform to another. Companies may pay developers to create "physical" outlets within the Metaverse, and in some high-traffic regions, "real estate" deals will be costly. The Metaverse is a distinct virtual realm that operates independently from the physical world. However, actions within this virtual domain can have tangible consequences in reality (Behl, Pereira, Jayawardena, et al., 2023b). Additionally, the Metaverse has its self-sustaining economic system that upholds the regulations of the virtual world. Nevertheless, several important questions arise regarding the governance of the Metaverse, including the establishment of rules and the design of its underlying code (Behl, Pereira, Jayawardena, et al., 2023b).

Expanding the Metaverse will result in a substantial increase in investment across various sectors. First and foremost, it will result in an additional surge in the virtual goods market. The present magnitude of virtual goods stands at approximately US$50 billion and is projected to expand to US$190 billion by 2025. Furthermore, it can accelerate the advancement of AR/VR. The worldwide AR/VR market is projected to reach a spending of US$12 billion in 2020 and is anticipated to grow at a CAGR of 54% from 2020 to 2024. In 2020, the total number of AR/VR devices shipped was 5.12 million, and it is expected to reach 43.2 million units by 2025 (De Felice et al., 2023). Additionally, the realization of the Metaverse will necessitate a significant increase in data storage and computing requirements, thereby fostering the accelerated growth of cloud computing. Furthermore, the content or platform builders can construct a captivating virtual environment that seamlessly combines social, entertainment, advertising, e-commerce, and other features. As the user value chain expands, their business value experiences exponential growth.

The year 2021 is recognized as the inaugural year of the Metaverse. Currently, in the emerging era of expansive navigation, humans are endeavoring to enter the realm of digital technology (Jayawardena et al., 2023). The Metaverse is a complex amalgamation of various technologies, currently in its embryonic stage (Jayawardena et al., 2023). However, it is still far from being fully accessible to humans. The realization of the Metaverse necessitates utilizing multiple techniques, including 5G, VR/AR, and cloud computing. Notably, the core technologies of AR/VR have yet to establish a definitive business model (Huang et al., 2023). These technologies have recently gained access to the doorway and pathway of the Metaverse, but the true Metaverse necessitates additional elements (Jayawardena et al., 2023). If the Internet allows for online office work, shopping, and teaching, the advancement into the Metaverse era should involve complete permeation and integration. This entails achieving full interconnection of all aspects of the Internet, technological compatibility, and even the realization of a genuine 3D world (Jayawardena et al., 2023). The immersion experience aims to establish a connection between the physical and virtual worlds, both linked to the Internet. China's top mobile development service provider has recently emerged.

Aurora Mobile effectively integrated the push feature into the self-created game demo on the Roblox platform (Huang et al., 2023). This feature enables the virtual information in the game to transcend the boundaries between the virtual and real worlds, allowing for dialogue and interaction between the two. It also facilitates the development of the "Metaverse" concept (Behl, Jayawardena, Pereira, et al., 2023a, Behl, Jayawardena, Shankar, et al., 2024b).

Within the Metaverse, individuals possess the capacity to partake in activities that extend beyond mere online conversations. Additionally, individuals have the opportunity to engage in immersive encounters within the virtual realm by utilizing technologies such as VR, AR, mixed reality (MR), and other similar advancements. The forthcoming Metaverse will possess cross-platform compatibility and entirely rely on user-generated content (Oh et al., 2023). Users can accomplish tasks and encounter and comprehend the results in the actual physical environment (De Felice et al., 2023). The Metaverse will offer a comprehensive and deeply engaging experience for individuals. Individuals can effortlessly create unlimited virtual representations without any limitations based on location (Behl, Jayawardena, Bhardwaj, et al., 2024; Behl, Jayawardena, Pereira, et al., 2023). Blockchain technology's intelligent contract can be utilized to create an economic system that seamlessly combines the virtual and real worlds in terms of economic, social, and identity systems, ensuring the accuracy and truthfulness of the content. The Internet of Things facilitates incorporating digital technology into our daily routines. In the future, every person will participate in the virtual world called the Metaverse, using a digital identity to generate various sources of income from virtual possessions (Wang & Wang, 2023). They can create, own, and exchange various virtual items. Advanced technology will be smoothly integrated into the human body, manifesting human consciousness in the Metaverse. The Metaverse holds an alluring vision and a promising future (Periyasami & Periyasamy, 2022), but its implementation in commercial applications requires the progress of hardware and technology.

4. Conclusion

VR platforms have not demonstrated a significant number of active users (Wang & Wang, 2023). Despite the expectations of numerous analysts, even more sizable corporations, the gaming industry is anticipated to be at the forefront of progress, with newer games potentially focusing less on gameplay and more on creating social environments (Wang & Wang, 2023). Organizations have a significant opportunity to adapt their business models and operational capacity to function within the Metaverse (Jayawardena et al., 2023). This can potentially bring transformative impacts on marketing, tourism, leisure, and hospitality (Jayawardena et al., 2023). In addition, new VR platforms will emerge from the business world to facilitate instruction in educational institutions and corporations. This is analogous to an actor who embodies disparate roles while upholding a uniform interpretation and employing the same emotions. The Metaverse will only materialize on a significant magnitude (Behl, Pereira, Jayawardena, et al., 2023b).

From a broader perspective, the Metaverse is currently in its nascent phase of advancement due to insufficient technological capabilities, incomplete industry expertise, and the high cost of equipment. The physical and virtual domains will progressively merge through the advancement of communication, cloud computing, AI, blockchain, and other technologies (Behl, Pereira, Jayawardena, et al., 2023). This integration will encompass various aspects of daily life, including entertainment, education, work, and trading, within the Metaverse system. Ultimately, this will give rise to a vast and diverse digital world (Behl, Jayawardena, Shankar, et al., 2024; De Felice et al., 2023). In VR, legal frameworks should operate with the same level of effectiveness as they do in the physical world. Because we are discussing undiscovered virtual realms, it is suggested that a competent supervisory board be established to investigate and evaluate technology's influence on human psychology (De Felice et al., 2023). Given that the Metaverse is relatively new, we can expect specific impacts. However, it is necessary to consistently and possibly in real-time examine the influence of the negative on human behavior (De Felice et al., 2023). This chapter's discussion on fostering opportunities and mitigating risks should have been interpreted as a prediction.

References

Allam, Z., Sharifi, A., Bibri, S. E., Jones, D. S., & Krogstie, J. (2022). The metaverse as a virtual form of smart cities: Opportunities and challenges for environmental, economic, and social sustainability in urban futures. *Smart Cities, 5*(3), 771–801.

Barta, S., Ibáñez-Sánchez, S., Orús, C., & Flavián, C. (2024). Avatar creation in the metaverse: A focus on event expectations. *Computers in Human Behavior, 156*, 108192.

Bau, S., & Power, R. (2024). Diversity in gaming and the metaverse. In N. Lee (Ed.), *Encyclopedia of computer graphics and games* (pp. 602–604). Springer International Publishing.

Behl, A., Jayawardena, N., Bhardwaj, S., Pereira, V., del Giudice, M., & Zhang, J. (2024). Examining the failure of gamification in implementing innovation from the perspective of problematization in the retail sectors of emerging economies. *Technovation, 129*, 102902.

Behl, A., Jayawardena, N., Pereira, V., Jabeen, F., Jain, K., & Gupta, M. (2023). Engaging and motivating crowd-workers in gamified crowdsourcing mobile apps in the context of logistics and sustainable supply chain management. *Annals of Operations Research*, 1–31 (online).

Behl, A., Jayawardena, N., Shankar, A., Gupta, M., & Lang, L. D. (2024). Gamification and neuromarketing: A unified approach for improving user experience. *Journal of Consumer Behaviour, 23*(1), 218–228.

Behl, A., Pereira, V., Jayawardena, N., Nigam, A., & Mangla, S. (2023). Gamification as an innovation: A tool to improve organizational marketing performance and sustainability of international firms. *International Marketing Review* (ahead-of-print).

Besson, M., & Gauttier, S. (2024). Business meetings in the metaverse: Stakeholder views evolve. *Journal of Business Strategy, 45*(3), 178–189.

Carrión, C. (2024). Research streams and open challenges in the metaverse. *The Journal of Supercomputing, 80*(2), 1598–1639.

Chung, J. M. (2022). Cloud computing and edge cloud technologies. In J. M. Chung (Ed.), *Emerging metaverse XR and video multimedia technologies: Modern streaming and multimedia systems and applications* (pp. 279–304). Apress.

Cui, L., Zhu, C., Hare, R., & Tang, Y. (2023). MetaEdu: A new framework for future education. *Discover Artificial Intelligence, 3*(1), 10.

De Felice, F., Petrillo, A., Iovine, G., Salzano, C., & Baffo, I. (2023). How does the metaverse shape education? A systematic literature review. *Applied Sciences, 13*(9), 5682.

Dwivedi, Y., Hughes, L., Baabdullah, A., Ribeiro-Navarrete, S., Giannakis, M., Al-Debei, M., Dennehy, D., Bhimaraya, M., Buhalis, D., Cheung, C., Conboy, K., Doyle, R., Dubey, R., Dutot, V., Felix, R., Goyal, D. P., Gustafsson, A., Hinsch, C., Jebabli, I., ... Wamba, S. F. (2022). Metaverse beyond the hype: Multidisciplinary perspectives on emerging challenges, opportunities, and agenda for research, practice and policy. *International Journal of Information Management, 66*, 102542.

Gao, H., Chong, A. Y. L., & Bao, H. (2024). Metaverse: literature review, synthesis and future research agenda. *Journal of Computer Information Systems, 64*(4), 533–553.

Guan, C., Liu, W., Yu, Y., & Ding, D. (2024). Tokenomics in the Metaverse: understanding the lead–lag effect among emerging crypto tokens. *Financial Innovation, 10*(1), 88.

Huang, Z., Xiong, C., Ni, H., Wang, D., Tao, Y., & Sun, T. (2023). Standard evolution of 5G-advanced and future mobile network for extended reality and metaverse. *IEEE Internet of Things Magazine, 6*(1), 20–25.

Jacobson, C. M. (2011). Virtual worlds and the 3-D Internet. In Information Resources Management Association (Ed.), *Virtual communities: Concepts, methodologies, tools and applications* (pp. 1855–1879). IGI Global.

Jayawardena, N. S., Thaichon, P., Quach, S., Razzaq, A., & Behl, A. (2023). The persuasion effects of virtual reality (VR) and augmented reality (AR) video advertisements: A conceptual review. *Journal of Business Research, 160*, 113739.

Jo, H., Park, S., Jeong, J., Yeon, J., & Lee, J. K. (2024). Metaverse gaming: analyzing the impact of self-expression, achievement, social interaction, violence, and difficulty. *Behaviour & Information Technology*, 1–15 (online).

Kim, D. Y., Lee, H. K., & Chung, K. (2023). Avatar-mediated experience in the metaverse: The impact of avatar realism on user-avatar relationship. *Journal of Retailing and Consumer Services, 73*, 103382.

Kim, J. (2021). Advertising in the metaverse: Research agenda. *Journal of Interactive Advertising, 21*(3), 141–144.

Luik, P., & Taimalu, M. (2021). Predicting the intention to use technology in education among student teachers: A path analysis. *Education Sciences, 11*(9), 564.

Oh, Y. K., Yi, J., & Kim, J. (2023). What enhances or worsens the user-generated metaverse experience? An application of BERTopic to Roblox user eWOM. *Internet Research* (ahead of print).

Onu, P., Pradhan, A., & Mbohwa, C. (2023). Potential to use metaverse for future teaching and learning. *Education and Information Technologies*, 1–32.

Park, J., & Kim, N. (2024). Examining self-congruence between user and avatar in purchasing behavior from the metaverse to the real world. *Journal of Global Fashion Marketing, 15*(1), 23–38.

Periyasami, S., & Periyasamy, A. P. (2022). Metaverse as future promising platform business model: Case study on fashion value chain. *Businesses, 2*(4), 527–545.

Richter, S., & Richter, A. (2023). What is novel about the Metaverse?. *International Journal of Information Management, 73*, 102684.

Soni, S., Shukla, K., Yadav, U., & Ahluwalia, H. S. (2022). Virtual reality in social media marketing: The new age potential. In R. Tiwari, N., Duhan, M. Mittal, A. Anand, & M. A. Khan (Eds.), *Multimedia computing systems and virtual reality* (pp. 79–97). CRC Press.

Turjya, S. M., Pandey, A. S., Bandyopadhyay, A., Swain, S., & Banik, D. (2024). Technologies that will fuel the future metaverse and its potential implementation in the healthcare system. In *Healthcare services in the metaverse* (pp. 1–25). CRC Press.

Wang, S., & Wang, W. (2023). A review of the application of digital identity in the metaverse. *Security and Safety*, *2*, 2023009.

Yoo, K., Welden, R., Hewett, K., & Haenlein, M. (2023). The merchants of meta: A research agenda to understand the future of retailing in the metaverse. *Journal of Retailing*, *99*(2), 173–192.

Zhang, Q. (2023). Secure preschool education using machine learning and metaverse technologies. *Applied Artificial Intelligence*, *37*(1), 2222496.

Chapter 2

The Impact of Metaverse on Businesses

Sridharan A.[a] and Sunita Kumar[b]

[a]Professor – Practice, NSB, Bengaluru
[b]School of Business and Management, Christ (Deemed to be University), Bangalore

Abstract

The Metaverse, a dynamic convergence of real and digital spaces powered by Augmented Reality (AR) and Virtual Reality (VR), presents a transformative frontier for businesses to expand consumer engagement. It offers a three-dimensional web-powered realm where users can immerse themselves in real-life scenarios and simulations from the convenience of their own devices, fostering real-time interaction and uninterrupted business operations. Integrating technologies like VR, AR, Cloud, Blockchain, and IoT, the Metaverse has already made significant strides across industries, providing consumers with unique digital experiences. Businesses can leverage this to enhance their brand awareness, establish stronger customer connections, and provide immersive shopping experiences, making traditional advertising appear antiquated. Major global companies have already embraced this technology, and the Metaverse represents an innovative digital platform with limitless possibilities, rapidly evolving with enabling technologies. This chapter delves into the potential of the Metaverse to bolster brand development and its recent growth, exploring the practical applications for businesses in the near future.

Keywords: Metaverse; metaverse internet; augmented reality; virtual reality; metaverse customers

Introduction

What Is Metaverse?

The metaverse seems to have become the lexicon overnight. But if we go back in history to 1992, sci-fi writer Neal Stephenson created this term to define the dystopian world. Today, when we talk about the "metaverse," our mind immediately springs to a 3D digital world where people experience a blend of work and play and feel a world of real and permanent. This helps individuals to train for and do tasks such as high-risk surgeries and participate in simulated practices like skydiving while feeling the actual physical sensations.

Metaverse combines hybrid and digital space to enhance business opportunities by expanding the consumer market. Metaverse is a three-dimensional web-powered space based on Augmented Reality (AR) and Virtual Reality (VR). Metaverse engages users in the online realm and gives them experiences of all real-life situations and simulations. Thus, consumers, from the comforts of their homes, can go shopping, attend events and concerts, go on adventures and create personal avatars and worlds. The importance of metaverse is that it helps us to do all things in real-time with other users. It has multiple support for businesses, and there is no pause in the metaverse. The users can log in and log out at any time, which means businesses can conduct their programs more efficiently and effectively. The business houses can shape the new world around them. Currently, the greatest advantage to businesses is that they can use any device to access metaverse platforms. A smartphone or laptop will help to enter the metaverse.

VR, AR, Cloud, Blockchain, and IoT are all part of the metaverse.

Several industries like Gaming, E-Commerce, Education, Communication, Fitness and Sports, and Entertainment have already gained the most using digital platforms. The metaverse offers consumers a whole new life experience as they get to live through their digital selves. Businesses can exploit this opportunity to connect with customers by providing enhanced digital services to enhance brand awareness and exposure. Companies can offer various adventures and exciting interactions to create an edge over the competition and potentially generate a new loyal customer base.

Today, media is highly cluttered, and businesses are not sure whether they get any mileage out of their advertisement campaigns. The metaverse is a god-sent opportunity to businesses as it takes the customers through the brands' world first-hand, thus turning customers into activeG participants in the brand's stores and identity building. Customers can explore and look into the qualities being offered by various brands before making an actual purchase.

World's leading technological companies like Google, Microsoft, Nvidia and, more famously, Meta, bet in a big way on Metaverse's growth and success and have invested billions of dollars into developing software and hardware for the Metaverse (Q.ai, 2022). In fact, as per the opinion voiced by few knowledgeable experts, the metaverse market will be worth US $800 billion in the next five years and potentially will create over US $1 trillion in Gross Domestic Product (Bloomberg Intelligence, 2021; Tong, 2022).

The new norm created by the metaverse world is a whole new shopping experience for customers, like virtual shopping assistants and showrooms. Now, users can try on clothes, put on make-up and drive new cars online. Customers will see their potential purchases in 3D and explore them from every angle before making the actual purchase from a real store.

Customers can make real-life or metaverse purchases while on platforms. Hence, businesses can use the digital world as yet another shopping platform to promote, offer, and sell their products.

As per Ball (2022), the Metaverse is a massively scaled and interoperable network of real-time rendered 3D virtual worlds, which can be experienced synchronously and insistently by any number of consumers with a sense of online presence.

The above definition gives way to the word "Metaverse" as a network of digitally mediated spaces that immerse users in a real-time experience. This leads to four conceptualizations of the Metaverse: (1) Digitally mediated, (2) spatial, (3) immersive, and (4) real-time.

Digitally Mediated

Consumer experiences in the Metaverse are facilitated by digital technology. The facilitation implies that consumers use the technology to interact with the technology (using the platform as a channel to interact with others (Hoffman & Novak, 1996).

High-fidelity 3D computer graphics are often used to illustrate Metaversal spaces (Ball, 2022). Though not a prerequisite, Metaversal experiences rely on Extended Reality (XR) technologies like VR and AR to help create and display digital portrayals of space, objects and people (Zhao et al., 2022). VR helps users to an entirely digitally mediated environment while obstructing any view of the real world (Sadowski & Stanney, 2002). AR drapes digital visual content onto the user's physical space so that both are simultaneously visible (Bimber & Raskar, 2005). In all cases, digital technology acts as both a source and conduit for consumer experiences. Although consumers often represent themselves with avatars that mimic their physical likeness, they may also adopt whimsical personas (unicorn horns or an animal head). They can interact with digital objects that exhibit imaginative functions. Thus, a Metaversal experience runs on the imagination of its creators and inhabitants.

The Metaverse Is Spatial

The metaverse represents a collection of digitally arbitrated spaces. In traditional social media platforms, the content is primarily posted on personal and institutional profiles, pages, and feeds (Peters et al., 2013; Sohn, 2014). However, in the Metaverse, users interact in three-dimensional "virtual worlds" similar to those common in video games (Messinger et al., 2008). Unlike in the physical world, users are unhindered by their actual geographic position as they can move around in their virtual world within the digitized space at any given time (Gursoy et al., 2022). An example of this world is the growing size of the Metaversal real estate market (Frank, 2022), which mirrors specific properties of the physical world real estate market (plots with greater visitor traffic are worth more than those with lesser visitor traffic) (Kamin, 2021). Since the brain often responds correspondingly to virtual and physical experiences (Blascovich & Bailenson, 2011), environmental cues are likely to influence consumers' behavior in the Metaverse as they do in the offline world (Spence et al., 2014). Experts argue that Metaverse will create innovations in the fields of urban design, architecture, landscape design, and interior design in the future (Cutieru, 2022; Schumacher, 2022; Spence et al., 2014).

The Metaverse Is Immersive

One of the distinctive features of the Metaverse is that it immerses users in an experience. A technology is said to be immersive if it effectively places the user in a virtual atmosphere (Bowman & McMahan, 2007). Immersion is an exhilarating feature for users as it gives them a sense of presence, known as the psychological experience of "being there" (Cummings & Bailenson, 2015). A system is said to be immersive if it produces rich simulations through sensory modalities (Cummings & Bailenson, 2015). This means both the quality and quantity of sensory inputs enhance the Metaversal experience of users via screen or headset (Zhao et al., 2022). The experience of immersion can be enhanced by making the users hear ambient background sound (Dinh et al., 1999). This digital sound in the physical world gives a greater immersion experience to the users (Fritz et al., 2023). Researchers have found that haptic sensations (vibrations or motions to the users) can increase the immersion sense in technology-mediated experience (Basdogan et al., 2000; Hadi & Valenzuela, 2020). Various startups are experimenting with olfactory devices that will help users to even smell in the Metaverse (Stone, 2022). Many of these products are relatively niche and new. Still, experts feel that if more sensory modalities are activated in the user, the more likely the user is to feel like they are actually in the real world (Wirth et al., 2007). Immersion in the Metaverse is also enabled by deploying an embodied representation of each user into the digitized space in the form of an avatar. Avatars are anthropomorphic digital representations symbolizing a user's presence in the digitized space (Messinger et al., 2008). In the world of Metaverse, the users select their own avatars (Hackl et al., 2022) and experience a "loss of self" (MacCallum-Stewart & Parsler, 2008), and the user may even cease to distinguish between self and avatar (Bartle, 2003; Belk, 2013).

The Metaverse Is Real-Time

The final distinctive characteristic of the Metaverse is that it operates in *real time*. This sequential factor is two-pronged, having both temporal synchronicity (time experienced is consistent across all users; Hoffman & Novak, 1996) and temporal persistence (time flows unidirectionally without the ability to traverse backwards; Kivetz & He, 2017). Metaverse is primarily concerned with the flow of time within itself, which means the users have the same experience. For instance, when a user is "walking," the walk is rendered at the same time for both acting user and viewer, meaning the movement is processed exactly in sync (Dennis et al., 2008). Thus, the consumers have a sense of strong social presence with others when they view live-streamed content, compared to pre-recorded content (Brundl et al., 2017; Park & Johar, 2022). Moreover, temporal synchronicity helps in getting the immediate attention of consumers, thus resulting in better responsiveness (Zeithaml, 2000), and increasing the feeling of trust (Wongkitrungrueng & Assarut, 2020).

Learning Objectives

a. What is metaverse, and how is it expanding its horizon?
b. What are the benefits to businesses through embracing Metaverse?
c. What are the benefits to consumers through Metaverse being provided by firms?

The Necessity of New Technology

Globally, companies like Nike, Hyundai, Gucci, Samsung, Ferrari, Coca-Cola, Louis Vuitton, and Tommy Hilfiger have effectively embraced metaverse technology to promote their brands. The metaverse is an innovative and exciting new digital platform with limitless possibilities for businesses. As already mentioned in the last paragraph, major companies worldwide are trying to explore the new opportunities being offered by the metaverse.

Gartner, the research firm, predicts that over 25% of people will spend at least an hour a day in the metaverse by 2025 and major tech businesses do not want to miss out on this golden opportunity and are trying to jump on the bandwagon.

The global metaverse market is expected to touch US $1,527 billion by 2029 from the current US $100 billion at a CAGR of 48%. This phenomenal growth can be attributed to the surge in online gaming adoption by consumers and rising consumer preference for online product shopping.

Metaverse technology is rapidly evolving, and it may not be long until AR glasses are as ubiquitous in the workplace as notebook computers and smartphones are today.

This chapter explores the possibilities of the metaverse helping businesses to develop their brands. The chapter also looks at the growth of Metaverse in the recent past and tries to understand whether Metaverse's active use will take at least a few more years before businesses can put it into practical use.

The metaverse, a convergence of hybrid and digital spaces powered by AR and VR, has emerged as a game-changer in the realm of business and branding. This chapter explores the manifold opportunities and transformative potential of the metaverse in expanding the consumer market and elevating the brand experience.

The metaverse, though it is still evolving, has the potential to revolutionize the way organizations function.

One of the most significant impacts of the metaverse on the apparel business will be in the area of marketing and sales. Brands can create immersive virtual experiences, allowing shoppers to try on clothes and attend virtual fashion shows. This will create a personalized shopping experience for customers, and it could lead to increased sales. In India, Len's Kart allows consumers to use online wearing of glasses and select glass that suits their face.

Another impact of the metaverse on the apparel business will be in the area of product design and development. Brands will be able to use VR and AR to create and test new designs without having to produce physical prototypes. This could save brands time and money and lead to more innovative and creative products.

The metaverse could also have a substantial influence on the apparel supply chain. Brands will be able to use VR to track the movement of goods through the supply chain, and they could also use AR to provide customers with information about the products they are buying, such as their origin and sustainability credentials. This could lead to a more efficient and transparent supply chain.

Brands embracing the metaverse early on could gain a significant competitive advantage.

Review of Literature

Nike has created a virtual world called Nikeland on the Roblox platform. In Nikeland, users can play games, try on virtual Nike products, and even build their own Nike stores. Gucci has partnered with the metaverse platform VRChat to create a virtual Gucci Garden. In the Gucci Garden, users can explore virtual Gucci products, attend virtual fashion shows, and even meet virtual celebrities. Balenciaga has released a line of digital clothing that can be worn by avatars in the metaverse. This digital clothing can be purchased using cryptocurrency.

We can expect to see even more innovative and creative uses of metaverse technology by apparel brands with the evolution and development of this technology.

Virtual Shopping Experiences

Virtual shopping experiences (VSEs) are becoming increasingly popular as consumers seek more convenient and immersive shopping methods (Verhagen & Roest, 2019). VSEs can take many forms, from online product configurators to VR and AR experiences (Kwak et al., 2019).

One of the key benefits of VSEs is that they allow consumers to try on products before they buy them, which can be especially helpful for products such as clothing and eyewear (Verhagen & Roest, 2019). VSEs can also help consumers to visualize how products will look in their homes or on themselves (Kwak et al., 2019).

Another benefit of VSEs is that they can be more engaging and interactive than traditional shopping experiences (Verhagen & Roest, 2019). For example, VR experiences can allow consumers to explore virtual stores and products in a realistic way (Kwak et al., 2019). AR experiences can allow consumers to visualize products in their own environment (Verhagen & Roest, 2019).

A growing body of research is exploring the impact of VSEs on consumer behavior (Verhagen & Roest, 2019). For example, one study found that VSEs can increase customer satisfaction and purchase intent (Kwak et al., 2019). Another study found that VSEs can help consumers make better purchase decisions by feeding them with more product information (Verhagen & Roest, 2019).

However, there are also some challenges associated with VSEs (Kwak et al., 2019). For example, developing and maintaining VSEs can be expensive (Verhagen & Roest, 2019). Additionally, VSEs may not be suitable for all products or consumers (Kwak et al., 2019). For example, consumers who are not comfortable with technology may find VSEs to be confusing or frustrating (Verhagen & Roest, 2019). Overall, VSEs offer several potential benefits to consumers and retailers. However, businesses need to understand the challenges of VSEs before employing them.

Virtual stores and showrooms in the metaverse can provide immersive and interactive shopping experiences. Research by Borowiecki et al. (2020) suggests that simulated shopping can increase engagement and purchasing behavior, particularly among young consumers.

Customization and Personalization

VR and AR are increasingly being used for customization in various industries, including fashion, furniture, and automotive. VR and AR allow consumers to visualize and customize products in a more immersive and interactive way than traditional methods (Khoo & Huang, 2012).

The advantage of using customized VR and AR is that it allows consumers to see how a product will look and feel before they buy it. This can help to reduce the risk of disappointment and returns. For example, VR can be used to try on clothes or furniture before buying them, while AR can be used to visualize how a new car will look in their driveway (Lee & Ryu, 2016).

Another benefit of using VR and AR for customization is that it can help consumers create more unique and personalized products. For example, VR can be used to design custom clothing or furniture, while AR can be used to personalize products with custom text or images (Kim & Kim, 2018).

Examples of VR and AR Customization in Different Industries

Fashion: VR and AR can be used to try on clothes, shoes, and accessories before buying them. This can help consumers to find the right fit and style and to avoid returns (Arnaoutis & Gavriel, 2019).

Furniture: VR and AR can be used to visualize furniture in a home before buying it. This can help consumers to see how the furniture will look and fit in their space (Huang et al., 2013).

Automotive: VR and AR can be used to customize cars and trucks. For example, consumers can use VR to choose the color, wheels, and other features of their new vehicle (Kim & Choi, 2018).

Challenges of VR and AR Customization

One of the challenges of VR and AR customization is that it can be expensive to develop and implement. Additionally, VR and AR headsets can be expensive and cumbersome for consumers to use. Another challenge of VR and AR customization is that it can be difficult to create realistic and accurate simulations of products. This can lead to disappointment for consumers if the product does not look or feel the way they expected.

Despite the challenges, VR and AR customizations have the potential to revolutionize the way consumers shop and buy products and marketers can expect increased sales through increased levels of customer satisfaction and delight.

The metaverse can offer highly personalized experiences. For apparel businesses, this means the ability to provide customized clothing options to customers. Studies by Lee et al. (2019) show that personalization positively impacts customer satisfaction and loyalty.

Supply Chain and Production

The metaverse could impact the entire apparel supply chain, from design and manufacturing to distribution. Virtual prototyping and 3D printing technologies can streamline the production process. Research by Lu et al. (2019) highlights the potential benefits of integrating virtual technologies in fashion supply chains.

Brand Engagement

Building a presence in the metaverse can enhance brand engagement. Companies can create virtual events, fashion shows, or even branded virtual worlds. Kim and Ko (2019) found that immersive brand experiences positively influence brand loyalty.

Data and Analytics

The metaverse generates vast amounts of data on user behavior and preferences and organizations will get huge benefits and competitive edge with the help of such massive information. Research by Davenport and Harris (2019) emphasizes the importance of data analytics in the metaverse.

The Potential Benefits of Metaverse for Business Houses

Immersive Entertainment

The entertainment industry has appreciated Metaverse as a cutting-edge technology. For instance, VR, an immersive technology associated with the metaverse, can be utilized in theme parks. Virtual parks will be appreciated by customers who do not want to go on a long journey but still would like to enjoy events and exhibitions like sports or concerts.

E-commerce

In the virtual space, the sellers and buyers can meet and interact and choose brands of customers' choice.

E-Commerce Platforms Can Go for Metaverse in the Following Ways

Product demonstrations and showrooms: Ecom can create virtual showrooms where products can be displayed and demonstrated. The customer need not visit the showroom during his busy business schedule and/or waste time due to traffic snarls.

Online Auctions

Metaverse platform makes it easy for both sellers and buyers to get connected easily and transact business.

Virtual Storefronts

The virtual stores help customers to imagine the kind of material that will suit them and accordingly order items, and this means the customer is not disappointed when the material arrives as they selected the same based on color, design, and size.

Customizable Shopping Experiences

As already mentioned above, customers can customize their purchases and derive the pleasure of their choice without regretting it later.

Increased Customer Engagement

The pleasure of interaction in an immersive environment is huge for the customers. It is not only new, it is also unique, and the experience of customers leads to more sales and loyalty.

Real Estate

Organizations can create virtual showings of properties for potential customers, who can access the properties through the virtual world from anywhere in the world. This is a huge support to marketers as they create virtual tours of the property that will help the customers understand what it would be like to live in a particular property.

Business Operations

Companies can seek Metaverse's help for marketing, product development, and customer services.

Education and Training

The learners can connect to educational experts worldwide without leaving their homes, thus getting knowledge and information from a wealth of experienced and talented experts. Moreover, metaverse can create customized content for each learner, tailored to suit the requirements of each individual.

The Importance of Metaverse to the Business

Metaverse offers a new to businesses to communicate and collaborate with customers from anywhere globally virtually. It also offers firms numerous activities like building a real business world. For example, businesses can build and monetize a recreational area where others can come and play a game or open a VR clothing store. Even a real estate company can offer architectural structure or its digital creation in the metaverse.

Improve the Customer Experience and Find New Marketing Opportunities

Products become brands primarily due to the unique experience that consumers get, and hence, businesses accord top priority to the value addition that consumers get from their products. Research shows that 86% of consumers are ready to spend more on a brand than its competitive brand for the great positive experience they get out of the brand. These can be

- proactively addressing consumer concerns,
- fast and excellent service,
- personalized attention and service,
- transparency and honesty,
- easy access to organizational support.

Metaverse helps firms connect well with the public, though not physically, but immersively. Similarly, customers can also have interactive options with the business.

Very importantly, metaverse helps you to gather consumer data very quickly, efficiently and accurately. This customized experience will help organizations to (1) optimize marketing strategies and resources and (2) provide personalized and customized service to customers.

If firms continue to use old, traditional and outdated marketing strategies, they will be left way behind by new millennials as they have no time for advertisements on television, print media or purchase through brick-and-mortar shops. Thus, firms need to update their social media marketing strategies to reach not only millennials but also millions to expand their business horizon.

The following marketing statistics show how society is embracing the digital world, and there lies lessons for marketing companies to get connected through social media platforms.

- eCommerce rose from $432 billion in 2019 to $24,029 billion in 2021 and is poised to touch $62,415 billion by 2030, rising at a CAGR of 11%, as per the research report of Sky Quest;
- Community is very important today, as is shown by the quantum jump in Facebook subscribers, and it holds good promise for marketers;
- Shopping of 95% of Gen Z is based on the inputs they get from social media.

Metaverse and Brand Authenticity

Around 86% of consumers prefer to buy authentic brands. In this connection, metaverse helps in creating trust in brands and that too with transparency, as consumers can, through VR, converse and understand the brand qualities and indulge in purchases. Metaverse will give consumers insights into the company's workings, what it stands for, and the products being made. These insights will ensure the consumers that they buy only authentic products from a genuine company.

If Businesses Need the Benefits of Metaverse

1. Collaborate with Metaverse Platform

If the business houses would like to hop on to metaverse platforms, they have better opportunities and windows today than ever, with such big developers like

- The Sandbox
- Decentraland
- Cryptovoxels
- Meta's Horizon Worlds
- Roblox
- Microsoft Metaverse partners.

The firms can extraordinarily build their businesses and create shareholders' wealth by creating virtual products on the above platforms. The fashion builders Gucci utilize metaverse very effectively to promote their brands. They purchased digital land on the Sandbox to give shoppers an immersive experience. Gucci also sold NFTs like collectibles designed off real products that the consumer's avatar uses or displays.

The metaverse platform also helps to host virtual events, which enables products to be marketed online and get connected with other businesses. The fashion shows, or the concerts held by Ariana Grande and Marshmallow, tasted grand success when they were hosted virtually.

2. Build VR and AR Experiences

Businesses can start building a framework for utilizing metaverse by integrating metaverse technology into marketing, enabling them to transit into a fully immersive digital world.

For example, AR Food Packaging is highly popular with consumers as consumers interact with products through smartphones, play games, collect nutrition information and watch videos of recipes.

Metaverse VR Technology gives a virtual experience to consumers as they zoom in and out of the item and interact with it to see how it works.

3. Metaverse and Connectivity

Metaverse creates a boundaryless global village and one virtual community, connecting people from across states and nations. In order to build brand connectivity and community, it is essential for organizations to find easy ways of communication, and that can happen through the metaverse platform.

Have the Businesses Fostered a Sense of Community and Connectivity among Consumers so that They Take Full Advantage of VR and AR to Create a Brand Image in the Minds of Consumers?

4. Improve Mobile Brand Access

Technology is ever-changing. Consumers who purchased desktops or laptops have shifted to mobile devices. With such action of embracing technologies so quickly by the population, there is no doubt that consumers will sooner than later shift to metaverse to gain new purchasing experiences. However, marketing people should also be ready to embrace and conduct business on Metaverse.

5. Hybrid Virtual Business Model

Since the pandemic, most of the companies operate in a hybrid mode that combines remote with in-office work. Meetings with employees on the Metaverse platform are being held like they would be in an in-office setting. Though this is not fully implemented by organizations, the metaverse creates an environment for a seamless workplace.

In order to make the hybrid operations successful, businesses need to

- Have collaboration tools like chats and file-sharing apps;
- Have data management systems that operate in the cloud.

(1) Case Study: Successful Marriage of Gucci and NFT

During the 2023 Metaverse Fashion Week, Gucci collaborated with NFT (Non-Fungible Token) giant Yuga Labs, creators of the famous NFT Bored Apple Yacht Club collections and currently owners of CryptoPunks and Meebits. Since NFTs are not interchangeable, they cannot be duplicated.

(2) Case Study: Amazon Says we are Ready

Not to be left behind, the online platform Amazon's AR helps customers the mental comfort by placing virtual furniture in their homes before the actual purchase.

(3) Exploring Zara's Metaverse Fashion: Bridging Reality and Digital Fantasy

Zara, the fashion designer, has been extensively using the metaverse platform after having ventured into the same in December 2022. The individual capsule collection called "Meta Collection" will be made available on the ZEPETO app, which Zara earlier used along with the South Korean creative collection, Ader Error. Zara also offers a few makeup products, such as eye shadows or fake nail sets, through the Metaverse platform and features three additional digital elements: a wall, a floor and a photo booth. This has been created to enhance the immersive experience for customers.

Metaverse and Consumers

What does the future of consumer behavior look like? One way to find out is to take a peek into the metaverse, where people can explore new virtual worlds and interact with others in ways that were not possible before.

With advancements in technology and with better scientific temperament, consumers find it exciting to interact with digital interfaces. Metaverse-based interactions help consumers to understand and express who they are. There is growing evidence that avatar embodiment has a great impact on how consumers see themselves. Studies by Nosek et al. (2016) have shown that people who spend more time in virtual worlds are more likely to report higher levels of self-esteem, and another study by Ding et al. (2020) has indicated that consumers' self-efficacy. Birk et al. (2018), in their studies, mentioned that people who own avatars tend to show increased engagement.

Szolin (2022) in their research found that Consumers have the "Proteus Effect," where consumers have been observed to consistently change their behavior based on their digital avatar's characteristics. This is very important for marketers to give consumers a pleasant experience through VR so that consumers get hooked to their products and services.

Hence, the Question is, How Fluid will Consumers' Behaviors and Identity Be in the Metaverse?

As per the research by razorfish.com, when a question was posed to Gen Z gamers on the gain they obtain from online gaming, the common answer obtained was self-exploration. Marketers need to exploit this new persona, both authentic and inauthentic and tap into the newfound confidence for promoting their brands through the metaverse.

Consumer rendezvous in virtual worlds is nothing new now. However, the shift from niche interest to mainstream relevance was ignited by the pandemic and the resultant social distancing restrictions and also due to the parallel spurt in the popularity of online gaming platforms (Belk, 2013; Blascovich & Bailenson, 2011; Messinger et al., 2008), which actually helped the consumers relieve their boredom by playing online games and spending real money in virtual settings.

What Motivates Consumers to Enter the Metaverse?

Many consumers stroll traditional social media as an escape from reality and fully get immersed in entertainment, but at the same time, indulge in other activities through a feed on their mobile phones. However, the immersive nature of the Metaverse prohibits such casual engagement. Thus, Metaversal consumers are normally less distracted, moreover, in a less cognitively depleted state than social media users. It is absolutely essential for marketers to understand how different segments of consumers differ in their overall motivation to engage in Metaversal experiences. For example, those who are lonely and alone are likely to show an increased tendency to live in the world of Metaverse. Demographic segmentation shows that Metaverse is dominated by a younger group (Adams, 2022), while older generations are attracted to the immersive – and often transportive qualities of Metaversal experiences (Rand, 2022).

Will the Metaverse Change Consumers' Shopping Behavior?

Metaverse holds huge potential as a virtual online marketplace where consumers can use their avatars to browse virtual stores, purchase virtual products and spend virtual currencies (Hofstetter et al., 2022).

Researchers are of the opinion that Metaverse could evolve into a virtual marketplace that is decoupled from the activities of the physical world, where consumers buy and sell non-tangible assets (NFTs) that have no mapping onto tangible products in the physical world. There is also a huge possibility for marketers that the Metaverse will be composed of a constellation of immersive extensions of firms' current online marketing efforts in which consumers shop and browse digital analogs of stores but with the goal of buying physical products (Cottrell, 2022), where consumers can purchase both physical and digital goods. Some non-Metaverse retail outlets have paired physical purchases (Nike Sneakers) with NFT-based virtual twins so that consumers can simultaneously acquire matching goods for their physical self and their avatar (Wilson, 2022).

In order to make digital touchpoints more meaningful and realistic, some offline service providers have integrated Metaversal rewards (exclusive NFTs) as part of their customer loyalty programmes (Starbucks Odyssey).

While the purchases in the physical world and Metaverse are dissimilar, some researchers are of the opinion that consumers might use conspicuous virtual purchases to compensate for what they cannot afford in the physical world (Belk, 2013).

Metaversing—Is a Journey and not a Destination

Technology is always evolving. From listening to music on a radio to transistor to Walkman to Two-in-One, it has now moved to mobile phones. And, tomorrow VR will ensure music can be picked up from nowhere and listen anywhere. When the World Wide Web was introduced in 1989, it worked more as a provider of information, and consumers can retrieve and consume the same without the ability to interact. Today, consumers communicate, collaborate and create information (Choudhury, 2014). The current technological landscape offers very little glimpse into what Metaverse can do to the business or to the consumers and what is the future it holds? It is also very hazy how Metaverse and business models will merge to create a unique proposition to the consumers, enhancing shareholder wealth. There is a great possibility that with its boundaryless and data-rich environment, Metaverse will make a unique environment and platform for organizations to reach out in an otherwise competitive world. Organizations will have to think differently to understand consumer behavior, breaking themselves from the shackles of traditional way of marketing. However, like all online innovations, there are likely to be offsetting, unforeseen consequences that are currently hard to predict.

The metaverse also raises ethical and privacy concerns, which could impact businesses. Researchers like Baumann and Salminen (2019) discuss the need for ethical considerations in the metaverse.

In conclusion, while the metaverse is still in its nascent stage in 2024, there is substantial academic interest in its potential impact on businesses, including the apparel industry. Researchers anticipate that it could transform various aspects of the industry, from consumer experiences to supply chain management.

We strongly believe and advocate that future researchers can play a seminal role in shaping the research ideas/concepts discussed in our paper, and we do hope our research paper will inspire new ideas and investigations on this new digital frontier for the good of society.

References

Adams, P. (2022). What gen Z wants to see from brands as metaverse attachments grow. *Marketing Dive*. https://www.marketingdive.com/news/gen-z-brand-metaverse-preferences-Fortnite-Roblox/622294/

Arnaoutis, I., & Gavriel, A. (2019). Virtual reality in fashion customisation: Current state and future prospects. *Fashion Theory*, 23(3), 351–370.

Ball, M. (2022). *The Metaverse: And how it will revolutionize everything*. Liveright.

Bartle, R. A. (2003). *Designing virtual worlds*. New Riders Publishing.

Basdogan, C., Ho, C. H., Srinivasan, M. A., & Slater, M. (2000). An experimental study on the role of touch in shared virtual environments. *ACM Transactions on Computer-Human Interaction (TOCHI)*, 7(4), 443–460. https://doi.org/10.1145/365058.365082

Baumann, N., & Salminen, J. (2019). Ethical and privacy concerns in the digital and metaverse age: A focus on business ethics, consumer protection, and intellectual property. *International Journal of Information Management*, 45, 142–145.

Belk, R. (2013). Extended self in a digital world. *Journal of Consumer Research*, 40(3), 477–500. https://doi.org/10.1086/671052

Bimber, O., & Raskar, R. (2005). Spatial augmented reality: Merging real and virtual worlds. In *Spatial augmented reality: Merging real and virtual worlds* (pp. 1–371). A K Peters/CRC Press. https://doi.org/10.1201/b10624

Birk, M. V., & Mandryk, R. L. (2018). *Combating attrition in digital self-improvement programs using avatar customisation* [Conference session]. Proceedings of the 2018 CHI Conference on Human Factors in Computing Systems (pp. 1–15). ACM.

Blascovich, J., & Bailenson, J. (2011). *Infinite reality: Avatars, eternal life, new worlds, and the dawn of the virtual revolution*. HarperCollins.

Bloomberg Intelligence. (2021). *Metaverse may be $800 billion market, next tech platform insights*. https://www.bloomberg.com/professional/blog/metaverse-may-be-800-billion-market-next-tech-platform/

Borowiecki, K. J., Crespo Cuaresma, J., & Hübler, O. (2020). Virtual visits and online purchases of art and culture. *Journal of Cultural Economics*, 44(1), 157–182.

Bowman, D. A., & McMahan, R. P. (2007). Virtual reality: How much immersion is enough? *Computer*, 40(7), 36–43. https://doi.org/10.1109/MC.2007.257

Brundl, S., Matt, C., & Hess, T. (2017). *Consumer use of social live streaming services: The influence of co-experience and effectance on enjoyment* [Conference session]. Proceedings of the 25th European Conference on Information Systems (ECIS) (pp. 1775–1791). ECIS.

Choudhury, N. (2014). World wide web and its journey from web 1.0 to web 4.0. *International Journal of Computer Science and Information Technologies*, 5, 8096–8100.

Cottrell, J. (2022). Integrating the Metaverse into omnichannel retail. *Fast company*. https://www.fastcompany.com/90771010/integrating-the-metaverse-into-omnichannel-retail

Cummings, J. J., & Bailenson, J. N. (2015). How immersive is enough? A meta-analysis of the effect of immersive technology on user presence. *Media Psychology, 19*(2), 272–309. https://doi.org/10.1080/15213269.2015.1015740

Cutieru, A. (2022). The architecture of virtual environments: Designing for the Metaverse. *Arch Daily.* https://www.archdaily.com/980632/the-architecture-of-virtual-environments-designing-for-the-metaverse

Davenport, T. H., & Harris, J. (2019). Competing on analytics in the metaverse. *MIT Sloan Management Review, 60*(4), 1–7.

Dennis, A. R., Fuller, R. M., & Valacich, J. S. (2008). Media, tasks, and communication processes: A theory of media synchronicity. *MIS Quarterly: Management Information Systems, 32*(3), 575–600. https://doi.org/10.2307/25148857

Ding, D., Brinkman, W.-P., & Neerincx, M. A. (2020). Simulated thoughts in virtual reality for negotiation training enhance self-efficacy and knowledge. *International Journal of Human-Computer Studies, 139*, 102400.

Dinh, H. Q., Walker, N., Hodges, L. F., Song, C., & Kobayashi, A. (1999). *Evaluating the importance of multi-sensory input on memory and the sense of presence in virtual environments* [Conference session]. Proceedings – Virtual Reality Annual International Symposium (pp. 222–228). https://doi.org/10.1109/VR.1999.756955

Frank, R. (2022). Metaverse real estate sales top $500 million, MetaMetric solutions says. *CNBC.* https://www.cnbc.com/2022/02/01/metaverse-real-estate-sales-top-500-million-metametric-solutions-says.html

Fritz, W., Hadi, R., & Stephen, A. T. (2023). Sound in motion: How spatial audio improves consumer responses to digital advertising.

Gursoy, D., Malodia, S., & Dhir, A. (2022). The metaverse in the hospitality and tourism industry: An overview of current trends and future research directions. *Journal of Hospitality Marketing & Management, 31*(5), 527–534. https://doi.org/10.1080/19368623.2022.2072504

Hackl, C., Lueth, D., Bartolo, T., Arkontaky, J., & Siu, Y. (2022). *Navigating the metaverse: A guide to limitless possibilities in a web 3.0 world.* Wiley.

Hadi, R., & Valenzuela, A. (2020). Good vibrations: Consumer responses to technology-mediated haptic feedback. *Journal of Consumer Research, 47*(2), 256–271. https://doi.org/10.1093/JCR/UCZ039

Hofstetter, R., de Bellis, E., Brandes, L., Clegg, M., Lamberton, C., Reibstein, D., Rohlfsen, F., Schmitt, B., & Zhang, J. Z. (2022). Crypto-marketing: How non-fungible tokens (NFTs) challenge traditional marketing. *Marketing Letters, 2022*, 1–7. https://doi.org/10.1007/S11002-022-09639-2

Hoffman, D. L., & Novak, T. P. (1996). Marketing in hypermedia computer-mediated environments: Conceptual foundations. *Journal of Marketing, 60*(3), 50–68.

Huang, W., Khoo, A., & Ong, S. H. (2013). Augmented reality-aided furniture customisation. *Computers & Graphics, 37*(5), 490–500.

Kamin, D. (2021). Investors snap up Metaverse real estate in a virtual land boom. *The New York Times.* https://www.nytimes.com/2021/11/30/business/metaverse-real-estate.html

Khoo, A., & Huang, W. (2012). *Virtual reality for fashion customisation* [Conference session]. Proceedings of the 2012 ACM SIGCHI Conference on Human Factors in Computing Systems (pp. 1041–1044). ACM.

Kim, A. J., & Ko, E. (2019). Impacts of immersive experience on brand engagement and brand loyalty. *Journal of Research in Interactive Marketing, 13*(1), 4–22.

Kim, J. Y., & Kim, J. H. (2018). The effect of augmented reality shopping experience on consumer satisfaction and purchase intention: An empirical study. *International Journal of Retail & Distribution Management, 46*(1), 118–133.

Kim, S. J., & Choi, E. (2018). The effect of augmented reality on consumer purchase intention in the automotive industry. *International Journal of Automotive Technology & Management, 18*(8), 445–461.

Kivetz, R., & He, D. (2017). *Being in the moment: The effects of ephemeral communication in social media.* Marketing Science Institute.

Kwak, D. H., Kim, S. Y., & Shin, D. H. (2019). The impact of virtual shopping experiences on consumer behaviour: A systematic review of the literature. *Journal of Retailing and Consumer Services, 50*, 171–179.

Lee, S., Lee, H. H., & Lee, J. (2019). Effects of personalised recommendations on consumer purchase decisions: A psychophysiological study of consumer choice. *Information & Management, 56*(1), 103–113.

Lee, S. M., & Ryu, K. (2016). The effect of virtual reality on consumer purchase intention in the clothing industry. *Computers in Human Behavior, 58*, 318–326.

Lim, Y. K., & Kim, J. H. (2016). The effects of virtual reality shopping experience on consumer satisfaction and purchase intention: An empirical study. *International Journal of Retail & Distribution Management, 44*(2), 173–192.

Lu, Y., Liu, S., Zhang, L., & Zhang, Y. (2019). Virtuality reality (VR) in fashion retailing: A research agenda. *International Journal of Production Economics, 214*, 95–110.

MacCallum-Stewart, E., & Parsler, J. (2008). Role-play vs gameplay: The difficulties of playing a role in world of Warcraft identity. In H. G. Corneliussen & J. W. Rettberg (Eds.), *Digital culture, play, and identity: A world of warcraft reader* (pp. 225–246). MIT Press.

Messinger, P. R., Ge, X., Stroulia, E., Lyons, K., Smirnov, K., & Bone, M. (2008). On the relationship between my avatar and myself. *Journal for Virtual Worlds Research, 1*(2). https://doi.org/10.4101/JVWR.V1I2.352

Nosek, M. A., Robinson-Whelen, S, Hughes, R. B., & Nosek, T. M. (2016). An internet-based virtual reality intervention for enhancing self-esteem in women with disabilities: Results of a feasibility study. *Rehabilitation Psychology, 61*(4), 358–370.

Park, E. S., & Johar, G. V. (2022). *The (virtual) crowd: Speed of synchronous chat affects popularity in livestreams* [Conference session]. ACR. https://www.acrwebsite.org/assets/ACR2022/FINAL%20PROGRAM-detailed_virtual-11-15.pdf

Peters, K., Chen, Y., Kaplan, A. M., Ognibeni, B., & Pauwels, K. (2013). Social media metrics: A framework and guidelines for managing social media. *Journal of Interactive Marketing, 27*(4), 281–298. https://doi.org/10.1016/J.INTMAR.2013.09.007

Q.ai. (2022). What long-term investors need to know about the metaverse. *Forbes*. https://www.forbes.com/sites/qai/2022/08/25/what-long-term-investors-know-about-the-metaverse/?sh=45dda8217877

Rand, K. (2022). How seniors are creating an inclusive metaverse. *Forbes*. https://www.forbes.com/sites/forbestechcouncil/2022/08/25/how-seniors-are-creating-an-inclusive-metaverse/?sh=3e134bf1931e

Sadowski, W., & Stanney, K. (2002). Presence in virtual environments. In K. M. Stanney (Ed.), *Handbook of virtual environments – design, implementation, and applications* (1st ed., pp. 831–846). CRC Press. https://doi.org/10.1201/9780585399102-51

Schumacher, P. (2022). The Metaverse as opportunity for architecture and society: Design drivers, core competencies. *Architectural Intelligence, 1*(1), 1–20. https://doi.org/10.1007/S44223-022-00010-Z

Sohn, D. (2014). Coping with information in social media: The effects of network structure and knowledge on perception of information value. *Computers in Human Behavior, 32*, 145–151. https://doi.org/10.1016/J.CHB.2013.12.006

Spence, C., Puccinelli, N. M., Grewal, D., & Roggeveen, A. L. (2014). Store atmospherics: A multisensory perspective. *Psychology & Marketing, 31*(7), 472–488. https://doi.org/10.1002/MAR.20709

Steuer, J. (1992). Defining virtual reality: Dimensions determining telepresence. *Journal of Communication, 42*(4), 73–93.

Stone, Z. (2022). Inside the smell-o-verse: Meet the companies trying to bring scent to the metaverse. *Fast Company*. https://www.fastcompany.com/90744828/inside-the-smell-a-verse-meet-the-companies-trying-to-bring-smell-to-the-metaverse

Sundararajan, A. (2022). How your brand should use NFTs. *Harvard Business Review*. https://hbr.org/2022/02/how-your-brand-should-use-nfts

Szolin, K., Kuss, D. J., Nuyens, F. M., & Griffiths, M. D. (2022). Exploring the user-avatar relationship in video games: A systematic review of the Proteus effect. *Human–Computer Interaction, 38*, 1–26.

Tong, G. C. (2022). Metaverse could pump $1.4 trillion a year into Asia's GDP: Deloitte. *CNBC*. https://www.cnbc.com/2022/11/14/metaverse-could-pump-1point4-trillion-a-year-into-asias-gdp-deloitte.html

Verhagen, T., & Roest, D. (2019). The impact of virtual shopping experiences on customer satisfaction and purchase intent: A meta-analysis. *Journal of Business Research, 104*, 71–83.

Wilson, M. (2022). Nike dotSwoosh will sell NFT shoes starting 'under $50'. *Fast Company*. https://www.fastcompany.com/90809804/nike-dotswoosh-will-sell-nft-shoes-starting-under-50

Wirth, W., Hartmann, T., Böcking, S., Vorderer, P., Klimmt, C., Schramm, H., Saari, T., Laarni, J., Ravaja, N., Gouveia, F. R., Biocca, F., Sacau, A., Jäncke, L., Baumgartner, T., & Jäncke, P. (2007). A process model of the formation of spatial presence experiences. *Media Psychology, 9*(3), 493–525. https://doi.org/10.1080/15213260701283079

Wongkitrungrueng, A., & Assarut, N. (2020). The role of live streaming in building consumer trust and engagement with social commerce sellers. *Journal of Business Research, 117*, 543–556. https://doi.org/10.1016/J.JBUSRES.2018.08.032

Zeithaml, V. A. (2000). Service quality, profitability, and the economic worth of customers: What we know and what we need to learn. *Journal of the Academy of Marketing Science, 28*(1), 67–85. https://doi.org/10.1177/0092070300281007

Zhao, Y., Jiang, J., Chen, Y., Liu, R., Yang, Y., Xue, X., & Chen, S. (2022). Metaverse: Perspectives from graphics, interactions and visualization. *Visual Informatics, 6*(1), 56–67. https://doi.org/10.1016/J.VISINF.2022.03.002

Part B

Technologies Driving the Metaverse

Chapter 3

Augmented Reality: Shaping the Metaverse

Ganesan Muruganantham and B. Dinesh Kumar

Department of Management Studies, National Institute of Technology, Tiruchirappalli 620 015, Tamil Nadu, India

Abstract

Metaverse is an immersive technology that has transformed the way we connect, interact, and work, providing massive opportunities for different sectors. The prevailing trends in the metaverse encompass various aspects such as multi-user virtual environments facilitating real-time interaction between users and digital objects, the utilization of virtual and augmented reality (AR) technology to generate immersive and captivating experiences, social and gaming encounters, virtual currencies, data, and analytics for personalization and targeting of experiences, live streaming, e-commerce, and other related developments. AR is a key component of the metaverse. Because of its increased accessibility and interactivity, AR has the potential to operate as a bridge between the present and the future. AR superimposes the virtual objects in the real environment, enabling mixed-reality experiences that enable users to have immersive experiences.

This chapter examines the role of AR in metaverse platforms. It navigates through the multifaceted platforms within the metaverse and underscores its transformative potential in various sectors, fueled by the demand for remote working tools and the growing embrace of Web 3.0 technologies. It also explores the technical elements of integrating AR, providing a comprehensive explanation of how AR-enabled devices like glasses, headsets, and smartphones are used to generate immersive user experiences.

Keywords: Augmented reality; metaverse; mixed reality; Web 3.0 technology; digital universe; virtual avatar; non-fungible tokens; immersive personalization

1. Introduction

The Metaverse encompasses a virtual realm wherein individuals can engage and interact with virtual worlds. It is a digital environment where the users can interact with a computer-generated universe. It is a science fiction term for a shared virtual space with many different virtual worlds and experiences that are all linked to each other. The metaverse is a huge, scalable, interoperable network of real-time rendered 3D virtual worlds. In this digital world, an unlimited number of people can experience virtual settings concurrently and persistently, each with a unique presence (Linda Tucci, 2023). The Metaverse simultaneously maintains identity, history, entitlements, objects, communications, and payments, creating a seamless and immersive user experience (Dwivedi et al., 2023).

The metaverse has been described as

> a massively scaled and interoperable network of real-time rendered three-dimensional (3D) virtual worlds that can be experienced synchronously and persistently by an effectively unlimited number of users with an individual sense of presence, and with continuity of data, such as identity, history, entitlements, objects, communications, and payments. (Ball, 2022, p. 29)

The Metaverse relies on augmented reality (AR) to add 3D models, animations, and data to real-world items (Mckinsey, 2023). AR improves the user experience by linking the real and virtual worlds in the vast Metaverse. According to Mckinsey (2023), total immersion, interactive real-time, and user agency are the key elements of metaverse, and it is driven by four major innovations.

First and foremost, the decentralized web application stack of Web3 empowers consumers with control over identification and data, seamlessly integrating with the metaverse and fostering value exchange within communities or ecosystems. Complementing this, spatial computing introduces a three-tiered technological stack, bridging user experiences between the real and digital realms. The Digital Twin of a Person (DToP) facilitates near-real-time synchronized multi presence, enriching interactions across both digital and physical contexts. Finally, the Digital Twin of a Customer (DToC) serves as a dynamic virtual representation, learning and predicting customer behavior. Together, these breakthroughs position the metaverse as a transformative technological force (Mckinsey, 2023).

In the constantly evolving environment of the metaverse, a variety of platforms have emerged, each providing users with distinctive experiences and opportunities. In India, the Metaverse market is anticipated to reach US$1.57 billion in 2023, growing at 50.3% % to US$337.76 billion by 2030 driven by AR, Virtual Reality (VR), Mixed Reality (MR), and the rise in demand for tools that help people work from home and the remote working tools (Blue Wave Consulting, 2023). Web3 denotes the upcoming evolution of the internet, constructed on blockchain technology and collectively governed by its user community (The Statesman, 2023). It allows metaverse platforms to extend existing platforms with AR, assisting reality-based conversations among users. AR is one of the main technologies that could play a significant role in the development and experience of the metaverse. AR integration into the metaverse entails overlaying virtual items and information over the user's real-world perspective utilizing AR-enabled devices such as glasses, headsets, and smartphones, resulting in MR experiences.

AR enables users to create personalized virtual avatars, interactive virtual objects, and real-time social interactions (Onirix blog, 2023). It could contribute significantly to the Metaverse by improving the user experience through the seamless integration of real-world elements, fostering dynamic social interactions, enabling virtual commerce experiences, and revolutionizing entertainment and gaming within this interconnected digital universe. With the Metaverse growing matured and the possibility of changing into a fully immersive MR and AR ecosystem, companies and people may use this technology more and more (Mckinsey, 2023). This could be an amazing opportunity for brands and marketers to build stronger relationships with customers by giving them new ways to interact with and engage with the business. Understanding how AR fits into the larger framework of the Metaverse is essential to comprehend how it enriches immersion, blurs the lines between the virtual and real, and changes the future of human-computer interactions in the global, networked digital universe. In this chapter, we explore the evolution, key pillars, and diverse applications of the Metaverse across various sectors, accompanied by mini-case studies to illustrate its real-world impact.

2. Evolution of the Metaverse

The notion of the Metaverse has experienced a notable transformation, originating from early conceptualizations and advancements in technology. In the year 1938, the French poet Antonin Artaud made a prediction regarding the future potential of VR, specifically highlighting its ability to create intricate and captivating environments. In the year 1962, filmmaker Morton Heilig introduced the Sensorama, a technological innovation that replicated a three-dimensional motorbike ride, thereby establishing a foundation for the development of immersive experiences. In the year 1984, Jaron Lanier's VPL Research made a significant contribution to the field of VR by introducing headgear and gloves for immersive experiences. The advent of Tim Berners-Lee's World Wide Web in 1989 brought about a significant transformation in the realm of online communication and interaction.

The term "Metaverse" was introduced by Neal Stephenson in his novel Snow Crash in 1992, where he presented a conceptualization of a collective virtual multiverse (Dwivedi et al., 2022). Active Worlds, the first proto-meta world, emerged in 1995, enabling users to log in, explore virtual environments, and create their own worlds with custom content. In 1997, Richard Garriott introduced the word "MMO" to describe Ultima Online, which is widely regarded as the inaugural massively multiplayer online game. In the year 2003, the platform known as "Second Life" was introduced, enabling individuals to generate and engage with simulated environments. It allows users to explore the world with their avatars and interact with items and other users. Roblox, which was introduced in

2006, achieved rapid success due to its accessible platform for constructing virtual environments.

The Oculus, a 3D headset with an affordable price point, came into being in 2012 and was subsequently acquired by Facebook in 2014. The advent of the inaugural Non-Fungible Token in 2014 marked the commencement of a novel epoch in the realm of virtual assets. The introduction of Ethereum in 2015 enabled the development and deployment of decentralized applications. In 2016, the popular mobile game Pokémon GO successfully integrated AR technology with the immersive experience of real-world gaming. In 2018, Axie Infinity emerged as a trailblazer in the realm of play-to-earn games by introducing the integration of Non-Fungible Tokens. In 2019, the virtual world phenomenon known as Fortnite, developed by Epic Games, gained significant popularity. Subsequently, in 2021, Meta underwent a rebranding process, and Microsoft introduced a new technology called Mesh. The collaboration established in 2022 between Siemens and Nvidia in the context of the industrial metaverse exemplifies the continuous merging of technology, creative thinking, and the capacity for collaboration within the increasing Metaverse domain. The Metaverse has evolved substantially since Neal Stephenson coined the word Metaverse in 1992, with notable milestones being the release of Second Life (2003), Roblox (2006), inexpensive VR with Oculus (2012), and AR integration in Pokémon GO (2016). Recent developments, such as Meta's rebranding in 2021 and the adoption of Microsoft's Mesh technology, highlight the ongoing growth of the Metaverse ecosystem. The diverse functions and impactful roles of AR tools, showcasing their contributions to the overall educational experience within the metaverse, are encapsulated in Fig. 1.

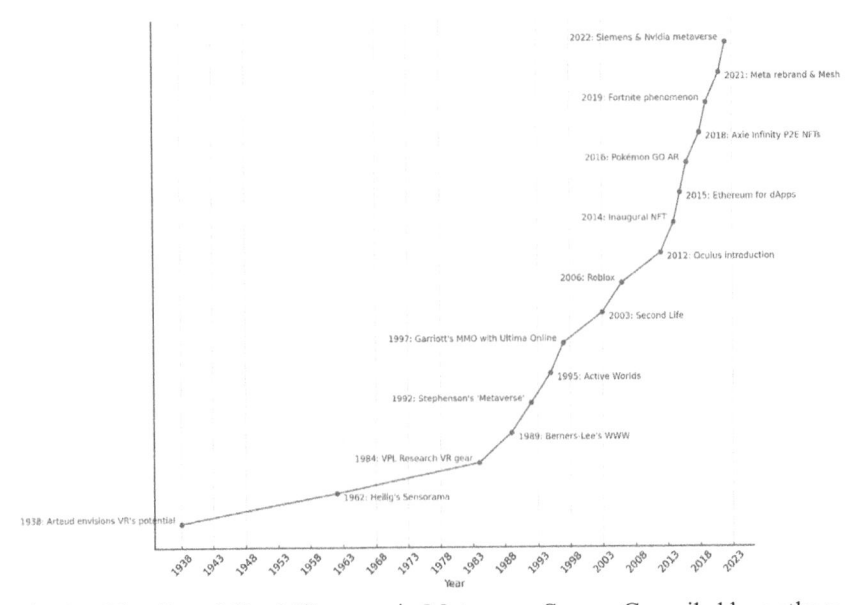

Fig. 1. Timeline of Key Milestones in Metaverse. *Source*: Compiled by authors.

3. Key Pillars of Metaverse

The Metaverse, as envisioned by Gartner, stands on a robust foundation supported by key elements that shape its multifaceted landscape (Ashutosh Gupta, 2022). These pillars jointly form a dynamic digital universe, from the fundamental characteristics of digital currency, infrastructure, and device independence to the immersive realms of games, digital humans, and social events. As non-fungible tokens reshape ownership and digital assets take center stage, the Metaverse's influence expands into online commerce, workplace dynamics, and the seamless integration of natural language processing, ushering in a new era of interconnected and immersive experiences (Ashutosh Gupta, 2022). The following are the key pillars of the metaverse.

3.1. Digital Currency

Within the metaverse, digital currency denotes a type of currency that exclusively exists in a digital or virtual state within the virtual world (Dwivedi et al., 2022). It is used for trade, transactions, and other business-related tasks. There are many kinds of digital currencies in the metaverse. They are used to buy and sell virtual things, services, and assets.

3.2. Marketplace/Digital Commerce

The concept of a metaverse in the realm of e-commerce refers to a virtual shopping environment that enables consumers to engage in activities such as browsing, purchasing, and personalizing items, services, and experiences facilitated by technologies such as AR and VR.

3.3. Non-Fungible Tokens

Non-fungible tokens (NFTs) are unique digital certificates of ownership that operate on the blockchain. The tokens are generated through a process known as minting, which typically involves digital files such as images, videos, or GIFs producing a proof of ownership and originality using cryptocurrency, frequently Ethereum, and then being transferred or sold to the new owner. The key Functions of NFTs in the Metaverse are virtual Property, In-Game Assets, Artwork, and Collectibles Digital representations of people, Management of events, and virtual tickets.

3.4. Infrastructure

In the metaverse context, infrastructure encompasses the fundamental technology and architecture that underpins virtual environments (Arkenberg & Arbanas, 2023). This includes servers, networks, and systems to facilitate the functionality of all the elements in the metaverse to offer an engaging experience to the users.

3.5. Gaming

Metaverse gaming creates a space where individuals can come together and engage in competitive online games. It offers "Massive Multiplayer Online experiences" and 360-degree perspectives which allow users to have the option to connect with friends for gaming, socializing, or embarking on other exciting adventures (Dwivedi et al., 2022).

3.6. Digital Assets

According to Gartner, digital assets in the metaverse refer to any digitally stored and uniquely identifiable elements that companies can leverage to generate value. Digital assets are mainly classified into digital collectibles and virtual spaces. It includes Non-Fungible tokens, virtual money, virtual real estate, digital art, etc. Users can buy, sell, and interact using blockchain technology. For instance, JP Morgan was the first bank to purchase a lounge in Decentraland.

3.7. Concerts, Social, and Entertainment Events

With the ever-changing technological landscape, the concept of the Metaverse has arisen as a unique arena for social interactions, business, and entertainment. In the metaverse, events take place in a networked, immersive virtual environment where users can interact with each other in real time using avatars. A notable example is the virtual concert by Travis Scott in Fortnite, which is one of the most popular video games globally. The event drew in a staggering 12 million live viewers and featured breathtaking visuals, engaging interactive elements, and an impressive virtual stage that was truly larger than life.

3.8. Virtual shopping

Companies can set up online stores and sell their merchandise there. It offers a virtual shopping experience to the users where they can explore interact, try things on, and buy things. It is similar to shopping online, but a lot more fun and exciting. By integrating artificial intelligence technology into virtual shopping experiences, the metaverse can present customers with personalized recommendations and persuade them to make purchases. Brands such as Gucci, Addidas, Nike, Luis Vitton, and Samsung have acquired virtual space for their metaverse shopping.

3.9. Workplace

VR environments that allow individuals to work from anywhere in the world is called workplace metaverse. It is an immersive virtual space where it can be tailored to specific requirements offering flexibility, creativity and enhanced productivity. Horizon Workrooms—Meta, NextMeet, Tangle, and PixelMax are some of the examples of metaverse workplace.

3.10. Social Media

Metaverse social media is a virtual realm where your interactions with others take place in a 3D digital environment. Instead of simply texting or posting pictures, users have the option to immerse yourself in a virtual space where they can chat, work, or play. It is a unique blend of reality and virtual gaming, where each conversation and gathering takes on a tangible, real-world quality. Users can create their own avatars, a "digital version of themselves" where they can move around, interact with others like they do in their real life.

3.11. Digital Humans

The term "digital human" refers to computer-generated avatars that are made to look and act like real individuals. It can be used to create virtual assistants and customer service representatives. They are employed in the metaverse for a range of functions, including virtual social engagement, virtual customer service, virtual events to offer more personalized and immersive experiences.

3.12. Natural Language Processing

Natural Language Processing enables the Artificial Intelligence to understand the human language and respond. The application of NLP in Metaverse are machine translation, information extraction, chatbot, sentiment analysis and audio processing (Soliman et al., 2024). Thus, it ensures a smooth and personalized customer experience.

4. Potential Role of AR in Enhancing the Metaverse Experience

AR, as its name implies, is a technology designed to enhance reality. In simpler terms, AR enables users to perceive an upgraded version of the real world by incorporating interactive digital elements. Through an AR application, users can access visual, auditory, and other sensory interactive information within real-world environments, elevating the overall experience. AR can be conceptualized as "a medium that integrates virtual content realistically into a user's field of view, ranging from very functional uses (assisted reality) to highly realistic experiences (MR) where virtual elements are almost indistinguishable from real ones" (Rauschnabel et al., 2022). Unlike VR, AR overlays an image of the viewer onto an electronically generated setting, as opposed to creating an entirely virtual scene in VR (Milgram, 1994). This unique feature of AR is particularly useful for retailers and consumers alike, as it allows consumers to try on products virtually without having to physically wear them in store (Verhagen et al., 2014).

There are two major types on the superimposition of AR namely marker-based and marker less AR. The marker less AR is classified into four types namely Projection-based, location-based, overlay and contour-based AR (Nextech3D.ai, 2022).

Marker-based AR: It works when the marker is scanned. For example, when a QR code is scanned by an AR enabled device, it generates an augmented experience like an image or a 3D model is superimposed on a physical environment. This type of AR is mainly used in Gaming, advertising, and education.

Markerless AR: It combines digital data with real-time information from devices in the real world that are registered to a physical place. This technique uses the camera, geolocation, and accelerometer of a device to ascertain positional data, encompassing the orientation of various objects and the spatial relationship between them. Subsequently, the system invokes the technique of simultaneous localization and mapping (SLAM) in order to analyze and comprehend the three-dimensional surroundings (Nextech3D.ai., 2022). In the meantime, the AR content is presented above the tangible viewpoint and can be observed from any location or perspective.

The two key types of markerless AR are projection-based AR and Location-based AR.

Projection-based AR: Projection-based AR exploits the creation of 3D graphics by projecting immersive light onto a flat surface. Subsequently, SLAM is employed to identify human engagement with the augmentation. For example, Projection-based AR can be utilized to generate holograms that serve both professional and recreational objectives.

Location-based AR: The content of location-based AR is confined to a particular physical space. It defines visual positions in the immediate environs and creates a map of the outside world. Upon identifying a correspondence with the mapped location, the device overlays corresponding digital imagery. The most widely recognized instance of location-based AR is Pokémon GO.

The application of AR in metaverse is redefining the business formats and functioning of various sectors such as gaming, retail, entertainment, education, etc. For instance, in education sector, AR tailors' content to learner's tastes and delivers feedback, resulting in an enjoyable and personalized learning experience. Similarly, in retail, AR enables users to virtually try-on clothing, accessories, and other items using the camera and AR features of their device. The application of AR in various sectors is elaborated in Table 1.

4.1. Digital Avatars

Avatars are the digital characters of users that is created using AR technology. It can be altered to look like users, resulting in a more personal and friendlier experience that connects with the end user. It affords users the ability to establish distinct attributes, including personality, appearance, attire, and accessories, thereby enabling a manifestation of their inclinations. AR avatars strengthen our sense of presence in the virtual world while also bringing a creative and personalized touch. Avatars will likely become increasingly important as technology develops, helping to shape the direction of AR and change our perception of the virtual world. Digital Avatars are being utilized by industries such as gaming, entertainment, Education and Training, Marketing (Market. us, 2023).

Table 1. The Role of AR in Various Metaverse.

Sector	AR Application	Description	Examples
Education	Interactive and personalized learning	AR enhances education by making learning enjoyable, interactive, and personalized. It turns learning into a game, offering points, badges, and challenges as rewards. Immersive stories or scenarios, like solving mysteries or virtual travel, engage learners. AR tailors content to individual preferences and provides feedback, creating a fun and personalized learning experience.	Google Expeditions VirBELA Classcraft ImmerseMe Brainly Osso VR Top Hat Harmony SEL CoSpaces Edu
Retail and E-commerce	Virtual Try-Ons	Enables users to virtually try on apparel, accessories, and other things using their device's camera and AR capabilities.	Roblox Decentraland NIKELAND
Workplace Metaverse	Immersive Workplace	AR enriches virtual offices with real-time collaboration, spatial computing, and remote assistance, fostering efficient work interactions.	PixelMax NextMeet
Gaming and Entertainment	Gaming	By utilizing cameras, microphones, and GPS to comprehend the real world. It then integrates game visuals and sounds, creating an interactive and blended gaming experience within the surrounding environment.	Decentraland, Axie Infinity, Sandbox, Battle Infinity

Source: Compiled by authors.

4.2. Metaverse Workplace

A virtual workspace known as the "Metaverse workplace" allows members of the organization to interact, collaborate, and work together just as if they were in the same physical space (Mark Purdy, 2022). AR is an integral component of the metaverse of the workplace, as it improves task execution, communication, and collaboration. Leveraging AR, the metaverse workplace revolutionizes collaboration through the seamless integration of the physical and virtual environments. The immersive attributes of AR augment virtual workspaces, facilitate instant collaboration, fortify spatial comprehension, and offer remote support. It enhances the induction process by streamlining data visualization and providing new employees with immersive experiences. AR assumes a pivotal role in this ever-evolving digital environment, transforming the virtual workstation into one that is not only productive but also captivating and interconnected.

AR transforms virtual offices, increasing their appeal and functionality while allowing for real-time collaboration via capabilities such as 3D model sharing. Spatial computing in AR enhances navigation and encourages organic interactions, resulting in a seamless integration of the virtual and actual worlds. AR's role includes remote support, data visualization, and onboarding, making it an adaptable tool for developing engaging, immersive, and collaborative work environments. The diverse roles of AR within the workplace Metaverse are elucidated below in Table 2.

Table 2. Functions of AR in the Metaverse Workplace.

Features	Role of AR in the Workplace Metaverse
Immersive Workplace	AR adds features to virtual offices, making them more engaging and practical.
Enhanced Collaboration	AR facilitates real-time collaboration, allowing team members to share 3D models and digital content in virtual meetings.
Spatial Computing	AR utilizes spatial computing to understand physical space in the metaverse, enhancing navigation and encouraging organic interactions.
Assistance	AR enables remote assistance, allowing experts to guide and assist employees or field workers in real-time using visual directions or notes.
Data Visualization	AR transforms complex data into interactive images, providing a natural way for workers to view and analyze data overlays in the workplace metaverse.
Onboarding	AR enhances the onboarding process by providing engaging and immersive experiences for new employees, introducing them to work procedures and company culture.

Source: Compiled by authors.

Thus, the role of AR in the workplace metaverse is crucial because it makes the virtual workplace immersive and enhances collaboration, training, and automation to make the work environment more efficient (Mark Purdy, 2022). From comprehending AR in the workplace metaverse to real-world applications, let us examine a case study that shows how AR has transformed workplace engagement.

4.2.1. Mini Case Study 1: NextMeet: Reshaping the Workplace Environment

Background: The metaverse has given us new ways to change the way we work, especially to deal with the problems that come up with remote and mixed work arrangements. NextMeet, an Indian immersive reality platform, has embraced this technological shift to deal with the growing concerns about workers becoming disconnected and alone because of the pandemic-caused trend of working from home.

Challenge: Getting employees to stay interested in the 2D world of video calls has proven to be very hard. Also, employees feel isolated and disconnected while working from remote or hybrid mode.

Solution: The immersive platform offered by NextMeet enables employees to seamlessly navigate virtual offices and meeting rooms in real time. They can also interact with virtual help desks, deliver live presentations from the dais, engage in networking activities with colleagues in a lounge, or navigate through conference centers or exhibitions using a customizable avatar.

Operational Mechanism: The Metaverse platform can be conveniently accessed through Windows, a laptop, or a mobile device. Participants have the option to select an avatar before entering a certain area through which they can network, engage, and navigate in the virtual platform.

Role of AR: AR can boost workplace productivity by overlaying digital information over a user's real environment. It combines the real and digitally immersive realms in a single location, offering novel opportunities for interaction and involvement.

Conclusion: The emerging metaverse presents organizations with a chance to redefine the equilibrium between hybrid and distant work, enabling them to reclaim the impromptu, interactive, and enjoyable aspects of team-based work and learning, while still preserving the adaptability, efficiency, and convenience associated with remote work.

Source: https://hbr.org/2022/04/how-the-metaverse-could-change-work

4.2.2. Mini Case Study 2: PixelMax: Redefining the Workplace Experience

Background: PixelMax, a UK-based firm, tackled the issues of remote work by developing a virtual workspace in the metaverse to reduce video meeting fatigue and improve team interactions.

Challenge: The increase in remote work has resulted in employees experiencing tension and challenges in maintaining a healthy work-life balance due to the lack of spontaneous communication.

Solution: PixelMax offered innovative features such as "Bump into" Experiences, Well-Being Spaces, and Live Status Tracking to create a virtual office that promotes greater collaboration and employee well-being.

Operational Mechanism: Team members communicate in real time with avatars, imitating unplanned workplace chats. Well-being spaces provide locations for leisure, and users can place virtual orders for delivery to their real-world location.

Role of AR: AR improves the immersive experience by making "bump into" experiences more realistic, reducing tension and promoting a collaborative virtual environment.

Conclusion: PixelMax's innovative approach reduces stress, improves teamwork, and offers a forward-thinking vision for the future of workspaces.

Key takeaways: Virtual avatars facilitate real-time interactions, establishing an immersive platform conducive to collaboration and networking. The metaverse workplace addresses challenges associated with remote and hybrid work through its personalized approach to employee experiences and connectivity.

Source: https://hbr.org/2022/04/how-the-metaverse-could-change-work

4.3. Gaming

AR is a captivating element in the metaverse game domain, as it seamlessly merges the digital and physical realms, resulting in engrossing and dynamic encounters. It seamlessly blends digital and real-world elements in metaverse gaming, making the experience more immersive and letting players interact with virtual things in a real way. GPS is used for unique tasks in location-based games, which encourages exploration. AR encourages social interaction by enabling users connect with virtual characters, and AR wearables make gaming more hands-free and immersive. Table 3 illustrated the role of AR in metaverse gaming. AR effectively revolutionizes metaverse gaming through the dismantling of obstacles that exist between the virtual and physical realms; as a result, players are treated to a gaming experience that is more immersive, interactive, and socially connected. The multitude of roles played by AR in the Gaming Metaverse is outlined below in Table 3.

4.3.1. Mini Case Study 3: Sandbox: The Gaming Metaverse

Background: The Sandbox is a unique virtual environment and gaming platform that enables users to create, own, and monetize their gaming experiences. The goal was to give the creators proper ownership of their work through NFTs and reward them for contributing to the community.

Challenge: To develop a platform enabling users to generate, distribute, and generate revenue from their games and experiences.

Solution: The metaverse enables users construct Sandbox Metaverse characters, structures, and landscapes. Users have the ability to acquire virtual land within the metaverse, which can subsequently be used for constructing buildings and generating immersive encounters. Creators of this virtual land is also benefited by monetary rewards. Also, users can socialize by attending events, playing games, and exploring with one another.

Table 3. The Role of AR in Gaming Metaverse.

Features	Role of AR in Metaverse Gaming
Integration of Real-world	In metaverse gaming, AR allows digital elements to interact with the physical world. Players can see virtual characters, objects, and events superimposed on their physical surroundings, making the game more dynamic and exciting.
Immersion	AR enhances the sensation of immersion in metaverse gaming by superimposing digital information on the actual world. Players can explore and interact with virtual items as if they were real-world objects, bringing authenticity to the gaming experience.
Location-based Gameplay	AR enables playing games in the metaverse based on where you are. Games can use GPS and real-world sites to create challenges, quests, and events that are only available in certain places. This makes players want to explore the area around them.
Social Interaction	AR facilitates social engagement within metaverse gaming by permitting users to observe and engage with one another's virtual avatars in physical environments. Social integration among participants can manifest in both local and global settings, thereby cultivating a sense of community.
AR Wearables	Wearable technology that works with AR, like AR glasses or headsets, can make games more immersive and hands-free. These gadgets can add information right into the player's field of view, combining the real and virtual worlds in a smooth way.

Source: Compiled by authors.

Operational Mechanism: This Metaverse platform lets users generate content with VoxEdit, a powerful 3D modeling tool. Users can upload, publish, and sell VoxEdit voxel models on the Sandbox Marketplace. Game Maker enables individuals to generate their own 3D games without incurring any costs.

Role of AR: AR ensures seamless integration of virtual aspects in the real world and dynamic interaction, resulting in immersive experiences.

Conclusion: The Sandbox metaverse allows users to generate their content, to upload, buy and sell. The creators get monetary benefits. Thus, it provides an exceptional user experiences by integration of virtual and real worlds.

Key takeaways: AR facilitates user interaction with the Metaverse platform, enhancing the level of personalization and immersion in the experience.

Source: https://www.blockchain-council.org/metaverse/sandbox-metaverse/

4.4. Virtual Shopping

The metaverse is poised to become a thriving hub for e-commerce. Businesses can establish virtual shops and sell their products. Customers have the opportunity to explore these virtual stores, test out products, and make purchases using virtual currency. It is similar to online shopping, but with a delightful twist of excitement and exploration. With the help of digital overlays, their perception of products is enhanced, creating a more engaging and realistic encounter. AR technology enables users to visualize virtual items in real-world environments, providing them with the opportunity to preview the appearance and fit of products prior to making a purchase decision. Virtual try-ons, interactive product demonstrations, and personalized recommendations, all powered by AR technology, combine to form a dynamic and captivating shopping experience.

The integration of AR in virtual shopping not only enhances the user experience but also serves to bridge the gap between online and offline retail. Since the metaverse is parallel to the actual world, as consumers spend more time digitally, they will gradually replicate the resemblances of their real lives in the digital realms. Status symbols such as digital apparel, cosmetics, household furniture, and jewellery will resemble real-world purchases and belongings greatly (Dwivedi et al., 2022). As a result of the reproduction of real-world habits, virtual possession is expected to increase. A virtual Gucci handbag recently sold in Roblox for 350,000 Robux (about $4,500), which is $800 more than the same genuine handbag in the real world (Cathy Hackl, 2021). Metaverse also offers a marketplace for the sale of digital twins, which are digital replicas of real-world objects (Dwivedi et al., 2022). Consumers can browse digital merchandise and buy physical versions of the products on exhibit. By bringing a tactile and visual dimension to the digital shopping journey within the expansive landscape of the metaverse, this integration offers a unique and immersive shopping experience.

4.4.1. Mini Case Study 4: Nikeland: Transforming Sports Arenas

Background: Nikeland, the Roblox metaverse developed by Nike, revolutionizes brand interaction by furnishing a venue where enthusiasts can convene, interact socially, and partake in exclusive brand encounters. Launched in 2021, Nikeland attracted more than seven million visitors.

Challenge: To introduce real-world lifestyles into virtual environments is the challenge identified by Nikeland.

Solution: Nikeland is a Roblox-based "purpose-built metaverse" where fans can network, socialize, and engage in campaigns. Visitors might see sports stars like LeBron James and buy special digital items to customize their avatars. Nikeworld products can be worn in other Roblox locations, turning visitors into digital brand advocates. They can also test their responses and tactics by playing various games for extra items and awards.

Operational Mechanism: Nikeland enables users to play games, create avatars, and style them in exclusive Nike clothes and accessories. Each Nikeland visitor gets their own "yard" to display their collections and design to fit their style. Users can try-on virtual garments for their avatars. Also, the game players may accomplish impressive motions in-game, such as long jumps or sprints, by moving their device and bodies in real life.

The Role of AR: Digital showroom available makes the users to explore and personalize the Nike products. The Nikeland enables users to try-on the virtual garments like clothes and accessories for their avatars.

Conclusion: Nike aims to leverage technology to create unique shopping experiences that foster strong customer-brand connections. This will increase their likelihood of seeking out the renowned swoosh logo the next time they need sporting goods – whether in the physical or digital realm.

Key Takeaways: Nikeland offers a one-of-a-kind opportunity for Nike as a platform for more meaningful community participation. Nike clearly understands the significance of meeting customer demands in the modern industry. For many well-known brands, Nikeland has become the standard of excellence when it comes to measuring online performance.

Source: https://www.forbes.com/sites/bernardmarr/2022/06/01/the-amazing-ways-nike-is-using-the-metaverse-web3-and-nfts/?sh=52cf5db256e9

4.5. Education

AR plays a crucial role in educational metaverse as it enables the learners to have engaging and immersive learning experiences. The AR devices such as AR glasses enables learners to explore, learn and interact with the virtual content. For instance, learners can explore virtual field trips being in the classrooms. AR has the potential to ignite creativity and foster innovation among students. It empowers them to craft their own captivating experiences, including 3D models, avatars, animations, and simulations. The use of VR and AR in education has proven that it can completely change how students learn and teachers teach. Students can interact with educational content in a more immersive way in the Metaverse. This makes learning more fun, interactive, and easy to get to. The application of AR tools and its contribution to the educational metaverse is summarized in Table 4.

Table 4. Key AR Tools and its Functions in Education Metaverse.

AR Tools	Functions in Education Metaverse
Smart Wearable Devices	Serve as a bridge between physical and virtual worlds
AR Glasses	Enable seamless interaction with educational content
Modeling and Rendering Technologies	Visualize complex concepts, historical sites, and abstract ideas
Real-time Tracking, Sensors, IoT	Facilitate embodied and multimodal interaction for hands-on learning

Source: Compiled by authors.

The Metaverse is transforming the field of education through the development of immersive, interactive, and captivating learning encounters that surpass limitations imposed by geographical borders. The ongoing advancement of technology presents boundless opportunities for the integration of the Metaverse into educational settings, hence facilitating a more interconnected, inclusive, and dynamic learning environment. AR application in real-time educational metaverse is given in Table 5.

Table 5. AR Application in Real-Time Educational Metaverse Platforms.

AR Application	Platform	Description
Augmented Field Trips	Google Expeditions	Explore locations in both virtual and AR, bringing educational content to life in an immersive way
Collaborative Learning in AR	VirBELA	Engage in real-time collaboration within a 3D environment using AR, fostering global connections among students
AR Language Learning	Mondly VR Language Learning	Immerse in language scenarios with native speakers through AR, enhancing language acquisition and cultural experiences
Gamified Learning with AR	Classcraft	Gamify the learning experience through quests and collaboration, promoting teamwork and critical thinking skills
Virtual Internships in AR	ImmerseMe	Access virtual internships and job shadowing experiences in various industries through AR
AR-Powered Remote Tutoring	Brainly	Connect with tutors globally using AR tools, facilitating real-time collaboration and personalized support
Inclusive Learning with Immersive Reader	Microsoft Immersive Reader	Improve reading comprehension with AR features like text-to-speech and adjustable fonts for inclusive education
AR Skills Training in Surgical Simulations	Osso VR	Practice surgical procedures in realistic AR simulations, enhancing skills and precision in a risk-free environment
Interactive Textbooks with AR	Top Hat	Utilize AR-powered interactive textbooks that adapt to individual learning preferences, offering immediate feedback
AR Labs for Science Education	Labster	Conduct virtual science experiments in immersive AR labs, deepening understanding of complex scientific concepts

Source: https://capsulesight.com/metaverse/15-examples-of-the-useof-metaverse-in-education/.

4.5.1. Mini Case Study 5: Antier: Revolutionizing the Way of Education

Background: The metaverse development firm Antier focuses on building immersive virtual learning environments. They have created state-of-the-art virtual classrooms that allow students to participate in a 3D educational environment.

Challenge: To create immersive and engaging virtual environment for education

Solution: Antier's VR-powered classes offer a range of features to enhance the learning experience. These include interactive whiteboards, avatars for students and teachers, and collaborative tools for real-time collaboration. Schools have the flexibility to customize their metaverse systems, ensuring that every student enjoys a one-of-a-kind and captivating learning journey.

Operational Mechanism: The integration AR allows the students to experience with educational contents like 3D images and virtual classrooms.

The Role of AR: AR seamlessly combines virtual elements with the real world, resulting in a digital representation of real-time space. It enables the recognition of gestures and movement from users, enhancing the learning experiences with a more engaging approach.

Conclusion: Antier's metaverse solutions have gained recognition for their ability to boost student engagement and enhance learning outcomes across different educational environments.

Key Takeaways: The educational metaverse revolutionizes educational experiences through virtual learning hubs, creating opportunities for long-distance education and interactive learning models.

Source: https://www.antiersolutions.com/build-in-metaverse/#:~:text=We%20offer%20Somnium%20metaverse%20development,experience%20with%20the%20NFT%20marketplace

4.6. Entertainment

One of the most fascinating applications of AR metaverse technology in movies is interactive storytelling (Dwivedi et al., 2022). Instead of being passive observers, viewers might become proactively involved in the plot of the film, making decisions that determine its outcome. This would drastically transform the usual viewing experience, giving viewers agency and control over their pleasure.

4.6.1. Virtual World Simulation

Disney recently obtained a patent for a "virtual-world simulator in a real-world venue," indicating that the company is starting to work on making a Metaverse system. In this creative use of AR, people who visit Disney theme parks can interact with AR characters by using a special app on their phones. This unique method makes Disney stand out because it turns the Metaverse, which is mostly virtual, into a real-world experience. Disney's virtual world's magic is seamlessly blended with their theme parks' real-world settings. This is an example of how AR is a key part of connecting digital and real-world experiences in the Metaverse as it changes.

4.6.2. Interactive Events

The concept of Metaverse for events involves the integration of AR & VR technologies to deliver a captivating and engaging experience for event participants. Furthermore, at present, the concept of the metaverse for events can be defined as cutting-edge technology that facilitates the creation of a dynamic virtual space where users can engage with one another and digital elements in real time. The metaverse is a versatile platform that can host a wide range of events, including trade shows, concerts, conferences, and various other gatherings. To effectively connect with fellow attendees, participate in presentations and sessions, and explore virtual booths or exhibits. Participants can create avatars to represent themselves and navigate a virtual environment. The metaverse has become a thriving technology offering a wide range of applications, making it an excellent investment and event tool.

5. Opportunities in Metaverse

The metaverse offers a plethora of chances across multiple sectors, hence defining new possibilities in the digital landscape. Businesses can create virtual shops in the sphere of commerce, reaching a global audience and altering the e-commerce experience. Immersive education opportunities emerge, providing novel and engaging learning experiences. The metaverse facilitates distant cooperation in the workplace, fostering unprecedented levels of productivity and connectivity (Jackie Wiles, 2023). The gaming and entertainment industries thrive on new experiences that blur the barriers between truth and fiction (Jackie Wiles, 2023). Furthermore, the metaverse fosters new channels for social contact, allowing groups to thrive and engage. The potential for enterprise, innovation, and exploration appears infinite as the metaverse evolves, providing a dynamic canvas for individuals and corporations alike.

6. Conclusion

Delving comprehensively into the transformative nature of the Metaverse, this chapter emphasizes its role as an expansive and interoperable digital realm influenced by AR. The anticipated expansion of the Metaverse market, specifically in India, highlights its increasing importance propelled by AR, VR, and MR technologies. The incorporation of AR into the Metaverse is becoming a central area of attention, providing users with customized avatars, interactive virtual components, and immediate social engagements.

AR is a highly popular and rapidly growing technology within the field of Extended Reality. Customers began to possess AR devices. This enables the development of a metaverse with a larger user base. Based on its economic value, AR can already be used in many fields, including education, health care, marketing, and more. This could also help the metaverse a lot as it tries to make a name for itself in the business world. Beyond only enhancing the immersive experience, AR has a plethora of other, more novel uses in the metaverse. As AR continues to expand, it serves as the bridge connecting the physical world with the virtual realm.

References

Arkenberg, C., & Arbanas, J. (2023). *What does it take to run a metaverse?* Retrieved November 29, 2023, from https://www2.deloitte.com/us/en/insights/industry/technology/metaverse-infrastructure.html

Ashutosh Gupta. (2022). *What is a Metaverse?* Retrieved November 29, 2023, from https://www.gartner.co.uk/en/articles/what-is-a-metaverse

Ball, M. (2022). *The Metaverse: And how it will revolutionize everything.* Liveright Publishing.

Blue Wave Consulting. (2023). *India metaverse market.* Retrieved November 29, 2023, from https://www.blueweaveconsulting.com/report/india-metaverse-market

Cathy Hackl. (2021). *Metaverse weekly: Virtual Gucci pursues, digital people, direct to avatar ecosystem, Nerf, NFTs and Beyond.* Retrieved November 29, 2023, from https://www.forbes.com/sites/cathyhackl/2021/06/01/metaverse-weekly-virtual-gucci-pursues-digital-people-direct-to-avatar-ecosytem-nerf-nfts-and-beyond/?sh=3e0bd10372c9

Dwivedi, Y. K., Hughes, L., Baabdullah, A. M., Ribeiro-Navarrete, S., Giannakis, M., Al-Debei, M. M., Dennehy, D., Metri, B., Buhalis, D., Cheung, C. M. K., Conboy, K., Doyle, R., Dubey, R., Dutot, V., Felix, R., Goyal, D. P., Gustafsson, A., Hinsch, C., Jebabli, I., ... Wamba, S. F. (2022). Metaverse beyond the hype: Multidisciplinary perspectives on emerging challenges, opportunities, and agenda for research, practice and policy. *International Journal of Information Management, 66*(July), 102542.

Dwivedi, Y. K., Hughes, L., Wang, Y., Alalwan, A. A., Ahn, S. J., Balakrishnan, J., Barta, S., Belk, R., Buhalis, D., Dutot, V., Felix, R., Filieri, R., Flavián, C., Gustafsson, A., Hinsch, C., Hollensen, S., Jain, V., Kim, J., Krishen, A. S., ... Wirtz, J. (2023). Metaverse marketing: How the metaverse will shape the future of consumer research and practice. *Psychology and Marketing, 40*(4), 750–776.

Jackie Wiles. (2023). *What is a metaverse? and should you be buying in?* Retrieved November 29, 2023, from https://www.gartner.com/en/articles/what-is-a-metaverse

Market.us. (2023). *Digital avatar market: Reshaping the future of virtual identity and interaction.* Retrieved November 29, 2023, from https://www.linkedin.com/pulse/digital-avatar-market-reshaping-future-virtual-identity-interaction/

Mark Purdy. (2022). *How the metaverse could change work.* Retrieved November 29, 2023, from https://hbr.org/2022/04/how-the-metaverse-could-change-work

Milgram, P., & Kishino, F. (1994). A taxonomy of mixed reality visual displays. *IEICE Transactions on Information and Systems, 77*(12), 1321–1329.

Mckinsey. (2023). *What is the metaverse?* Retrieved November 29, 2023, from https://www.mckinsey.com/featured-insights/mckinsey-explainers/what-is-the-metaverse

Nextech3D.ai. (2022). *What are the different types of augmented reality?* Retrieved November 29, 2023, from https://www.nextechar.com/blog/what-are-the-different-types-of-augmented-reality

Onirix blog. (2023). *Avatars in augmented reality: Their applications and how to create them.* Retrieved November 29, 2023, from https://www.onirix.com/avatars-in-augmented-reality-their-applications-and-how-to-create them/#:~:text=AR%20avatars%20not%20only%20add,we%20experience%20the%20digital%20world

Rauschnabel, P. A., Felix, R., Hinsch, C., Shahab, H., & Alt, F. (2022). What is XR? Towards a framework for augmented and virtual reality. *Computers in Human Behavior, 133*(January), 107289.

Soliman, M. M., Ahmed, E., Darwish, A., & Hassanien, A. E. (2024). Artificial intelligence powered Metaverse: Analysis, challenges and future perspectives. *Artificial Intelligence Review, 57*(2), 36.

Tucci, L. (2023). *What is the metaverse? An explanation and in-depth guide.* Retrieved November 29, 2023 from https://www.techtarget.com/whatis/feature/The-metaverse-explained-Everything-you-need-to-know

The Statesman. (2023). *Web3, Metaverse market to reach US $200 billion in India by 2035: Report.* Retrieved November 29, 2023, from https://www.thestatesman.com/business/web3-metaverse-market-to-reach-us-200-billion-in-india-by-2035-report-1503186890.html

Verhagen, T., Vonkeman, C., Feldberg, F., & Verhagen, P. (2014). Present it like it is here: Creating local presence to improve online product experiences. *Computers in Human Behavior, 39*, 270–280.

Chapter 4

Artificial Intelligence and the Metaverse

K. K. Shihab, Anil Vashisht, Arif Hasan and Astha Joshi

Amity Business School, Amity University, Gwalior, Madhya Pradesh, India

Abstract

As the Metaverse emerges as a prominent paradigm, Artificial Intelligence (AI) plays a pivotal role in shaping its landscape. This chapter explores the convergence of AI and the Metaverse, exploring the symbiotic relationship between these two transformative technologies. From virtual assistants to immersive experiences, AI-driven innovations are redefining how individuals interact and navigate within the Metaverse. This chapter also assesses the challenges and prospects brought about by AI in the Metaverse which is impacting both businesses and society on a broader scale.

Learning Objectives:
1. Understanding the role of Artificial Intelligence in shaping the Metaverse.
2. Exploring AI-driven applications and technologies within virtual environments.
3. Analyzing the difficulties and ethical concerns linked to AI within the Metaverse.
4. Evaluating the potential impact of AI on businesses and societal dynamics within the Metaverse.

Key Takeaways for Readers:
1. AI serves as a cornerstone technology in building immersive and interactive experiences within the Metaverse.
2. Ethical considerations surrounding AI usage in the Metaverse require careful attention to ensure inclusivity and privacy.

3. Businesses can leverage AI capabilities to enhance user engagement and optimize virtual operations in the Metaverse.
4. Effective collaboration among AI developers, businesses, and policymakers is essential to tackle the evolving challenges and prospects in the AI-driven Metaverse landscape.

Keywords: Artificial intelligence (AI); machine learning (ML); natural language processing (NLP); metaverse; augmented reality (AR); virtual reality (VR); generative adversarial networks (GANs)

Introduction

In the vast expanse of the digital realm, a new frontier had emerged – the Metaverse. A merging of augmented reality (AR), virtual reality (VR), and interconnected digital spaces signifies a fundamental change in our perception and interaction with digital spaces. At the core of this revolutionary terrain is Artificial Intelligence (AI), a ubiquitous force driving innovation, personalization, and immersion within virtual worlds.

The concept of the Metaverse, popularized by science fiction literature and media, is rapidly evolving from a speculative vision to a tangible reality. With the proliferation of immersive technologies and interconnected digital platforms, the boundaries between physical and virtual realities are becoming increasingly blurred. Within this dynamic ecosystem, AI serves as a cornerstone technology, imbuing virtual environments with intelligence, agency, and responsiveness.

At its core, the Metaverse is a manifestation of human creativity and ingenuity, offering limitless possibilities for exploration, collaboration, and expression. From virtual social gatherings to immersive gaming experiences, the Metaverse encompasses a diverse array of virtual spaces and interactions, each powered by AI-driven technologies. Virtual assistants, intelligent avatars, and procedural generation algorithms are just a few examples of how AI is shaping the fabric of the Metaverse, enabling new forms of interaction, storytelling, and commerce.

According to recent projections by market research firm MarketsAndMarkets, the global market for VR and AR technologies is at USD 12.9 billion and USD 25.1 billion in 2023 and is projected it to reach USD 29.6 billion and USD 71.2 billion by 2028, growing at compound annual growth rate (CAGR) of 18.0% and 23.2%, respectively, during the forecast period (2023–2028), fueled by growing demand for immersive experiences across diverse industries (MarketsAndMarkets, 2023). This surge in adoption underscores the transformative impact of virtual environments on consumer behavior, business operations, and societal interactions, signaling the dawn of a new era in human–computer interaction.

As we embark on this journey into the Metaverse, it is essential to understand the symbiotic relationship between AI and virtual environments. AI not only enhances the realism and interactivity of virtual experiences but also enables new modes of creativity, communication, and expression. However, along with its transformative potential, AI in the Metaverse also presents a host of challenges and ethical considerations.

Algorithmic biases, data privacy concerns, and digital inequalities are just a few of the complex issues that arise in the AI-driven Metaverse landscape. Moreover, the blurring of boundaries between virtual and physical realities raises profound questions about identity, agency, and societal norms in the digital age. As we navigate these challenges, it is imperative to foster collaboration, dialogue, and responsible AI governance to ensure that the Metaverse remains a vibrant, inclusive, and equitable space for all.

In this chapter, we will explore the multifaceted relationship between AI and the Metaverse, examining the transformative potential, challenges, and opportunities inherent in their convergence. From AI-powered virtual assistants to immersive content generation technologies, we will delve into the myriad ways in which AI is reshaping the landscape of virtual environments. Through case studies, analyses, and discussions, we will uncover the implications of AI in the Metaverse for businesses, society, and the future of human–computer interaction.

Let us start and explore the heart of the AI-driven Metaverse, where innovation knows no bounds, and the possibilities are limited only by our imagination.

AI-Powered Virtual Assistants in the Metaverse

In the immersive realms of the Metaverse, AI-powered virtual assistants stand as digital guides, companions, and facilitators, enriching user experiences and streamlining interactions within virtual environments. These intelligent entities, endowed with machine learning (ML), natural language processing (NLP), and conversational AI capabilities, play a pivotal role in enhancing engagement, accessibility, and convenience for users navigating the vast expanses of the digital realm.

Advanced NLP

AI-powered virtual assistants leverage sophisticated NLP algorithms to understand and interpret user queries, commands, and conversational nuances. Whether assisting users in virtual shopping experiences, providing navigation guidance in virtual worlds, or facilitating social interactions within digital communities, these virtual assistants possess the linguistic proficiency to comprehend and respond to user inputs in real time. Through continuous learning and adaptation, they evolve their language understanding capabilities, ensuring more natural and contextually relevant interactions with users.

Personalized Recommendations and Assistance

A significant strength of AI-powered virtual assistants lies in their ability to deliver personalized recommendations, assistance, and support tailored to individual user preferences and needs. By analyzing user data, interaction histories, and contextual cues, these virtual assistants can anticipate user intent and proactively offer relevant information, suggestions, and guidance. Whether recommending personalized content in virtual entertainment platforms or providing virtual concierge services in immersive virtual worlds, these AI-driven assistants enhance user satisfaction and engagement by catering to individual preferences and interests.

Conversational User Interfaces (CUI)

AI-powered virtual assistants often employ CUI to facilitate natural and intuitive interactions between users and virtual environments. Through text-based chat interfaces, voice commands, or avatar-mediated interactions, users can engage with virtual assistants in a manner that closely mirrors human-to-human communication. This conversational approach not only improves user immersion and engagement but also nurtures a feeling of companionship and connection between users and their virtual assistants, creating more enriching and enjoyable experiences within the Metaverse.

Dynamic Adaptation and Learning

One of the defining features of AI-powered virtual assistants is their capacity for dynamic adaptation and continuous learning. Through iterative feedback loops and reinforcement learning mechanisms, these virtual assistants refine their understanding, responses, and behaviors over time, becoming more adept at fulfilling user needs and preferences. Whether learning from user interactions, analyzing real-time data streams, or incorporating feedback from developers and users, AI-driven virtual assistants evolve and improve their capabilities, ensuring more personalized, contextually relevant, and effective assistance within the dynamic and ever-evolving landscape of the Metaverse.

In essence, AI-powered virtual assistants serve as indispensable companions and facilitators in the Metaverse, enriching user experiences, enhancing accessibility, and fostering engagement within virtual environments. Through their advanced NLP capabilities, personalized recommendations, conversational interfaces, and adaptive learning mechanisms, these intelligent entities empower users to navigate the intricacies of the digital realm effortlessly, confidently, and with satisfaction, heralding a new era of human–computer interaction in the immersive landscapes of the Metaverse.

AI-Powered Avatars and Social Interactions

In addition to virtual personal shoppers and immersive retail experiences, AI-powered avatars and social interactions are crucial in influencing user engagement and community dynamics within the Metaverse. These intelligent avatars, driven by advanced AI algorithms and NLP capabilities, serve as digital representations of users, enabling them to interact, communicate, and collaborate with others in virtual environments.

Intelligent Avatar Personalization

AI-powered avatars leverage ML algorithms and user data to personalize appearance, behavior, and communication styles, creating unique and lifelike representations of users within the Metaverse. By analyzing user preferences, social connections, and interaction histories, intelligent avatars can adapt their appearance, gestures, and speech patterns to align with individual user preferences and personality traits, enhancing user immersion and authenticity in virtual social interactions.

Conversational AI and NLP

AI-powered avatars incorporate conversational AI capabilities and NLP techniques to facilitate seamless and naturalistic communication between users in virtual environments. Using NLP algorithms, avatars can comprehend and reply to user queries, engage in real-time conversations, and participate in group interactions within virtual social spaces. By enabling natural language interactions, AI-powered avatars foster meaningful connections, collaboration, and community engagement in the Metaverse.

Emotional Intelligence and Social Cues

AI algorithms imbue avatars with emotional intelligence and social cues, enabling them to perceive and respond to subtle cues in user interactions, such as facial expressions, tone of voice, and body language. By interpreting social signals and emotional cues, intelligent avatars can convey empathy, understanding, and rapport in virtual social interactions, enhancing user satisfaction and fostering deeper connections within virtual communities.

Community Management and Moderation

AI-powered avatars serve as community moderators and facilitators, ensuring positive and inclusive social interactions within virtual environments. Using sentiment analysis and content moderation algorithms, intelligent avatars can detect and address inappropriate behavior, harassment, or toxic interactions in real-time, creating a safe and welcoming environment for users to connect, collaborate, and socialize in the Metaverse.

By integrating AI-powered avatars and social interactions into the fabric of the Metaverse, virtual platforms can create immersive, engaging, and socially vibrant environments that mirror the richness and complexity of real-world interactions. Whether connecting with friends, attending virtual events, or collaborating on projects, users can experience the power of AI-driven social interactions to foster community, creativity, and collaboration in the digital realm.

Immersive Content Generation in the Metaverse

Immersive content generation stands at the forefront of innovation within the Metaverse, revolutionizing the creation of virtual environments, characters, and narratives through the combination of AI and advanced rendering techniques. This process encompasses a diverse array of technologies and methodologies aimed at constructing dynamic, interactive, and visually stunning digital landscapes that captivate users and foster immersive experiences within virtual worlds.

Generative Adversarial Networks (GANs)

GANs stand as a cutting-edge AI technique used extensively in immersive content generation within the Metaverse. GANs comprise of two neural networks – one is a generator and other is a discriminator – trained collaboratively to generate realistic and diverse virtual content. In the context of the Metaverse, GANs are employed to create lifelike landscapes, buildings, characters, and objects, enriching virtual environments with intricate details, textures, and visual realism. By harnessing the power of GANs, creators can accelerate the content creation process and produce visually stunning virtual worlds that rival the complexity and richness of the physical world.

Procedural Generation Techniques

Procedural generation techniques play a vital role in scaling the creation of immersive content within the Metaverse by generating vast and diverse virtual landscapes, environments, and assets algorithmically. These techniques leverage mathematical algorithms and procedural rules to generate content dynamically, allowing the generation of vast and varied virtual worlds with minimal manual intervention. From terrain generation and vegetation distribution to architectural layout and urban planning, procedural generation enables creators to generate vast and varied virtual environments that offer endless exploration and discovery for users within the Metaverse.

AI-Driven Character Animation and Behavior

AI-driven character animation and behavior simulation are instrumental in bringing virtual worlds to life within the Metaverse. Advanced AI algorithms enable realistic and nuanced character animations, expressions, and interactions, enhancing immersion and believability for users engaging with virtual environments. Whether interacting with non-player characters (NPCs) in virtual game worlds, socializing with virtual avatars in virtual communities, or experiencing immersive storytelling narratives, users are immersed in dynamic and lifelike virtual experiences facilitated by AI-driven character animation and behavior simulation.

Dynamic Content Adaptation and Personalization

Another key aspect of immersive content generation in the Metaverse is dynamic content adaptation and personalization, wherein virtual environments and experiences are tailored to individual user preferences, behaviors, and interactions in real-time. AI algorithms analyze user data, interaction patterns, and contextual cues to dynamically adapt and personalize virtual content, ensuring that each user's experience within the Metaverse is unique, engaging, and relevant to their interests and preferences. By harnessing the power of AI-driven personalization, creators can create more immersive, captivating, and user-centric virtual experiences that resonate with users on a personal level within the dynamic and ever-evolving landscape of the Metaverse.

In summary, immersive content generation in the Metaverse represents a convergence of AI, procedural generation, and advanced rendering techniques, empowering creators to build dynamic, interactive, and visually stunning virtual worlds that captivate users and foster immersive experiences. Through the integration of GANs, procedural generation, AI-driven character animation, and dynamic content adaptation, creators can push the boundaries of creativity and innovation, creating virtual environments that offer endless exploration, discovery, and immersion for users within the boundless realms of the Metaverse.

Personalized Experiences and User Profiling in the Metaverse

In the dynamic and interconnected realms of the Metaverse, personalized experiences and user profiling play a vital role in shaping user interactions, content delivery, and virtual environments. Leveraging advanced AI algorithms and data analytics techniques, virtual platforms within the Metaverse strive to tailor user experiences to individual preferences, behaviors, and interests, fostering deeper engagement, satisfaction, and immersion for users navigating virtual spaces.

Data-Driven Personalization

At the core of personalized experiences in the Metaverse lies data-driven personalization, wherein user interactions, preferences, and behaviors are meticulously analyzed to deliver tailored content, recommendations, and interactions. Through the collection and analysis of user data, including browsing history, interaction patterns, and social connections, virtual platforms can acquire understanding of individual preferences and interests, empowering them to curate personalized experiences that resonate with each user's unique tastes and preferences.

Contextual Relevance

Personalized experiences in the Metaverse extend beyond mere content recommendations, encompassing contextual relevance that adapts to the user's immediate environment, activities, and social interactions. By leveraging real-time data streams, location-based services, and contextual cues, virtual platforms can dynamically adjust content delivery, user interfaces, and interactions to align with the user's current context and situational needs. Whether delivering relevant information in virtual navigation systems, tailoring virtual advertisements based on user location, or adapting gameplay challenges to match user skill levels, contextual relevance enhances user engagement and satisfaction by ensuring that interactions are meaningful, timely, and contextually appropriate.

Behavioral Profiling and Predictive Analytics

User profiling in the Metaverse involves the creation of detailed behavioral profiles that capture user preferences, tendencies, and engagement patterns across virtual environments. By analyzing user interactions, content consumption, and engagement metrics, virtual platforms can construct behavioral profiles that provide insights into user preferences, motivations, and decision-making processes. These behavioral profiles serve as the foundation for predictive analytics, enabling virtual platforms to anticipate user needs, preferences, and behaviors and proactively tailor content, recommendations, and interactions to align with user expectations. Whether predicting future content interests, suggesting social connections based on shared interests, or personalizing virtual environments based on past interactions, predictive analytics empower virtual platforms to deliver more relevant, engaging, and personalized experiences for users navigating the complexities of the Metaverse.

Ethical Considerations and User Privacy

While personalized experiences and user profiling provides numerous advantages in relation to user engagement and satisfaction, they also raise important ethical considerations related to user privacy, data protection, and algorithmic fairness. The collection and analysis of user data in the Metaverse must be conducted in a transparent, responsible, and privacy-preserving manner, with robust safeguards in place to protect user privacy, mitigate the risk of data breaches, and ensure algorithmic fairness and transparency. Additionally, users should possess authority over their personal information and the option to refrain from data collection and profiling activities if desired, fostering trust, transparency, and accountability in the virtual platforms they interact with.

In conclusion, personalized experiences and user profiling are essential components of the Metaverse, enhancing user engagement, satisfaction, and immersion by delivering tailored content, recommendations, and interactions that resonate with individual preferences and interests. By leveraging advanced AI algorithms, data analytics techniques, and contextual insights, virtual platforms can create more meaningful, relevant, and engaging experiences for users navigating the diverse and interconnected landscapes of the Metaverse, driving innovation and transformation in the realm of human–computer interaction.

Challenges and Ethical Considerations in the AI-Driven Metaverse

As the Metaverse evolves into a complex and interconnected digital ecosystem, the inclusion of AI brings forth a myriad of challenges and ethical considerations that need to be thoughtfully tackled to guarantee the responsible and equitable development of virtual environments. From algorithmic biases to data privacy concerns, navigating the ethical landscape of the AI-driven Metaverse requires a concerted effort to uphold principles of fairness, transparency, and accountability while mitigating potential risks and safeguarding user rights.

Algorithmic Biases and Fairness

One of the foremost challenges in the AI-driven Metaverse is the presence of algorithmic biases that can perpetuate discrimination, inequality, and exclusion within virtual environments. AI algorithms trained on biased or incomplete datasets might unintentionally sustain and magnify prevailing biases, resulting in unfair treatment, disparate outcomes, and marginalization of certain user groups. Addressing algorithmic biases requires careful consideration of dataset diversity, algorithmic transparency, and fairness-aware ML techniques to ensure that AI systems make equitable decisions and uphold principles of fairness and inclusivity within the Metaverse.

Data Privacy and Security

The collection, storage, and utilization of user data in the AI-driven Metaverse raise significant concerns related to data privacy, security, and consent. Virtual platforms within the Metaverse often gather vast amounts of personal data, including user interactions, preferences, and behavioral patterns, to personalize experiences and optimize content delivery. However, inadequate data protection measures, security breaches, and unauthorized entry to user data can jeopardize user privacy and undermine trust, and expose individuals to risks of identity theft, surveillance, and manipulation. Strengthening data privacy regulations, deploying robust encryption and security protocols, and empowering users increased control over their personal data are essential steps to safeguard user privacy and promote trust in the AI-driven Metaverse.

Digital Inclusion and Accessibility

Ensuring equitable access and participation in the AI-driven Metaverse poses significant challenges related to digital inclusion, accessibility, and affordability. Virtual environments that rely heavily on AI technologies may inadvertently exclude individuals with disabilities, limited digital literacy, or inadequate access to technology, exacerbating digital divides and widening inequalities within virtual communities. Addressing digital inclusion requires designing virtual platforms with accessibility features, providing support for various user requirements and preferences, and expanding access to affordable internet connectivity and digital devices to guarantee that all individuals can actively engage in and reap the benefits of the opportunities afforded by the AI-driven Metaverse.

Ethical Use of AI in Content Creation

The usage of AI technologies in content creation within the Metaverse raises complex ethical questions related to intellectual property rights, creative ownership, and authenticity. AI algorithms capable of generating virtual environments, characters, and narratives may blur the distinction between human-authored content and AI-generated creations, challenging traditional notions of authorship and creative expression. Additionally, AI-generated content may inadvertently perpetuate cultural stereotypes, misinformation, or harmful narratives if not carefully monitored and curated. Balancing the benefits of AI-driven content creation with ethical considerations require setting up explicit guidelines for attribution, ownership, and responsible use of AI-generated content within the Metaverse, fostering a culture of ethical creativity and innovation.

Algorithmic Transparency and Accountability

Promoting transparency and accountability in AI algorithms deployed within the Metaverse is essential to ensure that users can understand, interpret, and challenge algorithmic decisions that impact their virtual experiences. However, numerous AI systems function as opaque entities, making it challenging for users to understand the decision-making process or to hold AI developers and platform operators accountable for algorithmic errors or biases. Enhancing algorithmic transparency and accountability requires implementing mechanisms for auditing AI systems, providing explanations for algorithmic decisions, and fostering greater collaboration and accountability among AI developers, platform operators, and regulatory authorities to ensure that AI technologies serve the public interest and uphold ethical standards within the Metaverse.

In conclusion, addressing the challenges and ethical considerations inherent in the AI-driven Metaverse necessitates a comprehensive strategy that encompasses technical innovation, regulatory oversight, and involvement of stakeholders. By prioritizing principles of fairness, transparency, and accountability, virtual platforms and AI developers can foster a more ethical and inclusive digital ecosystem that empowers users, promotes trust, and advances collective well-being within the evolving landscapes of the Metaverse.

Business Opportunities and Innovation in the AI-Driven Metaverse

The emergence of the Metaverse, coupled with advancements in AI, presents a myriad of business opportunities and avenues for innovation across diverse industries. As virtual environments become increasingly integrated and immersive, businesses are utilizing AI technologies to improve customer experiences, streamline operations, and foster growth in the digital realm. From virtual commerce to collaborative workspaces, the AI-driven Metaverse offers a fertile ground for businesses to explore new frontiers, expand their reach, and unlock innovative solutions to meet evolving consumer demands and market dynamics (Gupta, 2023).

Virtual Commerce and E-Commerce Integration

In the AI-driven Metaverse, virtual commerce represents a significant opportunity for businesses to reach global audiences, engage customers in immersive shopping experiences, and drive sales in virtual environments. Virtual stores, digital marketplaces, and interactive shopping experiences powered by AI-driven technologies enable businesses to showcase products, personalize recommendations, and facilitate transactions within virtual spaces. Integrating e-commerce platforms with virtual environments enhances convenience, accessibility, and engagement for consumers, while offering businesses new channels for revenue generation and brand exposure in the digital landscape (Gupta, 2023).

Immersive Brand Experiences and Marketing Campaigns

AI-powered technologies enable businesses to create immersive brand experiences and interactive marketing campaigns within the Metaverse, fostering deeper engagement, brand loyalty, and customer relationships. From virtual events and experiential activations to personalized advertising and product placements, businesses can leverage AI-driven content generation, user profiling, and predictive analytics to deliver tailored experiences that resonate with target audiences. By harnessing the creative potential of the Metaverse, businesses can amplify brand visibility, drive brand advocacy, and differentiate themselves in the competitive digital marketplace.

Virtual Collaboration and Remote Work Solutions

The AI-driven Metaverse offers innovative solutions for virtual collaboration, remote work, and team collaboration, enabling businesses to overcome geographical barriers, enhance productivity, and foster collaboration in virtual environments. AI-powered virtual collaboration platforms, AR workspaces, and immersive meeting experiences facilitate seamless communication, knowledge sharing, and collaboration among distributed teams. By integrating AI-driven features such as NLP, real-time translation, and intelligent task automation, businesses can streamline workflows, enhance decision-making, and drive innovation in remote work settings.

Data Analytics and Business Intelligence

AI technologies are very essential for facilitating data-driven decision-making and business intelligence within the Metaverse, empowering businesses to extract actionable insights, identify trends, and optimize performance in virtual environments. Advanced AI algorithms, ML models, and predictive analytics tools analyze vast volumes of data generated within virtual spaces, uncovering valuable insights into customer behavior, market trends, and business opportunities. By leveraging AI-driven data analytics, businesses can make informed decisions, optimize resource allocation, and drive strategic growth initiatives in the dynamic and rapidly evolving landscape of the AI-driven Metaverse.

AI-Powered Customer Service and Support

In the AI-driven Metaverse, businesses can enhance customer service and support through AI-powered virtual assistants, chatbots, and intelligent automation solutions. These AI-driven technologies provide personalized assistance, resolve customer inquiries, and deliver seamless support experiences within virtual environments. By leveraging sentiment analysis, conversational AI capabilities, and NLP, businesses can improve customer satisfaction, reduce response times, and streamline customer interactions in the digital realm.

AI-Powered Avatars

AI-powered avatars open up new business opportunities for virtual service providers, content creators, and platform developers within the Metaverse. By offering customizable avatar creation services, avatar clothing and accessories, and avatar-based virtual experiences, businesses can capitalize on the growing demand for personalized and immersive social interactions in virtual environments. Additionally, AI-driven analytics and data insights derived from avatar interactions provide valuable market intelligence and user behavior insights, enabling businesses to optimize marketing strategies, personalize content offerings, and drive revenue growth within the burgeoning Metaverse ecosystem.

In conclusion, the AI-driven Metaverse presents a wealth of business opportunities and avenues for innovation across diverse industries. By harnessing the transformative power of AI technologies, businesses can unlock new revenue streams, enhance customer experiences, and drive growth in the digital landscape. Whether through virtual commerce, immersive brand experiences, collaborative workspaces, data analytics, or customer service solutions, businesses can leverage AI-driven innovations to thrive in the dynamic and interconnected world of the AI-driven Metaverse, shaping the future of commerce, communication, and collaboration in the digital age (Gupta, 2023).

Mini Case Study: AI-Powered Virtual Retail Experiences

Case Study Overview

In the AI-driven Metaverse, virtual retail experiences are undergoing a paradigm shift, redefining the way consumers shop, interact, and engage with brands in virtual environments. This case study explores how AI-powered technologies are revolutionizing the retail landscape within the Metaverse, enhancing customer engagement, personalization, and satisfaction.

Key Components

Virtual Personal Shoppers

According to a survey by Accenture, 64% of consumers are interested in receiving personalized recommendations from virtual shopping assistants. AI-powered virtual assistants serve as virtual personal shoppers, guiding users through personalized shopping experiences and providing tailored recommendations based on individual preferences, style preferences, and previous purchase history

(Accenture Newsroom, 2022). These virtual assistants utilize NLP and ML algorithms to comprehend user preferences, offer product suggestions, and assist with virtual try-on experiences. By simulating the in-store shopping experience in a virtual environment, virtual personal shoppers enhance user engagement and satisfaction, driving sales and fostering brand loyalty.

Dynamic Product Visualization

Research by Gartner predicts that by 2023, 25% of online sales in key verticals will be driven by virtual try-on experiences (Gupta et al., 2023; Hasan, 2018). Advanced rendering technologies and AI-driven product visualization tools enable users to interact with virtual products in lifelike environments, enhancing the online shopping experience and mitigating the limitations of traditional e-commerce platforms. Through VR and AR simulations, users can virtually try on clothing, visualize furniture in their living spaces, and preview products in different colors, sizes, and configurations (Gartner Newsroom, 2022). By providing immersive and interactive product experiences, dynamic product visualization technologies increase user confidence, reduce purchase hesitancy, and drive conversion rates in virtual retail environments.

Personalized Recommendations and Dynamic Pricing

A study by Deloitte found that 36% of customers are more inclined to make a purchase if offered personalized recommendations. AI algorithms analyze user behavior, purchase history, and preferences to provide personalized product recommendations and dynamic pricing strategies tailored to individual users (Deloitte Press, 2015). By leveraging ML models and predictive analytics, virtual retailers can optimize pricing strategies, maximize revenue, and offer targeted promotions and discounts to incentivize purchases. Additionally, AI-powered recommendation engines improve opportunities for cross-selling and up-selling, suggesting complementary products and accessories depending on user preferences and browsing patterns.

Data-Driven Insights and Analytics

As per a McKinsey report, companies that extensively utilize the customer analytics are more likely to generate profits above the average. AI-driven analytics platforms aggregate and analyze user data from virtual shopping interactions, providing in-depth understanding of customer preferences, purchasing behavior, and market trends. These data-driven insights enable virtual retailers to identify emerging consumer trends, improve inventory management, and customize marketing campaigns to target specific audience segments. By leveraging AI-driven analytics, virtual retailers can make data-driven decisions, optimize performance, and drive strategic growth initiatives within the competitive landscape of the AI-driven Metaverse retail industry.

Case Study Implications

AI-powered virtual retail experiences offer numerous benefits for both consumers and businesses within the Metaverse. For consumers, virtual retail experiences provide convenience, accessibility, and personalized assistance, enhancing the online shopping experience and bridging the gap between digital and physical retail environments. For businesses, AI-powered virtual retail experiences drive sales, increase customer engagement, and provide valuable data insights into consumer preferences and behavior, enabling businesses to optimize operations, improve decision-making, and drive strategic growth initiatives in the dynamic and rapidly evolving landscape of the AI-driven Metaverse retail industry.

Conclusion

The convergence of AI and the Metaverse heralds a new era of innovation, engagement, and transformation within the digital landscape. Through the lens of virtual retail experiences powered by AI technologies, we have explored the myriad ways in which the Metaverse is reshaping the retail industry, enhancing customer engagement, personalization, and satisfaction.

In the AI-driven Metaverse, virtual personal shoppers serve as digital concierges, guiding users through personalized shopping experiences, and revolutionizing the way consumers engage with brands and products in virtual environments. Leveraging advanced AI algorithms and NLP capabilities, virtual personal shoppers offer tailored recommendations, interactive styling advice, and real-time assistance, empowering users to explore, discover, and purchase products with confidence and ease.

From personalized recommendations to interactive try-on experiences, virtual personal shoppers enhance user engagement, satisfaction, and conversion rates within the virtual retail landscape. By leveraging AI-driven analytics, ML algorithms, and real-time data insights, virtual retailers can optimize the shopping experience, tailor marketing strategies, and drive strategic growth initiatives based on a deep understanding of consumer preferences and market trends.

As we look toward the future, the potential of AI-powered virtual retail experiences within the Metaverse is boundless. By embracing AI technologies, businesses can unlock new revenue streams, drive brand loyalty, and shape the future of retail commerce in the digital age. However, unlocking this potential demands a collective endeavor to tackle ethical considerations, privacy concerns, and algorithmic biases, ensuring that virtual retail experiences remain inclusive, transparent, and equitable for all users.

In conclusion, the convergence of AI and the Metaverse offers unprecedented opportunities for innovation, collaboration, and growth across diverse industries. By harnessing the transformative power of AI technologies, businesses can create immersive, personalized, and data-driven experiences that redefine how consumers interact with brands and products in virtual environments, shaping the future of commerce, communication, and collaboration in the era of digital advancements. As we traverse through this dynamic and rapidly evolving landscape, let us embrace the possibilities of the AI-driven Metaverse and strive to build a future that is inclusive, innovative, and empowering for all.

References

Accenture Newsroom. (2022). Consumer interest in "virtual living" intensifies. *Accenture Survey Finds*. Retrieved April 2022, from https://newsroom.accenture.com/news/2022/consumer-interest-in-virtual-living-intensifies-accenture-survey-finds

Deloitte Press. (2015). Making it personal – One in three consumers wants personalized products. *Deloitte*. Retrieved July 2015, from https://www2.deloitte.com/uk/en/pages/press-releases/articles/one-in-three-consumers-wants-personalised-products.html

Gartner Newsroom. (2022). Gartner predicts 25% of people will spend at least one hour per day in the metaverse by 2026. *Gartner Newsroom*. Retrieved February 2022, from https://www.gartner.com/en/newsroom/press-releases/2022-02-07-gartner-predicts-25-percent-of-people-will-spend-at-least-one-hour-per-day-in-the-metaverse-by-2026

Gupta, S. S. (2023). *Artificial intelligence in ecommerce*. Retrieved July 2023, from https://www.scaler.com/topics/artificial-intelligence-tutorial/ai-for-ecommerce/

Gupta, D., Singhal, A., Sharma, S., Hasan, A., & Raghuwanshi, S. (2023). Humans' emotional and mental well-being under the influence of artificial intelligence. *Journal for ReAttach Therapy and Developmental Diversities*, 6(6s), 184–197.

Hasan, A. (2018). Evaluation of factors influencing exclusive brand store choice: An investigation in the Indian retail sector. *Vision*, 22(4), 416–424.

MarketsAndMarkets. (2023). *Augmented (AR) and virtual reality (VR) market*. Retrieved October 2023 from https://www.marketsandmarkets.com/Market-Reports/augmented-reality-virtual-reality-market-1185.html

Chapter 5

Metaverse and Internet of Things: A Way to Smart Cities

Anubha Anubha[a], Govind Nath Srivastava[b] and Daviender Narang[a]

[a]*Jaipuria Institute of Management, Ghaziabad, Uttar Pradesh, India*
[b]*Symbiosis Institute of Business Management, Noida Campus; Symbiosis international University, India*

Abstract

The Metaverse and Internet of Things (IoT) have emerged like a tidal wave, and it is creating a transformative impact on society and industry. The metaverse and IoT changed the way companies were operating earlier and customers were living their lives. On the other hand, Metaverse enriches the customer experience by offering a matchless virtual experience using augmented reality and state-of-the-art technology. The metaverse and the IoT can be used in various sectors such as manufacturing, transportation, retailing, health care, banking, and automobiles to make cities smart. Metaverse and IoT provide real-time data, reduces operational cost and errors, improves efficiency, and helps industries to make intelligent decisions. Although the IoT and Metaverse offer significant benefits, it is not free from limitations. Ethical dilemmas, privacy issues, data breaches, and difficulty in extracting relevant data impose serious challenges that need to be addressed. There is an urgent and dire need to create a trade-off between the interest of the business and the privacy and security of customers. This chapter aims to discover the potential of Metaverse and IoT in various sectors (e.g., healthcare, transportation, and electronics). This study will bring significant insights to researchers and policymakers by exploring the likely benefits of IoT and metaverse in diverse sectors to develop smart cities. This chapter will also explain the challenges of metaverse and IoT, which can be addressed by integrating data analytics tools optimally and efficiently.

Keywords: Metaverse; Internet of Things; smart cities; customer experience; data analytics

---

The Metaverse Dilemma: Challenges and Opportunities for Business and Society, 69–83
Copyright © 2025 by Anubha Anubha, Govind Nath Srivastava and Daviender Narang
Published under exclusive licence by Emerald Publishing Limited
doi:10.1108/978-1-83797-524-220241005

1. Introduction

In a hypercompetitive and technologically advanced society, customer experience (CX) is a method of winning the game. Here is where the metaverse can play a significant role by providing one of its kind CX. To offer superior CX via incorporating personalization, adventure, and interactivity in their communications with customers, more and more businesses are turning to the emerging metaverse. In essence, through metaverse, customers may communicate, interact socially, and exchange digital products and services in varied contexts. As such, first, Metaverse can enhance CX by providing new ways for searching and exploring products, second, by creating a more meaningful fusion of physical and virtual experiences, and third, by reviving relationships between people and brands through artificial intelligence (AI)-enabled bots. However, the Metaverse has a few challenges that need to be combatted to take its fullest advantage.

One of the darkest challenges is the metaverse's capacity to incorporate the data into the virtual world by extracting it from the physical world. Such extracted data must be planned, relevant, secured, and accurate to offer the best CX. The interconnected and powerful Internet of Things (IoT) architecture helps the metaverse in combating this challenge. As such, IoT device flow will also make up a significant portion of the data ingestion. Such data must be represented in an eloquent pattern within the metaverse. Businesses are nowadays investing heavily in Metaverse projects that offer data intelligence solutions which enable them to offer superior CX. Based on the above, it can be inferred that data are the most valuable asset that needs to be extracted and used wisely to connect digital and physical worlds. In such a scenario, building a more sophisticated IoT infrastructure that can readily accommodate the complexities of the digital world is crucial for empowering Metaverse. IoT will enable consumers to move between the two worlds without hassles. The utilization of digital avatars within the IoT framework will play a key role in reshaping the future landscape of the Internet and enhancing CXs through the metaverse.

IoT is impacting diverse industries across the globe like a tidal wave due to its ability to connect billions of devices. The IoT is creating a transformative impact on operational efficiency, cost, decision-making, and security concerns. IoT helps in the collection, analysis, and exchange of data. The integration of data analytics with the IoT may address various security concerns like cyber threats, hacking, identity theft, and breaches.

IoT and Metaverse are as such similar technologies that are about to transform how people communicate and collaborate. This chapter aims to explore the potential of IoT and Metaverse in various sectors (for example, healthcare, transportation, and electronics). In other words, it intends to study the impact of IoT and metaverse in the development of smart cities. This study will bring significant insights to policymakers and researchers by exploring the likely benefits of IoT and metaverse in diverse sectors to develop smart cities. This chapter will also explain the challenges of metaverse, which can be addressed by integrating data analytics tools with the IoT.

2. Metaverse: A Trend

The term "Metaverse" can be defined as a virtual world that is connected to our physical reality. It is an idea that has been around for some decades and has experienced significant advancements. Science fiction writer Neal Stephenson originally used the term "Metaverse" in his 1992 book *Snow Crash*. The Metaverse, as described in this book, was a virtual reality (VR) environment where individuals could communicate with each other and with things created by computers (Huddleston, Jr., 2021). The Metaverse, as envisioned by Stephenson, served as a model for multiplayer online gaming and VR platforms.

With the development of the internet and the popularity of online gaming in the 1990s, the idea of the Metaverse gained traction. A business named Worlds Inc. introduced "WorldsChat," a virtual world that let users communicate with one another in a three-dimensional setting, in 1995. Launched in 2003, Second Life is one of the virtual worlds that were inspired by the success of WorldsChat. Because of the growth of blockchain technology and non-fungible tokens (NFTs), Metaverse has got more attention recently.

Blockchain technology enables the creation of decentralized virtual worlds, allowing users to own and trade virtual assets using bitcoin. Additionally, NFTs have opened up fresh opportunities for creators to monetize their contents by making virtual assets rare and distinctive. Technological developments and the inventiveness of users and developers have propelled the Metaverse's progress. The Metaverse is set to grow even more dynamic and immersive as blockchain technology, and NFTs have gained traction, further obfuscating the boundaries between the virtual and real worlds.

The metaverse can transform today's online transactions into immersive, real-time interactions by fostering a more emotionally pleasant and exciting connection between customers and marketers. The metaverse's virtual world is highly immersive which allows people to connect, interact and experience new opportunities regularly on a global scale (Moore, 2022; Sparkes, 2021; Wang, Yang, et al., 2022; Xu, 2022). The metaverse includes several modern technologies like digital twins, blockchain, VR, 3D modeling, NFTs, edge computing, augmented reality (AR), cloud computing, AI, and simulation (Gadekallu et al., 2022; Liu et al., 2022; Lv et al., 2022; Wang, Su, et al., 2022; Zallio & Clarkson, 2022). It has been predicted that around one-fourth population will invest a minimum of one hour in the metaverse by the year 2026 (Gartner, 2022). Even, the big tech companies are investing heavily in the metaverse, like, Qualcomm, Meta (Facebook), and Microsoft (Polona et al., 2022).

Here are a few insights about how metaverse can enhance CX. First, the metaverse makes personalization possible improving CX. While personalization enhances CX, organizations may now precisely and relevantly focus their marketing efforts and customer offerings thanks to developments in intelligent automation. Avatars are a popular tool used by gaming and fashion firms in the metaverse, providing new avenues for even more personalization. Second, with metaverse, marketers can offer a high-quality, unified omnichannel experience throughout the customer journey in varied channels. It recognizes that a lot of consumers will communicate with a business in a variety of ways even if they frequently have a preferred channel. Online, in-store, over the phone, and soon in the metaverse are all possible connecting points for a customer's journey.

Third, the metaverse presents marketers with novel and captivating scenarios for creating loyalty programs, wherein rewards might take the form of virtual events and digital assets. This will exponentially enhance CX. The initiative of luxury brand Gucci, Gucci Garden on Roblox can be considered as a very good example to understand the role of metaverse in improving CX. Fourth, metaverse can offer instant and context-sensitive customer support which will improve the CX. The metaverse can assist marketers in delivering information and content in an immersive, interactive way in addition to being a useful tool for sales and entertainment. The customers can get immediate answers to frequently asked inquiries rather of having to wait in a real or virtual line. Customers may see the main characteristics and technical specifications of their cars with Toyota's AR software, which also assists them in making selections about what to buy. Besides, metaverse can enhance CX by increasing urban resilience and emergency response skills by simulating city operations and disaster situations.

3. Smart Cities: A Need in the Metaverse World

A smart city employs digital technologies to improve the quality of its residents' lives. It is an urban area with improved accessibility, a better climate, improved government services and modern infrastructure which helps quicken economic growth and enhance sustainability[1] (Yaqoob et al., 2023). Cities are already using technologies like IoT blockchain, AR, and digital twins to assist them with municipal tasks like resource management in transportation, healthcare, and tourism to name few. Metaverse will revolutionize the development of smart cities. In addition, cities can use the Metaverse in a variety of ways, from straightforward ones like putting government services online to more complex ones like utilizing the Metaverse's 3D capabilities to predict how decisions will affect our communities. For example, In Seoul, South Korea, the metaverse has enhanced the city's experience. The city is going to invest $3.3 billion by the year 2030 to be a metaverse city. In such a metaverse city, people need not stand in lines, nor do they need to wait for buses. They can connect and interact with others without leaving their homes (Menzel, 2023; O'Donovan, 2023). All this will lead to an enhanced CX. On a similar line, the UAE is planning to develop a virtual city in the metaverse (O'Donovan, 2023).

4. Applications of Metaverse in Smart Cities: A Superior CX

In essence, the real world is being virtualized and digitalized through Metaverse. "Metaverse" is made up of two words: "Meta" and "Verse" (Lenger, 2022). The

---

[1] https://www.microsoft.com/en-us/industry/government/resources/smart-cities#:~:text=A%20smart%20city%20is%20an,the%20cities%20of%20the%20future.

Metaverse presents a picture of an immersive communal area where individuals can move around and connect with both, the Metaverse and the real world, in the future scenario. A lot of things will change due to the emergence of Metaverse. These changes may be experienced in five main categories: economy, innovation, culture, life, and cities. This chapter is mainly focusing on cities as the authors are of the view that smart cities will alleviate many problems of today's urban population by bringing a transformation in many aspects of cities including, retail, transport, healthcare etc. Modern civilization requires smart cities, which are built to efficiently apply the newest information technology to solve the problems posed by growing urbanization and globalization in city industries (Yigitcanlar, 2015). In such technologically advanced smart cities, having a great CX is a pressing need. In such a scenario, the metaverse has a significant role as it can offer a superior CX via personalization, adventure, transaction, and interactivity in communications with customers. Therefore, more and more businesses are turning to the creation of metaverse, like, Qualcomm, Meta (Facebook), and Microsoft (Polona et al., 2022). In essence, the metaverse is a collection of 3D virtual environments where customers may communicate, interact socially, and exchange digital products and services in varied contexts. As such, Metaverse can enhance CX by providing new avenues for exploring products, creating a more evocative synthesis of physical and virtual worlds, and by stimulating dealings between people and brands via AI-enabled bots. Metaverse has the capability to offer great CX by bringing revolutionary changes in many facets of smart cities, like smart homes, transportation, healthcare, banking, and tourism which will be discussed in detail.

4.1. Metaverse and Smart Homes

Metaverse can make homes smart by empowering customers to control devices at the convenience of their fingertips. Such homes will allow customers to personalize the environments which will enhance overall CX. In such smart homes, customers will be able to connect virtually with almost every electronic device and gadget. The immersive interface of Metaverse will enable residents to take a virtual tour of the entire home while sitting on a comfy sofa. They can customize their homes for better CX, Metaverse will enable them to monitor the security of their homes which will give them more satisfaction. They will be in a position to have real-time 360-degree views of their homes 24 × 7. Residents will be able to manage the usage of energy due to the metaverse. For example, if metaverse widgets are connected to the actual smart thermostat, such widgets can help raise the temperature of smart homes with a handful of hand motions (Bizzaco, 2021). Even cleaning a home with the support of Metaverse in itself a memorable experience without fatigue, as a resident can interact with a vacuum robot or a smart mop via a controlled panel and can control its functioning by giving desired commands (Bizzaco, 2021).

4.2. Metaverse and Transportation

Meta mobility can result in a revolution in the transportation sector through remote-controlled robots and cars. Meta mobility will bridge the gap between the physical and digital worlds. This will help travelers in finding more eco-friendly and efficient routes that will not only provide them with unique experience but will also result in the optimum utilization of scarce resources (Pamucar et al., 2023). Similarly, through VR, it is easy to monitor the movement of people at airports which will help the system to be on alert mode, if any emergency arises. Furthermore, this will make their journeys more cost-effective and will, in turn, improves their CX (Pamucar et al., 2023). As such, metaverse can potentially improve CX by enhancing customer engagement. For example, travel companies are offering three-dimensional virtual tours of sites and hotels in order to enhance CX by providing pre-travel planning information.

4.3. Metaverse and Smart Automobiles

According to the President of Hyundai Motor Group, Chang Song (2022), meta-mobility will make space, time, and distance all very irrelevant. Hyundai (2022) will connect robots to the metaverse and it will improve meta mobility. This in turn will allow people to travel from the real world to the virtual one without any boundaries. Thus, they will be having an immersive experience.

Metaverse has also improved the experience of customers while driving vehicles. This has brought a drastic and productive change in the automotive sector. Metaverse has enabled automobile manufacturers to embed gaming and entertainment in vehicles to improve CX (Mourtzis et al., 2022). Now it is possible to repair a vehicle without touching it physically and remotely, thanks to the metaverse (Lee & Kundu, 2022). Metaverse, thus, can offer multiple facilities that were not available earlier and thereby provide unique and memorable CX (Yaqoob et al., 2023).

4.4. Metaverse and Retail

The amalgamation of metaverse and retail can revolutionize the way customers shop, select a brand, interact with a brand, and experience the entire retail journey. It combines the convenience of online shopping with immersive technology and social facets of physical retail. In an era where more deals and varieties are available, customer attention, retention, experience satisfaction, and loyalty are the most important areas for retail to focus on (Yoo et al., 2023). Retail can manage all the above mentioned aspects easily and effectively via applying metaverse technology. Retailers can use personalized digital avatars to fit their offerings and improve CX. Retailers can create virtual stores within the metaverse. This will enable customers to browse, search, select, and finally purchase products in the virtual environment. Metaverse can offer immersive and interactive shopping experiences to customers. They can virtually try on clothing, test products, and explore merchandise before making a final purchase. Retailers can set up virtual showrooms to increase their visibility on a global scale (Barrera & Shah, 2023). Metaverse enables retailers to offer personalized shopping experiences which make customers more engaged. Retailers can use AR in the metaverse to enable customers to try on various products like clothing, cosmetics, or other accessories virtually before they decide to purchase.

4.5. Metaverse and Healthcare

The healthcare sector can experience a complete transformation using metaverse technology. Metaverse will bring revolutionary improvements in the healthcare sector and, thus, will offer a memorable CX (Chengoden et al., 2023; Wu & Ho, 2023). Metaverse makes pre-surgical mapping for serious health problems (e.g., brain tumors and cardiovascular diseases) possible which can be utilized to offer personalized treatment based on a virtual diagnosis. Metaverse can prove to be a boon for cardiac surgeons who can perform operations anywhere without leaving their place. Metaverse can be used to offer training to the physicians of the next generation. All this will bring revolutionary improvement in the healthcare industry and will create superior CX.

5. Linkage Between IoT and Metaverse

As discussed earlier, Metaverse, being a virtual world allows people to network with each other using 3D technology in real time. On the other hand, the IoT constitutes a network comprising physical devices, vehicles, buildings, and other tangible objects interconnected via the internet. These objects have the capability to gather and exchange data. IoT and Metaverse complement to each other. The Metaverse will function as a three-dimensional user interface for IoT devices, facilitating a novel, tailored user experience within the IoT realm. Concurrently, IoT will empower the Metaverse to analyze and engage with the physical environment. Together, IoT and the Metaverse will streamline the process of making data-informed decisions, requiring less effort and training from individuals. In the next section, focus was given on the application of IoT in varied industries.

IoT is a collection of appliances, and software which facilitate the exchange of data without human-to-human or human-to-computer interface. The IoT consists of many technologies that helps to trace, screen, and manage and enables companies to make intelligent and collaborative decisions (Molano et al., 2018). The IoT connects devices of people with machines without human intervention. IoT converts raw data into understandable facts and then makes intelligent decisions.

Metaverse and IoT can be applied in vast areas such as agriculture, healthcare, transportation, military, transportation, retailing, home automation, disaster management, environmental monitoring, surveillance, waste management, vehicular systems, and pilgrim monitoring systems (Hameed et al., 2019). The primary objective of metaverse and IoT is to improve the human beings' lives quality. Metaverse along with IoT brought smart cars, smart buildings, and smart homes which made life easy and convenient for everyone and thus, enhanced CX. It offers a bundle of benefits to companies as it strengthens supply chain management, improves the effectiveness of operations, minimizes operational costs, and helps the firms to offer defect-free services to customers. It manages the inventory and reduces needless faults in goods' delivery (Ayers & Odegaard, 2017). Traditional supply chain suffers from several deficiencies such as overstocking, stock out situation, and delays in delivery. These problems increase complexity and uncertainty (Abdel-Basset et al., 2018). Metaverse and IoT address all these issues associated with the supply chain. It also enriches CX through customer engagement and by providing real-time information to customers (Deshwal, 2016). IoT improves customer interactions and leads to value co-creation (Balaji & Roy, 2017). Many retail firms are using metaverse and IoT to improve the conversion ratio and enhance customer service experience (Polona et al., 2022; Saeed et al., 2019). As modern retailers are facing hyper-competition, it is not enough to offer the products that customers want. Retailers must give reasons to customers to buy the goods by offering them a better shopping experience using state-of-the-art technology. Sales are primarily driven by customer engagements which generate superior CX. The metaverse and IoT can connect and engage millions of customers. According to research conducted by the University of Michigan in 2021, the customers who are engaged spent 19% more as compared to the customers who are not engaged.

6. Applications of the IoT

The recent advancement in near-field communication technology (NFC), AI, web development, open-source server programs, and web development created a profound impact in the area of IoT. It is not only solving company-specific problems, environmental problems but also societal problems up to a great extent. The application of the IoT is discussed below.

6.1. IoT and Retailing

In the Indian context, retail is the second largest employer in the country after the agricultural sector. India is known as nation of the shops as there are more than 19 million shops in the country out of which only 4% are large shops. In India, organized retail is growing at the rate of 25% per annum and all the modern retailers are deploying IoT to increase sales and reduce the defection rates in the operation be it exchange, billing, or customer loyalty programs. Retailers are capitalizing mix of mobile apps and analytical tools to drive sales, optimize inventory, and engage customers. In the modern retail business, retailers use unique propositions of technologies such as touchscreen kiosks, AR, weather-targeted promotion, and personalization. Investment in IoT concerning retail is done primarily for the five purposes, namely, product tracking, customer engagement, mobile payment, asset management, and fleet and yard management. In the present context, retail companies are investing huge capital in RFID technology and cloud-based IoT. RFID offers significant benefits to retailers in managing back-end operations like inventory management, and theft prevention. It also helps to avoid the situation of stock out and ensure the availability of the product based on demand pattern. Roy et al., (2016) and Hoffman (2019) cited various applications of IoT in retail which are explained below.

McDonald's used weather-specific targeting strategies to drive sales. They sent contextual messages regarding the offer for a glass of soda if customers were near the store and the weather was sunny. The redemption offers on the mobile phone increased by 700%. Starbucks also sent the number of personalized offers on the mobile app which increased the sales exponentially. Walmart also uses predictive analytics, and big data to predict the sale of perishable items based on weather conditions, social media trends and customer demographic information. It is noteworthy to mention that only customer satisfaction associated with the product is not the ultimate objective of the retailer and hence retailers must find ways to offer unique and holistic experiences to customers through managing different touch points of the customers.

6.2. IoT and Military

Wireless technologies are used for monitoring and tracking the health of armed personnel but these technologies suffer from certain limitations such as complex infrastructure and limited bandwidth. These problems could be removed by using advanced IoT architecture. The use of IoT in the war helps in risk assessment and improves the extremely crucial response time. The deployment of an IoT-based system identifies the enemies, monitors the health condition of armed personnel, and synchronizes interconnection between armed forces and the defense system (Castiglione et al., 2017). Advanced helmets with sensors can be used to trace location of the army and prompt action can be taken to save their lives as per the need (Iyer & Patil, 2018).

6.3. IoT and Healthcare

IoT can be used for remote health monitoring and for developing smart hospitals. The use of IoT in the healthcare industry is discussed in this section. Generally, a remote health monitoring system is used to screen the health condition of patients belonging to an elder cohort who might be suffering from diabetes and neurological deficiency, heart disease, etc. (Malasinghe et al., 2019). Devices like accelerometers, Kinect cameras, pulsometers, and pedometers are connected to the bodies of patients which are further processed for better understanding of patient health conditions (Casacci et al., 2015; Kozlovszky et al., 2015; Otoom et al., 2015; Ramesh et al., 2012; Sannino et al., 2015; Szydło & Konieczny, 2015; Thelen et al., 2014). Next, two ingestible sensors can be helpful in taking the internal images of the patient body. It provides the information about functioning of the digestion system of a patient. Furthermore, smart hospitals can be developed using smart technology. The first stage begins with booking an appointment with the doctor based on availability and payment of the consultancy fee through the app. In the later stage medical report of the patient related to blood pressure, blood sugar, pulse rate, and ECG can be uploaded on real real-time basis for the reference of the doctor for the appropriate treatment plan.

6.4. IoT and Home Automation

The IoT changed the way people were living in their homes and operating home appliances. Customers can control all the home appliances such as TV, refrigerators, AC, and ovens from remote locations using the graphical user interface. It not only saves energy consumption but also reduces environmental pollution. All the home appliances are connected through the Internet using a network. Some of the important sensors used for controlling home appliances are temperature sensors, lux sensors, water level sensors, etc. The main advantage of home automation is that monitoring is possible from the remote location using face detection, and motion detection. The use of IoT improves the security system as it sends alert messages on real real-time basis. In the case of theft, the number plate of the vehicle can be detected.

6.5. IoT and Waste Management

Waste management is a major issue around the globe be it solid waste or electronic waste. IoT-based trash-based monitoring systems provide information about unfilled/filled trash bins. Based on the data, vehicles could be deployed to collect the solid waste from several locations.

6.6. IoT and Smart Meter

A smart meter improves transparency and monitoring and is beneficial for both the customer and the service provider. Customers can track the consumption of electricity/gas/water daily and they can pay the bill online. All the information related to energy consumption is sent to the central monitoring system of the service provider. Smart meters acquire information regarding usage patterns through the internet.

6.7. IoT and Surveillance

Security agencies are focusing much on surveillance as security threats are emerging in different forms and characters. The growing cases of terrorist activities across the world are a major area of concern. The security agencies are using face recognition technology to track the movement of any suspicious person/object. In China, 50% of the population is covered through face recognition technology. The surveillance device connected through the internet captures the data regularly. The data can be in audio or video form. The data are transmitted to the central monitoring station through the cloud server. Surveillance-based systems ensure the security of public infrastructure/railway terminals/airports through continuous monitoring and alert messages.

6.8. IoT and Vehicular Communication System

The IoT brought a revolution in vehicular communication through vehicle-to-vehicle, vehicle to sensor and vehicle-to-internet communication (Preeti & Harish, 2016). Vehicular communication can be categorized into two categories. The first category is intra-vehicular communication that provides information about road conditions, driver drowsiness, tyre pressure, water temperature, etc.

The second category is inter-vehicular communication. The important benefit of this is inter-vehicle connectivity in which the vehicle can connect with nearby vehicles to provide information regarding lane change to prevent accidents (Bai & Krishnamachari, 2010). The use of IoT can upgrade the vehicle to transform it into a smarter vehicle.

6.9. IoT and Pilgrims Monitoring

Pilgrim's monitoring is a major challenge keeping in mind the mass gathering of pilgrims at a particular place. In a country like India, any negligence of security agencies may lead to mass destruction. Kumbh Mela is the largest religious mass gathering on the earth. In Praygraj, India, 120 million pilgrims attended the Kumbh Mela. To control and manage such huge mass gatherings and to maintain law and order situations is not possible through manual intervention and thus internet-based technology comes into the picture. The IoT-based pilgrims monitoring system can manage and control the pilgrim crowd effectively.

7. Growth Prospects of Metaverse and IoT

Together, Metaverse and IoT created a transformative and revolutionary impact on industries and society in today's digital world. It has been predicted that around one-fourth population will invest a minimum of one hour in the metaverse by the year 2026 (Gartner, 2022). Even, the big tech companies are investing heavily in the formation of a metaverse, for example, Qualcomm, Meta (Facebook), and Microsoft (Polona et al., 2022), signaling the significance of metaverse in delivering superior CX. According to Gartner research and advisory firm, more than 24 billion things would be connected through the internet by IoT. The global IoT market is expected to be to $650 billion in the year 2026 from $300 billion in 2021. It is expected that the market of IoT will grow exponentially at the rate of 17.2% (CAGR) from 2023 to 2032.

8. Limitations

The IoT and Metaverse created significant impacts on varied industries. The data collected by IoT are utilized by Metaverse to create a virtual world where users interact with each other in real-time. There is the possibility of breaches of the data which hurt the possibility of the person. We attempted to shed light on IoT and Metaverse and its application in healthcare, retail, military, transportation, and limitations associated with IoT and Metaverse. Though the metaverse and IoT offer unimaginable opportunities to make cities smart, it is not free from challenges. As the data of smart homes becomes completely synced with the metaverse, the privacy and security of such smart homes can be at risk. Therefore, metaverse should be equipped with such security layers to protect against breaches of security and privacy to offer the best CX. Due to security breaches, hackers may control the device and can execute unlawful activities. The negative consequences of the metaverse and IoT include privacy issues, profile tracking, face recognition, localization and tracking, etc. Klein et al. (2018) discussed six categories of challenges associated with the IoT. These challenges are classified into six categories, namely, IoT ecosystem, product development, internal capabilities, value proposition, technology infrastructure, and the generation of revenue.

Profiling and tracking: The identity of the person can be traced and his association with a particular group/institution can be identified. This imposes serious challenges as the association of a person with a particular group/community can be misused due to political/religious interests. Moreover, based on the profiling of customers, insurance companies may charge a high premium to those customers who are expected to suffer from certain diseases.

Localization: With the help of advanced technology, the location of the individual can be tracked. Individuals can settle at any place and can move from one place to another place as per their desire. Government authority/security agency can restrict the movement of any person due to undisclosed reasons which is a violation of human rights. There is an urgent need to create a trade-off between business interests and the privacy of individuals.

Data transmission: Secured transmission of the data is a major concern. Due to breaches of the data, personal information can be disclosed to untrusted people and private information might be misused. The Cambridge Analytica scandal where the private data of millions of users were stolen is an alarming call for everyone. There is a dire need to create a protocol/framework to protect the privacy of people.

9. Conclusion

Metaverse, IoT, artificial intelligence and predictive analytics created a revolution in the industry. It changed the way companies were operating earlier. Metaverse and IoT bring better insight, help the company to make intelligent decisions, reduce operational costs and errors and manage the inventory effectively. IoT removes the inventory problems associated with stock out, overstocking, and delay in delivery. Metaverse and IoT can be used in a variety of sectors such as manufacturing, retailing, transportation, agriculture, healthcare, military operations, etc., which makes cities smart and enhances CX. Metaverse and the IoT is also creating transformative impacts on society and the environment which in turn is creating new avenues for customers in terms of more varieties, more options, more facilities, cleaner environment, more sustainability, more security, more safety, better treatments and hence, enhanced CX. Although these technologies: metaverse and IoT offer significant benefits for smart cities and improve CX, they are not free from limitations. There is a possibility of data breaches and loss of data; personal information can be disclosed to untrusted people who may misuse the data. There is a dire need to protect the privacy of individuals by creating a protocol/framework for interconnection among machines to further make CX memorable.

References

Abdel-Basset, M., Manogaran, G., & Mohamed, M. (2018). Internet of Things (IoT) and its impact on supply chain: A framework for building smart, secure and efficient systems. *Future Generation Computer Systems, 86*(9), 614–628.

Ayers, J. B., & Odegaard, M. A. (2017). *Retail supply chain management.* CRC Press.

Bai, F., & Krishnamachari, B. (2010). Exploiting the wisdom of the crowd: localized, distributed information-centric VANETs [Topics in Automotive Networking]. *IEEE Communications Magazine, 48*(5), 138–146.

Balaji, M. S., & Roy, S. K. (2017). Value co-creation with Internet of things technology in the retail industry. *Journal of Marketing Management, 33*(1-2), 7–31.

Barrera, K. G., & Shah, D. (2023). Marketing in the metaverse: Conceptual understanding, framework, and research agenda. *Journal of Business Research, 155*, 113420.

Bizzaco, M. (2021). *What does the metaverse mean for smart homes?* https://www.digital-trends.com/home/will-the-metaverse-affect-smart-home/

Casacci, P., Pistoia, M., Leone, A., Caroppo, A., & Siciliano, P. (2015, July). Alzheimer patient's home rehabilitation through ICT advanced technologies: The ALTRUISM project. In *Ambient assisted living: Italian forum 2014* (pp. 377–385). Springer International Publishing.

Castiglione, A., Choo, K. K. R., Nappi, M., & Ricciardi, S. (2017). Context aware ubiquitous biometrics in edge of military things. *IEEE Cloud Computing, 4*(6), 16–20.

Chengoden, R., Victor, N., Huynh-The, T., Yenduri, G., Jhaveri, R. H., Alazab, M., Bhattacharya, S., Hegde, P., Maddikunta, P. K. R. & Gadekallu, T. R. (2023). *Metaverse for healthcare: a survey on potential applications, challenges and future directions.* IEEE Access, 11, 12765–12795.

Deshwal, P. (2016). Customer experience quality and demographic variables (age, gender, education level, and family income) in retail stores. *International Journal of Retail & Distribution Management, 44*(9), 940–955.

Gadekallu, T. R., Huynh-The, T., Wang, W., Yenduri, G., Ranaweera, P., Pham, Q. V., da Costa, D. B. & Liyanage, M. (2022). *Blockchain for the metaverse: A review.* arXiv preprint arXiv:2203.09738.

Gartner. (2022). *Gartner predicts 25% of people will spend at least one hour per day in the metaverse by 2026.* https://www.gartner.com/en/newsroom/press-releases/2022-02-07-gartner-predicts-25-percent-of-people-will-spend-at-least-one-hour-per-day-in-the-metaverse-by-2026#:~:text=By%202026%2C%2025%25%20of%20people,research%20vice%20president%20at%20Gartner

Hameed, S., Khan, F. I., & Hameed, B. (2019). Understanding security requirements and challenges in Internet of Things (IoT): A review. *Journal of Computer Networks and Communications, 2019*, 1–14.

Huddleston, Jr. T. (2021). *This 29-year-old book predicted the 'metaverse'—and some of Facebook's plans are eerily similar.* https://www.cnbc.com/2021/11/03/how-the-1992-sci-fi-novel-snow-crash-predicted-facebooks-metaverse.html

Hyundai. (2022). *Human reach' through robotics & metaverse at CES 2022.* https://www.hyundai.news/eu/articles/press-releases/hyundai-shares-vision-of-new-metamobility-concept-through-robotics-and-metaverse-at-CES-2022.html#:~:text=The%20idea%20behind%20Metamobility%20is,real%20world%20and%20virtual%20reality

Iyer, V. R., & Patki, J. (2016). Reaching the Poor with Microfinance: a case of rural south India. *International Journal of Business Ethics in Developing Economies, 5*(2), 29–37.

Klein, A. Z., Pacheco, F. B., & da Rosa Righi, R. (2018). On developing business models for Internet of things-based products: Process and challenges. *Journal of Information Systems and Technology Management, 14*(3), 439–461.

Kozlovszky, M., Kovacs, L., & Karoczkai, K. (2015). *Cardiovascular and diabetes focused remote patient monitoring* [Conference session]. VI Latin American Congress on

Biomedical Engineering CLAIB 2014, Paraná, Argentina 29, 30 & 31 October 2014 (pp. 568–571). Springer International Publishing.

Lee, J., & Kundu, P. (2022). Integrated cyber-physical systems and industrial metaverse for remote manufacturing. *Manufacturing Letters, 34*, 12–15.

Lenger, A. D. (2022). Digital transformation in the digital world the metaverse: The new era on the internet. In R. Pettinger, B. B. Gupta, A. R. Babeș-Bolyai, & D. Cozmiuc (Eds.), *Handbook of research on digital transformation management and tools* (pp. 199–217). IGI Global.

Liu, Y., Shen, Y., Guo, C., Tian, Y., Wang, X., Zhu, Y., & Wang, F. Y. (2022). MetaSensing in metaverses: See there, be there, and know there. *IEEE Intelligent Systems, 37*(6), 7–12.

Lv, Z., Xie, S., Li, Y., Hossain, M. S., & El Saddik, A. (2022). Building the metaverse by digital twins at all scales, state, relation. *Virtual Reality & Intelligent Hardware, 4*(6), 459–470.

Malasinghe, L. P., Ramzan, N., & Dahal, K. (2019). Remote patient monitoring: A comprehensive study. *Journal of Ambient Intelligence and Humanized Computing, 10*, 57–76.

Menzel, G. (2023). *The metaverse has very real applications, and Seoul is one city on the path to prove it*. https://www.capgemini.com/insights/expert-perspectives/how-the-city-of-seoul-is-bringing-the-metaverse-to-life/#:~:text=In%20Seoul%2C%20South%20Korea%2C%20the,buses%2C%20or%20even%20leaving%20home

Molano, J. I. R., Lovelle, J. M. C., Montenegro, C. E., Granados, J. J. R., & Crespo, R. G. (2018). Metamodel for integration of internet of things, social networks, the cloud and industry 4.0. *Journal of Ambient Intelligence and Humanized Computing, 9*, 709–723.

Moore, K. (2022). *The next economy: Creating new ways to shop, work, and play*. https://www.fastcompany.com/90771640/the-next-economy-creating-new-waysto-shop-work-and-play

Mourtzis, D., Panopoulos, N., Angelopoulos, J., Wang, B., & Wang, L. (2022). Human centric platforms for personalized value creation in metaverse. *Journal of Manufacturing Systems, 65*, 653–659.

O'Donovan, T. (2023). *Virtual smart cities using metaverse, digital twins*. Retrieved from https://www.biznesstransform.com/virtual-smart-cities-using-metaverse-digital-twins/

Otoom, A. F., Abdallah, E. E., Kilani, Y., Kefaye, A., & Ashour, M. (2015). Effective diagnosis and monitoring of heart disease. *International Journal of Software Engineering and Its Applications, 9*(1), 143–156.

Pamucar, D., Deveci, M., Gokasar, I., Delen, D., Köppen, M., & Pedrycz, W. (2023). Evaluation of metaverse integration alternatives of sharing economy in transportation using fuzzy Schweizer-Sklar based ordinal priority approach. *Decision Support Systems, 171*, 113944.

Polona, C., André, M. T., & Maria, N. (2022). *Metaverse: Opportunities, risks and policy implications*. European Parliamentary Research Service.

Preethi, V., & Harish, G. (2016, August). *Design and implementation of smart energy meter* [Conference session]. 2016 International Conference on Inventive Computation Technologies (ICICT) (Vol. 1, pp. 1–5). IEEE.

Ramesh, M. V., Anand, S., & Rekha, P. (2012, September). *A mobile software for health professionals to monitor remote patients* [Conference session]. 2012 Ninth International Conference on Wireless and Optical Communications Networks (WOCN) (pp. 1–4). IEEE.

Roy, A., Zalzala, A. M., & Kumar, A. (2016). Disruption of things: A model to facilitate adoption of IoT-based innovations by the urban poor. *Procedia Engineering, 159*, 199–209.

Saeed, F., Mohammed, F., & Gazem, N. (Eds.). (2019). Emerging trends in intelligent computing and informatics: Data Science, Intelligent Information Systems and Smart Computing.

Sannino, G., De Falco, I., & De Pietro, G. (2015). A supervised approach to automatically extract a set of rules to support fall detection in an mHealth system. *Applied Soft Computing, 34*, 205–216.

Song, C. (2022). *Hyundai motor shares vision of new metamobility concept, 'expanding human reach' through robotics & metaverse at CES 2022*. https://www.hyundai.news/eu/articles/press-releases/hyundai-shares-vision-of-new-metamobility-concept-through-robotics-and-metaverse-at-CES-2022.html#:~:text=The%20idea%20behind%20Metamobility%20is,real%20world%20and%20virtual%20reality

Sparkes, M. (2021). What is a metaverse? *Newscientists, 251*(3348), 18.

Szydło, T., & Konieczny, M. (2015). Mobile devices in the open and universal system for remote patient monitoring. *IFAC-PapersOnLine, 48*(4), 296–301.

Thelen, S., Czaplik, M., Meisen, P., Schilberg, D., & Jeschke, S. (2014). Using off-the-shelf medical devices for biomedical signal monitoring in a telemedicine system for emergency medical services. *IEEE Journal of Biomedical and Health Informatics, 19*(1), 117–123.

Wang, Y., Su, Z., Zhang, N., Xing, R., Liu, D., Luan, T. H., & Shen, X. (2022). A survey on metaverse: Fundamentals, security, and privacy. *IEEE Communications Surveys & Tutorials, 25*(1), 319–352. http://dx.doi.org/10.1109/COMST.2022.3202047

Wang, X., Yang, J., Han, J., Wang, W., & Wang, F. Y. (2022). Metaverses and DeMetaverses: From digital twins in CPS to parallel intelligence in CPSS. *IEEE Intelligent Systems, 37*(4), 97–102.

Wu, T. C., & Ho, C. T. B. (2023). A scoping review of metaverse in emergency medicine. *Australasian Emergency Care, 26*(1), 75–83.

Xu, M., Ng, W. C., Lim, W. Y. B., Kang, J., Xiong, Z., Niyato, D., Yang, Q., Shen, X., & Miao, C. (2022). A full dive into realizing the edge-enabled metaverse: Visions, enabling technologies, and challenges. *IEEE Communications Surveys & Tutorials, 25*(1), 656–700.

Yaqoob, I., Salah, K., Jayaraman, R., & Omar, M. (2023). Metaverse applications in smart cities: Enabling technologies, opportunities, challenges, and future directions. *Internet of Things, 23*, 100884.

Yigitcanlar, T. (2015). Smart cities: An effective urban development and management model? *Australian Planner, 52*(1), 27–34.

Yoo, K., Welden, R., Hewett, K., & Haenlein, M. (2023). The merchants of meta: A research agenda to understand the future of retailing in the metaverse. *Journal of Retailing, 99*(2), 173–192.

Zallio, M., & Clarkson, P. J. (2022). Designing the metaverse: A study on inclusion, diversity, equity, accessibility and safety for digital immersive environments. *Telematics and Informatics, 75*, 101909.

Chapter 6

Unleashing Digital Frontiers: Bridging Realities of Augmented Reality, Virtual Reality, and the Metaverse

Arjun J. Nair[a], Sridhar Manohar[a], Amit Mittal[a] and Rishi Chaudhry[b]

[a]*Chitkara Business School, Chitkara University, Punjab, India*
[b]*Institute of Management Studies and Research, Maharshi Dayanand University, Rohtak, India*

Abstract

This chapter adopts a historiographical methodology, meticulously retracing the lineage of Augmented Reality (AR) from the 16th century and scrutinizing the conceptual genesis of Virtual Reality (VR) in the mid-20th century. It rigorously scrutinizes the fundamental principles and applications of AR and VR, extending the discourse to encompass the foundational tenets and ramifications of the burgeoning Metaverse. Thoroughly examining ethical considerations and challenges, there is an emphasis on perpetuating research, judicious implementation, and establishing ethical frameworks. Elucidating the profound ramifications of AR on sundry industries, the transformative potential of VR in crafting immersive environments, and the emergent interconnected virtual realm of the Metaverse, key principles such as spatial mapping, interaction modalities, and cross-platform interoperability are accentuated. Ethical challenges inherent in Metaverse development, notably digital identity, and privacy are identified. The narrative steadfastly underscores the significance of perpetuated research and ethical considerations in steering the evolutionary trajectory of avant-garde technologies. The findings hold far-reaching implications for diverse sectors, encompassing navigation, marketing, healthcare, architecture, education, and entertainment. The Metaverse's potential to reconfigure digital experiences ubiquitously and its consequential impact on privacy and content moderation accentuate the exigency for circumspect consideration in development and implementation.

The Metaverse Dilemma: Challenges and Opportunities for Business and Society, 85–112
Copyright © 2025 by Arjun J. Nair, Sridhar Manohar, Amit Mittal and Rishi Chaudhry
Published under exclusive licence by Emerald Publishing Limited
doi:10.1108/978-1-83797-524-220241006

This chapter fervently advocates for responsible usage and the facilitation of equitable access. This chapter contributes to the scholarly corpus by synthesizing historical perspectives, core principles, and ethical considerations across the domains of AR, VR, and the Metaverse. The unique emphasis on sustained research endeavors and the establishment of ethical frameworks adds distinctive insights, thereby guiding the sagacious evolution of these paradigm-shifting technologies.

Keywords: Augmented reality; virtual reality; metaverse; ethical considerations; transformative technologies

Chapter Learning Objectives

1. Understanding Historical Foundations
   - Define the historical origins of AR from the 16th century.
   - Recognize the evolution of AR applications across industries.
2. Exploring AR Principles
   - Identify and explain fundamental principles of AR, including registration, interaction, context-awareness and spatial mapping.
3. Applications of AR
   - Explore diverse applications of AR in navigation, marketing, healthcare, architecture and education.
   - Understand the impact of AR on user experiences in different sectors.
4. Challenges in AR Technology
   - Analyze challenges in AR development, focusing on hardware limitations, user experience, privacy concerns and content creation.
   - Propose potential solutions to overcome challenges in AR implementation.
5. Future Developments in AR
   - Anticipate and discuss potential advancements in AR technology, including hardware improvements, 5G connectivity, AR cloud, spatial computing and AI integration.
6. VR Evolution and Applications
   - Trace the historical development of VR from its conceptualization in the mid-20th century.
   - Examine VR applications in healthcare, education, gaming and entertainment.
7. Core Principles of VR
   - Define and elucidate core principles of VR, including immersion, presence, interactivity, realism, sensory feedback, user comfort, accessibility, ethics, and content creation.
8. Challenges and Advancements in VR
   - Identify challenges in VR hardware and content creation.
   - Explore potential advancements in VR technology, encompassing hardware comfort, affordability, AI integration, and user-generated content platforms.

9. Introduction to the Metaverse
   - Define the metaverse as a virtual collective shared space.
   - Explore foundational concepts of the metaverse, such as immersion, interoperability and interconnectedness.
10. Metaverse Platforms and Implications
    - Investigate existing metaverse platforms (e.g., Second Life, Roblox, Decentraland, Fortnite, and VR Chat).
    - Analyze the implications of these platforms on user-generated content, virtual economies and digital ownership.
11. Potential and Core Concepts of the Metaverse
    - Understand the potential of the metaverse in building interconnected virtual universes.
    - Define and discuss core concepts of the metaverse, including persistent digital experiences, social interactions, virtual economies, trust and cross-platform interoperability.
12. Ethical Considerations in the Metaverse
    - Recognize and analyze ethical considerations in the development and adoption of the metaverse.
    - Formulate ethical guidelines for digital identity, privacy, content moderation, economic inclusivity, and intellectual property.
13. Synthesis of AR, VR, and the Metaverse
    - Synthesize the knowledge gained from AR, VR, and the metaverse sections.
    - Understand the seamless fusion of real and digital worlds, predicting transformative possibilities.
14. Research, Implementation, and Ethical Considerations
    - Emphasize the importance of continuous research in AR, VR, and metaverse technologies.
    - Advocate for responsible implementation and ethical considerations to ensure equitable access and responsible usage.
15. Future Prospects and Transformative Possibilities
    - Envision the future prospects of AR, VR, and the metaverse in reshaping human experiences.
    - Anticipate novel intersections of technology and human experiences in the evolving digital landscape.

Key Takeaways

This comprehensive exploration delves into the intricate realms of AR, VR, and the nascent Metaverse, providing nuanced insights into these transformative technologies. Commencing with the historical antecedents of AR, tracing its roots to the 16th century, the narrative unveils its trajectory into a pivotal force across navigation, marketing, healthcare, architecture, and education. This chapter accentuates fundamental AR principles such as registration, interaction, context-awareness and spatial mapping, integral in crafting immersive and cohesive experiential domains. The chapter illuminates VR's potential to engender immersive learning environments, facilitate medical procedures and revolutionize the gaming industry. Key principles, such as spatial mapping, interaction modalities, real-time engagement dynamics, and hardware advancements, are expounded upon within the contextual tapestry of VR's evolution. The exploration extends into the Metaverse, an emerging interconnected virtual universe gaining ascendance. Core concepts, including cross-platform interoperability, digital economies, social interactions, and virtual entertainment, are meticulously discussed, underscoring their instrumental role in shaping this burgeoning digital realm. The Metaverse's potential to construct an expansive, interconnected virtual cosmos accessible across diverse devices and platforms is scrutinized, emphasizing its transformative impact not only on entertainment but also on education, healthcare and commerce. Ethical considerations and challenges intrinsic to the Metaverse's development are subjected to rigorous examination, acknowledging the pivotal import of digital identity, privacy safeguards, and content moderation mechanisms. Throughout the chapter, the narrative underscores the significance of ongoing research, judicious implementation practices and ethical considerations as indispensable components steering the perpetual evolution of these technologies. While AR, VR, and the Metaverse proffer seemingly boundless opportunities, their trajectories must be guided by robust ethical frameworks and concerted research endeavors to ensure equitable access and judicious deployment. This safeguards that the evolution of these technologies accrues societal benefits while diligently addressing latent risks and challenges. The amalgamation of the tangible and the digital domains is manifesting as an increasingly seamless endeavor, heralding transformative possibilities. As the sojourn through the realms of AR, VR, and the Metaverse endures, the abiding importance of research, judicious implementation, and ethical considerations persist as the lodestars guiding this intersection of technology and human experiences into novel and uncharted territories. The future holds exciting prospects, where technology and human experiences intersect in novel and unprecedented ways.

1. Introduction

Augmented Reality (AR) stands as a technological marvel that superimposes digital information, encompassing intricate 3D models, images, and textual data, onto the authentic physical milieu, thereby augmenting the user's perceptual and interactive experiences within their surroundings (Zak, 2013). Esteemed across diverse domains such as education, healthcare, gaming, and industry, AR has garnered substantial attention due to its transformative potential in reshaping the paradigms of learning, work and entertainment. The inception of AR traces back to the 1960s with the pioneering work of Ivan Sutherland, who conceptualized the first head-mounted display (HMD) systems (Peddie & Peddie, 2017). Subsequent evolution has been marked by remarkable strides in both hardware and software technologies. The seminal Virtuality Continuum by Milgram and Kishino (1994) laid the conceptual groundwork for amalgamating virtual and real environments, fundamentally shaping AR's contemporary definition and comprehension. Within the realm of AR, the synergy of hardware and software components is pivotal to its operational efficacy. AR relies on a spectrum of hardware components, spanning smartphones, tablets, HMDs, and intelligent eyewear. While initial AR applications predominantly operated on HMDs, the ubiquity of smartphones has catalyzed the widespread adoption of mobile AR (Azuma, 1997; Rampolla & Kipper, 2012). On the software front, AR applications assume responsibility for tracking, recognizing and rendering virtual objects seamlessly into the tangible world. Commonly employed tracking and registration techniques encompass markers, GPS, and computer vision methodologies (Schmalstieg & Hollerer, 2016). In education, AR is increasingly leveraged to augment learning experiences, creating interactive and immersive environments that enhance students' comprehension and engagement (Billinghurst & Duenser, 2012). In healthcare, AR finds utility in medical training, surgery guidance and patient education, furnishing real-time information to medical practitioners and yielding improved patient outcomes (Hsieh & Wei, 2017; Manohar et al., 2023). The global phenomenon of AR gaming, exemplified by applications like Pokémon Go, blurs the conventional demarcations between digital and physical domains, engaging users in unprecedented ways (Ghosh & Jhamb, 2022; Nair et al., 2023a). In industrial sectors, AR is revolutionizing operations by augmenting worker productivity, furnishing real-time information and facilitating maintenance and repair tasks (Jhamb et al., 2022). However, despite its immense promise, AR confronts challenges including user experience issues, privacy concerns and hardware limitations. Future trajectories of AR development are anticipated to surmount these challenges through advancements in wearables, sophisticated computer vision algorithms and enhanced integration with artificial intelligence (AI) and the Internet of Things (IoT) (Ghosh et al., 2022; Nair et al., 2023b). The trajectory of AR's evolution since its inception underscores its undeniable potential across diverse domains, asserting its escalating significance in our daily lives as technology relentlessly progresses, thereby transmuting our interactions with information and the world at large.

Virtual Reality (VR) manifests as an immersive technological marvel that has undergone significant metamorphosis, providing users with interactive computer-generated environments (McRobert, 2007). Its applications span diverse domains including gaming, healthcare, education, and training. Rooted in mid-20th-century concepts with notable contributions from trailblazers VR has witnessed increased accessibility through advancements in computing and display technologies, exemplified by contemporary high-quality headsets like Oculus Rift and HTC Vive (Gutierrez, 2023; Shalender & Yadav, 2019). Hardware components such as headsets and motion tracking devices, coupled with software applications and environments tailored for immersive experiences, form the structural foundation of VR. Its utilization extends to gaming, healthcare (for pain management and therapy), education and training, as well as architecture and design, fundamentally altering user interactions within virtual worlds.

The concept of the Metaverse, an amalgam of AR and VR within a shared virtual space, has garnered substantial attention, with major corporations like Meta (formerly Facebook) investing in its realization. The Metaverse extends beyond mere entertainment and social interaction, influencing healthcare through AR-enabled medical training and remote consultations, while VR proves efficacious in the treatment of psychological disorders. In fields such as architecture, engineering, and design, these immersive technologies facilitate virtual prototyping and simulations. As these technologies proliferate, concerns pertaining to privacy and ethics arise due to the extensive collection of personal data and potential psychological effects. The Metaverse introduces complex questions concerning digital ownership, identity, governance, and its overarching impact on future economies and societies (Bibri et al., 2022). These transformative technologies redefine our perceptions, interactions and coexistence within the digital and physical realms, holding the potential to reshape the very nature of reality itself.

The confluence of AR, VR, and the Metaverse constitutes a transformative force reshaping industries and ushering in a revolution in human experiences. These immersive technologies proffer avant-garde modalities for engaging with both the digital and physical realms, exerting profound influences across diverse sectors. The Metaverse, an expansive virtual domain transcending singular environments, functions as a nexus between tangible and digital realities, unfurling unprecedented opportunities for interaction, collaboration and creative endeavors (Fink, 2021). In the educational sphere, the orchestrated integration of AR, VR, and the Metaverse engenders immersive learning environments through simulations and interactive pedagogical modules (AlGerafi et al., 2023). Healthcare stands to gain substantial benefits as AR and VR contribute to surgical procedures and therapeutic interventions, while the Metaverse facilitates remote consultations and data sharing (Bansal et al., 2022). Within the industrial landscape, the triumvirate of AR, VR, and the Metaverse undergoes a metamorphosis of manufacturing, maintenance and training processes, thereby amplifying worker productivity (Qadir & Fatah, 2023). The panorama of entertainment and gaming undergoes a revolutionary overhaul, presenting interconnected virtual realms and introducing novel prospects for digital interaction. Retail experiences a paradigm shift as AR enhances in-store engagement, VR crafts virtual shopping environments and the Metaverse introduces social shopping experiences. However, challenges encompassing privacy, security, accessibility, and standardization necessitate meticulous attention. Nevertheless, this convergence serves as a crucible transforming industries and human experiences across a myriad of domains. As technology evolves, a future characterized by heightened interconnectedness and immersiveness beckons, obfuscating the demarcation between the physical and digital realms and unlocking uncharted possibilities for innovation and engagement.

The exploration serves as an exhaustive exposition elucidating the intricate and swiftly progressing terrain of AR, VR, and the emergent metaverse. These technological paradigms have engendered a metamorphosis in our interaction modalities with both the digital and tangible realms. The inquiry commences with AR, retracing its lineage to the 16th century when Giambattista della Porta propounded the manipulation of light for illusionary effects (Galson, 2016). Subsequently, probing into the concept of registration, a pivotal procedure involving the alignment of virtual content with the authentic world, while also delving into interaction dynamics, context-awareness and spatial mapping as integral components of AR is followed. The narrative accentuates the multifarious applications of AR, spanning navigation, marketing, healthcare, and education. The focus then transitions to VR, meticulously evaluating its transformative influence across diverse sectors. The examination encompasses VR's role in gaming, healthcare, education, and architecture, with an in-depth analysis of core principles such as spatial mapping, real-time interaction, and hardware advancements contextualized within the evolutionary trajectory of VR. The discourse subsequently expands into the metaverse, an imminent interconnected digital cosmos, exploring fundamental concepts like cross-platform interoperability, digital economies, social interactions, and virtual entertainment. Profound implications arising from the creation of an expansive and interconnected virtual universe are expounded upon, alongside a critical examination of ethical considerations and challenges inherent in the metaverse's development. Thereby, addressing issues encompass digital identity, privacy, and content moderation. The future portends thrilling prospects wherein the boundaries of the tangible world undergo redefinition, engendering novel and unparalleled intersections between technology and human experiences. Within the rapidly evolving panorama of contemporary technology, the digital domain undergoes a profound and perpetual metamorphosis orchestrated by groundbreaking innovations that dissolve the hitherto distinct demarcation between the tangible and digital spheres. Standing at the vanguard of this revolutionary transformation are AR, VR and the nascent conceptualization of the Metaverse. Collectively, these technologies redefine individuals' perception and engagement with digital content, intricately interweaving the realms of the digital and the tangible. fusion of immersive technologies with the physical world carries profound implications spanning not only entertainment and leisure but also extending to education, healthcare, commerce and a plethora of other sectors. The amalgamation of immersive technologies, notably AR and VR, with the tangible world bears profound ramifications across diverse sectors, extending beyond the realms of mere entertainment and leisure to exert a transformative influence on education, healthcare, commerce, and the preservation of cultural heritage. In the educational domain, these technologies inaugurate an epoch of immersive learning experiences, wherein students can navigate historical sites and partake in hands-on simulations, thereby revolutionizing established pedagogical methodologies. Healthcare practitioners reap the benefits of VR's surgical training simulations and applications in exposure therapy, fostering skill refinement and elevating patient outcomes. Within the commercial landscape, AR facilitates virtual try-ons and interactive product catalogs, thereby metamorphosing the landscape of online retail. The entertainment sector undergoes a paradigm shift courtesy of VR, endowing users with immersive gaming encounters and participatory narratives. Architects and designers strategically employ AR and VR for virtual prototyping and client presentations, thereby catalyzing a revolution in design and construction methodologies. Furthermore, these technologies contribute substantially to cultural preservation through the establishment of virtual museums and exhibitions, thereby transcending conventional limitations of geography and temporality. This fusion of immersive technologies with the corporeal world not only amplifies the efficacy of these sectors but also fundamentally redefines how individuals engage, learn, and experience the multifaceted dimensions of existence. This fusion of immersive technologies with the physical world carries profound implications spanning not only entertainment and leisure but also extending to education, healthcare, commerce, and a plethora of other sectors. Beyond their immediate applications, the profound influence of AR, VR, and the Metaverse permeates our societal and cultural fabric. The study embarks on a journey of exploration, delving into the historical evolution, current status and tantalizing future prospects of these immersive technologies.

2. AR: Merging Realities in the Digital Age

AR represents a technological innovation that overlays digital content onto the user's perceptual interface with the authentic world. This digital content manifests diversely, spanning images, videos, 3D models, text, and a plethora of other formats. The cardinal tenet underpinning AR is to furnish an interactive and immersive encounter by enriching the physical milieu with digital elements, thereby amplifying the user's sensory perception. In contradistinction to VR, which wholly engulfs users within a simulated environment, AR maintains an umbilical connection with the tangible world, affording users the ability to interact with digital facets while steadfastly anchored in reality (D'Onofrio et al., 2023). In general, AR stands as a polymorphic technological phenomenon that has undergone substantial strides and metamorphosis throughout its evolutionary trajectory. A comprehensive exploration of AR becomes imperative to fathom its intricate mechanisms and foundational principles, which constitute the bedrock for its operational dynamics and extensive applications. At its nucleus, AR denotes the fusion of the digital and physical realms, where virtual information seamlessly converges with the authentic environment, engendering an interactive milieu of mixed reality (Yang & Wang, 2023). This explication underscores the pivotal principle of AR, the instantaneous integration of computer-generated data or virtual entities with the user's real-world perceptual experience.

2.1. Historical Evolution of AR

In the annals of history, the year 1584 witnessed the unveiling of Giambattista della Porta's treatise, "Magia Naturalis," wherein he propounds a groundbreaking notion. Della Porta (Zik & Hon, 2017) introduces the concept of a chamber, intricately furnished with a glass pane strategically positioned to manipulate the reflection of light rebounding from objects, thereby inducing the perceptual illusion that these entities exist in a spatial reality distinct from their authentic placement. This historical narrative constitutes one of the earliest documented articulations of AR. The elemental precept of utilizing a semi-transparent mirror for reflective purposes endures in contemporary contexts, notably in the realm of HMDs, albeit in a more compact form. The genesis of AR harks back to the 1960s, an epoch when the luminary computer scientist Ivan Sutherland conceived the inaugural HMD system, christened the "Sword of Damocles." While admittedly rudimentary when juxtaposed with the sophistication of contemporary standards, this pioneering invention laid the cornerstone for immersive AR encounters and constituted the nascent exploration into the amalgamation of the digital and physical domains (Sutherland, 1968).

The trajectory of AR unfolds as a narrative punctuated by pivotal milestones, illuminating its evolutionary journey (Table 1). Its initial foray into commercial prominence materialized in the late 1990s with the advent of the ARToolKit, an open-source tracking library catalyzing the development of marker-based AR applications. This heralded a paradigm shift, rendering AR accessible to a broader spectrum of developers and users alike. In the temporal landscape of 1990, Boeing researcher Tom Caudell introduced the terminology "augmented reality," envisaging the fusion of computer-generated imagery with the tangible world, thereby laying the conceptual bedrock for this nascent technology. A mere two years later, at the U.S. Air Force Research Laboratory, Louis Rosenberg pioneered the inaugural fully immersive AR system, transcending the boundaries of AR's nascent capabilities. The latter part of the 1990s witnessed a watershed moment with NASA's groundbreaking application of AR for navigation in the context of the X-38 spacecraft. This served as a catalyst for the unprecedented evolution of AR technology and its subsequent diverse applications. The march of the 21st century witnessed continued strides in AR's advancement. The year 2000 witnessed the launch of AR Quake, a revolutionary AR game that endowed players with backpack-contained computers and gyroscopes, coupled with HMDs, ushering in a heightened level of gaming immersion. The early 2000s saw the advent of AR applications for smartphones, democratizing AR experiences for the general populace. In 2008, Blippar introduced the first cloud-based AR app, expanding the horizons of AR development. The year 2012 marked a significant leap with the release of Blippar's cloud-based AR app, foreshadowing a new epoch in AR capabilities. Four years later, the collaborative effort of Niantic and Nintendo birthed Pokémon Go, an immensely popular location-based AR game that catapulted AR into the mainstream, captivating millions worldwide. The digital epoch witnessed an avalanche of AR applications permeating diverse sectors, transforming user interactions with the world. From social media filters embellishing users' faces to the immersive gaming escapades exemplified by Pokémon Go, AR seamlessly intertwines the real and virtual realms. Notably, technology behemoths Apple and Google embedded AR capabilities into their operating systems, rendering AR ubiquitous across myriad devices. The advent of HMDs and smart glasses, epitomized by Microsoft HoloLens, Magic Leap and Google Glass, inaugurated a new chapter in AR. These devices facilitated more immersive and hands-free AR experiences, particularly in industrial and enterprise domains. Applications in remote maintenance, training and other professional realms underscored their tangible benefits.

2.2. Current Applications of AR

The adaptability inherent in AR has rendered it a ubiquitous force, permeating an expansive array of industries and domains with its transformative potential. In the realm of Gaming and Entertainment, AR has emerged as a formidable catalyst, reshaping the landscape of interactive experiences. Exemplifying this is

Table 1. Year Wise Milestone of AR Development.

Year	Milestone
1862	John Henry Pepper and Henry Dircks create the Pepper's ghost illusion technique for theatre.
1945	Henry McCollum patents the first Stereoscopic Television Apparatus.
1958	Early Head-Up Displays (HUDs) used for military purposes.
1960	Morten Heiling patents a stereoscopic television HMD.
1961	Philco introduces the Headsight-Remote Camera Viewing system.
1962	Pepper's Ghost technique refined for modern projection AR.
1968	Ivan Sutherland and Bob Sproull develop the "Sword of Damocles," the first AR HMD.
1980s	AR concepts incorporated into films like "The Terminator" and "Robocop."
1992	The term "Augmented Reality" coined at Boeing.
1992	Introduction of the virtual fixture for immersive AR experiences.
1994	Ronald T. Azuma develops motion-stabilized displays and marker-based tracking.
1995	Fiducial tracking in video introduced by Bajura and Neumann.
1996	UNC develops hybrid magnetic-vision trackers for AR.
1996	MIT Wearable Computing Group founded by Steve Mann.
1997	The Touring Machine, a 3D mobile AR system, is developed.
1999	ARToolKit, the first open-source AR tracking library, is released.
2001	First attempts to build an AR browser with web technology.
2007	Introduction of early mobile AR technology.
2008	Wikitude, a mobile AR technology for location-based experiences.
2009	Layar company founded, allowing AR layering on print media.
2009	Release of Argon, the first open technology browser for AR.
2009	ARToolKit moves to Flash, broadening AR accessibility.
2011	Blippar introduces compelling AR experiences.
2011	Google creates the first smart glasses, Google Glass.
2014	Google Tango designed for standalone mobile AR platforms.
2014	DAQRI's smart helmet introduces stereoscopic AR overlay.
2014	Meta One ships, the first high-quality AR headset.
2015	Qualcomm releases Vuforia, an AR SDK for mobile devices.
2015	Microsoft HoloLens released, the first self-contained AR headset with depth mapping.
2016	Magic Leap One unveiled as a competitor to HoloLens.

Table 1. (*Continued*)

Year	Milestone
2016	Introduction of the AWE media platform for web-based immersive VR and AR.
2017	Apple launches ARKit, an AR platform for iOS devices.
2017	Chinese companies Baidu and Tencent unveil DuMiX AR and Tencent TBS AR.
2017	Google releases ARCore for Android devices.
2019	Microsoft HoloLens 2 begins shipping.

the paradigm-shifting AR gaming phenomenon, Pokémon GO, which captivated the collective imagination as players embarked on real-world quests to apprehend virtual creatures. Furthermore, within the hallowed halls of museums, AR is harnessed to deliver enriched visitor experiences through interactive exhibits and tours, thereby elevating the edification process and imbuing it with a heightened level of engagement (Wu et al., 2013). Healthcare and Medical Training stand as veritable domains where AR has unfurled its prowess. Within the precincts of healthcare, AR has proven its mettle in the realms of medical training and patient care. Medical practitioners are endowed with the capability to visualize intricate anatomical structures and replicate surgical procedures, thereby amplifying their comprehension and honing their skillsets (Lowe, 2012).

Education, being a crucible for innovation, witnesses the profound potential of AR. The transformative impact unfolds through the provision of interactive and immersive learning experiences. AR applications in education orchestrate a metamorphosis of history lessons, breathing life into pedagogical content. Students are empowered to explore and interact with intricate 3D models, fostering a depth of understanding that transcends conventional educational paradigms (De Waard et al., 2012).

AR, with unprecedented alacrity, has assimilated into diverse sectors, effecting a paradigm shift in the dynamics of human interaction with our immediate environs. Within the domain of navigation, AR, as exemplified by applications such as Google Maps and the incorporation of head-up displays in vehicles, bestows real-time directions, thereby elevating the efficacy of navigation endeavors and mitigating the propensity for disorientation. In the realms of marketing and retail, AR manifests its prowess by enthralling customers through interactive encounters, encompassing virtual try-ons for apparel and cosmetics, along with dynamic product catalogs that render the shopping experience more immersive. In the crucible of industrial and manufacturing contexts, AR assumes the role of a stalwart aide, facilitating tasks related to maintenance, repair and training, thereby augmenting operational efficiency and curtailing errors. Architects and designers leverage AR to superimpose digital architectural models onto tangible settings, an instrumental facet in client presentations. AR's evolutionary trajectory portends a plethora of possibilities across domains such as education, healthcare, gaming and industry. Central to AR's functionality are pivotal principles, including registration, interaction, context-awareness and spatial awareness. These principles meticulously align virtual content with the tangible world, ushering in avenues for interaction through diverse input methods, adapting dynamically to the user's environment and ensuring the perpetuity of spatial alignment. The imperative of real-time interaction underscores its cardinal role in user engagement, with AR systems adopting either marker-based or markerless modalities, the latter proffering heightened flexibility. Spatial awareness emerges as the linchpin, ensuring precise alignment of digital content with the physical milieu, with HMDs standing as conduits for immersive AR experiences. The sensory arsenal harnessed by AR comprises cameras, accelerometers, gyroscopes and GPS, diligently gathering data about the user's surroundings to facilitate dynamic responses to real-world vicissitudes. These foundational principles and technological underpinnings constitute the crucible wherein the ongoing evolution of AR unfolds, continually shaping our interactions with augmented environments. This, in turn, engenders a fertile ground for the germination of new applications and innovations. Be it the augmentation of navigation prowess, the metamorphosis of retail experiences, the streamlining of industrial processes, or the facilitation of architectural design, AR emerges as an omnipotent force in the digital epoch, beckoning with exciting prospects for the convergence of the tangible and virtual realms.

2.3. Case Example

2.3.1. AR: Enhancing Retail Experiences

IKEA's integration of AR technology into its retail strategy, epitomized by the IKEA Place app, represents a groundbreaking advancement in the realm of furniture shopping. This innovative approach is reshaping how consumers interact with the brand, offering them a dynamic and immersive experience that transcends traditional online shopping. At the heart of IKEA's AR initiative is the commitment to enhance user experience. The IKEA Place app was meticulously designed to provide customers with a seamless and intuitive platform for exploring the company's extensive catalogue of furniture and home decor items. With just a smartphone or tablet camera, users can effortlessly navigate through IKEA's offerings and visualize how products will fit into their living spaces. A key feature of the IKEA Place app lies in its ability to present true-to-scale 3D models of furniture. This feature ensures that users receive an accurate representation of the size, shape, and proportions of each item, empowering them to make informed purchasing decisions. By virtually placing furniture in their homes, customers gain valuable insights into how products will integrate with their existing decor and layout. Moreover, the IKEA Place app addresses a fundamental challenge of online furniture shopping: uncertainty. By allowing customers to preview products in their own homes, the app mitigates the risk of dissatisfaction and returns associated with purchasing items sight unseen. This reduction in uncertainty fosters trust and confidence in the IKEA brand, enhancing overall customer satisfaction. Beyond its practical utility, the IKEA Place app serves as a powerful marketing tool, positioning the company as a leader in innovation and customer engagement. The app's interactive features not only captivate users but also generate buzz and excitement around the brand. By embracing AR technology, IKEA demonstrates its commitment to meeting the evolving needs and expectations of modern consumers. Looking ahead, the potential for expansion and innovation within the realm of AR technology is vast. IKEA has the opportunity to further enhance the capabilities of the IKEA Place app, potentially incorporating features such as virtual room design consultations and integration with smart home devices. As AR continues to evolve, IKEA remains poised to capitalize on emerging trends and technologies, reaffirming its position as a pioneer in the retail industry.

3. Virtual Reality

VR, standing at the vanguard of technological innovation, has materialized as a metamorphic force with far-reaching implications across diverse fields. The annals of time have witnessed an accumulation of substantial attention, both in the realms of research and practical applications, propelling VR into realms once deemed the province of futuristic conjecture.

The genesis of VR traces back to the mid-20th century, a conceptual inception spearheaded by pioneers like Morton Heilig, envisioning the immersive realms of simulated environments. However, the crystallization of VR technology did not materialize until the 1990s, catalyzed by the advent of HMDs and data gloves, pivotal instruments facilitating user interaction with computer-generated environments, laying the groundwork for contemporary VR. Presently, the technological landscape has matured into intricate systems incorporating elements such as 3D audio, motion tracking and haptic feedback, endowing users with genuinely immersive experiences (Biocca & Levy, 1995). The healthcare domain has harnessed the latent potential of VR across diverse applications, with medical training and simulation at the forefront. Offering healthcare professionals a risk-free environment for honing surgical and procedural skills, VR's capacity to simulate complex medical scenarios has proven invaluable in augmenting the competencies and confidence of medical practitioners (Mao et al., 2014). Additionally, VR has ushered in innovative approaches to treating psychological and neurological conditions, exemplified by enhanced accessibility and efficacy of exposure therapy. Addressing disorders such as phobias, post-traumatic stress disorder and anxiety disorders, VR-based interventions have demonstrated commendable success (Parsons & Rizzo, 2008). In the educational domain, VR has burgeoned into a potent pedagogical tool, elevating learning experiences through immersive educational simulations. Providing students with avenues to explore historical events, conduct virtual science experiments and embark on simulated field trips, these applications not only captivate student interest but also enhance retention and comprehension (Fernandes et al., 2021).

The gaming and entertainment industry stands as a pivotal driving force propelling the evolution of VR technology. From gaming consoles to theme park attractions, VR has revolutionized entertainment experiences, introducing virtual worlds where users interact with both environments and fellow users. Theme parks have embraced VR to fashion exhilarating experiences on roller coasters and interactive rides, effectively obfuscating the demarcation between the tangible and digital realms (Cummings & Bailenson, 2016). However, the immersive nature of VR has engendered unique challenges, notably motion sickness, which has prompted research endeavors to enhance user comfort. Additionally, concerns pertaining to privacy, ethics and addiction have surfaced, necessitating judicious contemplation as VR becomes increasingly interwoven into our daily lives. In summation, VR has metamorphosed from a mere conceptual framework into a transformative technology with pervasive applications across myriad sectors. Its impact resonates from healthcare and education to psychology and entertainment. As the trajectory of VR technology continues its inexorable advancement, it beckons toward a future rife with exciting possibilities, concurrently instigating pertinent questions regarding its ethical and psychological ramifications. The collaborative endeavors of researchers, practitioners and developers are pivotal in unlocking the full potential of VR while navigating the challenges it presents, ensuring a promising trajectory for this groundbreaking technology. The foundational principles of VR represent cardinal tenets that not only underpin the technology but also steer its evolution and utilization. These principles form an indispensable framework for creating immersive and credible virtual experiences. Elaborated in Table 2, these core principles or parameters furnish a lucid overview of the bedrock concepts associated with VR. Guiding the development and utilization of VR technology, these principles play a pivotal role in fashioning immersive, enjoyable and ethically responsible virtual experiences. Their intrinsic significance lies in the assurance that VR continues to evolve, realizing its potential across diverse fields, ranging from entertainment and education to healthcare and beyond.

Table 2. Parameters and Its Description.

Parameters	Description
Immersion	Central principle in VR, referring to the extent to which a user feels mentally and emotionally absorbed in the virtual environment. Achieving a high level of immersion is essential for creating a convincing and realistic experience, accomplished through high-quality visuals, 3D audio and interactive elements engaging multiple senses (e.g., touch or haptic feedback).
Presence	The feeling of "being there" in the virtual environment. Closely related to immersion, it goes a step further by creating a sense of physical presence. Users experiencing a strong sense of presence forget they are in a virtual world and interact with it as if it were real. Achieving presence involves reducing the gap between the real and virtual worlds, making users forget they are wearing a headset or interacting with a computer.

Table 2. (*Continued*)

Parameters	Description
Interactivity	Core principle setting VR apart from traditional media, allowing users to actively engage with the virtual environment. Users should manipulate objects, navigate the space and influence the virtual world. Effective interactivity enhances the sense of agency and control within the VR experience, making it more engaging and immersive.
Realism	Refers to the extent to which the virtual environment mirrors the real world. Achieving a high degree of realism involves creating lifelike graphics, accurate physics and authentic interactions. The closer the virtual world aligns with real-world expectations, the more convincing and immersive the VR experience becomes.
Sensory Feedback	Plays a crucial role in VR, involving providing sensory cues to users through various means, such as haptic feedback devices, motion controllers, or scent generators. Engaging multiple senses makes VR experiences more immersive and believable, simulating sensations like touch, temperature, or even smells to enhance the overall experience.
User Comfort	VR design should prioritize user comfort, including minimizing motion sickness. Developers aim to achieve this through techniques like smooth locomotion and reducing latency. Ensuring the comfort of users is paramount for making VR experiences enjoyable and usable for extended periods.
Accessibility and Inclusivity	VR should be designed to be accessible to a wide range of users, including those with disabilities. Inclusive design principles involve features like adjustable settings, voice commands, or alternative control methods to ensure that everyone can enjoy VR experiences.
Ethics and Privacy	As VR technology advances, ethical considerations become increasingly important. Protecting user privacy and ensuring ethical behavior within VR environments are key principles. This involves addressing issues like data privacy, consent and preventing harmful or offensive content within VR experiences.
Content Creation	VR content creation is a core principle involving the development of tools and platforms that allow creators to design and build immersive experiences. Empowering content creators and developers fosters innovation and diversity in VR content.
Research and Innovation	Continuous research and innovation are central to the development of VR, staying at the forefront of technological advancements and understanding user behaviors and preferences. These principles ensure that VR technology evolves and meets the changing needs and expectations of users.

The multifaceted applications of VR encompass diverse domains, with a notable emphasis on training simulations. In the medical sector, practitioners hone surgical skills within a risk-free VR environment, while sectors such as the military and aviation leverage VR for intricate training scenarios. Educational applications extend beyond conventional boundaries, allowing virtual travel and exploration. The gaming industry experiences a transformative influence, providing players with interactive gameplay that blurs the line between the virtual and tangible (Calleja, 2007). Amid the COVID-19 pandemic, VR emerges as a crucial tool for virtual meetings and its therapeutic applications find expression in exposure therapy and pain management. Architects and designers utilize VR for heightened visualization and decision-making, while VR transforms storytelling into immersive narratives. In education, VR offers interactive learning experiences, fostering engagement and knowledge retention. Hazard-prone occupations benefit from VR training simulations, preparing individuals for high-risk scenarios. VR serves as a platform for immersive artistry, providing a virtual realm for creative experimentation. Additionally, VR preserves historical artifacts within virtual museums, overcoming geographical and temporal limitations. The versatility of VR applications spans industries, amplifying training, entertainment, education and cultural experiences (Marougkas et al., 2023). Despite challenges like motion sickness and high hardware costs, VR disrupts gaming, healthcare, and education. Challenges in healthcare include the need for clinical validation and robust data security. In education, challenges involve hardware costs and nuanced curriculum development. The trajectory anticipates a growing impact as technology becomes more accessible, with ongoing refinements to address challenges. The development of VR hardware faces challenges in achieving immersion, comfort and affordability. Content creation involves adapting narratives to the 360-degree environment, with AI integration automating content generation and user-generated content platforms diversifying experiences. The evolution of VR holds promise for revolutionary shifts in hardware and content creation, making immersive experiences more accessible and multifaceted.

3.1. Case Example

VR technology has indeed revolutionized medical training, and Osso VR stands out as a leading example in this transformative landscape. Osso VR is a cutting-edge surgical training platform designed to provide surgeons with a realistic and immersive environment for skill development and refinement. Its innovative approach to medical education has the potential to reshape the way surgeons are trained and prepared for real-world procedures. Osso VR offers a comprehensive suite of virtual simulations that accurately replicate various surgical procedures. From simple suturing techniques to complex surgical interventions, the platform covers a wide range of scenarios to cater to the diverse training needs of surgeons across different specialties. This breadth of simulation allows trainees to progressively build their skills and confidence in a controlled, risk-free environment before transitioning to actual patient care settings. One of the key strengths of Osso VR lies in its fidelity to real-world surgical conditions. The platform leverages advanced graphics, haptic feedback systems, and interactive interfaces to create an authentic surgical experience that closely mirrors the complexities and challenges of operating room environments. Surgeons can practice intricate maneuvers, hone their decision-making skills, and familiarize themselves with the latest surgical tools and techniques all within the safety of a virtual space. Furthermore, Osso VR facilitates collaborative learning and skill sharing among medical professionals. Surgeons can engage in virtual training sessions, participate in case-based discussions, and receive feedback from expert mentors and peers. This collaborative approach not only fosters a sense of community and camaraderie within the medical community but also promotes continuous learning and improvement among practising surgeons and trainees alike. Beyond its immediate impact on surgical proficiency, Osso VR has the potential to drive significant improvements in patient outcomes. By enabling surgeons to master new procedures and refine existing techniques in a controlled environment, the platform contributes to reduced error rates, shorter surgical times, and improved postoperative recovery for patients. Moreover, the skills acquired through virtual training translate directly into enhanced clinical competence and confidence among surgeons, ultimately benefiting the quality of care delivered to patients. As the field of VR continues to evolve, Osso VR remains at the forefront of innovation in medical education and training. With ongoing advancements in VR technology and simulation capabilities, the platform is poised to expand its scope and reach across different medical specialties and global healthcare settings. By harnessing the power of VR to democratize access to high-quality surgical training, Osso VR is driving a paradigm shift in medical education one that promises to elevate standards of care and transform patient outcomes for years to come.

4. The Metaverse

The concept of the metaverse, an amalgamated virtual collective space, has become a focal point of considerable attention within both technological and scholarly realms. Nonetheless, a universal consensus regarding its definition remains elusive, rendering it a subject perpetually under scholarly scrutiny. At its essence, the metaverse denotes a digitized domain wherein users seamlessly intertwine, partaking in activities that span interaction, socialization, work and recreation within a communal online expanse. Originating from the tapestry of science fiction literature, the metaverse has metamorphosed into a cardinal concept threading through discussions pertaining to the future trajectory of the internet. In the discerning observations of Ronald Azuma and David Evans, the metaverse unfolds as an immersive, three-dimensional and often enduring digital milieu, wherein users not only interact amongst themselves but also with digital content in an intricately woven tapestry (Egliston & Carter, 2022). The metaverse, at its thematic core, epitomizes the fabric of interconnectedness and the coalescence of shared experiences, enveloping denizens within the realms of a meticulously crafted virtual world.

A pivotal facet intrinsic to the metaverse lies in the concept of immersion, aspiring to endow users with an experiential realm that transcends the conventional confines of 2D interfaces, ushering them into the dimensional embrace of a 3D spatial context. The conceptual genesis of this immersive trajectory traces back to the articulation by (Milgram & Kishino, 1994) of the "Virtuality Continuum," a theoretical framework delineating the trajectory from the tangible realms of the physical world to the ethereal expanse of the entirely virtual. Within the metaverse, this continuum finds its apogee, ensconcing users within a milieu meticulously crafted through digital means, thereby facilitating complete immersion. Another salient conceptual tenet is interoperability, envisioning the metaverse as a digital cosmos governed by shared standards and interoperable systems. This conceptualization beckons forth a landscape wherein users seamlessly traverse diverse virtual realms and platforms without encountering impediments (Schroeder, 2008). The foundational premise here is the capacity for users to seamlessly transport their digital identities and assets across disparate instances within the metaverse – a linchpin for the realization of the overarching vision of a seamlessly unified metaverse (Agarwal et al., 2020).

Although the definition of the metaverse remains in a state of continual evolution, it is intricately interwoven with the fundamental concepts of communal spaces, immersive experiences and interoperability. With increasing investments spanning diverse industries, ranging from gaming to social media, dedicated to the metaverse's developmental trajectory, its comprehension and utilization are poised for ongoing expansion. Positioned as a digital frontier, the metaverse serves as an arena where users wield the power to redefine their online experiences and interactions, thereby exerting a palpable influence on the evolutionary trajectory of the internet. As this inchoate conceptual paradigm unfurls, its foundational principles are poised to assume a pivotal role in sculpting the contours of the digital terrain.

4.1. Building a Vast and Interconnected Virtual Universe

The conceptualization of an expansive and intricately interconnected virtual cosmos, commonly denoted as the metaverse, has sparked the intellectual curiosity of technophiles and the broader populace. Envisioned as a digitized domain accessible through varied devices and platforms, the metaverse transcends the limitations imposed by the physical realm. Within this interconnected virtual expanse lies the latent potency to redefine the very fabric of our existence, altering the dynamics of how we engage, labor and socialize within the crucible of the digital epoch (Frankel & Krebs, 2021). At its core, the aspiration to construct a metaverse pivots on the fundamental objective of endowing users with the capacity to seamlessly navigate diverse digital landscapes, akin to the nuanced traversal through varied physical spaces in the corporeal world (Table 3).

The foundational tenets of the metaverse encapsulate a profound paradigm shift in our engagement with digital phenomena and our interpersonal interactions within a virtual domain. In the ongoing evolution of these foundational principles, the metaverse emerges as a potential vanguard, a digitized frontier poised to recalibrate the demarcations between the virtual and physical domains. Within its dynamic confines, users are envisaged to forge a multi-faceted existence, simultaneously dwelling, laboring, and exploring, thus transcending the confinements inherent in the conventional structures of the internet.

Table 3. Description of Core Concepts of Metaverse.

Core Concepts of the Metaverse	Description
Persistent and Continuous Digital Experiences	Users maintain a consistent presence and identity across the metaverse, offering a sense of permanence and continuity.
Nurturing Social Interactions and Building Community	The metaverse promotes social interactions and community-building, fostering shared experiences and immersion.
Virtual Economies and Digital Commerce	It features virtual economies where users can buy, sell and trade virtual goods and services, mirroring real-world economics.
Establishing Trust and Credibility	Trust and credibility are built through digital identity and reputation systems, ensuring safe and reliable interactions.
Cross-Platform Interoperability	Different platforms and applications seamlessly connect, providing users with consistent experiences across the metaverse.
Immersive and Interactive Entertainment	The metaverse offers immersive and interactive entertainment experiences that transcend traditional forms of media.
Virtual Workspaces and Collaboration	It supports virtual workspaces and collaborative environments, addressing the evolving landscape of remote work.
Virtual Education and Learning	The metaverse revolutionizes education with interactive classrooms, immersive learning experiences and lifelong learning.
Personalized Virtual Environments	Users can customize their virtual surroundings, creating a more engaging and personalized digital experience.
Virtual Healthcare and Telemedicine	The metaverse extends to healthcare services, offering innovative and accessible solutions, such as telemedicine.
Fostering Innovation and Creativity	User-generated content and virtual world building tools empower users to actively contribute and shape the metaverse.

4.2. Investigating Existing Metaverse Platforms

The metaverse, conceived as an intricately interconnected digital cosmos, has ascended to salience within discourses delineating the future trajectory of the internet and virtual experiential realms. Various metaverse platforms have materialized, each manifesting distinctive attributes and ramifications. A pioneering exemplar is Second Life, inaugurated in 2003 by Linden Lab, which accentuates the primacy of user-generated content, affording denizens the latitude to fabricate, explore and engage within a digitally crafted landscape. The emphasis on customizable avatars, the genesis of virtual entities, and the cultivation of a vibrant societal milieu underscore the metaverse's allure, particularly with regards to user ingenuity and social interplay. In the metaverse tapestry, Roblox, founded in 2006, emerges as a focal point channeling attention toward user-generated content and communal experiences. By furnishing a space wherein users not only devise but also partake in games authored by their counterparts, Roblox engenders an ecosystem wherein the dual roles of creator and participant coalesce, fostering a crucible of innovation and cooperative endeavor intrinsic to the metaverse ethos. A paradigm distinguished by blockchain technology, Decentraland unfolds as a metaverse wherein users engage in the acquisition, development and trade of virtual land parcels. Exploiting the Ethereum blockchain, it institutes digital ownership through non-fungible tokens (NFTs), endowing virtual properties with a novel dimension of ownership and intrinsic worth. In doing so, Decentraland propels the potential reconfiguration of conventional perceptions surrounding the commodification and valuation of virtual real estate within the metaverse milieu.

Fortnite, a creation of Epic Games, has propagated the metaverse paradigm through its digital crucible of an online battle royale game. This intricate gaming milieu encompasses in-game occurrences, communal spaces and a creative mode wherein players can architect their own idiosyncratic worlds and experiences. Fortnite serves as a poignant exemplar, illuminating the latent potential residing in the amalgamation of gaming, social interplay and user-forged content within the expansive tapestry of the metaverse. In the realm of VR, platforms such as VR Chat manifest as conduits for social VR experiences, where denizens are afforded the agency to fabricate and explore interactive 3D environments while concurrently engaging in social discourse. The cardinal tenets of VR Chat orbit around the primacy of user-generated content, immersive interactions and the cultivation of an overarching sense of presence within the expansive expanse of virtual domains.

4.3. Implications of Existing Metaverse Platforms

The advent of these metaverse platforms portends profound implications for the unfolding tapestry of the digital terrain. These platforms not only exemplify the allure of user-generated content, expressive creativity and social exchanges within the metaverse but also accentuate the economic vistas entwined with virtual property possession and virtual economies, particularly discernible in platforms such as Decentraland and Second Life (Ducrée et al., 2022). Platforms propelled by blockchain technology, like Decentraland, introduce novel paradigms of digital ownership, scarcity and the prospective realization of dividends for users within the virtual property market. Furthermore, the triumph of platforms like Roblox serves as a testament to the metaverse's capacity to empower individuals as both architects and participants within a dynamic ecosystem of ingenuity. At the forefront of these platforms are user-generated content and collaborative endeavors, underscoring the pivotal role of nurturing creativity and endowing users with the agency to actively mold their virtual sojourns (Balfour et al., 2023). The convergence of gaming, social discourse, and user-generated content embodied by platforms like Fortnite and VR Chat elucidates the metaverse's potential to metamorphose into a multifaceted digital realm, transcending the confines of conventional demarcations and captivating a broad and diverse audience (Sykownik et al., 2022). As the metaverse continues its evolutionary trajectory, these extant platforms emerge as invaluable case studies, illuminating the metaverse's potential to redefine our interactions with digital experiences, property entitlement, creativity, and social affiliations. These profound implications proffer a tantalizing glimpse into a prospective future where the metaverse seamlessly integrates into the fabric of our digital existence, heralding novel opportunities and concomitant challenges.

4.4. Case Example

Roblox stands as a pioneering force in the burgeoning realm of the metaverse, redefining the boundaries of virtual experiences through its innovative platform. At its core, Roblox serves as both an online game platform and a robust game creation system, seamlessly blending elements of gaming, social networking, and digital creativity. With its unwavering focus on user-generated content and community engagement, Roblox has emerged as a dynamic virtual ecosystem where users are empowered to shape their own digital destinies. Central to Roblox's appeal is its democratization of game development and content creation. Unlike traditional gaming platforms that are primarily controlled by a select group of developers, Roblox opens the door to virtually anyone with a creative vision and a passion for gaming. Through intuitive tools and frameworks, users can easily design, build, and publish their own games, fostering a culture of creativity, experimentation, and collaboration within the Roblox community. The breadth and diversity of experiences available on Roblox are staggering. From immersive role-playing adventures and adrenaline-fueled action games to whimsical social hangouts and educational simulations, Roblox offers something for everyone. This vast library of user-generated content ensures that there is always something new and exciting to discover, fostering a sense of exploration and wonder among players of all ages. Moreover, Roblox serves as a dynamic social platform where users can connect, interact, and forge meaningful relationships in virtual space. Whether teaming up with friends to tackle epic quests or attending virtual concerts and events, Roblox provides a rich tapestry of social experiences that transcend the boundaries of traditional gaming. Through chat, voice communication, and collaborative gameplay, users can build bonds, share stories, and create memories that endure long after the game session ends. Moreover, Roblox empowers creators to monetize their creations and turn their passion for game development into a viable livelihood. Through the Roblox Developer Exchange program and the sale of virtual items, developers can earn real-world currency for their contributions, incentivizing creativity and innovation within the platform. This economic empowerment not only rewards talented creators but also fosters a vibrant ecosystem of digital entrepreneurship and opportunity. In many ways, Roblox Corporation serves as a trailblazer in showcasing the immense economic potential of the metaverse. By harnessing the collective creativity and ingenuity of its user base, Roblox has created a thriving virtual economy where imagination knows no bounds. As the metaverse continues to evolve and expand, platforms like Roblox will play an instrumental role in shaping the future of digital interactions, entertainment, and commerce, ushering in a new era of limitless possibilities in the virtual realm.

5. Discussion

The comprehensive exploration of AR, VR, and the emerging metaverse in this book chapter has illuminated the intricate evolution, underlying principles, transformative potential, challenges, and ethical considerations of these groundbreaking technologies. Delving into the historical origins of AR, dating back to the 16th century and tracing its contemporary applications across navigation, marketing, healthcare, architecture, and education, underscores its profound impact on diverse sectors. The discussion delves into the transformative potential of VR to create immersive learning environments, facilitate medical procedures, and revolutionize the gaming industry. Key principles such as spatial mapping, interaction, real-time engagement, and hardware advancements are meticulously explored in the context of VR's evolutionary trajectory. Extending the discourse to the metaverse, an interconnected virtual universe gaining prominence, elucidates the core concepts including cross-platform interoperability, digital economies, social interactions, and virtual entertainment. The discussion emphasizes the metaverse's potential to build a vast, connected digital realm accessible across devices and platforms, reshaping entertainment, education, healthcare, and commerce. Ethical considerations and challenges in metaverse development are scrutinized, acknowledging the paramount importance of digital identity, privacy, and content moderation. Throughout this chapter, the recurring emphasis on the significance of continued research, responsible implementation and ethical considerations emerges as essential components shaping the continued evolution of AR, VR, and the metaverse. While these technologies present boundless opportunities, the need for ethical frameworks and research efforts to ensure equitable access and responsible usage is underscored, safeguarding their evolution to benefit society while mitigating potential risks and challenges. The seamless fusion of the real and digital worlds, promising transformative possibilities, is a recurrent theme. As the exploration unfolds, the intricate interplay of technology and human experiences becomes increasingly apparent, pointing toward exciting prospects. However, the acknowledgment of the importance of research, responsible implementation and ethical considerations remains paramount as these technologies progress further into uncharted territories. The convergence of AR, VR, and the metaverse holds the potential to reshape how individuals interact with digital content and each other, offering a more integrated and enriched digital experience. This chapter concludes by encouraging readers to contemplate the future possibilities where technology and human experiences intersect in novel and unprecedented ways.

6. Key Challenges

Interoperability and Standardization: A fundamental challenge in the convergence of AR, VR, and the metaverse lies in the establishment of interoperability standards. As these technologies amalgamate, the assurance of seamless communication and data exchange across platforms becomes imperative. The lack of standardized protocols may impede the harmonious integration of AR, VR, and the metaverse.

Hardware Limitations: The heterogeneity in hardware requisites for AR, VR, and metaverse experiences presents a substantial challenge. Diverse devices, ranging from AR glasses to VR headsets, necessitate distinct technical specifications. Bridging these realities requires addressing compatibility issues and devising experiences capable of adapting to a myriad of devices without compromising quality or functionality.

User Experience Design: Formulating a unified and intuitive user experience across AR, VR, and the metaverse poses a considerable design challenge. Each reality boasts distinct interaction models and user interfaces. Achieving a seamless transition for users navigating between these disparate digital environments demands meticulous design to avert disorientation or confusion.

Privacy and Ethical Concerns: As the integration of these realities progresses, the collection and utilization of user data raise profound privacy concerns. Striking a delicate balance between providing personalized experiences and safeguarding user privacy is paramount. Ethical considerations, encompassing consent and content moderation within the metaverse, demand meticulous attention to ensure responsible technology usage.

Content Standardization: The creation and dissemination of content across AR, VR, and the metaverse encounter challenges related to standardization. Establishing common content formats, quality standards and distribution protocols is indispensable for a coherent and immersive user experience. The absence of content standardization may culminate in fragmentation, impeding the seamless flow of experiences between realities.

7. Future Prospects

Unified Experiences: The future envisions seamless transitions for users navigating between AR, VR, and the metaverse. Progress in technology and cross-industry collaboration may culminate in the development of unified platforms offering a coherent and uninterrupted digital experience, erasing the demarcations between these distinct realities.

Advancements in Hardware: Continuous progress in hardware technologies is anticipated to address extant limitations and augment the user experience. Lighter, more versatile devices endowed with enhanced processing power and sensory capabilities may contribute to a more accessible and integrated ecosystem, rendering AR, VR, and the metaverse more user-friendly.

AI and Personalization: The integration of AI is poised to play a pivotal role in bridging realities. AI algorithms can tailor content based on user preferences, behavior and environmental context, engendering personalized and context-aware experiences. This can contribute to a more natural and user-centric interaction within AR, VR, and the metaverse.

Collaborative Development: Collaboration among technology developers, content creators, and other stakeholders is indispensable for the future integration of these realities. Open standards and collaborative endeavors can culminate in a more interconnected ecosystem, fostering innovation and the creation of shared platforms benefiting users across AR, VR, and the metaverse.

Enhanced Connectivity: The widespread adoption of 5G and advancements in network technologies are likely to contribute to improved connectivity. High-speed, low-latency networks are vital for real-time interactions and content delivery in AR, VR, and the metaverse. Enhanced connectivity can pave the way for more immersive and responsive experiences across these realities.

7.1. Future for the Technology

The trajectory of technology development in AR, VR, and the metaverse is poised for remarkable advancements. The vision of unified experiences suggests a future where users seamlessly transition between these realities without encountering barriers or disruptions. This entails the convergence of AR, VR, and metaverse platforms into unified ecosystems, offering cohesive and uninterrupted digital experiences. Anticipated advancements in hardware technology are set to revolutionize the user experience across these realities. Lightweight, versatile devices with enhanced processing power and sensory capabilities will become more prevalent, making AR, VR, and metaverse experiences more accessible and integrated than ever before. The integration of AI stands as a cornerstone in bridging realities. AI algorithms will personalize content based on user preferences, behavior, and environmental context, leading to more natural and user-centric interactions within AR, VR, and the metaverse environments. Collaborative development efforts among technology developers, content creators, and other stakeholders are crucial for the integration of AR, VR, and the metaverse. Open standards and collaborative endeavors will foster innovation, leading to the creation of shared platforms that benefit users across these realities. Enhanced connectivity, driven by the widespread adoption of 5G and advancements in network technologies, will play a pivotal role in shaping the future of AR, VR, and the metaverse. High-speed, low-latency networks will facilitate real-time interactions and content delivery, paving the way for more immersive and responsive experiences across these realities.

7.2. Future for the Organization

For organizations operating within the AR, VR, and metaverse space, the future holds both opportunities and challenges. Embracing the paradigm shift toward unified experiences will be key for staying relevant and competitive in the evolving landscape. Companies that invest in cutting-edge hardware technologies and AI-driven personalization algorithms will be well-positioned to deliver compelling and immersive experiences to their users. By fostering collaboration among technology developers, content creators, and industry stakeholders, organizations can drive innovation and contribute to the development of shared platforms that enhance the user experience across AR, VR, and the metaverse. Moreover, organizations that prioritize the development of robust and scalable network infrastructure will be able to capitalize on the potential of enhanced connectivity to deliver seamless and responsive experiences to their users. By staying abreast of technological advancements and market trends, organizations can navigate the complexities of the AR, VR, and metaverse landscape and position themselves for success in the future.

8. Conclusion

This chapter delves into the intricate landscape of AR, VR, and the burgeoning metaverse, unraveling their evolutionary trajectories, foundational principles, transformative capacities, attendant challenges, and ethical intricacies. These once fanciful technologies, rooted in the realms of speculative fiction, have swiftly metamorphosed into indispensable facets of diverse industries and human interactions. The odyssey commences with an exploration of AR's historical lineage, stretching back to the 16th century and traces its evolution to contemporary applications in navigation, marketing, healthcare, architecture, and education. The elemental tenets of AR, encompassing registration, interaction, context-awareness, and spatial mapping, are meticulously dissected, accentuating their pivotal role in crafting immersive and cohesive experiential domains. This chapter scrutinizes VR's potential to engender immersive learning environments, facilitate medical procedures and revolutionize the gaming industry. Key principles, including spatial mapping, interaction paradigms, real-time engagement modalities, and hardware advancements, are elucidated within the evolutionary tapestry of VR. The narrative extends further into the metaverse, an emerging interconnected virtual universe attaining escalating prominence. It probes into the fundamental concepts underpinning the metaverse, such as cross-platform interoperability, digital economies, social interactions, and virtual entertainment, dissecting their ramifications in shaping this burgeoning digital expanse. The metaverse's potential to construct an expansive, interconnected virtual cosmos accessible across diverse devices and platforms is expounded upon, underscoring its transformative role not only in entertainment but also in realms such as education, healthcare and commerce. Ethical considerations and challenges intrinsic to the metaverse's development are subjected to scrutiny, acknowledging the pivotal import of digital identity, privacy safeguards and content moderation mechanisms. Throughout the chapter, the emphasis is placed on the paramount significance of ongoing research, responsible implementation practices and ethical considerations as indispensable components steering the perpetual evolution of these technologies. While AR, VR, and the metaverse present seemingly boundless opportunities, their trajectories must be guided by robust ethical frameworks and concerted research endeavors to ensure equitable access and judicious deployment. This ensures that the evolution of these technologies accrues societal benefits while diligently addressing latent risks and challenges. The amalgamation of the tangible and the digital domains is manifesting as an increasingly seamless endeavor, heralding transformative possibilities. As the sojourn through the realms of AR, VR, and the metaverse endures, the abiding importance of research, judicious implementation, and ethical considerations persist as the lodestars guiding this intersection of technology and human experiences into novel and uncharted territories.

References

Agarwal, Y., Beatty, C., Biradar, S., Castronova, I., Ho, S., Melody, K., & Bility, M. T. (2020). Moving beyond the mousetrap: Current and emerging humanized mouse and rat models for investigating prevention and cure strategies against HIV infection and associated pathologies. *Retrovirology, 17*(1), 1–11.

AlGerafi, M. A., Zhou, Y., Oubibi, M., & Wijaya, T. T. (2023). Unlocking the potential: A comprehensive evaluation of augmented reality and virtual reality in education. *Electronics, 12*(18), 3953.

Azuma, R. T. (1997). A survey of augmented reality. *Presence: Teleoperators & Virtual Environments, 6*(4), 355–385.

Balfour, L., Evans, A., Maloney, M., & Merry, S. K. (2023). *Postdigital intimacies for online safety*. Coventry University.

Bansal, G., Rajgopal, K., Chamola, V., Xiong, Z., & Niyato, D. (2022). Healthcare in metaverse: A survey on current metaverse applications in healthcare. *IEEE Access, 10*, 119914–119946.

Bibri, S. E., Allam, Z., & Krogstie, J. (2022). The metaverse as a virtual form of data-driven smart urbanism: Platformization and its underlying processes, institutional dimensions, and disruptive impacts. *Computational Urban Science, 2*(1), 24.

Billinghurst, M., & Duenser, A. (2012). Augmented reality in the classroom. *Computer, 45*(7), 56–63.

Biocca, F., & Levy, M. R. (Eds.). (1995). Virtual reality as a communication system. In *Communication in the age of virtual reality* (pp. 15–31). Taylor & Francis.

Calleja, G. (2007). *Digital games as designed experience: Reframing the concept of immersion*. [Unpublished Doctoral Thesis]. Victoria University of Wellington, Wellington.

Cummings, J. J., & Bailenson, J. N. (2016). How immersive is enough? A meta-analysis of the effect of immersive technology on user presence. *Media Psychology, 19*(2), 272–309.

De Waard, I., Koutropoulos, A., Hogue, R. J., Abajian, S. C., Keskin, N. Ö., Rodriguez, C. O., & Gallagher, M. S. (2012). Merging MOOC and mLearning for increased learner interactions. *International Journal of Mobile and Blended Learning (IJMBL), 4*(4), 34–46.

D'Onofrio, S., Vertucci, R., Ricciardi, S., & De Nino, M. (2023). Augmented reality for maintenance and repair. In *Springer handbook of augmented reality* (pp. 597–616). Springer.

Ducrée, J., Codyre, M., Walshe, R., & Barting, S. (2022). DeSci-Decentralized Science, preprint.

Egliston, B., & Carter, M. (2022). 'The metaverse and how we'll build it': The political economy of Meta's Reality Labs. *New Media & Society*, 14614448221119785.

Fernandes, H. S., Cerqueira, N. M., & Sousa, S. F. (2021). *Developing and using BioSIMAR, an augmented reality program to visualize and learn about chemical structures in a virtual environment on any internet-connected device.* ACS Publications.
Fink, S. J. (2021). *Physical to virtual: A model for future virtual classroom environments.* [Masters Theses, University of Massachusetts Amherst, Amherst].
Frankel, R., & Krebs, V. J. (2021). *Human virtuality and digital life: Philosophical and psychoanalytic investigations.* Routledge.
Galson, S. J. (2016). *Ovid's metamorphoses and the scientific revolution.* Princeton University.
Ghosh, P., & Jhamb, D. (2022). The role of stakeholders in enhancing service quality in hospitality education: An application of stakeholder theory. *Revista Turismo & Desenvolvimento, 38*, 9–21.
Ghosh, P., Jhamb, D., & Yu, L. (2022). Faculty behavioral intentions in hospitality education: Effect of service quality, service value, sacrifice, and satisfaction. *Journal of Hospitality & Tourism Education, 35*, 1–17.
Gutierrez, N. (2023). The Ballad of Morton Heilig: On VR's mythic past. *JCMS: Journal of Cinema and Media Studies, 62*(3), 86–106.
Hsieh, P.-L., & Wei, S.-L. (2017). Relationship formation within online brand communities: Bridging the virtual and the real. *Asia Pacific Management Review, 22*(1), 2–9.
Jhamb, D., Kampani, N., & Arya, V. (2022). Embracing the employee orientation: Does customer relationship matter in brand building? *Benchmarking: An international journal, 29*(2), 411–433.
Lowe, D. (2012). *Perceptual organization and visual recognition* (Vol. 5). Springer Science & Business Media.
Manohar, S., Nag, I., Mittal, A., & Nair, A. J. (2023). *Omni channeling healthcare: Chaining details, information and predictions for extemporize service delivery* [Conference session]. 2023 7th International Conference on Computing, Communication, Control And Automation (ICCUBEA).
Mao, Y., Chen, P., Li, L., & Huang, D. (2014). Virtual reality training improves balance function. *Neural Regeneration Research, 9*(17), 1628.
Marougkas, A., Troussas, C., Krouska, A., & Sgouropoulou, C. (2023). Virtual reality in education: A review of learning theories, approaches and methodologies for the last decade. *Electronics, 12*(13), 2832.
McRobert, L. (2007). *Char Davies' immersive virtual art and the essence of spatiality.* University of Toronto Press.
Milgram, P., & Kishino, F. (1994). A taxonomy of mixed reality visual displays. *IEICE TRANSACTIONS on Information and Systems, 77*(12), 1321–1329.
Nair, A. J., Manohar, S., & Mittal, A. (2023a). *Enhancing customer experience with teleportation technology: The future of travel and tourism industry* [Conference session]. 2023 Second International Conference on Smart Technologies for Smart Nation (SmartTechCon).
Nair, A. J., Manohar, S., Mittal, A., & Khanna, V. (2023b). *Revolutionizing tourism and hospitality services: Integrating AI in the metaverse* [Conference session]. 2023 6th International Conference on Contemporary Computing and Informatics (IC3I).
Parsons, T. D., & Rizzo, A. A. (2008). Affective outcomes of virtual reality exposure therapy for anxiety and specific phobias: A meta-analysis. *Journal of Behavior Therapy and Experimental Psychiatry, 39*(3), 250–261.
Peddie, J., & Peddie, J. (Eds.). (2017). Historical overview. In *Augmented reality: Where we will all live* (pp. 59–86). Springer.
Qadir, A. M.-A., & Fatah, A. O. (2023). Platformization and the metaverse: Opportunities and challenges for urban sustainability and economic development. *EAI Endorsed Transactions on Energy Web, 10*(1).

Rampolla, J., & Kipper, G. (2012). *Augmented reality: An emerging technologies guide to AR*. Elsevier.

Schmalstieg, D., & Hollerer, T. (2016). *Augmented reality: principles and practice*. Addison-Wesley Professional.

Schroeder, M. (2008). *Value theory*. Oxford University Press.

Shalender, K., & Yadav, R. K. (2019). Strategic flexibility, manager personality, and firm performance: The case of Indian Automobile Industry. *Global Journal of Flexible Systems Management, 20*, 77–90.

Sutherland, I. E. (1968). *A head-mounted three dimensional display* [Conference session]. Proceedings of the December 9-11, 1968, Fall Joint Computer Conference, Part I.

Sykownik, P., Maloney, D., Freeman, G., & Masuch, M. (2022). *Something personal from the metaverse: goals, topics, and contextual factors of self-disclosure in commercial social VR* [Conference session]. Proceedings of the 2022 CHI Conference on Human Factors in Computing Systems.

Wu, H.-K., Lee, S. W.-Y., Chang, H.-Y., & Liang, J.-C. (2013). Current status, opportunities and challenges of augmented reality in education. *Computers & education, 62*, 41–49.

Yang, F. X., & Wang, Y. (2023). Rethinking metaverse tourism: A taxonomy and an agenda for future research. *Journal of Hospitality & Tourism Research*, 10963480231163509.

Zak, E. H. (2013). Do you believe in magic? Exploring the conceptualization of augmented reality and its implications for the user in the field of library and information science. *Information Technology and Libraries, 33*(4), 23–50.

Zik, Y., & Hon, G. (2017). Giambattista Della Porta: A magician or an optician? In A. Borrelli, G. Hon, & Y. Zik (Eds.), *The optics of Giambattista Della Porta (ca. 1535–1615): A reassessment* (pp. 39–55).

Chapter 7

Non-Fungible Tokens and Blockchain: Foundations for a Sustainable Metaverse Economy

Rim Gafsi

Sousse University, Tunisia

Abstract

This chapter examines the significant role of non-fungible tokens (NFTs) and blockchain technology in fostering a sustainable economy in the metaverse. Blockchain allows the saving and transfer of decentralized and secure data. As a primary component of the metaverse economy, NFTs are distinct and secure virtual assets saved on the blockchain. These assets facilitate possessing, trading, and monetizing digital assets. These advancing technologies have also revolutionized the method by which creators and artists test and exchange their digital work, introducing a novel period of ownership and value in the digital realm. However, the negative environmental effects of some blockchain technologies constitute a considerable constraint, pushing a shift to a sustainable economy. Platforms like The Sandbox have implemented initiatives to address environmental concerns. As a case study, The Sandbox play-to-earn model with tokenized assets showcases its ability to create value and encourage user participation. It shows the ability of NFTs and blockchain to support a sustainable economy.

Keywords: Blockchain; non-fungible tokens; metaverse economy; The Sandbox; sustainability; digital assets

1. Introduction

The metaverse is greatly considered a virtual world promoting user interaction, exchange, creativity, and revolutionizing society (Wang et al., 2022). This immersive virtual environment has quickly developed. While firms like Meta, Microsoft, and Nvidia strongly enhance their metaverse concepts, other international companies are involved in Web3 metaverses such as The Sandbox. Lee et al. (2021) and Vidal-Tomás (2023) state that the success of metaverse is contingent upon the interplay of various technological factors: such as user interactivity, intensive reality, blockchain, artificial intelligence, computer vision, Internet of Things (IoT) and robotics, edge and cloud computing, and future mobile networks. These are the primary elements preceding metaverse's surpassing success.

To flourish, the metaverse needs a functional economy that verifies digital properties. Blockchain technology is seen as a crucial element of the metaverse (Huynh-The et al., 2023). It is a revolutionary technique that ensures security and anonymity (Gadekallu et al., 2022). Blockchain enables users to possess, develop, and commercialize secure, transparent, and decentralized digital assets. It also sustains the metaverse economy, where users can use cryptocurrencies and non-fungible tokens (NFTs) to trade products virtually.

In the metaverse, NFTs are considered unique digital representations of virtual assets supported by blockchain technology (Chalmers et al., 2022). For instance, the Dolce & Gabbana brand has marked an important change in the digital era with the utilization of NFTs. NFTs offer features such as rareness and singularity that are attached to the metadata and serve as a certificate of ownership for digital items (Vidal-Tomás, 2023). According to Aksoy and Under (2021), the launch of ERC-721 on the Ethereum blockchain was a crucial step for NFT technology, illustrated by popular games such as "CryptoKitties," which contributed to the increase in Ethereum blockchain transactions. Ethereum remains the principal platform for NFT creation, transferring unchangeable data to different files.

NFTs have transcended their origins as digital collectibles and entered diverse domains, shifting industries such as fashion, music, academia, real-world object tokenization, patents, memberships, loyalty programs, decentralized finance (DeFi), and metaverse items. They authenticate ownership, property rights, and identity (Kshetri, 2022). For example, in The Sandbox, blockchain-backed NFTs certify parcel ownership, establishing a virtual real estate market. The Sandbox is an Ethereum-based metaverse game where users can purchase, create, and interface with NFTs. The native ERC-20 token of The Sandbox, SAND, facilitates transactions involving NFTs.

Despite their benefits, these technologies have the potential to increase energy consumption, generate waste and pollution, increase inequalities between countries (Piketty & Saez, 2014), etc. The shift to a more sustainable economic system is increasingly desirable. Technological advances, especially blockchain technology and NFT, toward sustainability are progressively incremental, and many companies and platforms are trying to fulfill their sustainability goals (Geissdoerfer et al., 2018). To build a truly sustainable economy, we need to recognize the drawbacks of technology while also using innovation to elaborate solutions that reduce damage and foster environmental well-being. It is in this context that our chapter is situated. We define a sustainable economy in the metaverse as an economy that is developed on the principles of economic, social, and environmental sustainability. Thus, what role do NFTs and blockchain play in building a sustainable economy in the metaverse? To do so, we researched the importance of NFTs and blockchain technology and their impact on society. This chapter aims to explore the role of NFTs and blockchain technology in shaping a sustainable economy within the metaverse, using The Sandbox as a specific case study. This case allows us to deeply investigate the economic dynamics and understand the contributions of NFTs and blockchain to a particular metaverse platform.

This chapter presents, first, the theoretical framework. Second, it analyzes the virtual worlds of The Sandbox. Finally, the conclusion discusses the theoretical and practical implications.

2. Literature Review

2.1. Blockchain Technology in Metaverse

To begin with the word "blockchain" was first associated with Bitcoin but there is no clarity around the meaning due to various interpretations (Frizzo-Barker et al., 2020). In principle, a blockchain is understood as a decentralized digital ledger (Appelbaum & Smith, 2018; Frizzo-Barker et al., 2020) designed to store transactions in a safe and transparent way which may help reduce the role of intermediaries. It has also been described as the literal chain of blocks (Frizzo-Barker et al., 2020; Sun et al., 2018), which form disruptive technology (Frizzo-Barker et al., 2020; Hassani et al., 2018), and a secure and tamper-resistant list of connected blocks with unchangeable networks A bunch of factors including trust, security, and transparency are vital considering blockchain as a trust machine in peer-to-peer transactions (Frizzo-Barker et al., 2020; Hawlitschek et al., 2018; Scott et al., 2017).

The metaverse would not progress without using blockchain technology, as stated by Torky et al. (2023) and Hassanien et al. (2023). The blockchain helps combat fraud, secure digital ownership, and identity of users, as well as deal with the risk of money laundering and other issues. The blockchain is a good foundation for confidence and traceability in the metaverse providing transparency and data integrity (Hassanien et al., 2023). Through the use of smart contracts, blockchain removes the need for intermediaries to accomplish transactions and ensures the automated regulation in all areas of the virtual world such as trading, gaming and avatars. Blockchain's decentralization enables synchronization between the avatars. Such synchronization promotes accuracy and transparency. Moreover, blockchain's immutability helps in the creation of the virtual bridges, and the assets can be smoothly transferred within the metaverse.

Additionally, Mahjoub et al. (2022b) present several characteristics of blockchain technology: (1) ensures the permanence of data; (2) sustains transparency by maintaining copies of the ledger on various nodes; (3) decentralizes governance; (4) offers anonymity through the utilization of public and private keys;

(5) guarantees the credibility, timeliness, and comprehensiveness of data; (6) withstands component failures through its resilient design; and (7) enables faster settlement times in comparison to traditional banking systems, thereby enhancing overall operational efficiency.

2.2. NFTs Technology

Barbon and Ranaldo (2023) define NFTs as digital assets saved in blockchain tokens and leveraged by smart contracts to verify their source and possession. These tokens are the property of unique digital or physical items and are assessed based on factors such as scarcity, popularity, or existence in virtual environments (Momtaz, 2022). Each NFT is unique in its features and capabilities, enabling various utilizations such as asset representation and transaction facilitation. In the art industry, the utilization of NFTs guarantees the authenticity of digital collectibles using smart contracts (Chalmers et al., 2022). Cortnelius (2021) argues that NFTs are creative digital items with significant capabilities that lead to continuous discussions and investigations in many disciplines. Beyond ownership proof, NFTs leverage blockchain to offer benefits to holders in both the digital and physical realms, similar to membership cards that grant access to events, exclusive items, and discounts. NFTs act as digital keys to online spaces for engagement.

NFTs, a technology supported by Ethereum, employ smart contracts written in Solidity and then stored on the blockchain (Barbon & Ranaldo, 2023). These contracts adhere both standards: ERC-721 for non-fungible and ERC-1155 for semi-fungible tokens. With the help of NFT markets such as OpenSea or Rarible, a user generates NFT in a way that includes uploading the digital asset, setting up its features and paying gas fees and NFT price itself. The user submits an order through minting where the data such as the item's name, description, image, and metadata are transferred to smart contract for executing the demand to create a brand-new token and link it to a unique and immutable address within the network (Hartwich et al., 2024; Wang et al., 2021). Complying with a standard like ERC-721, which is considered for its "unique tokens" attribute, guarantees the production of a single and uniquely owned item. However, unlike ERC-1155 tokens where you can create multiple instances of a token, ERC-20 tokens do not have a concept of multiples. Instead of that, one can say the NFT creator can give the quantity of identical NFTs that can be generated (Hartwich et al., 2024; Kuhn et al., 2021).

In practice, Sestino et al. (2022) describe five distinct steps for creating NFTs on platforms such as MetaMask, Bitski, and OpenSea. An illustrative example can be found at www.opensea.io:

1. At the beginning, users must sign in to the specific site to begin the account registration process, set up the profile and then create a virtual wallet. It often needs no more that your personal email address. The process is quick and efficient.
2. In the second stage, users choose the favorite NFT and decide on the way of formation or conversion, e.g., image, video, audio, the document

containing such file types as Jpg, Png, Gif, Svg, Mp3, Mp4, Wav, Webm, Ogg, Glb, and Pdf.
3. With the third stage, the system gives users to set such parameters as a name, a short description of the digital persona, and a link to the personal website.
4. During the fourth stage, users will put any digital file that will be turned into a blockchain-based.
5. The last step is that users get their NFTs and specify the payment or they go for royalties, meaning that most of the times users pay with Ether which is a crypto like Bitcoin. Consequently, the NFT can be spread over the platform, bought or gift provided that will lead to the marketplace or sharing a link, which is automatically created, on the social networks. A person should use the NFT transfer function and give the certificate of ownership for the NFT to the buyer.

The NFT market has boomed since it started with Etheria on the Ethereum blockchain in 2015, reaching significant popularity in 2021 (Ante, 2022). Early projects like CryptoPunks and CryptoKitties, launched in 2017, highlighted scalability issues on Ethereum, spurring innovations like layer-2 scaling solutions adopted by Axie Infinity and the migration of NBA Top Shot to the FLOW blockchain (Ante, 2022; Axie, 2021). The NFT boom of 2021 saw landmark sales such as the auction of the first tweet, the Nyan Cat meme animation, and Kings of Leon's music rights as NFTs (Ante, 2022; El Khoury & Alareeni, 2023). This expansion reflects the trend of artists, creators, collectors, and investors embracing NFTs (Wilson et al., 2022), expanding beyond digital art to encompass virtual real estate, music, videos, and more (Rehman et al., 2021). Deventer et al. (2024) suggested that the involvement of famous personalities, renowned companies, and popular media lending legitimacy to NFTs, drawing in a broader range of peoples. The progress of blockchain technology has also played a crucial role in enhancing scalability and interoperability, elevating user satisfaction, and fostering the growth of NFT marketplaces. Collectively, these advancements mark a significant transformation, empowering creators with unparalleled prospects to monetize their digital assets.

The NFT market has boomed since it started with Etheria on the Ethereum blockchain in 2015, reaching significant popularity in 2021 (Ante, 2022). Early projects like CryptoPunks and CryptoKitties, launched in 2017, highlighted scalability issues on Ethereum, spurring innovations like layer-2 scaling solutions adopted by Axie Infinity and the migration of NBA Top Shot to the FLOW blockchain (Ante, 2022; Axie, 2021). The NFT boom of 2021 saw landmark sales such as the auction of the first tweet, the Nyan Cat meme animation, and Kings of Leon's music rights as NFTs (Ante, 2022). This expansion reflects the trend of artists, creators, collectors, and investors embracing NFTs (Wilson et al., 2022), expanding beyond digital art to encompass virtual real estate, music, videos, and more (Rehman et al., 2021). Deventer et al. (2024) suggested that the involvement of famous personalities, renowned companies, and popular media lends legitimacy to NFTs, drawing in a broader range of people. The progress of blockchain technology has also played a crucial role in enhancing scalability and interoperability, elevating user satisfaction, and fostering the growth of NFT marketplaces. Collectively, these advancements mark a significant transformation, empowering creators with unparalleled prospects to monetize their digital assets.

Furthermore, NFTs possess distinctive features crucial for participants in the digital ecosystem, whether involved in buying, selling, or creating these unique digital assets (Chandra, 2022; Shilina, 2022). The authors enumerate six characteristics presented as follows:

- *Uniqueness:* Each NFT, minted through smart contracts on blockchain platforms, represents a one-of-a-kind object with metadata akin to a certificate of authenticity. For instance, an NFT could symbolize the first SMS ever sent or be part of a collection like the Bored Ape Yacht Club, which consists of 10,000 unique virtual apes (Chandra, 2022).
- *Non-interchangeability:* NFTs have distinct smart codes, making them non-interchangeable and different from other digital assets or virtual products. For instance, within the Cyber Punks (digital artwork), each punk preserves its individuality and cannot be exchanged with other punks or with diverse categories of virtual assets, such as a Dolce & Gabbana jacket NFT or a Nike shoe NFT (Chandra, 2022).
- *Authenticity:* The data associated with each NFT are permanent and unalterable, establishing a robust defense against counterfeiting. Authentication involves assigning a token ID, a wallet address, and a smart contract code (Chandra, 2022). An authenticated NFT may have a token ID like 40,913, a wallet address such as 0xc6b0562605D35eE7101 38402B878ffe6F2E23807, and a smart contract address like 0x2a46f2ffd99e19a89476e2f62270e0a35bbf0756.
- *Scarcity:* NFTs' scarcity, defined by their unique nature, enhances their market value, offering creators flexibility in creating "one of one" or themed collections. Examples include Dolce Gabbana's "The Glass Suit," Macallan cask whisky NFT, and the Crypto Kitties NFT collection, gathered from over two million unique kitties (Chandra, 2022).
- *Resaleability:* Creators benefit from continuous income as NFTs can be repeatedly sold in the secondary market with automated royalty payments via blockchain. Different NFT marketplaces have varying royalty limits: OpenSea allows up to 10% and Nifty Gateway permits up to 50% (Chandra, 2022).
- *Collectability:* NFTs serve as a virtual system for collecting objects, offering economic and non-economic values, from investment to social status. Examples of NFT collections include "Hey Jude" Notes written by Paul McCartney, the Crypto Punks collection, consisting of 10,000 items and owned by 3,400 individuals, and NFT-enabled conference event tickets like BlockDown Croatia 2022 (Chandra, 2022).

Fig. 1 explains the taxonomy of the key topics of NFT.

2.3. Role of Blockchain and NFTs in the Sustainable Metaverse Economy

Blockchain technology offers significant benefits to companies by addressing security and transparency concerns across various sectors (Mahjoub et al., 2022b).

Definition	Unique digital assets within blockchain tokens, verified by smart contracts			
NFT creation process	Account and wallet creation	NFT setting	NFT configuration	Upload & transformation process	NFT distribution (selling)
Market Development	Technological evolution		Diversification of Use Cases	Celebrity and Brand Endorsement
Properties	Uniqueness	Non-Interchangeability	Authenticity	Scarcity	Resaleability	Collectability

Fig. 1. NFT Taxonomy. *Source:* Author construction.

It ensures data integrity, confidentiality, and accessibility through advanced cryptographic techniques and consensus algorithms (Mahjoub et al., 2022a). By implementing blockchain, companies can reduce costs, automate processes, and enhance security through smart contracts (Mahjoub et al., 2022b). Innovative technologies like tokenization and NFTs further enhance the digital ecosystem by providing digital permanence, preventing counterfeiting, and ensuring proof of ownership (Bamakan et al., 2021). Additionally, blockchain facilitates prompt and low-fee transactions using cryptocurrencies, as demonstrated by the CHAI app powered by Terra's blockchain network (Mahjoub et al., 2022b).

In the financial sector, blockchain streamlines financial processes by eliminating middlemen, preventing duplication, and securely recording transactions, thus reducing costs (Al-Jaroodi & Mohamed, 2019). Its applications range from digital currencies and stock trading platforms to insurance and settlements, enabling efficient global financial transactions (Al-Jaroodi & Mohamed, 2019). In the healthcare sector, blockchain revolutionizes the way to handle electronic medical records (EMRs) (Prisco, 2016). Al-Jaroodi and Mohamed (2019) show that some companies like Gem and Tierion utilize blockchain security to save and control health data, enabling patients to verify their medical reports confidentially. Most significantly, blockchain permanently saves all modifications made to health reports, which is essential for inspecting and keeping medical investigations safe and trustworthy (Al-Jaroodi & Mohamed, 2019). Blockchain technology and NFTs also play a significant role in optimizing logistics management. Blockchain allows enhanced traceability, flexibility, and competition and minimizes production costs, delays, and errors (Al-Jaroodi & Mohamed, 2019; Hackius & Petersen, 2017). The insertion of NFTs in supply chains considerably improves transparency by approving authentication and ownership. For example, Provenance and Hijro companies utilized blockchain platforms to transform their traditional logistics practices (Al-Jaroodi & Mohamed, 2019). In the manufacturing industry, blockchain technology fights against imitations, secures data, and fosters collaboration (Barenji et al., 2018; Li et al., 2018). For instance, Breitling employs NFTs to verify the authenticity of their watches. Similarly, another company called "Genesis of Things" combines blockchain with 3D printing and the IoT to revolutionize and automate the production process (Al-Jaroodi & Mohamed, 2019). Within the realm of construction, blockchain technology helps create and register contracts as well as supports more efficient construction supply chain management and construction equipment leasing (Al-Jaroodi & Mohamed, 2019; Wang et al., 2017). Blockchain technology also serves as a crucial facilitator in the telecommunications sector. It improves traceability, contract management, and governance (Ibrahim, 2017). Xiong et al. (2020) show that in agriculture, blockchain helps to improve profitability, ensure food security, and minimize waste. The pharmaceutical industry takes advantage of the blockchain by enhancing pharmaceutical supply chain management and facilitating data exchange for medication innovation (Al-Jaroodi & Mohamed, 2019). The blockchain serves as a favorable tool for Industry 4.0 by creating a secure and reliable environment for the insertion of systems and components among various companies. This fosters the development of a productive industrial ecosystem (Al-Jaroodi & Mohamed, 2019).

Chohan and Paschen (2021) indicate that NFTs can benefit enterprises by increasing their digital products and developing relationships between the real and virtual worlds. A significant example is Nike's success with exclusive NFT products (Hofstetter et al., 2022). Having virtual art pieces as NFTs allows users to see them in different digital environments, which develops interaction, builds trust, and turns them into faithful fans of the brand (Hollensen et al., 2022). Beyond virtual products, NFTs offer special experiences, such as access to exclusive content or encounters with celebrities (Dwivedi et al., 2022). According to Cheah and Shimul (2023), NFTs present brands with novel prospects for market growth and income generation. As consumers actively participate in diversified domains, NFT marketplaces permit them to purchase, obtain, and swap digital items, therefore improving the link between brands and consumers. Israfilzade (2022) explains that smart contracts improve the user experience and facilitate the creation of income via royalties and shared revenues, which allows the development of innovative models like decentralized autonomous organizations (DAOs) and extends participation in the NFT ecosystem (Chandra, 2022). The continued evolution of NFTs is impacting the digital asset landscape deeply and extensively, shaping the future of commerce and entrepreneurship within the metaverse economy.

The influence of NFTs on society exceeds economic implications. Indeed, Zhang et al. (2022) determine that NFTs not only allocate value to digital files such as music and artwork but also generate discussions about their cultural, market, and ethical importance, creating new rules and organizations for digital assets. Ambolis (2023) indicates that NFTs can be used with DAO, justifying the flexible feature of NFTs. This enables community governance, collective ownership, and the improvement of digital assets within various DAO types. Moreover, NFTs offer a platform for people to communicate globally. Their development has also driven decision-makers to believe in social responsibility and sustainability. Cypherock (2023) outlines that NFTs have revolutionized the field of content creation by making artistic expression more accessible to a wider audience. NFTs enable artists from all over the world to directly present and sell their work in NFT marketplaces by eliminating traditional intermediaries like galleries and auction houses. The decentralized nature of NFT allows artists to preserve complete control over their intellectual property.

Despite the numerous benefits of NFTs and blockchain technology for the metaverse economy, concerns persist about their environmental impact. Sustainability is being challenged due to the intensive use of energy in Proof-of-Work (PoW) systems for blockchains and NFTs. Truby et al. (2022) clarify that the commercialization of NFTs, which rely on Ethereum, has a considerable carbon footprint. The process of creating NFTs requires a significant amount of electricity because every transaction needs a lot of computing resources. The rise of NFT transactions, exceeding US$10 billion in 2021, has intensified the negative environmental impacts (Truby et al., 2022). This increased energy requirement, identical to that of a European household in a month for each NFT artwork purchased (Mallapaty, 2020), constitutes a menace to worldwide climate stabilization efforts aimed at keeping temperature increases to less than 2°C (Huynh et al., 2021).

Fortunately, the industries of blockchain and NFT are seriously seeking environmental solutions to face ecological problems, showing a proactive stance in reducing negative effects and promoting sustainability. According to Asif and Hassan (2023), some promising solutions have evolved in the blockchain, including Proof-of-Stake (PoS) blockchains like Cardano, Tezos, and Algorand, which utilize considerably less energy than current PoW models. To validate transactions, PoS does not require miners to solve complex mathematical problems since it requires lower energy consumption than PoW. Asif and Hassan (2023) add that to improve its security, Ethereum was updated with a new feature called "Casper," which assures that validators continually accept the state of the blockchain. Moreover, platforms like Palm, Flow, and Polygon have been created with sustainability as a fundamental value. They use PoS mechanisms and incorporate efficient NFT features. Thurman (2021) clarifies that these platforms employ PoS to commercialize NFTs on the blockchain because they utilize less energy and are safer than PoW used by Ethereum and Bitcoin. According to Thompson (2023), PoS platforms offer different advantages for NFT developers and collectors, such as reduced cost, faster transactions, and rich user experiences. The change of the Ethereum platform to PoS protocols instead of PoW and the United Nations Carbon Offset Platform (UNFCCC) initiative demonstrates efforts made to be more environmentally friendly (Kapengut & Mizrach, 2023).

These developments have demonstrated the critical significance of NFTs and blockchain technology in fostering a prosperous and sustainable economy. Using the Sandbox platform as a case study, we can understand how these technologies empower users, inspire innovation, and promote a sustainable virtual economy.

3. Case Study: The Sandbox

3.1. Case Description

The Sandbox was started in 2012 as a mobile game allowing players to earn rewards, it underwent a significant shift under the direction of Animoca Brands in 2018, ultimately developing into a cohesive and collaborative 3D virtual world conducted by its community. The platform embraces a play-to-earn model, rewarding users in cryptocurrency or NFTs for active engagement. The decentralized nature of The Sandbox challenges traditional gaming models, disrupting the concept of centralized ownership. ERC-721 NFTs, known as LAND, actively track parcels in the virtual landscape. The Sandbox operates on Ethereum but supports token movement between Ethereum and Polygon blockchains. The ecosystem relies on multiple tokens (Table 1), including SAND for transactions and activities, ASSETS for 3D voxel creations, LAND for virtual real estate ownership, CATALYSTS to determine asset scarcity, and GEMS for burning and contributing to the platform's economy. The Sandbox encourages users to create content using the VoxEdit 3D modeling tool. The blockchain ensures uniqueness and traceable ownership of assets, with transactions recorded transparently on the blockchain. The product portfolio includes VoxEdit for asset creation, The Sandbox Marketplace for NFT trading, and The Sandbox Game Maker for non-coders to develop 3D games. The platform offers users a vibrant world for exploration, interaction, and customization. The Sandbox is not just an interactive experience; it serves as a cornerstone in the emergence of a new digital economy, providing valuable insights into Metaverse features, including user-generated content management, asset ownership, and community engagement. The success of The Sandbox positions it as a compelling example for understanding and influencing the evolving trajectory of the metaverse.

Moreover, The Sandbox has achieved several milestones and partnerships, such as:

- launching its alpha version in June 2021, with over 40 games and 5,000 players (www.cnetfrance.fr),
- selling over 160,000 LANDs, which are parcels of virtual space where users can build their worlds (https://decrypt.co/),
- collaborating with stars like Snoop Dogg and Paris Hilton, and brands such as Adidas and Gucci (https://decrypt.co/).

The Sandbox has also inserted the beta version of its Marketplace, enabling artists affiliated with the "Artist Fund" to monetize their NFTs and minimize the quantity of minted NFT copies while enhancing the technical capabilities of the Marketplace (The Sandbox, 2021).

Table 1. The Sandbox Token Overview.

Crypto Token	Token Standard	Digital Assets
SAND	ERC20	Fungible tokens
GEM	ERC20	Fungible tokens
CATALYST	ERC1155	Non-fungible tokens
LAND	ERC 721	Non-fungible tokens
ASSET	ERC721	Non-fungible tokens

Source: Author construction.

3.2. Role of The Sandbox NFTs and Blockchain in Sustainable Metaverse Economy

Blockchain technology forms the foundational infrastructure of The Sandbox, establishing a secure and transparent environment for all metaverse transactions and interactions. This decentralized system ensures the secure recording of ownership for virtual assets, guarding against tampering or manipulation. The Sandbox further empowers users through the utilization of blockchain and NFTs, capitalizing on the emerging segment in the global game market. NFTs provide digital rareness, safety, and authentication, with each NFT being distinct, inseparable, and non-interchangeable, offering distinct and secure digital assets to users. The benefits of using NFTs within The Sandbox (Fig. 2), as outlined in the White Paper (2020), are as follows:

- **True Digital Ownership:** Users still possess true ownership of their digital items, even if the game is closed. Every game item is tokenized on the blockchain, enabling users to decide the method of marketing their items.
- **Security and Immutability:** Trading digital game items in markets managed by blockchain easily tokenizes them, minimizing the risks of fraud and robbery associated with scarcity and demand. The distributed ledger ensures security and immutability.
- **Trading:** Users on blockchain-based gaming platforms have fundamental control over their digital items, allowing them to purchase and sell assets freely without concerns about fraud or platform closures that could annul the value of in-game items.
- **Cross-Application Interoperability:** Blockchain allows games to exchange assets, like avatars, lands, and other game elements, between various games, making the digital environment vaster.

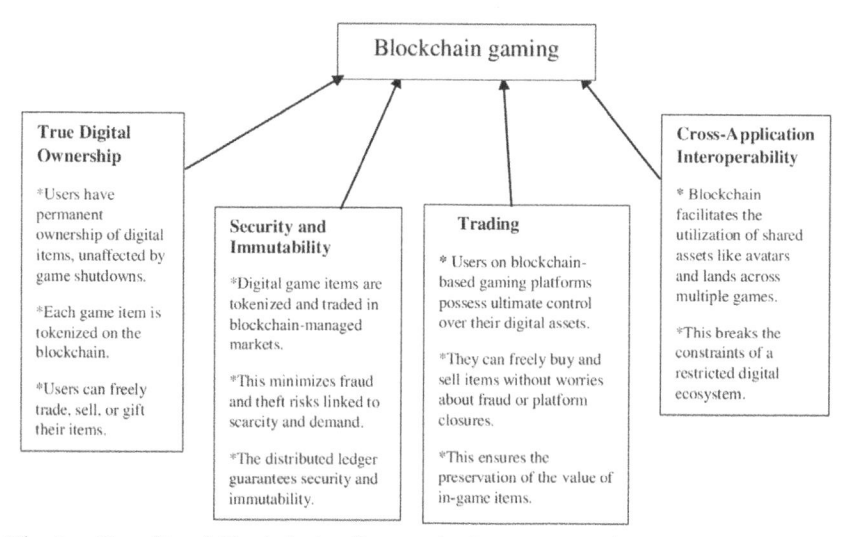

Fig. 2. Benefits of Blockchain. *Source:* Author construction.

The Sandbox metaverse operates with various tokens like LANDS, ASSETS, and the native SAND in which each token plays a specific role in shaping the virtual economy (Nakavachara & Saengchote, 2022).

NFTs are considered key contributors to The Sandbox's success by encouraging players to own, trade, and capitalize on various virtual assets, such as plots of land, wearables, and artwork. They offer creators not only the opportunity to monetize their creations but also a lucrative investment. According to Song et al. (2023), The Sandbox is a decentralized platform that is changing digital interactions and plays an important role in creating the direction of the metaverse. The major emphasis on content created by users, with the help of tools like VoxEdit, allows them to freely discover and personalize virtual experiences. This method gives power to users and enables game developers and artists to make money from their creations (Song et al. 2023). Christodoulou et al., (2022) determine that The Sandbox utilizes blockchain technology to guarantee transparency and easily traceable ownership of assets, solving problems in the digital world. According to Song et al. (2023), The Sandbox is not just about exploring virtually, it also helps create a new digital economy in the metaverse. The Sandbox's success demonstrates how to effectively handle user-generated content, asset property, and community involvement. The platform uses three main elements, namely, VoxEdit, Game Maker, and Marketplace, to create a space where people can trade SAND, LAND, and graphic assets (Christodoulou et al., 2022; White Paper, 2020). According to White Paper (2020), the SAND token is the main currency used in the metaverse. It allows people to commercialize virtual assets, NFTs, and services. It also allows users to participate in decisions about The Sandbox ecosystem's development. The platform inserts the concept of "play-to-earn," which allows players to acquire rewards and SAND tokens through contribution to gameplay, completion of quests, or development of valuable content. This novel strategy links gaming activities to the opportunity to earn, providing players with financial incentives for their investment of time and creativity (Song et al., 2023). The Sandbox's NFTs have many uses, such as being assets in games, virtual properties, and a platform for artists to expose their work. These NFTs are specific because they can be employed in different games and platforms without any difficulties. The funding round, which raised a whopping $93 million and was led by SoftBank, shows that there is a great interest in growing The Sandbox's virtual world which is based on NFTs (White Paper, 2020).

Recently, it was innovated by The Sandbox some ways to lower environmental effect and protect sustainable being. On the basis of the research published in 2021, the platform has decided to be part of the Polygon alliance and to migrate toward a cutting-edge NFT layer technology that concentrates on environmental sustainability. Being powered with this very advanced technology, the energy consumption is predicted to be as low as 0.1% of Ethereum's. Moreover, The Sandbox has invested in carbon credits on the level of technology like blockchain platforms, for example, Nori and Offsetra (The Sandbox, 2021). For this reason, ETS first and foremost aims to maintain the transparency of the process of compensation for emissions. The Sandbox has calculated the environmental impact from their NFTs for the year 2021, which amounted to around 350 tons of CO_2, and they have later bought carbon credits and started to offset since then (The Sandbox, 2021). Notably, The Sandbox has selected Offsetra to provide its nature-based CO_2 offsets which total 200 metric tons. Moreover, the Sandbox secured an extension of their partnership with WeForest, an NGO that has a mission to reforest areas, which they have cooperated back in 2014. As part of their joint effort, The Sandbox and Conservify Alliance have pledged to plant around 9,000 mangrove trees in Madagascar (The Sandbox, 2021). Consistent with the previous statement, The Sandbox set 1% of the proceeds of LANDS purchasing of the customers to be given to WeForest. These grant programs will be channeled toward projects that safeguard Ethiopia's, Zambia's, and Brazil's forests. The Sandbox also partners with other environmental conservation groups in order to further its goal of making a measurable change in our physical world (The Sandbox, 2021).

4. Conclusion

In this chapter, we have tried to emphasize the essential role of NFTs and blockchain technology in a sustainable economy in the metaverse, using The Sandbox as a case study. A sustainable economic system in the metaverse involves meeting the present generation's needs while ensuring that future generations can fulfill their necessities. The inclusion of NFTs and blockchain technology assumes a crucial role in building such an economy, as it has the potential to address social, economic, and environmental obstacles.

Far et al. (2023) outline that the user's involvement in governance and decision-making processes is boosted due to the decentralized nature of NFTs and blockchains. They offer enhanced transparency, security, and efficiency. This allows individuals to conduct transactions and make payments to distant recipients without the need for in-person authentication or secure channels (Far et al., 2023). The Sandbox metaverse platform utilizes NFTs and blockchain technology to establish a transparent, secure, and decentralized economic model. This model enables users to create and monetize digital assets and game experiences on the blockchain. To promote sustainability, The Sandbox advocates for Ethereum's transition to a PoS consensus mechanism. This transition aims to reduce energy consumption and emissions. The game also demonstrates its commitment to sustainability through its "The Sandbox Gets Greener" program, which pledges to plant a tree for every LAND sold in collaboration with environmental projects. The Sandbox emphasizes strong social aspects through its collaborative nature, active community of creators and users, digital ownership, and interoperability. By collaborating with celebrities and brands, The Sandbox creates a metaverse that serves as a hub of pop culture.

NFTs in the education sector serve as a method for verifying educational certificates and diplomas, establishing a secure framework for credential authentication, and enhancing the accessibility of educational records. While traditional paper certificates are vulnerable to loss, damage, and counterfeiting, NFTs present a tamper-resistant solution for educational credentials. By being saved on a secure blockchain ledger, NFTs guarantee the legitimacy and accuracy of diplomas. This not only streamlines verification processes for employers and institutions but also ensures easy access to records. Nevertheless, the integration of such technology necessitates overcoming obstacles such as technological adoption, ensuring inclusivity, establishing uniform formats, and addressing potential privacy issues. Leading programs at prestigious universities like the Massachusetts Institute of Technology (MIT) showcase the transformative potential of NFTs in revolutionizing the issuance and management of educational credentials moving forward.

Thus, the emerging sustainable metaverse economy needs additional progress and partnership to fully grasp the potential of NFTs and blockchain in the metaverse.

References

Aksoy, P. C., & Under, Z. O. (2021). NFTs and copyright: Challenges and opportunities. *Journal of Intellectual Property Law & Practice, 16*(10), 1115–1126.

Al-Jaroodi, J., & Mohamed, N. (2019). *Industrial applications of blockchain* [Conference session]. 2019 IEEE 9th Annual Computing and Communication Workshop and Conference (CCWC) (pp. 0550–0555).

Ambolis, D. (2023). *NFT-based DAOs: How NFTs are changing the game in Web 3.0*. https://blockchainmagazine.net/

Ante, L. (2022). Non-fungible token (NFT) markets on the Ethereum blockchain: Temporal development, cointegration and interrelations. *Economics of Innovation and New Technology, 32*, 1216. https://doi.org/10.1080/10438599.2022.2119564

Appelbaum, D., & Smith, S. S. (2018). Blockchain basics and hands-on guidance: Taking the next step toward implementation and adoption. *The CPA Journal; New York, 88*(6), 28–37. https://www.cpajournal.com/category/magazine/june-2018-issue/

Asif, R., & Hassan, S. R. (2023). Shaping the future of Ethereum: Exploring energy consumption in Proof-of-Work and Proof-of-Stake consensus. *Frontiers in Blockchain, 6*, 1151724. https://doi.org/10.3389/fbloc.2023.1151724

Axie. (2021). *The great migration - Ronin phase 2 is live!* https://axie.substack.com/p/migration

Bamakan, H., Mojtaba, S., Shima, Gh., & Sajedeh, M. (2021). Blockchain-enabled pharmaceutical cold chain: Applications, key challenges, and future trends. *Journal of Cleaner Production, 302*, 127021. https://doi.org/10.1016/j.jclepro.2021.127021

Barbon, A., & Ranaldo, A. (2023). Non-fungible tokens. In T. Walker, E. Nikbakht, & M. Kooli (Eds.), *The fintech disruption. Palgrave studies in financial services technology*. Palgrave Macmillan. https://doi.org/10.1007/978-3-031-23069-1_6

Barenji, V. A, Hanyan, G., Zonggui, T., Zhi, L., Wang, W. M., & Huang, G. Q. (2018). *Blockchain-based cloud manufacturing: Decentralization* [Conference session]. Conference: Advances in Transdisciplinary Engineering. https://doi.org/10.3233/978-1-61499-898-3-1003

Chalmers, D. C., Matthews, F. R., Quinn, J., & Recker, W. (2022). Beyond the bubble: Will NFTs and digital proof of ownership empower creative industry entrepreneurs? *Journal of Business Venturing Insights, 17*, e00309. https://doi.org/10.1016/j.jbvi.2022.e00309

Chandra, Y. (2022). Non-fungible token-enabled entrepreneurship: A conceptual framework. *Journal of Business Venturing Insights, 18*, e00323. https://doi.org/10.1016/j.jbvi.2022.e00323

Cheah, I., & Shimul, A. S. (2023). Marketing in the metaverse: Moving forward – What's next? *Journal of Global Scholar of Marketing Science, 33*(1), 1–10. https://doi.org/10.1080/21639159.2022.2163908

Chohan, R., & Paschen, J. (2021). What marketers need to know about non-fungible tokens (NFTs). *Business Horizons, 66*(9). http://dx.doi.org/10.1016/j.bushor.2021.12.004

Christodoulou, K., Katelaris, L., Themistocleous, M., Christodoulou, P., & Iosif, E. (2022). NFTs and the metaverse revolution: Research perspectives and open challenges. In M. C. Lacity & H. Treiblmaier (Eds.), *Blockchains and the token economy. Technology, work and globalization*. Palgrave Macmillan. https://doi.org/10.1007/978-3-030-95108-5_6

Cortnelius, K. (2021). Betraying blockchain: Accountability, transparency and document standards for non-fungible. *Information, 12*(9), 358. https://doi.org/10.3390/info12090358

Cypherock. (2023). *NFTs and the empowerment of content creators: Unlocking new opportunities*. https://www.cypherock.com/

Deventer, C., de Sousa, V. A., & Pirnay, L. (2024). NFTByBrands: Value identification framework for analysis and design of NFT initiatives. *International Journal of Electronic Commerce, 28*(1), 33–62. https://doi.org/10.1080/10864415.2023.2295070

Dwivedi, Y. K., Hughes, L., Baabdullah, A. M., Ribeiro-Navarrete, S., Giannakis, M., Al-Debei, M. M., Dennehy, D., Metri, B., Buhalis, D., Cheung, Ch. M. K., Conboy, K., Doyle, R., Dubey, R., Dutot, V., Felix, R., Goyal, D. P., Gustafsson, A., Hinsch, Ch., Jebabli, I., … Wamba, S. F. (2022). Metaverse beyond the hype: Multidisciplinary perspectives on emerging challenges, opportunities, and agenda for research, practice and policy. *International Journal of Information Management, 66*, 102542.

El Khoury, R., & Alareeni, B. (2023). *How the metaverse will reshape business and sustainability*. Springer Nature Singapore. https://doi.org/10.1007/978-981-99-5126-0

Far, S. B., Rad, A. I., & Asaar, M. R. (2023). Blockchain and its derived technologies shape the future generation of digital businesses: A focus on decentralized finance and the Metaverse. *Data Science and Management, 6*, 183–197. https://doi.org/10.1016/j.dsm.2023.06.002

Frizzo-Barker, J., Chow-White, P. A., Adams, P. R., Mentanko, J., Ha, D., & Green, S. (2020). Blockchain as a disruptive technology for business: A systematic review. *International Journal of Information Management, 51*, 102029. https://doi.org/10.1016/j.ijinfomgt.2019.10.014

Gadekallu, T. R., Huynh-The, T., Wang, W., Yenduri, G., Ranaweera, P., Pham, Q.-V., & Liyanage, M. (2022). Blockchain for the metaverse: A review. *arXiv preprint arXiv:2203.09738*. https://doi.org/10.48550/arXiv.2203.09738

Geissdoerfer, M., Vladimirova, D., & Evans, S. (2018). Sustainable business model innovation: A review. *Journal of Cleaner Production, 198*, 401–416. https://doi.org/10.1016/j.jclepro.2018.06.240

Hackius, N., & Petersen, M. (2017). *Blockchain in logistics and supply chain: trick or treat?* [Conference session]. Hamburg International Conference of LogisticsAt: Hamburg, GermanyVolume: Digitalization in Supply Chain Management and Logistics. 10.15480/882.1444

Hartwich, E., Ollig, P., Fridgen, G., & Rieger, A. (2024). Probably something: A multilayer taxonomy of non-fungible tokens. *Internet Research, 34*(1), 216–238. https://doi.org/10.1108/INTR-08-2022-0666

Hassani, H., Huang, X., & Silva, E. (2018). Banking with blockchain-ed big data. *Journal of Management Analytics, 5*(4), 256–275. https://doi.org/10.1080/23270012.2018.1528900

Hassanien, A. E., Darwish, A., & Torky, M. (2023). *The future of metaverse in the virtual era and physical world* (Vol. 123). Springer Nature. https://doi.org/10.1007/978-3-031-29132-6

Hawlitschek, F., Notheisen, B., & Teubner, T. (2018). The limits of trust-free systems: A literature review on blockchain technology and trust in the sharing economy. *Commerce Research and Applications, 29*, 50–63. https://doi.org/10.1016/j.elerap.2018.03.005

Hofstetter, R., de Bellis, E., Brandes, L., Clegg, M., Lamberton, C., Reibstein, D., Rohlfsen, F., Schmitt, B., & Zhang, J. Z. (2022). Crypto-marketing: How non-fungible tokens (NFTs) challenge traditional marketing. *Marketing Letters, 33*(4), 705–711. https://doi.org/10.1007/s11002-022-09639-2

Hollensen, S., Kotler, P., & Opresnik, M. O. (2022). Metaverse: The new marketing universe. *Journal of Business Strategy, 44*(3), 119–125. https://doi.org/10.1108/JBS-01-2022-0014

Huynh, A. N. Q., Duong, D., Burggraf, T., Luong, H. T. T., & Bui, N. H. (2021). Energy consumption and Bitcoin market. *Asia-Pacific Financial Markets*. https://doi.org/10.1007/s10690-021-09338-4

Huynh-The, Th., Gadekallu, R. T., Wang, W., Yenduri, G., Ranaweera, P., Pham, Q. V, Benevides da Costa, D., & Liyanage, M. (2023). Blockchain for the metaverse: A review. *Future Generation Computer Systems, 143*, 401–419. https://doi.org/10.1016/j.future.2023.02.008

Ibrahim, M. A. (2017). *Applicability of blockchain technology in telecommunications service management*. [M.S. thesis, Leiden Inst. Adv. Comput. Sci. Leiden Univ., Leiden, The Netherlands]. Retrieved February 2019, from http://liacs.leidenuniv.nl/assets/Uploads/AtefMohamed-non-confidential.pdf

Israfilzade, K. (2022). Marketing in the metaverse: A sceptical viewpoint of opportunities and future research directions. *The Eurasia Proceedings of Educational & Social Sciences (EPESS), 24*, 53–60.

Kapengut, E., & Mizrach, B. (2023). An event study of the ethereum transition to proof-of-stake. *Commodities, 2*, 96–110. https://dx.doi.org/10.2139/ssrn.4247091

Kshetri, N. (2022). Web 3.0 and the metaverse shaping organizations' brand and product strategies. *IT Professional, 24*(2), 11–15. https://doi.org/10.1109/MITP.2022.3157206

Kuhn, M., Funk, F., & Franke, J. (2021), Blockchain architecture for automotive traceability. *Procedia CIRP, 97*, 390–395. https://doi.org/10.1016/j.procir.2020.05.256

Lee, L. H., Braud, T., Zhou, P., Wang, L., Xu, D., Lin, Z., Kumar, A., Bermejo, C. & Hui, P. (2021). All one needs to know about metaverse: A complete survey on technological singularity, virtual ecosystem, and research agenda. *arXiv Preprint arXiv, 14*(8), 1–66. https://doi.org/10.48550/arXiv.2110.05352

Li, R., Song, T., Mei, B., Li, H., Cheng, X., & Sun, L. (2018). Blockchain for large-scale internet of things data storage and protection. *IEEE Transactions on Services Computing, 12*(5), 762–771. https://doi.org/10.1109/TSC.2018.2853167

Mahjoub, Y. I., Chargui, T., Bekrar, A., & Trentesaux, D. (2022a). Supply chain application of blockchain-based solutions for cyber-physical systems: Review and prospects. In T. Borangiu, D. Trentesaux, P. Leitão, O. Cardin, & L. Joblot (Eds.), *Service oriented, holonic and multi-agent manufacturing systems for industry of the future. SOHOMA 2021. Studies in computational intelligence* (Vol. 1034). Springer. https://doi.org/10.1007/978-3-030-99108-1_39

Mahjoub, Y. I., Hassoun, M., & Trentesaux, D. (2022b). Blockchain adoption for SMEs: Opportunities and challenges. *IFAC PapersOnLine, 55*(10), 1834–1839. https://doi.org/10.1016/j.ifacol.2022.09.665

Mallapaty, S. (2020). How China could be carbon neutral by mid-century. *Nature, 586*, 482–483. https://doi.org/10.1038/d41586-020-02927-9

Momtaz, P. P. (2022). *Some very simple economics of web3 and the metaverse*. https://ssrn.com/abstract=4085937

Nakavachara, V., & Saengchote, K. (2022). Is metaverse LAND a good investment? It depends on your unit of account! https://ssrn.com/abstract=4028587 or http://dx.doi.org/10.2139/ssrn.4028587

Piketty, T., & Saez, E. (2014). Inequality in the long run. *Science, 344*, 838e843. https://doi.org/10.1126/science.1251936

Prisco, G. (2016). The blockchain for healthcare: Gem launches gem health network with Philips Blockchain Lab. *BitCoin Magazine*. Retrieved February 2019, from https://bitcoinmagazine.com/

Rehman, W., Hijab, Z., Jaweria, I., & Narmeen, B. (2021). *NFTs: Applications and challenges* [Conference session]. 22nd International Arab Conference on Information Technology (ACIT). http://dx.doi.org/10.1109/ACIT53391.2021.9677260

Scott, B., Loonam, J., & Kumar, V. (2017). Exploring the rise of blockchain technology: Towards distributed collaborative organizations. *Strategic Change*, 26(5), 423–428. https://doi.org/10.1002/jsc.2142

Sestino, A., Guido, G., & Peluso, A. M. (2022). *Non-fungible tokens (NFTs) examining the impact on consumers and marketing strategies*. Palgrave Macmillan, Springer Nature Switzerland AG. https://doi.org/10.1007/978-3-031-07203-1

Shilina, S. (2022). A comprehensive study on Non-Fungible Tokens (NFTs): Use cases, ecosystem, benefits & challenges. http://dx.doi.org/10.13140/RG.2.2.15324.67206

Song, C., Shin, S.-Y., & Shin, K.-S. (2023). Exploring the key characteristics and theoretical framework for research on the metaverse. *Applied Sciences*, 13(13), 7628. https://doi.org/10.3390/app13137628

Sun, H., Wang, X., & Wang, X. (2018). Application of blockchain technology in online education. *International Journal of Emerging Technologies in Learning*, 13(10), 252–259. https://doi.org/10.3991/ijet.v13i10.9455

The Sandbox. (2021). *The sandbox gets greener - Reducing the carbon footprint of NFTs by 99% and regrowing forests across the globe*. https://medium.com/

Thompson, C. (2023). *Palm foundation to scale its native network to support NFT minting and trading*. https://www.coindesk.com/

Thurman, A. (2021). *ConsenSys announces layer-two NFT platform, palm, to compete with flow*. https://cointelegraph.com/

Torky, M., Darwish, A., & Hassanien, A. E. (2023). Blockchain technology in metaverse: Opportunities, applications, and open problems. In A. E. Hassanien, A. Darwish, & M. Torky (Eds.), *The future of metaverse in the virtual era and physical world. studies in big data* (Vol. 123). Springer. https://doi.org/10.1007/978-3-031-29132-6_13

Truby, J., Brown, R. D., Dahdal, A., & Ibrahim, I. (2022). Blockchain, climate damage, and death: Policy interventions to reduce the carbon emissions, mortality, and net-zero implications of non-fungible tokens and Bitcoin. *Energy Research & Social Science*, 88, 102499. https://doi.org/10.1016/j.erss.2022.102499

Vidal-Tomás, D. (2023). The new crypto niche: NFTs, play-to-earn, and metaverse tokens. *Finance Research Letters*, 47, 102742. https://doi.org/10.1016/j.frl.2022.102742

Wang, Q., Li, R., Wang, Q., & Chen, S. (2021). Non-fungible token (NFT): Overview. *Evaluation, Opportunities and Challenges*. arxiv preprint http://arxiv.org/abs/2105.07447

Wang, X., Feng, L., Zhang, H., Lyu, C., Wang, L., & You, Y. (2017). *Human resource information management model based on blockchain technology* [Conference session]. Proceedings – 11th IEEE International Symposium on Service-Oriented System Engineering (pp. 168–173). SOSE.

Wang, Y., Su, Z., Zhang, N., Xing, R., Liu, D., Luan, T. H., & Shen, X. (2022). A survey on metaverse: Fundamentals, security, and privacy. *IEEE Communications Surveys and Tutorials*. https://doi.org/10.1109/COMST.2022.3202047

White Paper. (2020). *The sandbox*. www.The_Sandbox_Whitepaper_2020

Wilson, K. B., Karg, A., & Ghaderi, H. (2022). Prospecting non-fungible tokens in the digital economy: Stakeholders and ecosystem, risk and opportunity. *Business Horizons*, 65(5), 657–670. https://doi.org/10.1016/j.bushor.2021.10.007

Xiong, H., Dalhaus, T., Wang, P., & Huang, J. (2020). Blockchain technology for agriculture: Applications and rationale. *Frontiers in Blockchain*, 3(7). https://doi.org/10.3389/fbloc.2020.00007

Zhang, J. F., Xu, Z., Peng, Y., Yang, W., & Zhao, H. (2022). Culture, digital assets, and the economy: A trans-national perspective. In T. Walker, F. Davis, & T. Schwartz (Eds.), *Big data in finance*. Palgrave Macmillan. https://doi.org/10.1007/978-3-031-12240-8_9

Part C

How Can Metaverse Contribute to Sustainability?

Chapter 8

Sustainability in the Metaverse: Challenges, Implications, and Potential Solutions

Poornima Jirli[a] and Anuja Shukla[b]

[a]Swiss School of Business Management, Geneva, Switzerland
[b]Jaipuria Institute of Management, Noida, India

Abstract

The Metaverse, an emergent Web 3.0 platform, offers users immersive virtual reality experiences. This study employs a case study approach to explore the concept of sustainability within the Metaverse. It examines the environmental, social, and economic implications of virtual interactions and the role of sustainable technologies in shaping user behavior and virtual economies. Through selected case studies, the research provides insights into the potential and challenges of integrating sustainable practices in the Metaverse, with implications for stakeholders ranging from policymakers to end-users.

Keywords: Metaverse; sustainability; case-study; virtual reality; environmental impacts; green technology

1. Introduction

The Metaverse, a concept once confined to science fiction, has become a significant focus of interest for educators, marketers, and the public. This evolving digital landscape transcends the physical world's limitations, offering immersive 3D environments where interactions and experiences reach new heights of engagement. Platforms like City Space, Second Life, and Roblox each provide distinct spaces for socialization, education, and entertainment, reshaping our digital interactions and expanding the boundaries of virtual possibilities (Benedikt, 2008; Schroeder et al., 2001).

The renaming of Facebook to Meta signifies the Metaverse's expanding influence and potential to become the next digital frontier, offering new dimensions for learning, working, and interacting through virtual reality (VR) and smartphones (Taylor, 2022). However, this rapid growth brings sustainability challenges across environmental, social, and economic dimensions. Originating from Neal Stephenson's "Snow Crash," the Metaverse now impacts diverse sectors, aligning with Society 5.0's vision of a balanced world supported by technologies like 6G and augmented reality (AR) (Metaverse and Society 5.0, 2023). Research indicates the importance of credibility in Metaverse investments and highlights new marketing opportunities beyond the physical world limitations (Dwivedi & Hughes, 2023; Efendioğlu, 2023; Shukla et al., 2024). This study addresses the need for sustainable expansion in the Metaverse, focusing on its impacts and exploring sustainable practices. We aim to ensure the Metaverse's development benefits the environment, society, and the economy, creating a more inclusive and sustainable digital future.

2. Evolution and State of the Metaverse

2.1. Conceptual Evolution of the Metaverse

The term "Metaverse," originally coined by Neal Stephenson, has grown beyond its fictional roots into a multifaceted digital ecosystem that defies a singular definition. Despite the absence of a consensus, the Metaverse is broadly viewed as the next phase of the internet—Web 3.0—blending the digital and physical worlds and reshaping various sectors through technological innovations by entities like Meta and Microsoft (Chen et al., 2021; De Giovanni, 2023). The Metaverse encompasses immersive environments, mirror worlds, augmented realities, and lifelogging, offering dynamic avatar interactions and novel applications like virtual real estate transactions (Jeon et al., 2021; Toraman & Geçit, 2023).

It functions as both a tool and a target, enhancing real-life activities such as education and healthcare, while simultaneously creating new revenue streams in gaming and business (Park & Kim, 2022). The evolution of the Metaverse signifies a shift toward a persistent, immersive platform that blends the virtual and the physical, impacting work, collaboration, and daily life (Gartner, 2022; Singh & Vanka, 2023).

2.2. Societal Dynamics and Impacts

The Metaverse, with its immersive environments, is revolutionizing social interactions and community dynamics, challenging traditional communication frameworks. This digital evolution, however, raises critical issues, including data security, privacy, and an expanding digital divide, creating obstacles to a fair digital environment. Metaverse played a critical role in societal structures. Also, the credibility of communicators influenced the significant effectiveness of the message that was conveyed in virtual settings (Lou & Yuan, 2019).

A new trend in social media influencers (SMIs) and micro-endorsers in the Metaverse blurs the distinction between the real and virtual worlds, impacting norms for advertising and engagement in the community (Raza & Zaman, 2021; Saima & Khan, 2020). According to researchers such as Weismueller et al. (2020) and Shareef et al. (2019), this shift highlights the nuanced relationship between source credibility and user engagement, having significant implications for the societal fabric of the digital era. The Metaverse extends beyond socialization to impact various aspects of life and work, raising challenges such as privacy, access to equal opportunities, and bridging the digital divide (Hollensen et al., 2022). Furthermore, it presents new security challenges, as the multifaceted nature of the Metaverse necessitates comprehensive strategies to protect against threats like identity theft and fraud (Sun et al., 2022). Due to the inherent vulnerabilities within the underlying blockchain technology, the technology may still result in significant losses, highlighting the need for robust security measures in these virtual environments (Du et al., 2017; Shukla et al., 2023). Integrating AR and VR technologies further complicates security, requiring advanced solutions for protecting information and verifying identities (Kozinets, 2022). Integrating digital and physical realities into the Metaverse will require extensive security and privacy measures to ensure a safe and stable user environment and maintain the integrity of this burgeoning digital ecosystem (Sun et al., 2022).

2.3. Challenges in the Metaverse

Metaverse technology presents challenges at work, including ergonomic issues that can lead to discomfort and reduced productivity (Pyun et al., 2022). Due to the extensive collection of data, privacy and security concerns are raised, making it necessary to strike a delicate balance between innovation and individual rights (Singh & Vanka, 2023). Furthermore, technostress poses significant risks to mental health and employee productivity, manifesting as techno-anxiety, techno-addiction, and techno-strain. Therefore, strategies to address such concerns are essential in Metaverse-enabled environments (Brivio et al., 2018; Dragano & Lunau, 2020). There is also the possibility that the Metaverse poses broader societal and geopolitical challenges, disrupting traditional structures and leading to new geopolitical tensions and ideological shifts (Corballis & Soar, 2022; Dear, 2022). To ensure that the Metaverse's evolution aligns with ethical, social, and environmental standards, we need a deeper understanding and a strategic approach.

The Meta Platforms, Inc. suggests that existing regulations should be leveraged while cautioning against rapidly introducing new, distinct frameworks that could discourage innovation. A broader industry perspective supports a balanced regulatory approach that encourages collaboration between the private sector and government to establish standards that foster the responsible growth of the digital economy. An emerging dialogue between corporations and regulators, particularly in Europe and the United States, indicates that a significant discourse is being initiated regarding the integration of the Metaverse into our existing legal and ethical frameworks so that it can contribute positively to society and the economy.

2.4. Sustainability in the Metaverse

The Metaverse's sustainability concerns encompass a wide range of issues, including the carbon footprint of the digital infrastructure, ethical data management, and the impact of virtual economies on real-world poverty and environmental degradation. The identification of these themes is crucial to understanding the Metaverse's potential contribution or detriment to global challenges (Accenture, 2021; Anshari et al., 2022; Arnold & Beauchamp, 2020; Racelis, 2010; Mishra et al., 2024). A Gartner report, published in 2023, emphasizes the growing importance of sustainability in the digital domains, recommending the use of eco-friendly IT practices and emphasizing the Metaverse's potential to foster new virtual economies by combining digital and physical realities (Sustainability, the Metaverse and Superapps Among Tech Trends for 2023, 2022).

According to Le Bei Sze, Jari Salo, and Teck Ming Tan, the Metaverse can be used to implement decentralized sustainable management within vertical farming, incorporating stakeholder capitalism theory as a basis. The Metaverse's unique characteristics, such as its creator economy and digitalized mindset, may profoundly influence vertical farming's sustainability. Sze et al. (2023) proposed that this new approach could revolutionize the agricultural sector by offering new business models and marketing strategies, resulting in more sustainable, efficient, and inclusive agricultural practices (Sze et al., 2023).

The Black Leaders Powering the Metaverse (Dennis, 2022) report outlines several ways that industry professionals and thought leaders are advancing discussions regarding diversity, inclusivity, and sustainability within virtual spaces. Through their initiatives, they are establishing new standards for ethical and sustainable practices in the Metaverse, fostering community and inclusion. They highlight the importance of a holistic approach to sustainability, addressing social, economic, and environmental concerns, and advocate for a more inclusive and sustainable digital future.

There exists a significant gap in research regarding the Metaverse's long-term environmental impacts, particularly regarding energy consumption and e-waste. There is a need to explore further the broader ecological consequences of the expansion of the Metaverse (EY, 2022 Shukla et al., 2024).

A second concern is that there has been little research on the impact of prolonged interactions within the Metaverse on societal structures, mental health, and real-life relationships. The psychological effects of these immersive virtual environments and how they affect human behavior and social dynamics require empirical studies.

As a third point, there is a lack of comprehensive research regarding how the Metaverse is influencing economic disparities both within its virtual spaces and in the real world. To ensure equitable growth and opportunity within these digital realms, it is essential to understand how virtual economies contribute to or alleviate real-world economic inequalities (Allam et al., 2022).

It is also important to note that global regulatory and ethical standards for navigating the Metaverse are in the early stages of development. More research is necessary to develop robust frameworks that ensure privacy, security, and equitable access for all users, thus fostering a safe and inclusive virtual environment (Anshari et al., 2022). Furthermore, there are few studies examining accessibility of the Metaverse for individuals with disabilities and its cultural inclusivity. Diverse and inclusive virtual spaces must be welcoming and accessible to all, regardless of physical abilities or cultural backgrounds (Racelis, 2010).

Furthermore, the interaction between the Metaverse and real-world systems, such as urban planning and education, has not been adequately explored. The study of virtual spaces can serve as a complement and enhance to real-world processes and infrastructure, bridging the divide between the physical and digital worlds (Lv et al., 2022)

3. Sustainability in the Metaverse

In today's rapidly evolving digital environment, the Metaverse presents unique opportunities for integrating sustainability. Developing sustainable virtual environments requires a Triple Bottom Line (TBL) approach that encompasses environmental, social, and economic dimensions (Elkington, 1997). The Metaverse progresses in a technological, sustainable, and inclusive manner as a result of this framework.

3.1. Environmental Sustainability in the Metaverse

By implementing green data centers and energy-efficient technologies, the Metaverse is actively reducing ecological impacts. In addition to reducing carbon emissions and utilizing renewable energy sources, these initiatives highlight the urgent need for eco-friendly advances in virtual spaces, highlighting the high energy demands of Metaverse infrastructure (Davis, 2019).

Metaverse is a platform that offers immersive experiences in education, healthcare, and economic development to support Sustainable Development Goals (SDGs). Virtual learning environments enhance educational opportunities (SDG 4), virtual consultations broaden healthcare access (SDG 3), and create new job opportunities (SDG 8) to contribute to economic growth (SDG 8), particularly in areas where traditional employment options are limited (Rane et al., 2024).

Several studies have indicated that it is crucial to adopt sustainable practices within the Metaverse, including energy-efficient design and the use of renewable energy, to mitigate the environmental impact of its technological infrastructure (Energy Star, n.d.-a; Energy Star, n.d.-b; Morini Bianzino, 2022; Stoll et al., 2022).

Furthermore, they discuss ways to reduce the overall carbon footprint by utilizing less energy-intensive blockchain mechanisms, such as proof-of-authority or proof-of-stake (Alkhateeb et al., 2022; Braud et al., 2022). The integration of digital twins in the Metaverse is also recommended to optimize energy usage, thus bridging the gap between the virtual and real worlds of sustainability (Chen, 2022; Zhao et al., 2023). Move to Earn(M2E) model which is innovative Carbon savings application was introduced to promote physical activity and address climate change challenge (Vico, 2023). In alignment with broader sustainability objectives, this application, which features a unique carbon footprint algorithm, encourages users to choose sustainable transportation methods.

3.2. Social Sustainability in the Metaverse

Metaverse social sustainability emphasizes the creation of inclusive and equitable virtual spaces that reflect the diversity of the global population. There should be a priority for accessibility and preventing systemic inequalities in the design and governance of these spaces, so that all users, regardless of their backgrounds, can participate meaningfully in them (Johnson, 2021). Users of the Metaverse benefit greatly from these practices to foster a sense of belonging and community (Shukla et al., 2024).

According to Al-Emran (2023), understanding the implications of technology on sustainability goes beyond simply accepting technology. This study presents a comprehensive framework that links technology use to sustainability's multifaceted dimensions and develops and evaluates the Technology-Environmental, Economic, and Social Sustainability Theory (T-EESST). The purpose of this innovative approach is to broaden the discourse within the field of Information Systems (IS), highlighting the significant influence that technology can have on the sustainability of the environment, economy, and society. Through its integration of sustainability into traditional technology acceptance models, the theory serves as an essential extension of traditional technology acceptance models.

This study by Kraus et al. (2023) provides an in-depth analysis of the evolution of research topics in technological forecasting and social change. By using a Structural Topic Model, they identify 18 dominant themes, tracing the transition from early emphasis on generic forecasting models to current priorities such as Industry 4.0 and green innovation. In response to evolving societal demands and technological advancements, technological forecasting research has undergone a paradigm shift. In addition to revealing shifts in research priorities and the field's growing complexity, their bibliometric analysis reveals the most influential articles over the years. Kraus et al. (2023) also examine the international trends in collaboration in technological forecasting, which demonstrates the expanding diversity and global involvement of this field.

In terms of its potential for fostering inclusive and equitable environments, the study by Pellegrino et al. (2023) emphasizes the Metaverse's potential for revolutionizing sustainable consumption patterns by creating inclusive and equitable environments. According to them, it is crucial to investigate how the Metaverse can enhance consumer behavior and motivation to adopt sustainable practices within these virtual environments. Pellegrino et al. (2023) suggest that the Metaverse presents an unprecedented opportunity for addressing social challenges by facilitating the interaction of diverse groups without the constraints of the physical world. This digital environment, however, must be developed responsibly to ensure accessibility and equity for all users, in order to prevent the exacerbation of existing social inequalities. To guide these interventions, the authors emphasize the necessity of integrating sustainable practices into virtual marketplaces and exploring regulatory frameworks. Additionally, Pellegrino et al. (2023) emphasize the importance of examining how the Metaverse impacts social dynamics, privacy, and ethical standards, indicating that robust ethical guidelines and standards are critical to contributing meaningfully to the sustainability of social and ethical values within these virtual spaces (Shukla et al., 2024).

3.3. Economic Sustainability in the Metaverse

On the economic side, the Metaverse introduces new models for executing transactions and exchanging value. Business innovation and sustainability opportunities are offered by the emergence of digital economies within virtual spaces. Through the use of virtualization, the Metaverse can promote more sustainable consumption behaviors by reducing physical waste and material consumption. Digital twins can also enhance operational efficiency and create new revenue streams by integrating them with real-world processes. Environmental impacts of the Metaverse's development, such as increased energy consumption and carbon dioxide emissions, are being closely examined. Research suggests that the sustainability of the Metaverse depends on the adoption of clear regulations and sustainable policies at an international level.

A comprehensive understanding of the Metaverse ecosystem's functioning and evolution, as well as the promotion of responsible practices within the industry, is essential to its long-term viability. This research could prove invaluable for technology companies, academics, and policymakers looking to forge a sustainable path forward for the Metaverse (Vlăduțescu & Stănescu, 2023). The metaverse's economic impact on sustainable consumption is discussed by Pellegrino et al. (2023), emphasizing its transformative potential for marketplaces and consumer behavior. Metaverses have the potential to promote the transition to sustainable economic models, such as the circular economy, by altering traditional consumption patterns and encouraging more sustainable practices (Shukla et al., 2024).

Using virtual environments to promote sustainable economic practices and reduce consumption's environmental impact is a crucial aspect of future research, according to the authors. A key aspect of understanding the Metaverse's overall sustainability is evaluating virtual platforms' life cycle and environmental impacts. There are concerns about the paradox of digitalization resulting in increased energy consumption and emissions, and a balanced evaluation of these technologies' sustainability impacts is recommended. Further, Pellegrino et al. (2023) discuss the potential economic benefits of the Metaverse, including the creation of new job opportunities and the growth of virtual tourism, both of which could contribute to economic growth and encourage sustainable consumption patterns. A collaborative approach between policymakers and researchers could ensure that the Metaverse's expansion aligns with sustainability goals, according to the authors. With this economic perspective, the study significantly contributes to the ongoing discussion on harnessing the Metaverse for sustainable development, highlighting both the opportunities and challenges for economic innovation in virtual environments.

3.4. Integrating the Triple Bottom Line in the Metaverse

A sustainability framework for the Metaverse incorporates the Triple Bottom Line approach, ensuring that advancements in virtual environments adhere to global sustainability standards of environmental integrity, social equity, and economic viability.

Fig. 1 depicts three dimensions, the first being the planet, the second being the people, and the third being the profit. The first aspect the environmental aspect focuses on reducing ecological footprints and improving energy efficiency. Metaverse data centers must address the energy demands and carbon emissions associated with the rapid expansion of virtual spaces. For reducing environmental impact, initiatives promoting renewable energy sources and efficient computing are essential (Davis et al., 2019).

A second objective of social sustainability is the creation of inclusive, equitable virtual spaces that reflect global diversity. While the Metaverse has the potential to transform society, replicating real-world inequalities poses several challenges. To promote inclusive user interactions, designers must focus on accessibility and community (Johnson, 2021).

The last aspect of the metaverse concerns virtual economies and the sustainability of economic activity within it. The digital transaction introduces new models that can reduce material consumption and promote the adoption of sustainable behaviors. Digital innovation can be leveraged to create new markets and

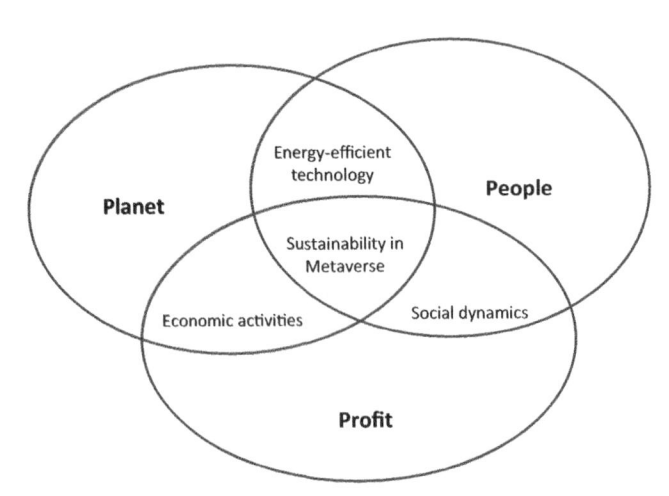

Fig. 1. Conceptual Model. *Source*: Author's compilation.

job opportunities, contributing to economic growth while upholding sustainability principles.

Sustainability in the Metaverse emerges at the intersection of Planet, People, and Profit, where environmental conservation, social responsibility, and economic activity merge (Shukla et al., 2024). Providing a balanced approach to the digital world contributes to the achievement of global sustainability goals, ensuring technology advancements are consistent with environmental integrity, social equity, and economic viability.

4. Case Studies

4.1. Mini Case Study 1: Green Metaverse Networking: Promoting Environmental Sustainability in the Metaverse

Background:
As a rapidly evolving digital ecosystem, the Metaverse combines VR, blockchain technology, and artificial intelligence. The Internet offers a wide range of interactive and transactional opportunities, but it also poses substantial environmental challenges. Zhang et al. (2022) address the need for sustainable practices within this digital expansion, with a particular focus on reducing the carbon footprint associated with its operation.

Challenge:
There are several challenges related to the Metaverse's increasing energy demands, which contribute to higher carbon emissions and significant environmental impacts. Several factors contribute to the energy requirement of blockchain technologies as well as the need for extensive data centers to support the Metaverse infrastructure. To maintain immersive experiences within the Metaverse, it is imperative to address these issues.

Solution:
GMN is a solution proposed by Zhang et al. (2022) to enhance the energy efficiency of the Metaverse's networking components. GMN is committed to lowering the environmental impact of the Metaverse through the implementation of green data centers, renewable energy sources, and energy-saving technologies.

Operational Mechanism:
A key aspect of the implementation of GMN is the application of sustainable practices at every level of the Metaverse. Utilizing green data centers, optimizing resources, and deploying energy-efficient computing and networking technologies are all part of this effort. They are essential to reducing the Metaverse's environmental footprint and promoting a more sustainable digital future.

Achievements and Future Directions:
The case study provides insight into the critical role that green technologies play in mitigating the environmental impacts of the Metaverse. By implementing GMN principles, Zhang et al. (2022) suggest that the Metaverse can significantly

reduce its carbon footprint, resulting in a more sustainable digital environment. The use of this approach contributes to the reduction of global carbon emissions and sets a precedent for future technological advancements within and beyond the Metaverse. The study emphasizes the importance of integrating environmental sustainability into the development of digital ecosystems, opening the door to further research and implementation of green technologies within the Metaverse.

4.2. Mini Case Study 2: Metaverse Ethics and Responsible Behavior

Background:
As a digital ecosystem that is expanding, the Metaverse presents a number of complicated challenges, especially in the area of user conduct and digital ethics. The impact of the integrating digital ethical education within the Metaverse based E-leaning was conducted which explored the potential of education initiatives to foster a more respectful and ethically aware virtual community in the Metaverse and considers the necessity for users to engage in more responsible and conscientious behavior in the Metaverse (Dahan et al.,2022).

Challenge:
There is a significant challenge in the Metaverse in ensuring that user behavior aligns with digital ethics, in order to promote a respectful and safe online environment. When ethical awareness is lacking, negative interactions may occur and the integrity of the community may be compromised. To cultivate a positive and responsible virtual community, it is thus imperative to instill a comprehensive understanding of digital ethics among users.

Solution:
Embedding digital ethics education within the Metaverse significantly influences user behavior (Dahan et al., 2022). The E-Learning modules incorporated ethical guidelines and dilemmas, which allowed users to demonstrate respect, responsibility, and a conscientious approach to community engagement and content management.

Operational Mechanism:
Metaverse's E-Learning platforms are integrated with digital ethics education as part of the operational strategy. Among these activities are the creation of ethical dilemma scenarios, incorporating community guidelines, and encouraging reflection on personal behavior. Education initiatives of this type aim to provide users with the knowledge and skills they need to navigate the Metaverse safely.

Achievements and Future Directions:
The evidence of the transformative power of digital ethics education in metaverse, for it to evolve into a space characterized by responsible and culturally sensitive interactions, the Metaverse needs to foster an environment in which users are well-informed of ethical standards (Dahan et al., 2022). According to the study, the expansion of digital ethics education across Metaverse platforms can significantly contribute to the formation of a globally responsible digital society. Several

future directions could be explored, including the scalability of these educational initiatives, the role of artificial intelligence in promoting ethics, and the design of metaverse platforms that inherently promote ethical behavior. Metaverse can become both a hub of technological innovation and a leading example of ethical community engagement by focusing on these developments.

4.3. Mini Case Study 3: Urbanization and virtual economies

Background:
Allam et al. (2022) focus their research on the intersection between virtual economies within the Metaverse and their impact on actual urban economic landscapes. This study examines how urban economic strategies, consumer trends, and property markets are influenced by consumer behavior and transactions in the Metaverse, which are echoed in the real world.

Challenge:
A key challenge involves understanding how virtual goods and services in the Metaverse affect real-world economic dynamics, particularly in urban settings. As virtual transactions become more prevalent, it raises questions about the sustainability of traditional economic models as well as the adaptations urban retailers and service providers must make in order to remain competitive.

Solution:
By conducting an in-depth analysis of the Metaverse and real-world consumer patterns, Allam et al. (2022) shed light on how virtual economies can influence the dynamics of physical markets. Several factors have influenced real-world investment strategies and urban development policies, including the importance of virtual real estate transactions.

Operational Mechanism:
Using insights from virtual consumer dynamics within the Metaverse, urban businesses can be informed. It is possible for retailers to forecast future market trends by understanding virtual buying patterns and preferences. The development of virtual real estate has also opened up new avenues for investors and urban planners, who have the opportunity to test out urban development concepts before actually implementing them in a risk-free virtual environment.

Achievements and Future Directions:
Allam et al. (2022) provide an in-depth understanding of how virtual economies can serve as a barometer for real-world urban market changes, fostering the symbiotic relationship between the virtual and physical realms. The findings of the case study suggest that the Metaverse could be a significant factor in shaping future urban economic strategies and development models, emphasizing the importance of urban stakeholders monitoring and participating actively in virtual economic activities. There is a potential for future research to explore the scalability of virtual real estate markets and their implications for urban development over the long term, as well as how the Metaverse can

serve as a platform to assist in sustainable urban planning and innovation in the future.

4.4. Mini Case Study 4: Technologies, Advances, and Future Directions of Green Metaverse Networking

Background:
According to Zhang et al. (2022), in the context of the burgeoning Metaverse, environmental sustainability challenges are posed by the underlying digital infrastructure. The research emphasizes the growing environmental concerns associated with the growing economic expansion of the Metaverse by critically evaluating the energy consumption of servers and network equipment essential to its operation.

Challenges:
Metaverse infrastructures pose significant environmental challenges due to their escalating energy demands. According to the study, it is urgently necessary to develop sustainable technologies to facilitate the Metaverse's expansion without exacerbating environmental degradation.

Solutions:
Zhang et al. (2022) propose a Green Metaverse Networking framework to integrate energy-efficient protocols and systems within the Metaverse infrastructure. This initiative ensures that the economic growth within the Metaverse is aligned with global sustainability efforts, thereby reducing resource consumption and lowering carbon emissions.

Operational Mechanisms:
Sustainable practices are incorporated into all levels of the Metaverse's infrastructure as part of the operational mechanism. A key component of this initiative is the implementation of energy-efficient technologies and the design of virtual goods and services that will promote environmental consciousness among users. Several findings of the research suggest that the Metaverse offers a platform for fostering sustainable consumer behavior, which may influence real-world actions and decisions.

Achievements and Future Directions:
Zhang et al.'s study (2022) lays the groundwork for future research and development to embed sustainability into the core of virtual economies. Toward environmental sustainability, the research advocates for a Green Metaverse Networking that supports economic growth. Based on the findings of this study, the Metaverse has the potential to catalyze environmental change on a real-world scale, illustrating the importance of aligning virtual economic activities with environmental objectives. A future study could examine the scalability of these sustainable practices and their impact on global sustainability initiatives, strengthening the Metaverse's position as a driver of environmental innovation and change.

5. Conclusion

The case studies presented offer insights into the potential impacts and opportunities of the digital ecosystem in the Metaverse. Three key areas present innovative solutions to the Metaverse, which is rapidly evolving. To begin with, the importance of incorporating energy-efficient technologies and practices is emphasized through initiatives like Green Metaverse Networking. To reduce the ecological footprint of these digital realms, these practices include the adoption of green data centers and renewable energy sources. The second reason is that the incorporation of digital ethics into Metaverse platforms has a significant impact on user behavior. Developing ethical guidelines and educational programs fosters a respectful, responsible, and inclusive digital community, enhancing the safety and inclusion of the virtual environment. The emerging economic models of the Metaverse highlight its profound impact on the real-world economy. By bridging the gap between virtual and physical market dynamics, this new domain offers new avenues for consumer behavior analysis, economic strategies, and virtual real estate investments.

6. Implications and Recommendations

Various stakeholders in the Metaverse's ecosystem can benefit from the findings presented in this paper. There is an opportunity for policymakers and regulators to develop and enforce guidelines that promote sustainability, ethical conduct, and economic fairness within the Metaverse. Regulation of virtual economic activity and the promotion of green technology can ensure a positive contribution to the real-world economy. Sustainable business practices and ethical virtual interaction guidelines should be incorporated into the Metaverse's business models, as well as sustainable economic practices that are applicable in both virtual and real contexts.

Researchers and academicians are called upon to conduct studies to assess the long-term effects of the Metaverse on society and the environment. Interdisciplinary studies that meld technological insights with social and environmental sciences could offer a comprehensive understanding of the Metaverse's benefits and challenges. The Metaverse should be educated about the repercussions of end-user and consumer actions, the importance of ethical online behavior, and the real-world consequences of virtual economic activities.

In conclusion, as the Metaverse opens up new avenues for innovation and interaction, it is important to place an emphasis on sustainability, ethics, and economic integrity (Shukla & Jirli, 2024). A platform that addresses these aspects can provide rich, immersive experiences, align with global sustainability objectives, and promote a fair and ethical digital environment.

References

Accenture. (2021). *Exploring the metaverse's impact on business.* Accenture Survey.
Al-Emran, M. (2023). Beyond technology acceptance: Development and evaluation of technology-environmental, economic, and social sustainability theory. *Technology in Society, 75*, 102383.

Alkhateeb, A., Catal, C., Kar, G., & Mishra, A. (2022). Hybrid blockchain platforms for the Internet of Things (IoT): A systematic literature review. *Sensors, 22*(4), 1304. https://doi.org/10.3390/s22041304

Allam, Z., Sharifi, A., Bibri, S. E., Jones, D. S., & Krogstie, J. (2022). The metaverse as a virtual form of smart cities: Opportunities and challenges for environmental, economic, and social sustainability in urban futures. *Smart Cities, 5*(3), 771–801. https://doi.org/10.3390/smartcities5030040

Anshari, M., Syafrudin, M., Fitriyani, N. L., & Razzaq, A. (2022). Ethical responsibility and sustainability (ERS) development in a metaverse business model. *Sustainability, 14*(23), 15805. 10.3390/su142315805.

Arnold, D. G., & Beauchamp, T. L. (2020). *Ethical theory and business* (10th ed.). Cambridge University Press.

Benedikt, M. L. (2008). Cityspace, cyberspace, and the spatiology of information. *Journal for Virtual Worlds Research, 1*(1). https://doi.org/10.4101/jvwr.v1i1.290

Braud, T., Lee, L. H., Alhilal, A., Fernández, C. B., & Hui, P. (2022). DiOS-An extended reality operating system for the Metaverse. *IEEE MultiMedia, 30*(2), 70–80. https://doi.org/10.1109/MMUL.2022.3211351

Brivio, E, Gaudioso F, Vergine, I., Mirizzi, C. R., Reina, C., & Galimberti, C. (2018). Preventing technostress through positive technology. *Frontiers in Psychology, 9*. https://www.frontiersin.org/articles/10.3389/fpsyg.2018.02569

Chen, A. (2022, January 16). How "GREEN" is the METAVERSE? The two sides of the environmental impact of the Metaverse. *Medium*. https://medium.com/geekculture/how-green-is-the-Metaverse-the-two-sides-of-the-environmental-impact-of-the-Metaverse-6a35913fd329

Chen, Y. H., Lin, C. Y., & Wang, T. I. (2021). Exploring consumer experience in the metaverse: The role of brand experience and self-identity congruity. *Journal of Business Research, 133*, 27–38.

Corballis, T., & Soar, M. (2022). Utopia of abstraction: Digital organizations and the promise of sovereignty. *Big Data and Society, 9*(1). https://doi.org/10.1177/20539517221084587

Davis, A., Murphy, J., Owens, D., Khazanchi, D., & Zigurs, I. (2009). Avatars, people, and virtual worlds: Foundations for research in metaverses. *Journal of the Association for Information Systems, 10*(2), 90–117. https://doi.org/10.17705/1jais.00183

De Giovanni, P. (2023). Sustainability of the metaverse: A transition to industry 5.0. *Sustainability, 15*, 6079. https://doi.org/10.3390/su15076079

Dear, K. (2022). Beyond the 'geo' in geopolitics: The digital transformation of power. *The RUSI Journal, 166*(6-7). https://doi.org/10.1080/03071847.2022.2049167

Dennis, R. (2022). Black leaders powering the metaverse. *U.S. Black Engineer & Information Technology, 46*(2), 64–67.

Dragano, N., & Lunau, T. (2020). Technostress at work and mental health: Concepts and research results. *Current Opinion in Psychiatry, 33*(4), 407. https://doi.org/10.1097/YCO.0000000000000613

Du, M., Ma, X., Zhang, Z., Wang, X., & Chen, Q. (2017). *A review on consensus algorithm of blockchain* [Conference session]. IEEE International Conference on Systems, Man, and Cybernetics (pp. 2567–2572). IEEE.

Dwivedi, Y. K., & Hughes, L. (2023). In search of a head start: Marketing opportunities in the metaverse. *NIM Marketing Intelligence Review, 15*(2), 18–23. https://doi.org/10.2478/nimmir-2023-0012

Efendioğlu, İ. H. (2023). The effect of information about metaverse on the consumer's purchase intention. *Journal of Global Business & Technology, 19*(1), 63–77.

Elkington, J. (1997). *Cannibals with Forks: The triple bottom line of 21st century business*. Wiley.

Energy Star. (n.d.-a). *Implement efficient data storage measures.* https://www.energystar.gov/products/implement_efficient_data_storage_measures

Energy Star. (n.d.-b). *16 more ways to cut energy waste in the data center.* https://www.energystar.gov/products/16_more_ways_cut_energy_waste_data_center

EY. (2022). *Metaverse: Could creating a virtual world build a more sustainable one?* Available at: https://www.ey.com/en_gl/insights/digital/metaverse-could-creating-a-virtual-world-build-a-more-sustainable-one#:~:text=As%20critical%20as%20environmental%20sustainability,retrofit%20them%20after%20exponential%20growth

Gartner. (2022). *What is a metaverse?* Retrieved from gartner.com

Hollensen, S., Kotler, P., & Opresnik, M. O. (2022). Metaverse – The new marketing universe. *Journal of Business Strategy* (ahead-of-print). https://doi.org/10.1108/JBS-01-2022-0014

Jeon, H.-J., Youn, H.-C., Ko, S.-M., & Kim, T.-H. (2021). *Blockchain and AI meet in the metaverse.* Intech Open.

Johnson, C. (2021). Metaverse: Introduction and current research. *Journal of Business Research, 133,* 1–5.

Kozinets, R. V. (2022). Immersive netnography: A novel method for service experience research in virtual reality, augmented reality and metaverse contexts. *Journal of Service Management, 34,* 100–125.

Kraus, S., Kumar, S., Lim, W. M., Kaur, J., Sharma, A., & Schiavone, F. (2023). From moon landing to metaverse: Tracing the evolution of Technological Forecasting and Social Change. *Technological Forecasting and Social Change, 189,* 122381.

Lee, U. K., & Kim, H. (2022). UTAUT in metaverse: An "Ifland" case. *Journal of Theoretical and Applied Electronic Commerce Research, 17*(2), 613–635.

Lou, C., & Yuan, S. (2019). Influencer marketing: how message value and credibility affect consumer trust of branded content on social media. *Journal of Interactive Advertising, 19*(1), 58–73.

Lv, Z., Xie, S., Li, Y., Hossain, M. S., & El Saddik, A. (2022). Building the metaverse using digital twins at all scales, states, and relations. *Virtual Reality & Intelligent Hardware, 4*(6), 459–470.

Metaverse and Society 5.0. (2023). Pivotal for future business model innovation. *Journal of Business Models, 11*(3), 62–76.

Mishra, A., Malik, N., & Shukla, A. (2024). Decoding individual motivations and responses to misinformation: Insights from thematic analysis. *Journal of Research in Interactive Marketing.* https://doi.org/10.1108/JRIM-09-2023-0312

Morini Bianzino, N. (2022, September 4). How the Metaverse could bring us closer to a sustainable reality. *VentureBeat.* https://venturebeat.com/virtual/how-the-Metaverse-could-bring-us-closer-to-a-sustainable-reality/

Park, S. M., & Kim, Y. G. (2022). A metaverse: Taxonomy, components, applications, and open challenges. *IEEE Access, 10,* 4209–4251. https://doi.org/10.1109/ACCESS.2021.3140175

Pellegrino, A., Stasi, A., & Wang, R. (2023). Exploring the intersection of sustainable consumption and the Metaverse: A review of current literature and future research directions. *Heliyon, 9,* e19190.

Pyun, K. R., Rogers, J. A., & Ko, S. H. (2022). Materials and devices for immersive virtual reality. *Nature Reviews Materials, 7*(11), 841–843. https://doi.org/10.1038/s41578-022-00501-5

Racelis, A. D. (2010). Business ethics and social responsibility. *Education About Asia, 15*(2), 251–260.

Rane, N. L., Choudhary, S. P., & Rane, J. (2024). Metaverse as a cutting-edge platform for attaining sustainable development goals (SDGs). *Journal of Advances in Artificial Intelligence, 2*(1), 27–46. https://ssrn.com/abstract=4644035

Saima, & Khan, M. A. (2020). Effect of social media influencer marketing on consumers' purchase intention and the mediating role of credibility. *Journal of Promotion Management*, 27(4), 503–523.

Schroeder, R., Huxor, A., & Smith, A. (2001). Active worlds: Geography and social interaction in virtual reality. *Futures*, 33(7), 569–587. https://doi.org/10.1016/s0016-3287(01)00002-7

Shareef, M. A., Mukerji, B., Dwivedi, Y. K., Rana, N. P., & Islam, R. (2019). Social media marketing: Comparative effect of advertisement sources. *Journal of Retailing and Consumer Services*, 46, 58–69.

Shukla, A., & Jirli, P. (2024). Ethical and social consequences of accelerated technology adoption. In *Driving decentralization and disruption with digital technologies* (pp. 166–189). IGI Global.

Shukla, A., Jirli, P., Mishra, A., & Singh, A. K. (2023). Blockchain: A structural topic modelling approach. In *International working conference on transfer and diffusion of IT* (pp. 238–245). Springer Nature Switzerland, Cham.

Shukla, A., Mishra, A., Rana, N.P. and Banerjee, S. (2024). The future of metaverse adoption: A behavioral reasoning perspective with a text-mining approach. *Journal of Consumer Behaviour*. Available at: https://doi.org/10.1002/cb.2336.

Singh, S., & Vanka, S. (2023). Metaverse and future of work: Avenues and challenges. *IUP Journal of Organizational Behavior*, 22(2), 107–118.

Stoll, C., Gallersdörfer, U., & Klaaßen, L. (2022). Climate impacts of the Metaverse. *Joule*, 6(12), 2668–2673. https://doi.org/10.1016/j.joule.2022.10.013

Sun, J., Gan, W., Chao, H. C., & Yu, P. S. (2022). Metaverse: Survey, applications, security, and opportunities. *arXiv preprint arXiv:2210.07990*.

Sze, L. B., Salo, J., & Tan, T. M. (2023). Under studied markets and marketing stakeholders: Achieving decentralized sustainable management in vertical farming through the metaverse. *AMA Summer Academic Conference Proceedings*, 34, 1174–1177.

Taylor, C. R. (2022). Research on advertising in the metaverse: A call to action. *International Journal of Advertising*, 41(3), 383–384. https://doi.org/10.1080/02650487.2022.2058786

Toraman, Y., & Geçit, B. B. (2023). User acceptance of metaverse: An analysis for e-commerce in the framework of technology acceptance model (TAM). *Sosyoekonomi*, 30(55), 85–104. https://doi.org/10.17233/sosyoekonomi.2023.01.05

Vlăduțescu, Ș., & Stănescu, G. C. (2023). Environmental sustainability of metaverse: Perspectives from Romanian developers. *Sustainability*, 15(15), 11704. https://doi.org/10.3390/su151511704

Weismueller, J., Harrigan, P., Wang, S., & Soutar, G. N. (2020). Influencer endorsements: How advertising disclosure and source credibility affect consumer purchase intention on social media. *Australasian Marketing Journal*, 28(4), 160–170.

Wohlgenannt, I., Simons, A., & Stieglitz, S. (2020). Virtual reality. *Journal of Business Research*, 106, 360–365.

Zhang, S., Lim, W. Y. B., Ng, W. C., Xiong, Z., Niyato, D., Shen, X. S., & Miao, C. (2022). Towards green metaverse networking: Technologies, advancements and future directions. (ahead of print).

Zhao, N., Zhang, H., Yang, X., Yan, J., & You, F. (2023). Emerging information and communication technologies for smart energy systems and renewable transition. *Advances in Applied Energy*, 9, 100125. https://doi.org/10.1016/j.adapen.2023.100125

Chapter 9

Metaverse and ESG Governance: Addressing Social and Environmental Challenges in the Virtual World

Supriya Lamba Sahdev[a], Ahdi Hassan[b], Chitra Krishnan[c], Jasmine Mariappan[d] and Ivan Salazar Chang[e]

[a]Alliance University, Bengaluru, Karnataka, India
[b]Global Institute for Research & Scholarship, Amsterdam, Netherlands
[c]Symbiosis Center for Management Studies, Noida, Symbiosis International (Deemed University), Pune, India
[d]University of Technology and Applied Sciences, Ibra, Oman
[e]Chair of esports and active gaming - University Polytechnic of Valencia, Spain

Abstract

The Metaverse, a virtual environment with enormous capabilities, can be defined as a world that has the power to change the manner individuals perceive technology, each other, and the surrounding world. This potential gives the possibility of significant ecology, social, and governance problems which should be resolved under an extensive sustainable development concept. This chapter is centered on the micro-level challenges of the Metaverse, such as the environmental, social, and governance (ESG) aspects, and proposes ways for the Metaverse to overcome the challenges. The methodology for this chapter is, therefore, the use of such literatures on the Metaverse, Metaverse Governance, and Sustainability. It is found that the biggest ESG challenges are going to be that of the metaverse and that there is a need to address these challenges to ensure a sustainable future. This chapter emphasizes the approaches to diminishing the environmental footprint of Metaverse, advocating diversity and empowerment, and providing sound governance and regulation in that field. The case studies elucidate about the effective projects which have made tremendous progress in these domains and can be an ideal model for a better Metaverse. This chapter underlines the point that ESG governance is one of the essential factors that can stand in the way of the Metaverse's sustainability in the long run. The case studies in this chapter provide you with a real-world basis how this can be to study approach and can serve as a guide for future development in this area.

Keywords: Metaverse; ESG governance; sustainability; environmental challenges; social challenges; governance challenges; inclusivity; diversity; cybersecurity

1. Introduction

Metaverse is a revolutionary idea of the digital space, which is beyond the limits of the physical world, painting the real virtual world with interactive, immersive, and interconnected elements in it. Metaverse as Stephenson (1992) would have conceived of, the Metaverse refers to the highly interconnected digital space in which people may interact with each other and digital entities in real-time, effectively removing the boundaries between physical and digital existence.

The extent to which the metaverse is significant is huge, touching numerous foundations of technology, society, and governance. From a technological point of view, the Metaverse is a game changer as it provides never-before-seen before opportunities for innovation. It introduces new immersive experiences to the user through Virtual Reality (VR), Augmented Reality (AR), and other similar technologies. Those advancements could have a high impact on fields such as gaming, entertainment, education, healthcare, and commerce (Rubin, 2018). However, along with the Metaverse concept, there is a whole other level of society ridings, which may be new avenues for social interaction, collaboration, and self-expression. In terms of the Metaverse, people can extend the boundaries of the location and be a part of lots of different communities, encouraging collaboration among them, as well as creativity and collective action (Steuer et al., 1995). Whether it is ethnic minority voices or those who are physically challenged, a fair degree of empowerment and inclusion is becoming increasingly possible among the global population (Bailenson, 2018).

Despite the Metaverse which is innovative and full of transforming prospects, is at the same time, suffering conjunct challenges that need to be fixed to have long-term sustainability and ethical development of the Metaverse. Eco-issues such as energy consumption and the necessity of virtual infrastructure which often come as a co-factor of a massive development of the Metaverse contribute to the doubt about the environmental effect (Bonneau et al., 2015). The notion of social issues is mentioned to indicate that special measures should be taken to create inclusive virtual environments, which depict the diversity of the real society. Finally and to sum up, leaders face other challenges such as safety breaches which is cyber security, privacy and regulatory gap therefore calls for formation of responsible structures and mechanisms to avoid risky acts.

With these challenges in mind and keeping it in mind, we should recognize that the Environmental, Social, and Governance (ESG) governance's significance of the Metaverse does not only stop there. ESG is a set of principles and practices that allow businesses to be transparent while they strive to produce long-term sustainable and ethical outcomes in their operations and decision-making processes (Shapsugova, 2023). Stakeholders may get some very positive outcomes and make the technology less risky, building trust, and making sure that the technology grows sustainably and equally with considering the ESG principles that would be involved in designing and operating the metaverse.

We will continue this discussion by analyzing the ESG challenges of the Metaverse topic, then we will address question about how to solve these challenges, and we will include some real-life examples which were efficient in solving a certain problem. At this point, we aim to bring the attention of everyone to the fact that it is the undisputed ESG governance that would be able to pave the way for further Metaverse development and, consequently, to the latter one being implemented to ensure compliance with the sustainable development goals in the digital world.

2. Environmental Challenges in the Metaverse

2.1. Carbon Footprint of Virtual Environments

The carbon footprint of the virtual environment in Metaverse refers to the amount of climate-changing gas like carbon dioxide (CO_2) emitted due to the energy needed to operate a virtual platform, graphics, and data processing. Virtual environments, in turn, require great computing power, and their energy depletion largely depends on the data centers that host the servers that support this virtuality (Ferri-Molla et al., 2024). As a consequence, the carbon emission of virtual ecosystems will increase and result in climate change and environmental deterioration.

2.2. Exploration of Environmental Impact

The fact is that virtual environments have way more eco-footprints than just noxious gas emissions and power consumption. It not only depletes resources but also increases electronic waste likewise, and it brings greater electronic data centers forest footprint (Belkhir & Elmeligi, 2018). The large energy demand of data centers makes them an environmental problem of posing cascade of concerns ranging from habitat destruction and water pollution (Shehabi et al., 2018).

2.3. Presentation of Strategies for Environmental Sustainability

To address the environmental challenges posed by the Metaverse, various strategies for environmental sustainability can be implemented:

a. Renewable Energy Adoption: Virtual environments can reduce their carbon footprint by transitioning to energy sources like solar, wind and hydropower to decrease their dependency on fossil fuels. Similarly, Oculus VR company which is owned by Meta Platforms-formerly Facebook company has pledged to power all its operations with 100% renewable energy.

b. Energy-Efficient Design: Making use of energy efficient design principles for virtual environment leads to energy saving through the optimization of resource utilization. This involves the code optimization, utilizing the power saving hardware technologies and data compression methods which require minimum data transmissions.
c. Virtualization and Cloud Computing: Virtualization can be used by employing cloud computing technologies to improve resource use and energy efficiency in virtual world. The environmental footprint of hosting virtual platforms is decreased through pooling server resources and dynamic distribution of resources as per demand (Katal et al., 2023).

2.4. Examples of Successful Initiatives

Several case studies exemplify successful initiatives aimed at promoting environmental sustainability in the Metaverse:

a) Google's Commitment to Renewable Energy: For a long time, Google has been at the forefront of using renewable energy, investing in large renewable energy projects to provide power to its data center and operations. An example is Google entering into agreements with renewable energy producers to purchase clean power and make Google Cloud platforms virtually sustainable, reducing carbon footprint (In et al., 2022).
b) The Greening of Minecraft: Minecraft, one of the most widely played sandbox video games, has taken steps to lessen the negative environmental effects tied to it. Mojang Studios, the developer of the game, collaborated with Blockworks, a creative team, to help produce immersive environments through which conservation, sustainability, and environmental awareness were promoted. The participants of these digital projects become aware of the presence of environmental issues and it challenges them to take real-life actions.
c) NVIDIA's Energy-Efficient GPUs: NVIDIA, an industry leading GPU maker, has developed VR- and gaming-optimized GPUs that are also energy efficient. Such GPUs are equipped with the latest technologies including variable rate shading and deep learning super sampling that aid in maximizing performance while reducing energy consumption. Then saving energy and emitting less carbon, developers do not have to put the performance at risk (Wang et al., 2021).

By implementing these strategies and learning from successful case studies, stakeholders in the Metaverse can work toward mitigating environmental challenges and fostering long-term sustainability in virtual environments.

3. Social Challenges and Inclusivity

3.1. Diversity and Inclusivity in Virtual Communities

With the rising number of online communities within Metaverse, we have noticed that this group of people can be a diverse and inclusive community for people with different backgrounds and identities. Within this space, people can work, meet, and afterward build together. Therefore, the creation of diverse and inclusive digital communities is a huge challenge in that we need to think about news sources, divisions, cultural barriers and algorithmic bias (Cezarotto et al., 2022).

3.2. Examination of Social Challenges

Social challenges related to diversity and inclusivity in the Metaverse include:

- Digital Divides: Differences in access and use of the internet and technology that are occasioned by socioeconomic imbalances can impede inclusive digital participation (Van & Van, 2019).
- Cultural Barriers: The cultural implication of people's languages along with the obstacles to virtual communication makes it harder for such groups to be involved to the point that some may feel excluded and alienated (Kim, 2023).
- Algorithmic Biases: Algorithms employed in virtual environments can be manipulated by the magnitude of the displayed factors that play a role such as gender, race or others, leading to unequal treatment and representation of the individuals within the virtual communities (Noble, 2018).

Importance of Creating Inclusive Virtual Spaces:

- Grasping the construction of truly inclusive virtual spaces becomes pivotal for the establishment of social equity, generation of the sense of belongingness and empowerment of overlooked communities in the Metaverse. Providing an inclusive virtual space helps people to be themselves, interact with other people constructively and contribute to collaborative activities without the fear of being excluded because of their differences.

Strategies for Promoting Social Equity:

> To promote social equity and inclusivity in virtual communities, various strategies can be employed:

- Accessibility Features: We should come up with accessible features like closed captioning and audio description, screen readers as well as language translators devices so that virtual space can be enjoyed by all people with disabilities and language barriers (Horton & Quesenbery, 2014).
- Community Engagement: Interacting with different communities including collecting feedback can enlighten the virtual platform providers' pertinent individual needs and tastes, and consequently they will be able to customize their services accordingly to fit the users (Kuniavsky, 2003).
- Representation and Diversity Initiatives: Encouraging divergent representation in the design of content including avatars, and virtual events may help to reflect the experiences of the excluded. Strategies like diversity scholarships, mentorship programs, and inclusive practicing can also work when it comes to the systemic inequality issue in the virtual community.

Examples of successful initiatives promoting diversity and inclusivity in the Metaverse include:

- Roblox: The Roblox gaming platform dedicates countless avatar customization options for the users who can create their avatar based on their unique identity and background. Interestingly, that is also part of Roblox's activity; it has virtual events and experiences that are meant to uplift cultural diversity and inclusivity such as the Pride Month celebrations and Black History Month events (Roblox, 2022).
- Second Life: The virtual world of Second Life has some community-centered initiatives motivated by and connected to the development of diversity, equity, and inclusion. Besides that, these groups are in charge of organizing events, discussions and campaigns to promote awareness and the conversation around social justice and representation issues among digital community members (Dick, 2021).

Through not only carrying out such plans but also making use of successful case studies, Metaverse stakeholders could promote virtual spaces that consider social justice and strengthen the influence of disadvantaged groups.

4. Governance Challenges and Regulation

The Metaverse, a sophisticated virtual space where individuals meet and do a lot of different activities, brings along its challenges, and the brotherhood is one of them that should be seriously addressed, to achieve a sustainable development of the Metaverse. This part is about these problems and finds out that governance frameworks should be efficient and gives good examples of successful ESG governance projects in the Metaverse such as comparing their results to lessons learned.

4.1. Governance Challenges

The Metaverse faces several governance challenges, including:

Cybersecurity Threats: Digital environments can easily be subjected to cybersecurity problems such as hacking, data breaches, and identity theft. The interconnectedness of huge volumes of personal data that are processed in Metaverse might profoundly exacerbate these risk factors (Herley et al., 2018).

Regulatory Uncertainty: The Metaverse regulatory environment is speckled and developing further, so the question of what represents legal requirements, jurisdictional issues, and compliance has been the source of concerns. Regulatory insufficiencies arise in the domains of personal data protection, intellectual property, as well as content moderation (Kalyvaki, 2023).

4.2. Need for Effective Governance Frameworks

The existence of effective governance structures becomes necessary for the Metaverse to adhere to certain ethical standards while at the same time implementing them within the virtual world. These frameworks provide strategies, standards, and ways to tackle governance problems and help to show transparency, accountability, and user protection. Core Features of governance that are effective include:

- Comprehensive Regulation: Through the establishment of comprehensive supranational regulative mechanisms that encompass various dimensions of online interactions, such as personal data protection, consumer rights, and platform accountability. The regulations do this by cutting risks, covering privacy issues, and creating clear rules for user interaction within the Metaverse (Protection, 2018).
- Collaborative Governance Models: The involvement of participants from industry, the academic sphere, and community representatives in the decision-making process using a cooperative governance model. Joint work promotes the increasing popularity of consensus building sharing of information, and implementation of collective actions to deal with government challenges (Song et al., 2017).

4.3. Case Studies of Successful ESG Governance Initiatives

Two case studies exemplify successful ESG governance initiatives in the Metaverse:

Decentraland's Governance Model: Decentralized Fluide, a platform that comes on the decentralized blockchain, incorporated governance mechanisms that are involved with community-based decisions. Via DAOs, users administer democratic processes as they get to propose and vote on governance proposals, for instance, platform development, content management as well as community governance (Goldberg & Schär, 2023).

Virtual Economy Research Network (VERN): VERN is all about the exchange of thoughts, researchers, professionals, and decision-makers getting together to conduct research and work out solutions related to virtual governance. Research Projects, Policy Recommendations, and Stakeholder Engagement should be some of the main strategies by which VERN will enable this; responsible governance practices and regulatory frameworks for the Metaverse.

4.4. Outcomes and Lessons Learned

It is evidenced by the good implementation of decentralized governance models and collaborative initiatives in the case studies mentioned above that governance challenges in the Metaverse can be addressed. By utilizing DAOs, Decentraland gives a chance for the users to have a say in platform management, which, in turn, demonstrates transparency and a high level of user engagement. By creating suitable working formats, VERN aims to develop interdisciplinary research, share knowledge in a distributed manner, and contribute to informed decision-making/regulatory reform, implying each factor in turn.

Our primary lessons from these cases, though include community participation, transparency, as well as the interdisciplinary participation of stakeholders in the governance and decision-making exercise. Governance models based on decentralization increase the involvement of users in the processes of the system, which leads to growing trust and satisfaction among participants. UNINT: The VERN project will pool the knowledge, resources, and models of responsible use within the community which eventually will increase the inventiveness and sustainability within the Metaverse.

Finally, governance frameworks with practical effectiveness are what matters most when combating cybersecurity threats, dealing with regulatory uncertainty, and for the overall governance for the metaverse. The implementation of a comprehensive framework of regulations and multi-stakeholder management may help create an environment where ethics and accountability are fostered, citizen rights are protected and innovation and creativity may flourish in virtual spaces.

5. Integrating ESG Principles in Metaverse Development

5.1. ESG Integration in Technology Design

- Imprinting ESG criteria on the Metaverse is essential in creating sustainable and responsible virtual ecosystems.
- Environmental Sustainability: Designers can make use of energy efficiency and resources reserve in creating virtual platforms and applications. This comprises of optimum code coding to facilitate low energy consumption, renewable energy for server hardware, and minimization of digital environment carbon footprint.
- Social Inclusivity: Designers will achieve a generation of virtual spaces that are welcoming and accessible to people with different backgrounds. The most important features are the use of avatars that you can customize to your liking, language translation tools, and accessibility features for all persons who are disabled. Through the support of diversity and inclusion, virtual environments can lead to the equality of social entities and increase the involvement of the users.
- Governance and Ethics: The developers should keep best ethical practices and the governance rules built into virtual spaces. This includes developing clear content moderation policies where one openly states what is been done, securing their user's data through serious data security measures, and respecting all ethics in transactions and interactions.

5.2. Role of Designers and Developers

Designers and developers play a critical role in creating sustainable virtual environments by:

- Prioritizing Sustainability: Designers may identify the base and put the sustainability considerations in process at the very stage of the product design, through to the implementation and operation. There should be a thorough evaluation of the environmental impact, the designation of energy-saving and resource efficiency opportunities as well as the usage of sustainable design practices throughout the development process.
- Innovating for Sustainability: Developers can not only explore better innovations but also find ways to leverage advanced technologies to create cleaner

environments and socially responsible Metaverse. In this regard, we are aiming to include VR experiences in which the environmental problems will be raised, gamifying sustainability behavior scenarios, and motivating users to include the pro-environment aspects in virtual environments.
- Collaborating Across Disciplines: Designers and prevailers must work together with specialists in, say, environmental science, social psychology and governance in order to maneuver ESG principles diligently. Collaboration across sectors, index of knowledge and skill, and one can craft the comprehensive approaches that tackle multi-dimensional challenges in the Metaverse.

5.3. Collaborative ESG Efforts

Importance of Collaborative Efforts:

Ensuring collaboration among all stakeholders is a key requirement for handling ESG problems and objects to successful Metaverse community development. A few points why collaborative initiatives are crucial:

- Holistic Perspective: Togetherness provides a platform where participants with unique skills and viewpoints could propel ESG initiatives. The collaboration of the stakeholders can lead to the achievement of a combined knowledge base and skills, and as a result, they will develop effective strategies for cross-sectoral management.
- Shared Responsibility: The ESG issues in Metaverse are going to be unperformed if the collaborative work of government agencies, civil society actors, business players, and users is not facilitated. The cooperative engagement will bring out the collaborative ventures that make partnerships and alliances avenues for joint decision-making, resource sharing, and impacting collectively on sustainability outcomes.

5.4. Partnerships and Initiatives

Several partnerships and initiatives contribute to responsible Metaverse development:

- Industry Collaborations: Electronic companies, content developers, and virtual platform managers cooperate in ESG projects as an example of achieving sustainability certifications, shifting toward green tech use, and creating green content. It is through these partnerships that habits that are industry-wide and best guidelines are initiated for environmental conservation and sustainable production.
- Government Partnerships: Different governments engage with block-chain or the gaming industry to formulate regulation and promotion laws as well as public-private partnerships that ensure the Metaverse is developed with sustainability in mind. Through joint efforts, the government and the stakeholders can develop policies to overcome fan gaps, empower compliance, and demand responsible business conduct within the space.

- Civil Society Engagement: Civil society groups like research, as well as educating the public, and awareness campaigns. Activities like educating personnel to promote sustainability, availability of sustainability ratings, or the dialogs with stakeholders, let company service providers and consumers stay transparent, accountable, and ethical.

Organizations can jointly fund, create partnerships, and work together to attain ESG targets, achieve sustainability of the Metaverse, and maintain it as a responsible virtual world where people live and conduct business. To properly implement ESG into the Metaverse building, we need designers, and stakeholders who are in different sectors, developers, and sectors to get involved. Through the process of sustainable-oriented, creative social inclusiveness, and promoting collaborative projects, Metaverse can develop into a responsive and collective digital ecosystem.

6. Future Perspectives and Recommendations

The development of the Metaverse is expected to continue evolving rapidly, driven by emerging trends and technologies. Some key future trends include:

- Advancements in VR and AR: VR and AR technologies integration will be the way the Metaverse experience will improve. This makes the VR interaction more genuine and natural. Hence, such a situation could be accompanied by higher performance in terms of energy consumption and natural resources with the consequence of deteriorating environment's condition.
- Blockchain and Decentralized Technologies: There will be a large part in those new circumstances to blockchain technology and decentralized platforms for Metaverse. Decentralized governance models, Nonfungible tokens (NFTs), and Blockchain-based virtual economies may be the introduction of opportunities for economic empowerment and digital ownership. An implication is that scaling them up can be a problem while maintaining security and complying with regulations can be problematic.
- Artificial Intelligence (AI) and Machine Learning (ML): These techniques also open up possibilities of more personalized, customized, and dynamic experiences in the Metaverse which helps in sustaining the users' levels of interest as well as making it possible to adjust content recommendation systems accordingly. Nevertheless, due to the possible algorithm biases, data privacy issues, as well as digital rights management measures, are likely to arrive, requiring decent ethical rules and regulation standards.

6.1. Potential ESG Implications

These emerging trends and technologies in the development of the Metaverse have several potential ESG implications:

- Environmental Impact: Blockchain-based platforms, VR/AR developments may lead to increase in consumption of energy and emission of carbon which

adds up to the environmental concerns. Changing these impacts requires that stakeholders focus on energy efficient design, renewable energy adoption and carbon offset mechanisms to mitigate them.
- Social Equity: The AI-driven algorithms along with the decentralized technologies that are used in the Metaverse may lead to the worsening of social inequality and existence of the digital divide. Having stakeholders ensure inclusivity, accessibility, and diversity is the best way for the virtual environment to foster social equity and digital inclusion.
- Governance and Ethics: On the one side, the vast bloc chains impose duress on transparency, accountability, and regulatory compliance due to the decentralized nature and autonomous decision-making power of the systems. These regulatory controls should be crafted into holistic governance structures, ethical guidelines and regulatory systems to deal with those challenges and sustain ethical norms in the Metaverse.

6.2. Recommendations for Stakeholders

- Invest in Research and Development: Stakeholders should invest in research and development initiatives to explore sustainable technologies, innovative solutions, and best practices for ESG integration in the Metaverse. Collaborative research partnerships and interdisciplinary collaborations can facilitate knowledge sharing and accelerate progress toward sustainability goals.
- Promote Collaboration and Knowledge Sharing: Encourage collaboration among industry players, government agencies, academia, and civil society organizations to share insights, resources, and expertise on ESG issues in the Metaverse. Platforms for stakeholder engagement, industry forums, and public-private partnerships can foster dialogue, cooperation, and collective action on sustainability challenges.
- Adopt ESG Standards and Certifications: Embrace ESG standards, certifications, and best practices to guide decision-making, benchmark performance, and demonstrate commitment to sustainability. Initiatives such as the ISO 14000 series for environmental management and the Global Reporting Initiative (GRI) for corporate sustainability reporting provide frameworks for measuring and reporting ESG performance in the Metaverse.

Key Findings:

In summary, ensuring a sustainable Metaverse requires proactive efforts from stakeholders to address ESG challenges. Key findings include:

- Environmental Stewardship: The priorities for the ecosystem participants should be directed toward energy efficiency, green energy adoption, and CO_2 reduction strategies to reduce the negative impact of the Metaverse.
- Social Inclusivity: Taking advantage of diversity, accessibility, and digital inclusion is indispensable that virtual infrastructures open everyone possible and serve different users' professions and needs.

- Ethical Governance: Solid governance structures, ethical rules, and regulatory procedures are junctures in holding the ethics high, protecting the rights of the users, also preserving the responsibility line.

Therefore, the final thought is that the ESG should be considered fundamentally and persistently for the long-term stability and success of the Metaverse. Doing this way means having to introduce ESG activities into technics creation, involving interested parties together and encouraging environmentally friendly processes which will lead to the Metaverse that is environmentally friendly, socially responsible, and ethically driven. Do we pledge to walk together in the development of a Metaverse that takes care of the interests of all the users as well as the coming generations?

References

Bailenson, J. (2018). *Experience on demand: What virtual reality is, how it works, and what it can do*. WW Norton & Company.

Belkhir, L., & Elmeligi, A. (2018). Assessing ICT global emissions footprint: Trends to 2040 & recommendations. *Journal of Cleaner Production, 177*, 448–463.

Bonneau, J., Miller, A., Clark, J., Narayanan, A., Kroll, J. A., & Felten, E. W. (2015, May). *Sok: Research perspectives and challenges for bitcoin and cryptocurrencies* [Conference session]. 2015 IEEE symposium on security and privacy (pp. 104–121). IEEE.

Cezarotto, M., Martinez, P., & Chamberlin, B. (2022). Developing inclusive games: Design frameworks for accessibility and diversity. In *Game theory-from idea to practice*. IntechOpen.

Dick, E. (2021). *Current and potential uses of AR/VR for equity and inclusion*. Information Technology and Innovation Foundation.

Ferri-Molla, I., Linares-Pellicer, J., & Izquierdo-Domenech, J. (2024). *Virtual reality and language models, a new frontier in learning*. Universidad Internacional de la Rioja.

Goldberg, M., & Schär, F. (2023). Metaverse governance: An empirical analysis of voting within decentralized autonomous organizations. *Journal of Business Research, 160*, 113764.

Herley, C., & Van Oorschot, P. C. (2018). Science of security: Combining theory and measurement to reflect the observable. *IEEE Security & Privacy, 16*(1), 12–22.

Horton, S., & Quesenbery, W. (2014). *A web for everyone: Designing accessible user experiences*. Rosenfeld Media.

In, S. Y., Peterman, A., & Monk, A. (2022). *Deploying corporate capital as clean energy catalyst: A case study of Google's impact roles in global energy transition*. Available at SSRN 4066014.

Kalyvaki, M. (2023). Navigating the metaverse business and legal challenges: Intellectual property, privacy, and jurisdiction. *Journal of Metaverse, 3*(1), 87–92.

Katal, A., Dahiya, S., & Choudhury, T. (2023). Energy efficiency in cloud computing data centers: A survey on software technologies. *Cluster Computing, 26*(3), 1845–1875.

Kim, S. J. (2023). The role of social media news usage and platforms in civic and political engagement: Focusing on types of usage and platforms. *Computers in Human Behavior, 138*, 107475.

Kuniavsky, M. (2003). *Observing the user experience: A practitioner's guide to user research*. Elsevier.

Noble, S. U. (2018). Algorithms of oppression: How search engines reinforce racism. In *Algorithms of oppression*. New York University Press.
Protection, F. D. (2018). *General data protection regulation (GDPR)*. Intersoft Consulting.
Roblox. (2022). *Roblox celebrates black history month and honors black creators and community members.* https://news.xbox.com/en-us/2022/02/01/xbox-celebrates-black-history-month-2022/
Rubin, P. (2018). *Future presence: How virtual reality is changing human connection, intimacy, and the limits of ordinary life.* HarperCollins.
Shapsugova, M. (2023). *ESG principles and social responsibility* [Conference session]. E3S Web of Conferences (Vol. 420, p. 06040). EDP Sciences.
Shehabi, A., Smith, S. J., Masanet, E., & Koomey, J. (2018). Data center growth in the United States: Decoupling the demand for services from electricity use. *Environmental Research Letters, 13*(12), 124030.
Song, H., Srinivasan, R., Sookoor, T., & Jeschke, S. (2017). *Smart cities: Foundations, principles, and applications.* John Wiley & Sons.
Stephenson, N. (1992). *Snow crash.* Bantam Spectra Books.
Steuer, J., Biocca, F., & Levy, M. R. (1995). Defining virtual reality: Dimensions determining telepresence. *Communication in the Age of Virtual Reality, 33*, 37–39.
Van Deursen, A. J., & Van Dijk, J. A. (2019). The first-level digital divide shifts from inequalities in physical access to inequalities in material access. *New Media & Society, 21*(2), 354–375.
Wang, Y., Karimi, M., Xiang, Y., & Kim, H. (2021, December). *Balancing energy efficiency and real-time performance in GPU scheduling* [Conference session]. 2021 IEEE Real-Time Systems Symposium (RTSS) (pp. 110–122). IEEE.

Chapter 10

Metaverse: Transformative Pathways for Skilling, Reskilling, and Upskilling in the Digital Age

Snigdha Dash[a], Prashant Dev Yadav[b], Rishi Manrai[c] and Aditya Kumar Gupta[d]

[a]*Galgotias University, Greater Noida, India*
[b]*Symbiosis Centre for Management Studies, Noida, Symbiosis International (Deemed University), Pune, India*
[c]*Amity Business School, Amity University Manesar, Gurgaon, Haryana, India*
[d]*Amity International Business School, Amity University, Noida, India*

Abstract

This chapter takes on the role of the metaverse in skill development, such as skilling, reskilling, and upskilling in the digital age. Metaverse is instrumental in revolutionizing skill development in the digital age and bringing the paradigm shift in learning. This chapter will cover the capability of the metaverse to transform the ways of learning and developing skills in the evolving digital landscape. Individuals can be part of tailor-made solutions for their needs through innovative methodologies and interactive experiences. This chapter takes through real cases to get deeper insights about conventional methods that transform how an individual experiences learning to acquire skills to get exposed to the rapidly changing digital world, allowing people to customize their learning experiences to adapt their unique requirements through cutting-edge methodologies and digitally responsive encounters. It then deliberates the importance of the metaverse in the individual-led industry in a manner that allows people to reach their potential. Individuals succeed in the evolution of the metaverse dynamic by continually upskilling granted to them.

Keywords: Metaverse; skilling; reskilling; upskilling; digital age; immersive learning

1. Introduction: Metaverse a New Digital Frontier

As a virtual immersive reality, the metaverse combines the cyber and physical worlds by acting as a social platform with game-like elements such as a seamless state of reality presentation, interaction, and marketplace. Its growth is persistent, as the world metaverse market is worth USD65.5 billion and is set to top USD936.6 billion by 2030 (Quakenbush & Oliver, 2023). This development has further magnified the digitalization trend, which dominates the economy, thereby creating a skills gap, especially with the emergence of Industry 4.0, fueled by Artificial Intelligence. It is also leading the adoption of technology across the sectors (Gupta, Aggarwal, et al., 2022; Manrai et al., 2022; Singh et al., 2023), and with technologies like metaverse coming onto the scene, some fundamental digital competencies are needed by individuals to function well in the constant digital evolution (Kabilan, 2023).

Metaverse has a game-changing potential that cuts across different sectors ranging from auto-mechanics to healthcare, with many potentials for the growing job market (Rodon et al., 2023). It provides an apt landscape of training and education, seeking skills inherently intrinsic to virtual reality concerning technology literacy, digital creativity, virtual collaboration, and technological adaptability (Barráez-Herrera, 2022). The integration of the metaverse in learning/training relates it to employee skill gap and workforce preparation, particularly in developing digital skills like 3D design and visualization skills (Cai et al., 2022).

On the other hand, these challenges should be remembered as the possibility of being disconnected from the real world, and the ambiguous line between what can be considered real and what is virtual should be reckoned with. The metaverse is still separate, with several barriers hindering the success of realizing an integrative digital multiverse. A concerted effort is being made by creating platforms for skill portability, developing unified certifications, and handling compliance and regulation issues (Zhang et al., 2022). The metaverse still projects a path where people are taught new skills, learn new things, and are equipped with the relevant information that would be easier to process in an age of dynamic technology (Zhang et al., 2022). Immersion technology, such as the metaverse, is the perfect choice for training and general education, reducing the skills gap and fitting individuals in the digital era (Kaddoura & Husseiny, 2023).

Inclusion in the learning ecosystem by giving more respect to migration of skills and standardization of certifications and accreditations, addressing legal and HR compliance issues, and extensive research making the individuals ready to be fit for jobs in the age of the digital world are only methods that enable people to get the prerequisite skills. Hence, the gradual changes in skill portability, standardization of certification and accreditation process, regulatory and HR compliance issues, and research of the metaverse must be considered by leaders, policymakers, and HR leaders to create a whole learning environment. The metaverse creates a new educational place for mutual communication, freedom of expression, and immersive scenarios (Kye et al., 2021).

In this chapter, we scrutinize the dynamics of the metaverse and its synchronization with new technologies to determine the revolutionary trends of skilling, reskilling, and upskilling. Additionally, in this chapter, we provide readers with the ideal topics for investigation, including:

- How does the Metaverse revolutionize skilling, reskilling, and upskilling pathways?
- What role does the metaverse play in the integration of workforce reskilling, and what is the maximum potential for organizations through its implementation?
- What does the metaverse introduce the most effective upskilling opportunities concerning the current or evolving digital landscape, and how can individuals grab them?
- What role does the metaverse play in solving professional development gaps through its integrative and innovative learning-based environment?
- What is the ultimate role of Metaverse education in preparing individuals for their career advancement concerning the skills and knowledge tapped?
- What effect does the metaverse have on career advancement, and how does it orient professional development for individuals? Additionally, what strategies can individuals use to enhance this growth?
- What are the benefits of the metaverse as a catalyst for continuous learning and growth, and how can individuals harness the potential to maximize learning in this environment?
- Finally, what are the implementation challenges and considerations based on the Metaverse education systems?

2. Transformative Pathways for Skilling in the Metaverse

Through a metaverse, the transformative route to improving skilling is vitally essential to the picture of people with the needed competencies to manage the dynamic digital space. Immersive education within the Metaverse features settings for interactive simulations and virtual classrooms, which involve the learners' practice of the acquired novel skills and are highly engaging. Furthermore, the few virtual academies and institutes specialized in Metaverse-related skills also offer training about topics like VR development, 3D modeling, and Blockchain technology. The Metaverse is where skills-focused communities and guilds can be met, providing networking, learning, and skill-building activities on their own. Cross-disciplinary training programs profess to integrate the skill sets from many fields simultaneously, preparing people for the hitherto unknown challenges of the Metaverse. The experiential learning projects, which will include the application of skills in practical contexts and the persisting learning and adaptability, will be the critical factors in remaining relevant in the rapidly evolving Metaverse world. Progressive skilling brings out their best, allowing them to grow and develop in the Metaverse and contributing to its continuous improvement and invention.

The metaverse also has the potential to revolutionize skilling, reskilling, and upskilling at scale during this digital age. Its features include a new form of social interaction and communication, more significant creative freedom and sharing, branded new experiences provision, and profoundly immersive through virtualization (Contributors, 2023). Nonetheless, there are also certain factors to consider and constraints to be aware of (Cai et al., 2022). These limitations include weaker social connections, privacy issues, and potential crimes due to the virtual space and anonymity. To use the metaverse to its full potential in education, educators should consider analyzing students' knowledge and developing classes aimed at problem-solving or teamwork on projects (Zhang et al., 2022).

Moreover, the creation of educational metaverse platforms is necessary to control and safeguard the use of student information. Teachers and educators must know about the existence of the metaverse and its learning opportunities (Cai et al., 2022). It is also necessary to focus on an essential shift in the approach to learning—traditional two-dimensional interaction with information must become more multidimensional through interactive and immersive forms (Kye et al., 2021). The education metaverse can form a three-dimensional and multidimensional learning environment similar to real-world teach-mimics, patterns, and pedagogy through technology support, interaction business, and rule design. These make the educational metaverse an immersive and interactive environment foundation where training participants and instructors can easily simulate the real-world teaching and learning environment. In this metaverse, real subjects and their virtual avatars can easily connect, collaborate, and learn in an enhanced form (Kabilan, 2023).

Using the metaverse in educational settings can be a game changer due to its three-dimensional, multidimensional, and real-time learning experience. The metaverse substantially reconfigures and transforms new skilling, reskilling, and upskilling pathways that offer a new environment for shaping social communication and collaboration, creative problem-solving, and a learning ecosystem. The metaverse can be considered a game changer due to its three-dimensional, multidimensional, and real-time learning experience. In other words, it creates a more immersive and interactive environment for education, highlighting students' opportunities to engage in collaborative problem-solving and exercise their creativity. Meanwhile, the comprised approach will also address the analysis of understanding the metaverse from the student side (Cai et al., 2022) and guarantee that platforms are there to safeguard student data and limit the risks of any misuse. Integration with the initial instructional practice will ensure that virtual reality immersion becomes a constant attribute of the learning process. Due to the experience, students become much more motivated and attentive, which can also positively affect their involvement and comprehension of the curriculum.

First and foremost, immersive learning allows students to interact with various virtual objects and settings, creating an excellent visual and tactile image of the studied phenomenon. The possibility of using digital avatars to represent themselves strengthens empathy and enhances cultural competence by trying on new identities and viewpoints. Besides, this tool also helps to eliminate the boundary between knowledge and its practical use: Students will be able to test their analytical and practical resources in the simulated metaverse settings (Kabilan, 2023; Kaddoura & Husseiny, 2023). The metaverse can indeed transform education into a three-dimensional, multidimensional, and real-time classroom

(Zhang et al., 2022). The use of the metaverse in education aligns with the principles of Education 4.0 and the fourth industrial revolution at an overarching level. Notably, the metaverse can integrate numerous exponential technologies such as artificial intelligence, 3D printing, and cloud computing. The metaverse can also overcome the limitations of traditional learning through a flexible and self-paced learning experience (Belmonte et al., 2023). Other technologies could also leverage the metaverse to advance learning in their own ways (Zhang et al., 2022). The metaverse in education offers a potential avenue for the transformation of skilling in the digital age.

3. The Role of the Metaverse in Reskilling the Workforce

Metaverse is the new emerging frontier where workforce redesign and performances are altered.

3.1. Immersive Learning Environments

It is the Metaverse gives a chance to virtually experience and interact within environments that are extraordinary, interactive, and simulated at the same time. Moreover, such a sensory mode assists in comprehension, which makes the process of studying more interesting and efficient than the classical one. Staff members can be trained in simulated environments that are the closest in look and feel to their workspace. Hence, the implementation of a practical, embodied learning curriculum is possible.

3.2. Accessible Training Programs

The main problem in traditional job training is what it takes to reach most employees who are in remote locations or workplaces. The Metaverse will be a path-opener as it will give you access to training programs all around the world without any relocation constraints. This benefits, in particular, the people, who live at the end of the world or having availability problems. The fact that members of the public can conduct the training within the Metaverse is ensured by one requirement that may be found in every Metaverse social networking platform – the internet connection.

3.3. Personalized Learning Paths

Metaverse will be able to offer learning to everyone in a more personalized fashion based on students' needs and learning styles. Through the use of data analytics and Artificial intelligence platforms within the Metaverse can acquire users' habits and performance. This is in turn enabling them to give personalized suggestions to improve these respective skills. With this customized method, each employee workers will receive coaching which is directly linked with his role, career expectations.

3.4. Collaborative Learning Opportunities

The spirit of collaboration and unity is actually the essence of solving problems and mastering skills in the workplace In the Metaverse, interaction among peers and mentors as well as experts is facilitated by enabling users to interact in real-time and space without regard of their geographical status. Through this platform, employees may be able to learn from each other; also, they can share knowledge and work collaboratively on projects; the main thing is that such a platform lets to cultivate a learning environment within an organization.

3.5. Cost-Effective Training Solutions

Providing traditional employee training may entail considerable expenditures, e.g., removal charges, traveling fees, and an instructor's remuneration. The Metaverse is a perfect example of a cheap alternative that removes many of these additional lease costs. In the future, businesses can focus on building virtual training platforms and interactive experiences that can be reused more than a single time with almost zero additional expenditures, which guarantees that reskilling employees in the workforce will be financially sustainable.

3.6. Adapting to Technological Advancements

The lifespan of technology is rapidly changing; therefore, the competency of workers has to keep on accelerating for them to be competitive in the workplace. The Metaverse, which spearheads the latest technological advances, allows for anything from AI to virtual reality and blockchain training. With the help of Metaverse's huge performance, organizations continue to stay right at the forefront of technology.

The metaverse has a role to reskill the workforce, it does so by providing the following: learning and skill development activities that a person can participate in. This goes beyond the bounds of reality by furnishing virtual learning and simulations, virtual real worker's orientation, and adaptive learning systems that bridges the knowledge gap and its application. Besides, the metaverse users will be provided with a variety of educational materials libraries in addition to experts understanding of every single subject which will ensure application of the new skills and capabilities desired in the digital world (Chua & Yu, 2023; Kaddoura & Husseiny, 2023). Within the context of education and skills, the metaverse, through its 3D presentation in an integrated learning environment in which one can easily hear, watch and see, provides a 360-degree format where one can interact and engage in workforce retraining which is active and experiential (Cai et al., 2022). This way, learners will be able to utilize the gained knowledge by participating in metaverses experience that indulges them in real life applications, enhancing their learning with practical skills.

On the top of that, there is plenty of place for the educational business in the Metaverse as it offers numerous opportunities. Initially, it helps us to the preparation of qualified experts with wherein they can set up their online business and perform in a safe, efficient, and trusted platforms thus gaining international clients. Whatsoever, aforementioned training enables the usage of respective operational competences in the workplace. VR can be a powerful learning tool for a wide range of industries including medicine, engineering, human resource management, and production. These are exactly the sectors that rely heavily on practical training, which in turn underlies knowledge and skill acquisition. The organizations can simulate training methods to assess the competency of their personnel's hands-on skills in dealing with rapid demand and industry changes. This helps to identify candidates who are ready to transfer from current operations to new mandates and operations based on the changes in the business. Along with the development of the metaverse, there will be many corporations that may apply the scenario for upskilling workers which means higher possibilities for them to come out as winners in an increasingly dynamic labor sector.

The metaverse permits some novel learning opportunities, which can evolve education into a set of skills fit for the cutting-edge digital era and upcoming years. Through metaverse as a means to develop abilities and skills concerning to digital community helps companies to stay on top in the fast pace of technology (Kye et al., 2021). While the barriers such as a limited social engagement, privacy control and identity stress (Belmonte et al., 2023) may have some drawbacks as far as the learning process is concerned within the virtual reality, it allows the learners to keep up with the pace in the age of the technology evolutions (Kye et al., 2021). In general, while there may be some disadvantages, the metaverse becomes a gateway of great development for skills teaching and education.

4. Upskilling Opportunities in the Age of the Metaverse

The metaverse is not only a one-dimensional world. Rather, one of the most spectacular aspects of the metaverse is that the digital age makes it possible to develop various skills. Those can be revitalized or even created (Purdy, 2022). The BCG framework sees the metaverse as comprising objects that does not just stop at the virtual classroom, but a host of learning resources including simulation experiences can be found in the metaverse that evidence shows lifted learning skills and capacities (Kye et al., 2021). We would go further and enunciate upskilling prototypes and practical use cases of all the community-driven innovation initiatives using the scenario of the metaverse. Companies have applied it to their training programs and the new way will be immersive experiences via a virtual reality scholarship where employees can train through various applications from understanding consumers and building campaigns to using digital platforms.

Furthermore, the metaverse allows us to improve our skills and learn collaboratively. For example, we can interact with professionals in our field and workmates in other countries to acquire new knowledge and learn new skills through mentorship. Similarly, we can use the metaverse to explore new marketing trends and modern marketing methods in the labor market. Business owners can also create virtual upskill workshops on the metaverse to fill skill gaps and address new trends in the digital marketing environment. As a result, any business can use the platform to upskill our marketing staff to align with the requirements and expertise of the new labor market in the digital era. The metaverse generally provides digital novices unrivaled opportunities to thrive in the digital era. Metaverse is the door to various new upgrade opportunities for the overall industries.

4.1. Virtual Reality (VR) Development

In general, the main source of supply and demand in the Metaverse is the virtual world. This applies so much to developers of VR systems; whose task is to raise immersion. It is worth mentioning that people with VR development skills, who can work in a variety of programming languages like C#, Unity, and Unreal Engine, can play active roles in creating virtual spaces, designing interactive simulations, and building VR apps. The metaverse is improving our skills and collaborative learning by letting us do so as well. For instance, the people who are in the same field or the country we live in could act as our mentors through whom we can get more knowledge and new skills by their counseling.

4.2. Augmented Reality (AR) Design and Development

AR technology brings the real world along with virtual objects together where the user blurs the boundary between reality and the digital world. Skills training in AR design and development can provide access to job applications in the areas of AR for training, education, gaming, marketing, and many others. It may be possible to expand the job opportunities in these areas. Mastery of AR developing frameworks such as ARKit, ARCore, and WebAR may prove more relevant.

4.3. 3D Modeling and Animation

The emblem of the world is generating 3D objects to build life-like experiences of the Metaverse. These people competent with 3D modeling, texturing, rigging, and animation may be designers of virtual environments, characters, objects, or effects depending on the company's projects. The utility of such software as Blender, Maya, 3ds Max, or ZBrush may be essential if one strives for a professional art content career.

4.4. Virtual World Architecture and Design

Just as physical spaces have their architects, virtual environments in Metaverse have their virtual architects who design these digital spaces. The training in virtual world architecture is a complex process, which should be based not only on knowledge of spatial design principles, UX design, and optimization but also on ensuring that these worlds have good scalability, are realistic and are as immersive as possible. Familiarization with platforms such as Spatial.io and Decentraland will make the field of AR/VR easier.

4.5. Digital Marketing in Virtual Spaces

As businesses start to create a presence in Metaverse, there is a growing gap of professionals who are skilled and knowledgeable in marketing their brands in a virtual environment. Virtual spaces provide new avenues for digital marketing upskilling. Among them, event management, avatar-based advertising, and life-like community engagement tactics can be highly profitable career options for companies.

4.6. Blockchain and Cryptocurrency

Cryptocurrency has a long way to go with blockchain (Singh et al., 2022). Decentralization, ownership, security, and governance are all key elements of the Metaverse that effectively implement blockchain technology. Experts in blockchain creation, smart contract coding, and crypto coins economics can help develop the decentralized virtual economies and platforms inside the Metaverse.

5. Bridging the GAP: The Metaverse in Professional Development

A digital environment, the Metaverse, that aims to close the gap between conventional professional development programs and the sector of the digital world that is rapidly unfolding is presented as a transformational tool. The merger of both physical and virtual realms brings forth unprecedented capabilities for humanity to overcome their limitations and raise new levels of skills and competencies. Regarding professional development, Metaverse is a vigorous arena for intuitive 3D environments where individuals can immerse themselves, and the learning acquisition process can be realized experientially and to the maximum. With VR simulations, AR applications, and how people can immerse from less to more, professionals may go as literal as possible. It also adds to the effectiveness of the training as participants gain both learning retention and practical skills to solve relevant problems in a safe environment.

The Metaverse apart from this also offers people collaboration options and networking prospects on a global scale. Professionals can build relationships with peers, mentors, and established experts from all over the world, chatting about, and learning from one another, as well as sharing valuable knowledge and practices on a moment's notice. The Metaverse creates a collaborative environment where individuals can meet other professionals, pool together different points of view, and learn from the negative and positive of others' professional lives. In addition, the Metaverse has got an array of specialized training modules and resources of education relevant to different sectors and skill sets a person might be interested in. It might be learning species of advanced coding mastering digital marketing systems and layouts or honing leadership skills, and generally, people can fish these resources from the Metaverse in furtherance of their professional development journey. Things such as online learning and advanced technologies and learning methods are among the resources offered. These resources are designed to be interactive and entertaining.

Moreover, in the Metaverse, individuals not only gain skills but also make significant contributions in the pursuit of career advancement and personal branding. Displays of professional's skills, projects, and achievements in virtual portfolios or virtual resumes can be very effective in making people hired in a competitive job market. Also, through virtual events like job fairs, networking events, and communities found inside the Metaverse, they will be able to explore their career options, build their networks, and further their career. Thus, living the Metaverse in career development is not an issue-free and uneven process. Sufficient access to technology, digital literacy skills, and honoring users' privacy rights are among the most essential things that should be carefully considered in providing professional development opportunities based on Metaverse. Furthermore, institutions must revise their teaching materials and facilities to add metaverse to the existing knowledge base, as it has the potential to influence to next generation (Aggarwal et al., 2021).

At the same time, the metaverse can fill in the gap in professional development, providing new learning experiences for its users. They can attend virtual conferences, workshops, and topical training programs, thus learning new skills and knowledge from the leading figures in the industry across the globe. Besides practicing language skills by engaging in natural dialogues, students are often requested to attend language fairs in the metaverse, which are exhibitions where educational institutions and companies present job opportunities to students (Purdy, 2022). The metaverse also offers professionals a platform to network and a collaborative way of marketing themselves and demonstrating their skills. With the metaverse's interactive and immersive capabilities, professionals experience real-time simulation and scenarios of actual challenges they would face in their professions. Subsequently, they get to increase their practical skills, improve their problem-solving abilities, and enhance their critical thinking abilities in a safe and controlled area. The metaverse also provides a continuous learning platform through virtualization and gamified technologies.

Furthermore, professionals can learn in virtual classrooms, access limitless educational resources, interact with instructors and other professionals, and engage in hands-on activities and simulations that improve their knowledge and competence in complex subjects. In addition, a metaverse will speed up the learning process involving a personalized and adaptive learning offering. As the metaverse will be able to identify each individual's strengths and weaknesses and their learning preferences, it will be more than capable of giving them learning pathways and content tailored to their needs. Most importantly, diversified learning experiences will optimize professional activities, enabling individuals to acquire knowledge and resources that suit their professional development journey. Therefore, the metaverse will transform professional development through innovative and diverse learning, theoretical and practical connections, and personalized, diverse learning approaches (Kye et al., 2021). The metaverse introduces opportunities for future professionals to develop their skills, knowledge, and careers. However, the metaverse is not limited by games and social events.

It has an unlimited future as a space for socializing, creativity, communication, and immersive experiences. These possibilities can heavily influence how professionals learn and develop in their relevant fields. Today, the metaverse represents an excellent opportunity for professionals to meet and network during their rapid changes. Additionally, the metaverse may help professionals to unite even if they are from another country or continent (Cai et al., 2022). The metaverse has great potential to revolutionize professional development by presenting new educational opportunities and promoting collaboration and practical skills acquisition (Kye et al., 2021).

6. The Case Study for Skilling, Reskilling, and Upskilling with Metaverse

6.1. Top Employers Leverage the Metaverse to Take Workforce Development to the Next Level

It is clear the metaverse is more than just gaming – with growing frequency; private companies are utilizing virtual and AR to deliver immersive, in-person training to their employees (see Table 1).

6.2. Developing Economies Are Increasingly Employing the Metaverse in Efficient Advance Workforce Development

Developing nations such as India, Rwanda, Morocco, Nigeria, and Ghana have all commenced using virtual labs in pioneering ways (see Table 2). Endeavors, including the India virtual labs project and initiatives such as Rwanda polytechnic, are

Table 1. Top Employers Using Metaverse for Workforce Development.

Company	Scope	Links of Interest
KLM	Pilot training	Article / Video
Volkswagen	Assembly training	Article / Video
UPS	Driving and logistics training	Article / Video
International Training Institute	Welding, air conditioning, electrical, plumbing, auto-mechanics training courses	Article / Video
The Refrigeration School	Welding, electrical, and air conditioning repair training	Programs / Video
Tulsa Welding School	Welding training	Video 1 / Video 2
KFC	Cooking training	Article / Video
Walmart	Customer service training	Article / Video 1 / Video 2

Source: Adopted from Unleashing the Metaverse for Skills and Workforce Development 2023 (https://blogs.worldbank.org/en/education/unleashing-metaverse-skills-and-workforce-development) in the public domain.

Table 2. Developing Economy's Use of Metaverse for Workforce Development.

Country	Name	Objective
Ghana	OpenSTEM Africa	Practical science knowledge for upper secondary level
India	Virtual Labs Project	Remote access to science and engineering labs for college and university students
Morocco	Design and Implementation of a Virtual Laboratory for Physics Subjects in Moroccan Universities	Low-cost virtual lab in an interactive physics learning environment for first year bachelor's students
Nigeria	StanLab	Quality STEM lab for secondary school students
Rwanda	Rwanda Polytechnic	Vehicle engine system lab for automobile technology diploma students

Source: Adopted from Unleashing the Metaverse for skills and workforce development 2023 (https://blogs.worldbank.org/en/education/unleashing-metaverse-skills-and-workforce-development) in the public domain.

deploying virtual laboratories for advanced technical and vocational skill development. These online labs provide learners access to first environments, enabling them to develop skills in science, engineering, and trades such as vehicle engine maintenance and repair. These and other initiatives use open-source and low-cost technologies to provide high-quality education in low-resource settings.

6.3. Skillveri – XR Simulators

Enhancing through Metaverse-powered XR simulators, Skillveri provides advanced training on precision skills such as welding and HVAC repair (HVAC, 2012; Skillveri, 2023). The company has 400 global installations and has availed enhanced skills to more than 2 million people, enough to increase productivity and quality. Skillveri's operations accentuate the potential of immersive technology in transforming skills acquisition, something potential job seekers, training facilities, and industries should consider.

7. Innovative Learning Environments: The Metaverse as a Skill Accelerator

Innovative Learning Environments: The Metaverse as a Skill Accelerator Innovative learning environments can use the metaverse to serve as a skill accelerator. Through immersive and interactive experiences, the metaverse platform enables set exposure that is not possible in the traditional sense. As such, the experiences enable learners to conduct real-world simulations to test their theorized skills when exposed to practical settings. In so doing, learners gain better and innate understanding, which promotes their memory and ability to compare concepts when solving real-world problems. The metaverse also offers a platform for collaborative learning, where diverse people can gather to learn collaboratively. The metaverse will ensure a parts and varied learning platform where people will be able to learn from each other and exchange opinions and perspectives. In addition, the learning experiences are expected to be more personalized as they will be tailored to fit the needs and preferences of the learners, and technology is a boon for SMEs (Gupta, Dash, et al., 2022).

Consequently, it will enhance productivity and efficiency in learning, and the learners will be able to interact with the content based on the learning style and pace. Besides, the metaverse will make it easier for learners to learn continuously, as any professional will have current knowledge and skills in their industry. Professionals will access virtual conferences, workshops, seminars, resources, and communities in the metaverse. Determining how the metaverse can be integrated into professional development settings is essential. Due to the pace and lack of accurate geographical walls in the current world, it will become more critical as learners engage and interact from different parts of the continent. Therefore, the metaverse can be a game-changer in how skilling and reskilling are performed and conducted. Individuals will acquire new skills, improve existing ones, and adapt to new trends in the digital era.

8. Preparing for the Future: Education in the Metaverse

Feel free to take the following resources. Indeed, the potential of the metaverse as a new educational environment is revolutionary in its impact (Camilleri & Divya Meena, n.d.). Restrictions, for example, may include weaker student communities, infringements on students' privacy, and even criminal activity in the virtual space. Due to anonymity and maladjustment to real life for identities that have not yet formed, students may enjoy committing illegal actions and avoid punishment. Teachers and educational institutions should use this knowledge for the good of all. They must study how students understand and draw the metaverse. Classes must be centered so that problems are solved together and students can be creative. Finally, students must create safe educational metaverse platforms that protect data. The metaverse's potential for education effect is not only possible; it could transform the whole experience by giving the chance to create more interactive learning (Cai et al., 2022).

There is still a need for research to explore the integration of educational spaces in the metaverse from a more comprehensive perspective (Kye et al., 2021). Other aspects that need to be further researched include the use of the metaverse in other educational stages, including secondary education, primary education, and professional training (Zhang et al., 2022). Altogether, the metaverse offers what sport offers to the virtual world by creating a new educational space to enjoy social communication, expand creativity, and have a unique experience due to deep immersion (Kye et al., 2021).

9. The Impact of the Metaverse on Career Advancement

In the digital age, the metaverse can change how careers are advanced. The metaverse will enable people of all ages to gain new qualifications and improve existing ones in a rapidly changing, interactive atmosphere. It will give people new chances to continue, reskill, and upskill through virtual training programs and simulated work environments such as simulated surgical rooms or spaceships (Zhang et al., 2022). It may result in improved and efficient learning of skills with the ability to allow one to engage by using their own hands and experiences and experience some skills in virtual reality. Similarly, people can now connect through virtual career fairs and professional metaverse platforms to look for job opportunities, get mentors, or network with professionals with similar ideas. In this case, the metaverse will transform the way people learn and enter the job market in a virtual environment that will be well-connected and vibrant. Nevertheless, the metaverse as a form of learning has limitations and challenges (Kye et al., 2021).

10. Metaverse: A Catalyst for Continuous Learning and Growth

In transforming digital technologies, the future metaverse can be a solution implementation of the opportunity to maintain the learning process and the individual's ability to develop. A new social communication moderator, a space for more freedom, creation, and sharing – realization of virtualization – can be a medium for integrating LLL and CSCD into the E-learning system (Zhang et al., 2022). Learning experiences can also be interactive and collaborative in the metaverse, where students can learn from one another, try various teaching subjects, solve problems, and pursue projects creatively, depending on the topic. Integration of technology is also need of the hour (Gupta et al., 2024).

Additionally, the metaverse allows students to access various educational opportunities and learning resources without regard for the territorial principle (Cai et al., 2022). For example, students can attend workshops online, take learning simulations, and play games that have been shown to enhance student learning.

Thus, the metaverse could also mean closing the gap between theory on education and its practical application to the real world (Belmonte et al., 2023). Students will also have the opportunity to apply what they have learned and practice working in virtual duty, similar to computer game scenario software, allowing them to gain experience and skills demanded by employers that are fully transferable (Kye et al., 2021). Therefore, the metaverse might revolutionize education opportunities and ways of mastering skilling, reskilling, and upskilling, positioning the young digital age to succeed.

11. Challenges and Considerations in Metaverse Education Systems

The introduction of the Metaverse into educational systems is thus a double-edged sword, offering a variety of benefits and difficulties which teachers and policymakers must manage swiftly and appropriately. Among the key problems is the creation of equal conditions for engaging students in learning experiences offered in the Metaverse, as the lack of homogeneity in technology access and the level of digital literacy in use can add inequality among learners into the existing educational inequalities. Besides, such an immersive nature of the Metaverse implies that the teachers and learners have to fulfill some essential digital skills requirements, therefore, it totally calls for really high-quality digital literacy teaching. The policy challenge that centers on privacy and safety is also featured; therefore, mechanisms need to be implemented that guarantee the protection of students' personal information and a secure virtual learning space. Furthermore, mainly, ensuring the quality of content and training in cyber environments becomes even more critical for better learning experiences.

Thus, to do this well, we need to align our curriculum well and apply pedagogical concepts seriously. Emphasizing on the expenditures linked to infrastructure and technology is another strike, especially in institutions with smaller incomes. Moreover, a surgeon's ethics and attitude toward treatment have a profound influence on how the patient views potential medical procedures. The next element of the e-learning ethic is inclusion, where learners can participate in the learning process without respect to their cultural and ethnic background. Stakeholders such as teachers, parents, and school administrators must actively leverage the transformative opportunities presented by the Metaverse in education to propel learning into the digital age.

However, any technology can raise specific issues and concerns. There are three main points to worry about and ensure the necessary measures are taken regarding the metaverse. The first is when a metaverse can cause weaker connections and get into the virtuality that harms genuine human relationships. In contrast, improper data privacy and attacks can also affect human privacy. Second, there may be issues concerning using the metaverse, such as committing a crime or having an identity and moral problems before students have established personalities. Third, since students may need help adapting to the real world after using a metaverse, there is a danger that students will be maladapted. Despite these issues, the metaverse has excellent potential for the further evolution of education. Educators will be able to reap the rewards of metaverse-based instruction. It is also the responsibility of teachers to implement the possibility of designing classes that promote learning by problem-solving, collaboration, and creativity. There is a chance that specially made metaverse platforms will have different levels of privacy and security that could be abused.

Despite the critical points in implementing metaverse education systems, such as weakened social connections, problems of confidentiality, and maladaptive shifts, the metaverse is invariably a new social communication space and a new environment for immersive and interactive learning. To implement it fully, the teacher should focus on more detailed work to study the student's metaverse understanding, develop interdisciplinary learning activities, and create secure learning platforms. Thus, it would be appropriate to conclude that the trend of the metaverse has transformed the educational space into a new social environment and learning place (Cai et al., 2022).

Therefore, education stakeholders must embrace the metaverse for the sake of teaching and learning transformation (Kye et al., 2021). In conclusion, based solely on this lit review, it can be stated that according to the perspectives above, the metaverse possesses the power to transform the very stage of education with a novel social communication channel and transformative learning (Zhang et al., 2022). The entire education spectrum is suggested to embrace the metaverse and explore how it transforms the instruction profession (Kye et al., 2021).

12. Conclusion

To sum up, Metaverse plays the role of a modern and innovative platform for improving the employee's skills. It fully matches the rapidly developing context of the digital age (Kye et al., 2021). This can enable virtualized learning to offer new ways for interactions, artistic expression, and creativity. At the same time, it can address the division among students in education through different collaborative channels. The integration with skilling initiatives would allow organizations and educational institutions to create diverse and exciting learning environments that would answer the needs of every learner. These measures provide a platform for the incubation of new talents and retaining of the already existing skills, thus giving rise to employment markets that are focused on growth and adaptability. Furthermore, Metaverse enables new communication paths and educational opportunities that can change and reshape the skilling, reskilling, and upskilling programs (Zhang et al., 2022). Therefore, the stakeholders involved in efforts to equip individuals with the necessary skills to succeed in the digital age should be champions of the Metaverse and call for revolutionary change. Through the Metaverse, we will open up new avenues for ability, allow people to triumph in the ever-changing digital world, and design a future based on education and labor that is more equal and creative.

References

Aggarwal, V., Yadav, P. D., Singh, V. K., & Dash, S. (2021). Sustainable behaviour and social media: A study of centennials attitudes towards sustainable advertising. *World Review of Entrepreneurship Management and Sustainable Development*, *17*(6), 777. https://doi.org/10.1504/wremsd.2021.118653

Barráez-Herrera, D. P. (2022, May 5). Metaverse in a virtual education context. *Metaverse*, *3*, 1807. https://doi.org/10.54517/met.v3i1.1807

Belmonte, J. L., Sánchez, S. P., Moreno-Guerrero, A., & Lampropoulos, G. (2023, January 31). Metaverse in education: A systematic review. *Revista de Educación a Distancia*, *23*(73). https://doi.org/10.6018/red.511421

Cai, S., Jiao, X., & Song, B. (2022, January 18). *Open another door to education – Applications, challenges and perspectives of the educational metaverse*. https://doi.org/10.54517/met.v3i1.1798

Chua, H. W., & Yu, Z. (2023, May 18). A systematic literature review of the acceptability of the use of metaverse in education over 16 years. *Journal of Computers*, *11*, 615. https://doi.org/10.1007/s40692-023-00273-z

Contributors, F. (2023, July 25). *How the metaverse is shaping the future of education.* https://www.financemagnates.com/forex/education-centre/how-the-metaverse-is-shaping-the-future-of-education/

Gupta, A. K., Aggarwal, V., Sharma, V., & Naved, M. (2024). Framework to integrate education 4.0 to enhance the e-learning model for industry 4.0 and society 5.0. In A. K. Gupta (Ed.), *The role of sustainability and artificial intelligence in education improvement* (pp. 151–167). Chapman and Hall/CRC.

Gupta, A. K., Aggarwal, V., Yadav, P. D., Naved, M., Dash, S., & Chandwani, T. (2022). *Effectiveness of technological based classroom engagement* [Conference session]. 2022 3rd International Conference on Intelligent Engineering and Management (ICIEM).

Gupta, A. K., Dash, S., Aggarwal, V., & Yadav, P. D. (2022). *Critical success factors influencing success of sMEs* [Conference session]. 2022 3rd International Conference on Computation, Automation and Knowledge Management (ICCAKM).

HVAC. (2012, July 2). *Refrigeration, & electrician training school.* Refrigeration School, Inc. (RSI). https://www.rsi.edu/

Kabilan, S. J. (2023, April 1). *Teaching and learning in the metaverse world: The future of new-gen education.* https://journaleet.in/download-article.php?Article_Unique_Id=JPR1966&Full_Text_Pdf_Download=True

Kaddoura, S., & Husseiny, F. A. (2023, February 13). The rising trend of metaverse in education: Challenges, opportunities, and ethical considerations. *PeerJ. Computer Science, 9*, e1252. https://doi.org/10.7717/peerj-cs.1252

KLM. (2021, March 16). *VR Owl.* https://www.vrowl.io/klm-pilot-vr-training/

Kye, B., Han, N., Kim, E., Park, Y., & Jo, S. (2021, December 13). Educational applications of metaverse: possibilities and limitations. https://doi.org/10.3352/jeehp.2021.18.32

Manrai, R., Yadav, P. D., & Goel, U. (2022). Factors affecting adoption of digital payments by urban women: Understanding the moderating role of perceived financial risk. *Technology Analysis & Strategic Management*, 1–13.

Purdy, M. (2022, April 5). *How the metaverse could change work.* https://hbr.org/2022/04/how-the-metaverse-could-change-work

Quakenbush, S., & Oliver, M. (2023, October 13). How the metaverse is revolutionizing employee upskilling and credentialing. *Training Industry.* https://trainingindustry.com/articles/learning-technologies/how-the-metaverse-is-revolutionizing-employee-upskilling-and-credentialing/

Rodon, G., Chinen, M., & Angel-Urdinola, D. (2023, September 12). *Unleashing the metaverse for skills and workforce development.* World Bank Blogs. https://blogs.worldbank.org/en/education/unleashing-metaverse-skills-and-workforce-development

Singh, P., Dash, S., Gupta, A. K., Singh, N., & Yadav, P. D. (2023, December). *Utilizing blockchain for effective urban street vendor management* [Conference session]. 2023 4th International Conference on Computation, Automation and Knowledge Management (ICCAKM) (pp. 1–5). IEEE.

Singh, V. V., Singh, H., Gupta, A. K., & Yadav, P. D. (2022). *Cryptocurrency as a hedging alternative-DCC GARCH model analysis using R programming* [Conference session]. 2022 5th International Conference on Contemporary Computing and Informatics (IC3I) (pp. 1529–1533). https://ieeexplore.ieee.org/abstract/document/10073144/

Skillveri. (2023, August 22). *World's leading metaverse XR simulation platform.* https://skillveri.com/

TechRepublic [@techrepublic]. (2020, May 20). How virtual reality is changing UPS employee training. *Youtube.* https://www.youtube.com/watch?v=Khwp8W5cfQ0

Volkswagen. (2021, May 25). *VR Owl.* https://www.vrowl.io/volkswagen-assembly-vr-training/

Walmart [@WalmartCorporate]. (2018a, February 9). Bringing VR to the classroom. *Youtube.* https://www.youtube.com/watch?v=QF45wunTMQk

Walmart [@WalmartCorporate]. (2018b, May 30). VR headsets train associates in-store. *Youtube.* https://www.youtube.com/watch?v=F1FQ5cYpvh4

Zhang, X., Chen, Y., Hu, L., & Wang, Y. (2022, October 11). The metaverse in education: Definition, framework, features, potential applications, challenges, and future research topics. *Frontiers in Psychology, 13,* 1016300. https://doi.org/10.3389/fpsyg.2022.1016300

Part D

Potential Present and Future of Metaverse Technology

Chapter 11

Metaverse and Wellness Tourism: An Investigation on Mixed Reality (MR) Health Care Approaches in the Tourism Industry

Saranya Thaloor

Department of Mass Communication, SK Somaiya College Somaiya Vidyavihar University, Mumbai, India

Abstract

The main purpose of this chapter is to study and analyze the impact of metaverse (mixed reality) on health tourism in the major tourist destinations in India and the global market. This chapter is made as a case study with detailed mentions of factors for tourism promotion for metaverse, sustainability, and crisis management. This chapter has tried to explain the role of the metaverse in tourism marketing and the cognitive level of influence the metaverse possesses among tourists which makes them prefer repeated visits. Also, the chapter tried to assess the existing conditions in the tourism industry which positively or negatively impact the health sector due to the role of metaverse. This chapter ends with giving inspirational notes to future researchers to examine the conceptual understanding of metaverse as a major tool for destination tourism emphasizing health, wellness, and happiness.

Keywords: Mixed reality; wellness tourism; augmented reality; wellness retreats; virtual reality; experiences; revisit intention

Introduction

The tourism industry is having a tremendous impact due to the revolutionizing power on creating repercussions by the entry of information and communication technologies (ICT). Drastic transformations in the tourism industry were highly visible due to the involvement of technological advancements in all sectors especially tourism development (Buhalis, 2003). Late in 17th century, when a team of people were given the opportunity to travel around Europe labeled as grand tour with the idea of educating and informing the world on history, art, and cultural practices of European countries, that was considered as the footprints for the beginning of tourism in the global level (Enzensberger, 1996). Nowadays people prefer traveling in the pretext of medical reasons and also for the sake for detoxing and relaxing themselves for the purpose of wellness and wellbeing (Koncul, 2012). As part of this ongoing trend, the flourishing of the tourism industry is offering more opportunities for blending tourism concept for the sake of health, wellness, and relaxation (Tabish, 2012). The idea of tour or travel becomes planned and organized from one place to another for medical aid, recovery, wellness and that gets accepted globally for its both physical and mental aid for health it offers (Carrera & Bridges, 2008). The terms like medical, wellness, preventive, and rehabilitation are all connected well with the idea of health tourism (TRAM, 2006). The current study aims to understand the role of metaverse (mixed reality) in the tourism sector especially in the field of health and wellness. The study also tries to analyze the role of the emotional status of a tourist and the various levels of instincts he or she possess that lead them to the experience of wellness or health tourism. The study also explained the preservation of the interest of the tourist which can also facilitate the tourist to go for revisit intention in the minds of tourists. The inferences and findings of this study can contribute to the addressing of the following research questions:

a) Does the variable called hedonic pleasure play a significant role in the generation of rehabilitation and support for the health tourism of a visitor?
b) Do financial status play a mediator role for the rehabilitation and support of the tourist by creating memorable experiences?
c) Do health avatars bring a change in the medical tourism field especially with reference to mixed reality and medical tourism?

> There are numerous studies on tourist satisfaction and engagement in health tourism. However, there is a lack of research on the impact of the metaverse on tourism in the health sector, health data management, and tourist privacy. This is the main area where the researcher is planning to conduct further research.

The Role of Mixed Reality in Tourism Sector

The presentation of the real world in an augmented way for the end users is defined as mixed reality. There will be a clear cut association between real and digitally created environments in mixed reality and it offers realistic experience for the users without compromising the beauty of the manifestation of the environment

(Rauschnabel, 2021). The involvement of technology in offering the mixed reality (MR) to the users are of a greater extent and level by equipping them with usage of various types of Hardware, multiple sensors to observe and analyze the environment (Rauschnabel, 2022). The realistic environment is mixed with technology and the experience is rendered to the audience without compromising the significance of 3D or similar content made out of augmented. The advancements of technology, namely, augmented reality (AR)/virtual reality (VR)/MR provides participatory and interactive involvement using digital technologies. All these provide their unique qualities and contributions to the tourism industry (Hausman & Siekpe, 2009). Technology has deeply contributed to the development of the travel and tourism industry to flourish over the decades due to the involvement of high-end technological tools to create interest and prevail the interest in the minds of the tourist visiting the destinations (Guerra et al., 2015). AR, VR, and MR provide participatory experiences without spoiling the comfort level of home but allowing visualizing the content more creatively (Huang et al., 2016; Tussyadiah et al., 2017). Technological advancement paves the way for better impact and influence of mixed reality on tourists while planning for a trip to the destinations. Even though the mixed reality factor can't play any important role in preventing the issues in this sector, but it is efficient enough to bring the feel and presence of physical environment to the end user (Huang et al., 2016). When explaining this study, the variable health is simply mentioned as "health is like money, we never have a true value until we lose it". The increased importance of healthy lifestyles and mindful eating has resulted in the preference of healthy choices for pampering themselves after tough work pressure. The popularity of the idea-3A (Action, Amusement, and Adventure) related to health and tourism over 3S (Sun, Sea, Sand) brings a clear picture about the high-level acceptance of technology called metaverse in the changing health sector (Białk-Wolf et al., 2016).

Mixed Reality and Health/Wellness Tourism

Regardless of the growing interest in discussing the various aspects of tourism using AR and VR, there is still a dearth of research studies on the potential benefits and drawbacks analysis of various aspects of tourism on a broader level. Many others have discussed and presented that mixed reality which is a combination of virtual and AR brings the experience of real and digital world immersion for the end user and giving them the opportunity to interact with the similar ones (Benckendorff et al., 2014).

High-end immersive technologies are playing a key role in transforming the communication network across many applications which can clearly influence or alter the experiences of the end user in different ways (Mahamoud, 2022). The real owners of various sectors can involve immerse technologies (AR, VR) for modification of the existing situations or increase stakeholder participation, launch of new products or facilities in the market to get more recognition among the users (Abdelmaged, 2021). The data of role of mixed reality in health care sector in Fig. 1 explain that there is a steady increase in the preference of MR in healthcare sector.

While coming to the most preferred functions of metaverse in health tourism, Fig. 2 mentioned below gives the exact purpose of health tourism preferred by the audience.

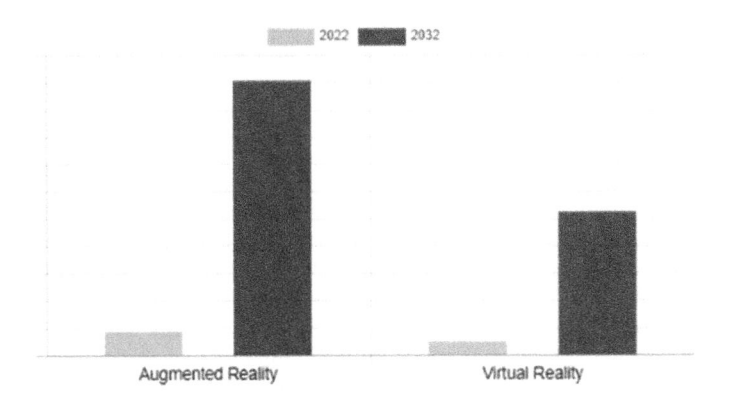

Augmented reality held the highest revenue in 2022 and is anticipated to continue its dominating over the forecast period

Fig. 1. Mixed Realty in Healthcare. *Source*: Mixed Reality in Healthcare Market Size, Share, Competitive Landscape and Trend Analysis Report by Type, by Component, by Application, by End User: Global Opportunity Analysis and Industry Forecast, 2023–2031. Jun 2023, Report Code: A11440, Author Name(s): Rohini Dnyandeo Kale and Surya Sanka.

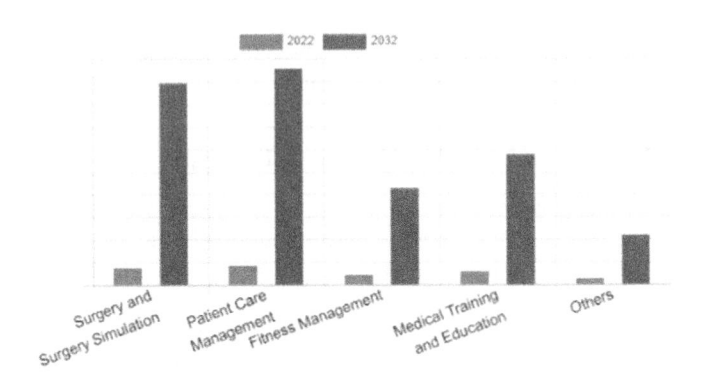

Patient care management held the highest revenue in 2022 and is anticipated to continue its dominating over the forecast period

Fig. 2. Mixed Realty in Healthcare Market. *Source*: Mixed Reality in Healthcare Market Size, Share, Competitive Landscape and Trend Analysis Report by Type, by Component, by Application, by End User: Global Opportunity Analysis and Industry Forecast, 2023–2031. Jun 2023, Report Code: A11440, Author Name(s): Rohini Dnyandeo Kale and Surya Sanka.

Wellness tourism research papers are in the field of tourism marketing and lack the study and analysis of comfort, wellness, and medication with tourism opportunities. The significance of mixed reality to foster medical tourism is also in the primary stages of development (Chi et al., 2020). The positive side of wellness and treatment tourism will have social, economic impact factors of human wellbeing which can bring in depth development of a nation as a whole concept (Kazakov & Oyner, 2021). The opportunity of travel and avail wellness treatments across the globe for affordable healthcare facility has drastically increased the popularity of the term-medical and wellness tourism (Intelligence, 2020). A healthcare mechanism without compromising qualitative services in low budget expenses with the aid of mixed reality can make the tourism industry flourish for years (Connell, 2023).

Metaverse: A Tool to Revamp the Travel Industry

Historical Insights of Wellness Tourism

The most common definition of tourism is mentioned as the attempt to experience and observe different cultural practices with the blend of treatment, wellness activities and leisure, and when the tourist comes out of his usual environment for a particular time period for a specific purpose (Shah & Shende, 2017). According to The Medical Tourism Global Market Report, 2023, the international medical tourism market is spontaneously growing USD 35.7 billion in 2022 to USD 40.1 billion in 2023 at a compound annual growth rate of 11%. The idea of medical or wellness tourism has a long history of existence in India as well as globally. The travel angle for treatments and wellness programs started getting momentum in the recent times in which the role of new media for the promotion of such initiatives are commendable (Nilsson, 1998). When coming to the history behind the origin of health tourism, it was found that Greek pilgrims who had traveled to Mediterranean town of Epidauria (Balaban & Marano, 2010). Many research papers had mentioned the close relationship between religion and health where sacredness in temple visits and healthy thermal baths associated to culture as well.

Later when health began to be incorporated with the tourism industry, it started bringing combination success stories with technology on a wide level. In that case, the role of metaverse in tourism, especially in health tourism, is making notable transformations in the sector which will benefit the country and global market too. The World Health Organization (WHO) was very keen in observing the impact of technology especially immersive technologies in the case of promoting health tourism. There are some parameters advised by WHO for maintaining balance in tourism growth with the interference of technology. It includes the maintenance of quality products and services, the formation of regulatory bodies and bringing filtered accreditation, ensuring that no compromise is being taken place in ethical considerations, integration of methods for better patient services (Timothy et al., 2006).

The Entry of Metaverse in Tourism Industry

In the travel and tourism industry, the term "metaverse" has become a heated topic of discussion (Buhalis, 2019). The role of metaverse in tourism industry was found to be a positive initiative which can bring potential advantages for the marketing process, opportunity for the different sectors of people to be a part of responsible tourism and creation of experiences that are similar to reality at the same time posing the issue of disadvantages on sustainable tourism initiatives too (Godze Ozdemir, 2022). The tourists experience the physical ambience of the destination through visual sensations supported by the metaverse leading to strong intention of purchasing power of the destinations in the mind of end user (Kim & So, 2022; Godovykh & Tasci, 2020).

The Indispensable Role of Metaverse in Sustainable Wellness Tourism

Several research papers have already been published in the analysis where the significance of metaverse on sustainable tourism is clearly mentioned. Metaverse can contribute to the opening up of alternative and local community participative measures and resource utilization for sustainable tourism. The utilization of resources and tourism products according to the United Nations (UN) Sustainable Development Goals (SDGs) could lead to the betterment of the tourism industry with the angle of preserving tourists products for many more generations (Loureiro et al., 2020).

The specific feature of "trial before usage" is the significant user selling point of metaverse in the tourism sector. In the context of sustainable tourism, metaverse also provides the opportunity for the tourists who possess interest to visit the destination but lack the action stage of reaching the destination (Gursoy et al., 2022). The role of metaverse in wellness tourism brings the relevance of metaverse to treat COVID-19 pandemic and mental health of the patients using VR (Ahmadi et al., 2022). A case study in United Arab Emirates (UAE) where the launch of metaverse hospital took place in doctor-patient discussion and consultation using virtual and AR avatars (Hasan, 2022). The avatar facility to chat with doctor opened up the opportunity to sustainable practices in medical sector especially giving clear picture on how the hospital is, the facilities in the hospital in the UAE hospital.

New Initiatives in Tourism with the Role of Mixed Reality in Health Sector

The transformation happening in ICT is having severe impact in the tourism sector which includes end user requirements to the destination management (Buhalis, 2003; Buhalis & Law, 2008). The combination of ICT and tourism termed as e-tourism is contributing to the revamping and reforming the management and marketing of tourism destinations in several innovative ways like the use of avatars, e-consultation, e-visualization of the destination and many more (Egger Buhalis, 2008).

Many research papers have already studied the utility of small technologies for accessible tourism. The concept of information poor among visually impaired tourists had gone for a complete revamp due to the new trend of Smartphone Accessible tourism (Lam et al., 2020). There were also case studies in Hong Kong on improving the traveling experience for challenged tourists where VR was employed well to make them motivate to enjoy the destination in all possible ways (Ribeiro et al., 2018).

In the case of wellness tourism, there exists three-layer architecture which brings the metaverse significant in this field. The layers of wellness metaverse (Duan et al., 2021) including interaction, metaverse ecosystem, infrastructure for the tourists. There are many innovations in health tourism that includes avatar doctor, the experience of digital hospital facilities by metaverse for the end users which ultimately augment the interest of the tourist to experience the reality aided by metaverse (Go & Gretzel, 2009).

There are many literatures available which highlighted the innovation of VR technology used across globe to offer relax mode of experiences to the end users (Beták et al., 2023). In the case of Thailand, through the immersive technology named – Bitkub Metaverse, the Tourism Authority of Thailand (TAT) launched projects in the year 2023 to establish zones and organize events in the physical and virtual worlds. Their goal was to use Metaverse technology's potential to revitalize Thailand's tourism industry. Together, a specialized structure was created on Bitkub. The metaverse will act as a central location for information about travel to Thailand by this initiative. Famous tourism destinations in Thailand were incorporated into Bitkub Metaverse to motivate users. Using digital coupons and NFTs, tourists can interact with Bitkub Metaverse attractions, which are presented as pop-up seasonal events. Activities are made by combining the virtual world with 3D images and videos from actual sites to encourage sustainable tourism all the year especially focusing on wellness tourism where the user aims for maximum space for bringing memorable experiences in the form of wellness and health improvements (Chulaphan et al., 2018).

Another example of South Korea can also be seen in this wellness tourism and role of immersive technologies for augmentation of better experiences on health improvement. This is consistent In Korea while (Kim & Hall, 2019) using AR and VR principles to enhance travel experiences, it makes use of metaverse technology to improve tourism in both the real and virtual worlds. It is up to the visitors to choose a tour guide in the language of their choice. After then, a virtual guide appears and gives thorough explanations of the location's significance where in the case of wellness it facilitates the patient or end user with better access to the resources (Suanpang et al., 2022).

Crisis Management in Tourism and the Role of Metaverse

In the context of crisis management in the tourism sector, there comes the significance of two major terms namely mobile tourism and stationary tourism in which moving tourism is the traditional method of tourism and traveling experiences and the latter specifically mentioning the enjoyment of tourism using technology. The chance of visiting a tourist destination is also there for stationary tourist inspired by the visual representation of the same (Monaco, 2021).

The role of phygital tourism is also significant during crisis times as it offers innovative methodologies to link physical and virtual environments form the foundation in creating memorable experiences in the mind of the end user (Moreira et al., 2021). In the case of the hospitality sector, a hotel company citizen is the pioneer to implement metaverse to promote tourism marketing in the form of avatars to position their brand in the market using technology more effectively (Utkarsh, 2021).

Challenges in Tourism Promotion Utilizing the Technology of Metaverse

The tourism industry includes the components mainly services, goods, travel experiences, travel and hospitality, entertainment, and the level of satisfaction and enjoyment of social, cultural, and environmental raw materials (Bellato et al., 2022). Along with this concept, the metaverse encompasses the significance of extra elements which can contribute to the most splendid tourism experiences beyond the physical spaces (Happ & Ivancsó-Horváth, 2018). Due to the effect of the pandemic, many of tourists still prefer alternative forms of tourism with less mobility, experiencing the features offered in four walls which can be considered as a major challenge of tourism due to pandemic (Urry & Griego, 2016). The major challenge in this field is the digital divide ratio between different categories of tourists. These groups of people face problems in navigating the technology-rich avatars, virtual space ethical constraints which can restrict the growth of tourism using immersive technologies (Doyle, 2009). The problem of restricting one's privacy due to the involvement of avatars along with cyber-attacks can be a major hindrance in tourism sector due to the increased role of metaverse (Rehm et al., 2015). Major case study to be added in this part is the features of google art and culture which can accelerate the tourism process which can also facilitate the end user to use the aid of technology for tourism destination exploration.

Survival Strategies of the Tourism Industry with the Aid of Metaverse

According to the tourism sector is considered as the major area of development and innovation under the metaverse. Due to the visual features and characteristics of the metaverse, there will be a transformation in customer preference for destinations in the coming years (Glover, 2022). The mixed feelings of end users to distinguish the real and manmade spaces will impact the cognitive process of the tourists which needs to be studied in detail. Tourism marketing should be focused on bringing measures to overpower the negative impacts of the metaverse where virtual and personal space will be mentioned (Buhalis et al., 2023). This understanding can bring major growth of the tourism sector even during crisis times (Rauschnabel, 2022). The precautionary aid of privacy and security boundaries should be catered by a technical expert so that metaverse will not negatively impact the tourism sector (Dwivedi et al., 2022). With all these measures, metaverse can a be the sole supporter for the tourism industry especially during a crisis where more virtual avatars can satisfy the tourists with memorable experiences (Sheper & Speros, 2022).

Immersive Technology for Sustainable Tourism

Sustainable tourism always seeks to adopt a holistic approach in bringing all the stakeholders in the tourism sector to work together in promoting the tourism growth for future generations also (Pollock, 2019). Technological advancements can be used to bring sustainable development in tourism by participating local population and reducing digital divide among the community (Gretzel et al., 2020). Immersive technologies which are highly visual and self-explanatory will aid more benefits for this sector leading to the qualitative growth of tourism (Mihalic et al., 2021). Immersive technologies have also contributed to the positioning of sustainable efforts in the tourism sector which will improve tourism sites, inhabitants, and their lifestyle and repeated visits of the tourists to the destinations (Balletto et al., 2022).

Major Tourism Practices for Sustainable and Responsible Tourism

Spenceley et al. (2002) explained that responsible tourism is a process through the fostering of enhanced tourism and destination experiences, empowering the local inhabitants, preserving natural resources, and better economic and societal outcomes. The impact of responsible tourism initiatives on local communities is considered the most significant one in the case studies available in the academic domain (Frey, George, 2010).

The studies available also say that the factors, the expenses to meet the demands of responsible tourism and the lack of authority support for the same restrict the states from bringing innovative tourism projects aiming for sustainable development. The campaign named "Travel for Life" initiated by the ministry of Tourism propagated the idea of creating a tourist crowd who are responsible for bringing awareness to the concept of sustainable tourism using various media platforms. This campaign was considered as successful one from the effort to convert the inflow of tourists more committed and socially responsible for destination marketing (Gagneet Kaur, 2022). Along with this campaign, other two initiatives namely responsible traveler campaign and the global tourism plastics initiative also impacted the flow of tourists post-COVID times stressing more on green and sustainable tourism initiatives. In the Indian context, Apollo's group of medical sectors invested in the greatest and most advanced technologies in the world. The Apollo Telemedicine Networking Foundation (ATNF), founded in 1999, was the pioneer in launching the country's first rural telemedicine center (Nair & George, 2016). The telemedicine program can be used to improve its medical tourism business. At this point, Apollo should aim to connect its medical tourism activities with telemedicine initiatives, as telemedicine offers a very good alternative for preliminary and post-treatment consultations which can be quoted well for medical tourism using technology.

Crisis Management Case Studies of Tourism Destinations

A crisis occurs when unexpected events affect the perceptions of various publics involved and that situation negatively affects the outcome and expectations (Coombs, 2012). According to Heath (1998), the principles needed to manage crises in the tourism sector are the sense of responsibility, the spirit of coordination, and the willingness to implement changes. The beginning of setting up a crisis management communication system using technology was considered the most novel method for tourism promotion in Kerala post-crisis times (Agarwal, 2018). The process of including all business sections under e-governance and e-booking in the tourism sector in the era of information superhighways was the most innovative idea adopted by many states for sustainable and profitable tourism (Gowrishankar, 2004).

In a case study on Greek tourism and the crisis management strategy, it was clearly stated that the factor of high-level loyalty played a major role in the crisis management mechanism in Greece along with the fostering and identifying of the concept micro-level destinations. The issue of the refugee crisis also pointed out in Greece but was well managed by the team resulting in more inflow of tourists to the destinations (Chung & Buhalis, 2008).

Kerala

The tourism industry in Kerala had met a continuous crisis which equipped them with technology and other similar immersive technologies to become more responsible and sustainable in the tourism sector. Due to its characteristic crisis.Ininked with many industries, the tourism sector is found highly vulnerable to crisis. In the case of Kerala tourism, it was clearly found that after the natural disaster, the tourists lost confidence and trust in selecting the destination for their vacation. The lack of credibility on safety and stay facilities which can contribute to not only state issue also national level defect too.

The two aspects of crisis management include proactive and reactive natures (Pauchant & Mitroff, 1992) where Kerala also had followed the same pattern of taking necessary precautions before the crisis comes because of the first flood effects. The reactive part of Kerala crisis management happened after one crisis occurred followed by the second one where they accepted the damage and achieved the state of stability back. There was a very effective campaign to manage the crisis due to monsoon floods in Kerala titled "Kerala's Open" which emphasized more on employment regeneration for better livelihood as a social responsibility in association with Samsonite also.

Kashmir and Assam

During the crisis times, Kashmir and Assam tourism had made moderate level of pre-crisis preparations in which the role of social media was considered as a notable role for tourism promotion (Abdul Gani et al., 2021). In the case of Assam, special emphasis was given to the identify and mitigate of earthquakes by making the tourists aware about the crisis with the help of various media specially social media.

In the case of Kashmir, where health tourism is developing gradually, the state follows the twin policy of lessening human made pollution and unrest and turmoil over the years. The State has thus adopted the twin principle of minimizing human suffering during disasters and reduction of financial losses through integration of DRR activities into development planning. After multiple crisis due to several wars in Kashmir, the tourism industry had a huge set back. The data clearly show that 26.73 lakh tourists have visited Kashmir in the year 2022 with a huge spike which can be attributed to crisis management strategies of the state.

Metaverse Shaping Tourism Policies and Facilities for Better Experiences

Contribution of Metaverse in Health Tourism Which Can Hold the Tourists with Better Experiences and Revisit Intention

The health and wellness industry are expected to show a huge spike reaching the net worth of $180 billion by 2024 which may reach $210 billion by 2027, even the pandemic had ceased the complete industry for more than two years (Vagena, 2021). There is also a tendency of more innovations in the field of tourism especially in medical tourism which can actually bring notable changes in this field (Millar, 2015). The experiences of tourists after the medical facility availing undergo a complete makeshift with the aid of metaverse where the option of try "prior to purchase" opportunity which they can try from their convenient place where booking is carried out along with the sense of motivation also (Gursoy et al., 2022). Metaverse can influence and advance healthcare services in the future. According to the World Health Organization (WHO) immersive technologies play a significant role to make the health patients in the usage of the technology. As a result, it finds that metaverse can facilitate the process of treatment in a fast and smooth way (Ahmadi et al., 2022).

As part of sustainable development, environmental issues at well-known tourist locations have raised awareness of sustainable tourism. Protecting the environment from negative development externalities, as well as ensuring environmental preservation, community involvement, and other benefits, were the primary objectives of sustainable development (Guo & Wang, 2021). It was not until the 1990s that the concept of "sustainable tourism" began to take shape, with an emphasis on mass tourism as opposed to tourism that grows sustainably. Thus, in the context of the tourism industry, sustainable tourism is a component of sustainable development. Its main goals are the protection of society, the economy, and the environment (Yang et al., 2023).

The application of sustainable development ideas in tourism firms is very uncommon. This is because tourism-related enterprises are only partially accountable for social and environmental protection expenses in their commercial calculations. In actuality, the most popular solutions are those that are low-cost (making pamphlets, labeling the location, etc.), aid in cost reduction (energy conservation in hotels, recycling), enable better brand positioning for businesses to set themselves apart from the competition, and elicit a favorable response from customers (Sharpley Telfer, 2008). These methods bring more awareness to the publics using social media which became an important interactive platform for discussions relating to tourism marketing (Leung et al., 2013). Later the importance of sustainable tourism using metaverse also came to highlight the importance of tourism promotion.

Empowering Tourism Industry for Sustainable Transformation

To boost the tourism sector, the Tourism Ministry of India has recently launched new programs such with Swadesh-Darshan and Prasad, they updated programs like hunar-se-rozgar Tak and continued to offer E-tourist Visas to several countries. They also created a mobile application for travelers and established an Incredible Indian Tourists helpline (Praveen & Kambar, 2019).

Due to overcrowding taking place in major tourism destinations and as a result, environmental deterioration is occurring in many developing nations, necessitating the development of sustainable tourism policies and resources, which are then very beneficial in promoting the allegiance of tourists (Buhalis, 2003). Nonetheless, sustainability concerns reveal heterogeneity across dimensions and require an appropriate structure. Every dimension has an impact that differs depending on the destination and the role and influence of the specific community (Kruja & Hasaj, 2010). Sustainable tourism gained more momentum with the aid of media and the information dissemination on tourism marketing which mentioned on creation of memorable experiences across the globe.

Media Intervention for Health Tourism Promotion Using Metaverse

In this information society, information through digital technologies and also using artificial intelligence has become a part and parcel of everyone's life (Al Emran et al., 2018). In the case of tourism, social media has played a major role in making people aware of the destinations and educated them with the happenings on spots to visit and facilities for the tourists. The entry of social media has led for a paradigm shift in the tourism communication strategies leading for more sustainable tourism practices' entry of metaverse (VR and MR) to tourism industry can be traced back to few years only (Koo et al., 2022).

It is important to note that India's travel and tourism sector ranks seventh globally and contributes approximately 9.8% of the country's GDP. In the next ten years, it is predicted to increase by 7.8% annually, making it the fourth largest in the world. This is anticipated to construct infrastructure to have a multiplier effect on India's socio-economic growth, generation of jobs and improvement of skills. In India, the approach to sustainable tourism is to offer visitors in ecotourism featuring wildlife, tribal tourism, village homestays, and silk tourism in a responsible manner (Carrerio, 2018). The entry of metaverse made the process of sustainable tourism more innovative and easy for the generation Z and alpha better than the generation Y who had depended completely on social media for tourism information (Buhalis & Law, 2008). The idea of metaverse and virtual experiences in the form of avatars for facilitating the potential of hospitality and tourism has started influencing the stakeholders and altering their perspective on tourism in a more positive way (Buhalis & Karatay, 2022). Tourism industry seeks the support of various media stakeholders in bridging the relationship between tourism and hospitality sector and employing metaverse for better results in the field (Davis et al., 2009). The feature of virtual presence and participation in metaverse has attracted tourism sector and adopted methodologies in the form of more travel experiences beyond physical challenges (Gössling & Schweiggart, 2022). The introduction of applications which showcases mobile features, immersive virtual experiences, virtual accommodation facilities using metaverse has clearly brought changes in the field of tourism. The role of media in bringing awareness on these properties also seems to be quite satisfactory (Shen et al., 2021). Media should play a prominent role in developing better metaverse environment and proper planning for studying the uses of metaverse for the tourism industry (Kwon & Koo, 2022). Many research papers have stressed the importance of media and metaverse tourism where the idea of metaverse in reconnecting the real world by inventing various models which are socially, politically, culturally, and economically significant for tourists (Shen et al., 2021). Media started giving the public information about 3D avatars facilitating tourism in a better way blending VR and the real experience in such a way resulting in better smooth interactions (Dwivedi et al., 2022). When social media used to infotain the audience the privilege of posting, tagging and vlogging on tourism destinations, metaverse gives more experiences where they can restrict their movement and enjoy the same feel and satisfaction (Kaplan & Shiff, 2016). This is more in the case of wellness tourism where the virtual experiences provide multiple opportunities on products, services and facilities in detail (Blackshaw & Nazzaro, 2006).

Awareness Programmes and Role of Media in Bringing Awareness on Metaverse Opportunities for the Tourists in Choosing Destinations

In the tourism sector, metaverse is still considered as in an infancy stage which can progress in the coming years to a stupendous level. Smart Tourism Destination (STD) incorporates innovation in information technology in the travel and tourism sector which can offer many developments and innovations interlinked with metaverse almost uses technology to bring utility, satisfaction and memorable experiences for tourists thereby contributing for the economic growth of a country. Using metaverse in healthcare sector, tourism brings more health assistance using advanced technology which can make people visit the destination for treatment or any wellness programme and also for relaxing themselves. Social media plays a major role in informing the audience about health care initiatives and treatment offers using metaverse (Sebastian & Rajagopalan, 2009). The increased and improved role of immersive technologies have made a revolutionized change in the field of tourism by making the facilities available for consumers very promptly (Dwivedi et al., 2022; Gursoy et al., 2022; Wei, 2022).

Recognizing Opportunities and Scope of Skill Management in Metaverse Tourism

When the tourism industry uses VR and AR for presenting tourism campaigns and information, then labeling of virtual tourism starts getting better coverage among the end users (Lu et al., 2022). These metaverse technologies help to consume the content in diverse methods by various strata of audiences (Ilkhanizadeh et al., 2020). It was found that these areas of excellent combination of real world and virtually made world in tourism sector can be focused in the coming years for more research contributions (Richards, 2018).

There is a new trend of gamification where the usage of AR and VR is combined for providing wellness information and fitness content completely guided by health experts. There is also an application using metaverse which brings the idea of walk or be mobile so that you can earn well also which provides financial incentives also to the stakeholders involved in it (Sigala, 2020). Medical institutions are trying to incorporate AR and VR in curriculum to make people aware of the possibilities of wellness and health tourism in our nation and also abroad. The feature of visualization of the procedures in the most available format makes metaverse more effective in tourism sector (Shin & Kang, 2020).

Implications to Industry Stakeholders in Tourism Sector

Integrated efforts by various stakeholders to bring stakeholders in a collaboration effort for eradicating patient's anxiety of experimenting the immersive technology in health sector and offer the most valuable experiences for the patient or end user. Industry professionals can offer training and workshops for medical students facilitating them to equip them with advanced technology usage for giving the best treatment opportunities for the end user. Industry experts can also concentrate on more marketing research in this field to understand the behaviors and preferences of end users preferring health tourism. Framing industry standards with incorporating technology in the health care sector also brings sustainable development in this field which can be performed by the experts from this industry.

Our research also suggests that industry marketers should think about leveraging technology interaction on social media to foster more on Artificial Intelligence and immersive technologies along with its co-creation and repurchase intention from a managerial standpoint in the field of health tourism. To promote positive cognitive information exchange among patients and wellness end users, marketers should think about interacting with them through interactive material that is contemporary, current, and amusing in the form of avatars and other telecommunication methods. The objective is to enhance consumers' cognitive processing, attachment, and activation (CBE), so fortifying their inclination to jointly generate brand value for mixed reality and make future repeated visits in tourism sector due to the involvement of mixed reality.

In the point of more investment and revenue, marketers need the help of influencers to find and distribute information about their favorite technology adopted in tourism through social media. This provides engaging material and makes MR interaction easier, such as end-user recommendations for specific items and incorporating the most recent news and changes in the field.

Conclusion

This paper has brought the cross-sectional approach to studying the effectiveness of metaverse in health tourism which is properly grounded on tourist psychology and marketing. As we had dealt with immersive technology and health tourism, this study offers the potential to improve health care availability for the end user with the aid of technology with global-level connectivity to boost the international tourism market.

When it comes to managerial implications, the study was able to understand the need for support for better policies and strategies in this sector in a public/private partnership mode. Despite advancements in the industry's expansion, patients' demands from different cultures and nations have become more varied, and their expectations for the caliber of medical travel have grown, reflecting cultural and familial preferences (Connell, 2013). The top preference for this sector is given for sustainable tourism practices which can be also seen visible in the efforts made by various destinations. The branding of Indian healthcare tourism using the blend of traditional and contemporary cultural roles also gain momentum in the study where the need for domestic advertising getting upgraded to high-end technology used brand promotion of this sector. The feature of physical and virtual spaces for health measures in tourism will make tourism marketing a top-grade strategy contributing to upward progress in national development. In the case of crisis and pandemic also metaverse proved to act as a major tool to facilitate the significance of health measures of destinations across the globe which will offer better amenities for the end user to healthcare and wellness. Taking advantage of this nexus between technology and health tourism is essential to opening new doors and meeting the changing demands of an increasingly interconnected world.

Key Takeaways and Inspiration for Future Research

Major research studies give this research a broad understanding of strategies that can be employed for the betterment of health tourism sector with the support of advanced technological developments.

The study brings the ideas like

- The joint marketing of medical tourism information system and tourism activities in all the major tourism destinations in India can bring the sector to an upward developmental process in the coming years.
- If the role of information technology with latest developments is catered with more expertise from the area, then the tourism will be the major development contributor in India and in global market.
- The role of Governmental organizations to cater and inspire to bring responsible tourism, green tourism, and other similar initiatives to manage crisis will reflect health sector also with tremendous developments.
- The adoption of localization angle in health tourism brings more end users to the industry where the local inhabitants involvement results in much more scope and significance for health tourism.
- Incorporating global level health practitioners and cultural health practices will yield more results in the industry, which was highly stressed throughout the study.
- The lesser-known tourist destinations can also be added to this area as an experiential effort without much role for culture.
- A scope for psychological empowerment of the tourists will also be done thereby making a holistic approach to study metaverse on tourism destination visits.
- SDGs can be defined as supportive data to mold better sustainable activities in tourism sector in the form of environment conservation and technology literacy.

- Efficient data driven decision making for better innovation in the field of health tourism.
- The proper and timely implementation and revision of policies in tourism with technology is also the need of the hour using various stakeholders in the industry.
- There needs to be widespread level of demonstration of safety aspects for patients and tourists on incorporating mixed reality in wellness tourism to avoid any unpleasant experience for the patients and tourists.
- The possibility of imagination using visual elements by the immersive technologies in wellness tourism also brings the scope of getting potential guests' preference for booking intentions.
- With the help of mixed reality in the tourism department, cross-border collaborations with other countries can also be recommended which can overall lead for tourism development using advanced technology.

References

Agarwal, B. (2018). Gender equality, food security and the sustainable development goals. *Current Opinion in Environmental Sustainability, 34*, 26–32. ISSN 1877-3435.

Abdelmaged, M. A. M. (2021). Examining the impact of omnichannel retailing on buying intention using binary models. *Empirical Quests for Management Essences, 1*(1), 13–23.

Ahmadi, A., Noetel, M., Parker, P., Ryan, R. M., Ntoumanis, N., Reeve, J., Beauchamp, M., Dicke, T., Yeung, A., Ahmadi, M., Bartholomew, K., Chiu, T. K. F., Curran, T., Erturan, G., Flunger, B., Frederick, C., Froiland, J. M., González-Cutre, D., Haerens, L., ... Lonsdale, C. (2022). A Classification System for Teachers' Motivational Behaviors Recommended in Self-Determination Theory Interventions. 10.31234/osf.io/4vrym.

Al-Emran, M., Mezhuyev, V., Kamaludin, A., & Shaalan, K. (2018). The impact of knowledge management processes on information systems: A systematic review. *International Journal of Information Management, 43*, 173–187.

Balaban, V. & Marano, C. (2010). Medical tourism research: A systematic review. International. *Journal of Infectious Diseases, 14*. 10.1016/j.ijid.2010.02.1784

Balletto, G., Ladu, M., Camerin, F., Ghiani, E., & Torriti, J. (2022). More circular city in the energy and ecological transition: A methodological approach to sustainable urban regeneration. *Sustainability, 14*(22), 14995. https://doi.org/10.3390/su142214995

Bellato, L., Frantzeskaki, N., Fiebig, C. B., Pollock, A., Dens, E., & Reed, B. (2022). Transformative roles in tourism: Adopting living systems' thinking for regenerative futures. *Journal of Tourism Futures, 8*, 312–329.

Benckendorff, P., Sheldon, P. J., & Fesenmaier, D. R. (2014). *Tourism information technology*. CABI.

Beták, N., Csapó, J., Horváth, Á., & Dávid, L. D. (2023). Virtual tour as a virtual experience of destination management organisations in Slovakia. *GeoJournal of Tourism and Geosites, 47*(2), 508–514. https://doi.org/10.30892/gtg.47218-1050

Białk-Wolf, A., Arent, M., & Buziewicz, A. (2016). *Analiza podaży turystyki zdrowotnej w polsce*. Polish Tourism Organization.

Blackshaw, P., & Nazzaro, M. (2006). *Consumer-generated media (CGM) 101: Word-of-mouth in the age of the web-fortified consumer*. Nielsen BuzzMetrics.

Buhalis, D. (2019). Technology in tourism-from information communication technologies to eTourism and smart tourism towards ambient intelligence tourism: A perspective article. *Tourism Review*. 10.1108/TR-06-2019-0258.

Buhalis, D. (2003). *eTourism: Information technology for strategic tourism management*. Pearson (Financial Times/Prentice Hall).
Buhalis, D., & Karatay, N. (2022, January). *Mixed reality (MR) for generation Z in cultural heritage tourism towards metaverse* [Conference session]. ENTER22 e-Tourism Conference (pp. 16–27). Springer, Cham.
Buhalis, D., & Law, R. (2008). Progress in information technology and tourism management: 20 years on and 10 years after the Internet – the state of eTourism research. *Tourism Management, 29*, 609–623.
Buhalis, D., Leung, D., & Lin, M. (2023). Metaverse as a disruptive technology revolutionizing tourism management and marketing. *Tourism Management, 97*, 104724.
Carrera, P., & Bridges, J. (2008). *Health and medical tourism: What they mean and imply for health care systems?* HanserVerlag.
Carrerio, H. (2018). Available at https://kaziranganationalparkassam.in/guest-reviews/
Chi, C. G.-Q., Chi, O. H., & Ouyang, Z. (2020). Wellness hotel: Conceptualization, scale development, and validation. *International Journal of Hospital Management, 89*, 102404. https://doi.org/10.1016/j.ijhm.2019.102404
Chulaphan, W., & Barahona, J. (2018). Contribution of disaggregated tourism on Thailand's economic growth. *Kasetsart Journal of Social Sciences, 39*(3), 401–406. 10.1016/j.kjss.2017.07.012.
Chung, J. Y., & Buhalis, D. (2008). *Information needs in online social networks*. Information Technology
Connell, J. (2013). Contemporary medical tourism: Conceptualisation, culture and commodification. *Tourism Management, 34*, 1–13.
Coombs, W. T. (2012). *Ongoing crisis communication: Planning, managing, and responding* (3rd ed.). Sage.
Davis, A., Murphy, J. D., Owens, D., Khazanchi, D., & Zigurs, I. (2009). Avatars, people, and virtual worlds: Foundations for research in metaverses. *Journal of the Association for Information Systems, 10*(2), 90–117. https://doi.org/10.17705/1jais.00183
Doyle, L., Brady, A.-M., & Byrne, G. (2009). An overview of mixed methods research. *Journal of Research in Nursing, 14*(2), 175–185. doi:10.1177/1744987108093962
Dwivedi, Y. K., Hughes, L., Baabdullah, A. M., Ribeiro-Navarrete, S., Giannakis, M., Al-Debei, M. M., Dennehy, D., Metri, D., Buhalis, B., Dimitrios ... Samuel. (2022). Metaverse beyond the hype: Multidisciplinary perspectives on emerging challenges, opportunities, and agenda for research, practice and policy. *International Journal of Information Management, 66*. https://doi.org/10.1016/j.Ijinfomgt.2022.102542
Dwivedi, Y. K., Hughes, L., Ismagilova, E., Aarts, G., Coombs, C., Crick, T., ... Duan, Y. (2021). Artificial Intelligence (AI): Multidisciplinary perspectives on emerging challenges, opportunities, and agenda for research, practice and policy. *International Journal of Information Management, 57*, 101994. ISSN 0268-4012.
Egger, R., & Buhalis, D. (2008). Part Six. *ETourism Case Studies: Management and Marketing Issues*, 417.
Enzensberger, H. M. (1996). A theory of tourism. *New German Critique, 68*, 117–135. https://doi.org/10.2307/3108667
Frey, P. & George, P. L. (2010). *Mesh Generation*. New York: Wiley-ISTE.
Gani, A., Asjad, M., & Talib, M. (2021). Prioritization and ranking of indicators of sustainable manufacturing in Indian MSMEs using fuzzy AHP approach. *Materials Today: Proceedings, 46*(15), 6631–6637. ISSN 2214-7853. https://doi.org/10.1016/j.matpr.2021.04.101; https://www.sciencedirect.com/science/article/pii/S2214785321029977
Glover, G. (2022, February). *Bank of America shares how to invest in the metaverse and 13 other disruptive technologies that could transform our lives and become a market worth over $6 trillion by 2030*. https://www.businessinsider.com/investing-strategy-tech-6g-metaverse-flying-cars-ai-moonshots-2021-9

Go, H., & Gretzel, U. (2009). *Web 3.0: Tourism in virtual worlds* [Conference session]. Proceedings of the HITA 2009 conference, Anaheim, CA, June 21–22.

Godovykh, M. & Tasci, A. (2020). Customer experience in tourism: A review of definitions, components, and measurements. *Tourism Management Perspectives*, 10.1016/j.tmp.2020.100694.

Gössling, S., & Schweiggart, N. (2022). Two years of COVID-19 and tourism: What we learned, and what we should have learned. *Journal of Sustainable Tourism*, 30(4), 915–931. https://doi.org/10.1080/09669582.2022.2029872

Gowrishankar, N. (2004). Medical tourism in India: Strategy for its development. Crisil Young Thought Leader Series, p. 6.

Gretzel, U., Fuchs, M., Baggio, R., Hoepken, W., Law, R., Neidhardt, J., Psonen, J., Zanker, M., & Xiang, Z. (2020). E-tourism beyond COVID-19: A call for transformative research. *Information Technology & Tourism*, 22, 187–203. 10.1007/s40558-020-00181-3

Guerra, J. P., Pinto, M. M., & Beato, C. (2015). Virtual reality-shows a new vision for tourism and heritage. *European Scientific Journal*, 11, 49–54.

Gungor, I., Berrin, G., Beyza, M., Buyukgebiz, Y., Selin, B., Miray, G. O., Gozde, I., Suna, O. O.. (2023). Evaluation of the effectiveness of artificial intelligence for ultrasound guided peripheral nerve and plane blocks in recognizing anatomical structures. *Annals of Anatomy – Anatomischer Anzeiger*, 250, 152143. ISSN 0940-9602, https://doi.org/10.1016/j.aanat.2023.152143; https://www.sciencedirect.com/science/article/pii/S0940960223000985

Guo, C., & Wang, H. A. (2021). *Study on the application of virtual reality in the marketing of rural cultural tourism in Hubei Province* [Conference session]. Proceedings of the International Conference on Culture-Oriented Science & Technology (ICCST), Beijing, China.

Gursoy, D., Malodia, S., & Dhir, A. (2022). The metaverse in the hospitality and tourism industry: An overview of current trends and future research directions. *Journal of Hospitality Marketing & Management*, 31, 1–8.

Happ, É., & Ivancsó-Horváth, Z. (2018). Digital tourism is the challenge of the future. A new approach to tourism. *Knowledge Horizons Economy*, 20, 9–16.

Hassan, S. M., Rahman, Z., & Paul, J. (2022). Consumer ethics: A review and research agenda. *Psychology Marketing*, 39, 111–130. https://doi.org/10.1002/mar.21580

Hausman, A. V., & Siekpe, J. S. (2009). The effect of web interface features on consumer online purchase intentions. *Journal of Business Research*, 62, 5–13.

Heath, R. (1998). *Crisis Management for Managers and Executives*. Financial Times, Pitman Publishing, London.

Huang, Y. C., Backman, K. F., Backman, S. J., & Chang, L. L. (2016). Exploring the implications of virtual reality technology in tourism marketing: An integrated research framework. *International Journal of Tourism Research*, 18(2), pp. 116–128.

Ilkhanizadeh, S., Golabi, M., Hesami, S., & Rjoub, H. (2020). The potential use of drones for tourism in crises: A facility location analysis perspective. *Journal of Risk and Financial Management*, 13(10), 1–13. 10.3390/jrfm1310024

Intelligence, M. (2020). Medical tourism market | Growth, trends, forecast (2020–2025). *Mordor Intelligence*. Retrieved August 8, 2020, from https://www.mordorintelligence.com/industryreports/medical-tourism-market

Kaplan, L., & Shiff, M. (2016). Mapping Ararat: An augmented reality walking tour for an imaginary Jewish homeland. *Anthrovision. Vaneasa Online Journal* (4.2).

Kim, M. J, & Hall, C. M. (2019). A hedonic motivation model in virtual reality tourism: Comparing visitors and non-visitors. *International Journal of Information Management*, 46, 236–249. https://doi.org/10.1016/j.ijinfomgt.2018.11.016

Kim, H., So, K. K. F. (2022). Two decades of customer experience research in hospitality and tourism: A bibliometric analysis and thematic content analysis. *International Journal of Hospitality Management, 100*, 103082. https://doi.org/10.1016/j.ijhm.2021.103082

Kazakov, S., & Oyner, O. (2021). Wellness tourism: A perspective article. *Tourism Reviews, 76*, 58–63. https://doi.org/10.1108/TR-05-2019-0154

Koncul, N. (2012). Wellness: A new mode of tourism. *Economic Research-Ekonomska Istraživanja, 25*, 525–534. https://doi.org/10.1080/1331677X.2012.11517521

Koo, C., Kwon, J., Chung, N., & Kim, J. (2022). Metaverse tourism: Conceptual framework and research propositions. *Current Issues in Tourism, 26*, 3268. https://doi.org/10.1080/13683500.2022.2122781

Kruja, D., & Hasaj, A. (2010). Comparisons of stakeholders' perception towards the sustainable tourism development and its impacts in Shkodra region, Albania. *Turizam, 14*, 1–12.

Kwon, J., & Koo, C. (2022). TechTalk with the editors of journal of travel research: The perspectives of technology by Dr. Nancy G. McGehee and Dr. James Petrick. *Journal of Smart Tourism, 2*(1), 1–3.

Lam, K. L., Chan, C.-S., & Peters, M. (2020). Understanding technological contributions to accessible tourism from the perspective of destination design for visually impaired visitors in Hong Kong. *Journal of Destination Marketing & Management, 17*, 100434, ISSN 2212-571X, https://doi.org/10.1016/j.jdmm.2020.100434. (https://www.sciencedirect.com/science/article/pii/S2212571X20300561)

Leung, D., Law, R., Van Hoof, H., & Buhalis, D. (2013). Social media in tourism and hospitality: A literature review. *Journal of Travel & Tourism Marketing, 30*, 3–22. 10.1080/10548408.2013.750919.

Loureiro, S. M. C., Guerreiro, J., & Ali, F. (2020). 20 Years of research on virtual reality and augmented reality in tourism context: a text-mining approach. *Tourism Management, 77*, 104028.

Lu, L., Lee, L., Wu, L., & Li, X. (2022). Healing the pain: Does COVID-19 isolation drive intentions to seek travel and hospitality experiences? *Journal of Hospitality Marketing & Management, 31*(5), 1–20. https://doi.org/10.1080/19368623.2022.2029726

Millar, M. R. (2015). The choice to travel: Health tourists and the spread of antibiotic resistance. *Public Health Ethics, 8*(3), 238–245.

Mihalic, T., Mohamadi, S., Abbasi, A., & Dávid, L. (2021). Mapping a sustainable and responsible tourism paradigm: A bibliometric and citation network analysis. *Sustainability, 13*, 853.

Mohammed, I., Mahmoud, M. A. & Hinson, R. E. (2022), The effect of brand heritage in tourists intention to revisit. *Journal of Hospitality and Tourism Insights, 5*(5), 886–904. https://doi.org/10.1108/JHTI-03-2021-0070

Monaco, S. (2021). *Tourism, safety and COVID-19: Security, digitization and tourist behaviour* (pp. 1–182). Routledge.

Moreira, C. O., Ferreira, R., & Santos, T. (2021). Smart tourism and local heritage: Phygital experiences and the development of geotourism routes. In L. Oliveira, A. C. Amaro, & A. Melro (Eds.), *Handbook of research on cultural heritage and its impact on territory innovation and development* (pp. 206–232). IGI Global.

Nair, R., & George, B. P. (2016). E-learning adoption in hospitality education: An analysis with special focus on Singapore. *Journal of Tourism, Heritage & Services Marketing, 2*(1), 3–13. https://doi.org/10.5281/zenodo.3763

Nilsson, O. S., & Solgaard, H. S. (1995). The changing consumer in Denmark. *International Journal of Research in Marketing, 12*, 405–416.

Pauchant, T., & Mitroff, I. (1992). *Transforming the crisis-prone organization: Preventing individual, organizational, and environmental tragedies* (p. 227). Jossey-Bass.

Pekerşen, Y., & Kaplan, M. (2022). The perceptions of a local community on tourism development: The case of Akyaka as a Cittaslow. *Community Development*, *54*(2), 292–311. https://doi.org/10.1080/15575330.2022.2071956

Pollock, A. (2019). Inclusive and regenerative urban tourism: Capacity development perspectives. *Medium*, *7*, 943–961.

Praveen, S., & Kambar. (2019). The study of sustainable tourism: concerning Karnataka state. *Indian Journal of Research*, ISSN: 2250-1991.

Rauschnabel, P. A. (2021). Augmented reality is eating the real world! The substitution of physical products by holograms. *International Journal of Information Management*, *57*, 102279.

Rauschnabel, P. A. (2022). XR in tourism marketing. In D. Buhalis (Ed.), *Encyclopedia of tourism management and marketing*. Edward Elgar.

Rehm, S. V., Goel, L., & Crespi, M. (2015). The metaverse as mediator between technology, trends, and the digital transformation of society and business. *Journal of Virtual Worlds Research*, *8*, 1–6.

Ribeiro, Í., Pereira, R., Vidal Freire, I., Oliveira, B., Casotti, C., & Boery, E. (2017). Stress and quality of life among university students: A systematic literature review. *Health Professions Education*, *4*. 10.1016/j.hpe.2017.03.002.

Richards, G. (2018). Cultural tourism: A review of recent research and trends. *Journal of Hospitality and Tourism Management*, *36*, 10.1016/j.jhtm.2018.03.005.

Sebastian, L., & Rajagopalan, P. (2009). Socio-cultural transformations through tourism: A comparison of residents' perspectives at two destinations in Kerala, India. *Journal of Tourism and Cultural Change*, *7*, 5–21. 10.1080/14766820902812037.

Shah, G., & Shende, K. (2017). A study on the importance of Food Tourism and its impact on Creating Career Opportunities amongst the Residents of Pune city. *International Journal of Research in IT and Management*, *7*(3), 192–208.

Shen, B., Tan, W., Guo, J., Zhao, L., & Qin, P. (2021). How to promote user purchase in Metaverse? A systematic literature review on consumer behavior research and virtual commerce application design. *Applied Sciences*, *11*, 23. https://doi.org/10.3390/app112311087

Sheper, A., & Speros, W. (2022). *The hotel industry enters the Metaverse*. https://hospitalitydesign.com/news/development-destinations/hotel-industry-nfts-metaverse/

Shin, H., & Kang, J. (2020). Reducing perceived health risk to attract hotel customers in the COVID-19 Pandemic Era. Focused on technology innovation for social distancing and cleanliness. *International Journal of Hospitality Management*, *91*, 102664. https://doi.org/10.1016/j.ijhm.2020.102664

Sigala, M. (2020). Tourism and COVID-19: Impacts and implications for advancing and resetting industry and research. *Journal of Business Research*, *117*, 312–321. https://doi.org/10.1016/j.jbusres.2020.06.015

Sohn, J.-I., Alakshendra, A., Kim, H.-J., Kim, K.-H., Kim, H.-D. (2021). Understanding the New Characteristics and Development Strategies of Coastal Tourism for Post-COVID-19: A Case Study in Korea. *Sustainability*, *13*, 7408. https://doi.org/10.3390/su13137408

Spenceley, A., & Goodwin, H., & Maynard, W. (2004). *Development of Responsible Tourism Guidelines for South Africa*.

Suanpang, P., Niamsorn, C., Pothipassa, P., Chunhapataragul, T., Netwong, T., & Jermsittiparsert, K. (2022). Extensible Metaverse implication for a smart tourism city. *Sustainability*, *14*, 14027. 10.3390/su142114027.

Tabish, S. A. (2012). Healthcare: From good to exceptional governance. *JIMSA*, *25*, 147–150.

Telfer, D., & Sharpley, R. (2007). Tourism and development in the developing world. *Tourism and Development in the Developing World*. 10.4324/9780203938041.

Timothy, D., & Olsen, D. (Eds.). (2006). *Tourism, religion and spiritual journeys* (1st ed.). Routledge. https://doi.org/10.4324/9780203001073

TRAM (Tourism Research and Marketing). (2006). *Medical Tourism: A global analysis, a report by tourism research and marketing.* Atlas Publication.

Tussyadiah, I. & Wang, D. & Jia, C. (2017). *Virtual Reality and Attitudes Toward Tourism Destinations.* 10.1007/978-3-319-51168-9_17

Urry, J., & Griego, M. (2016). *Mobilities: New perspectives on transport and society* (pp. 1–384). Routledge.

Utkarsh, S. M. (2021). A bibliometric review of research on COVID-19 and tourism: Reflections for moving forward. *Tourism Management and Perspective, 40*, 100912.

Vagena, A. (2021). Second-home tourism present and future. The case of Greece. *International Journal of Scientific Research and Management, 9*, EM-2021. 10.18535/ijsrm/v9i12.em2

Wei, C., Li, J., & Guo, X. (2022). Influence analysis of hotel and tourism economic development based on computational intelligence. *Security and Communication Networks,* 7549628, 9. https://doi.org/10.1155/2022/7549628

Yang, Y., Gowhar, A. W., Nagaraj, V., Mohammad, H., Sameer, S., Hossain, Md. E., Kamal, M., & Shah. S. M. R. (2023). Progress in sustainable tourism research: An analysis of the comprehensive literature and future research directions. *Sustainability, 15*(3), 2755. https://doi.org/10.3390/su15032755

Chapter 12

Metaverse: A Game Changer for Reshaping the Fashion Industry

Reema Varshney[a] and Nimisha Rana Chaudhary[b]

[a]*Vidya Institute of Fashion Technology, Vidya Knowledge Park, Meerut, Uttar Pradesh 250002, India*
[b]*Department of Home Science, Dayalbagh Educational Institute (Deemed University), Agra, Uttar Pradesh 282005, India*

Abstract

This chapter reviews the Metaverse's inception and digitalization's impact on the fashion and apparel retail industry. This review demonstrates how digital clothing rooted in the Metaverse assists industry environmental sustainability, the planet, and consumers, providing business strategies for growth through research in theory and an analysis of practices. Virtual checkout uses digital tools to help marketers and designers better understand their target audience. In the foreseeable future, the Metaverse of our works will be a well-known and safe space for budding designers. Designers will find it much simpler to bring their concepts to life thanks to the immediate relationship that Metaverse technology creates with humans.

Eco-friendly methods and technology found in the Metaverse will transform the industry. Expanding acceptance of Metaverse could lead to a 97% decrease in the amount of carbon dioxide in approximately per item 4,000 L of water, reducing its carbon footprint by around thirty percent during the company's design and development phases.

Digital apparel may be extremely helpful leading up to the real physical manufacturing of a garment, applied to sampling, marketing and modeling prior the actual variants are put into manufacturing, significantly lowering the environmental impact of a clothing item's entire lifecycle. Computer-generated representations of clothing cannot replace real garments entirely, and they can help reduce waste and help address overproduction-related difficulties.

The Metaverse Dilemma: Challenges and Opportunities for Business and Society, 205–222
Copyright © 2025 by Reema Varshney and Nimisha Rana Chaudhary
Published under exclusive licence by Emerald Publishing Limited
doi:10.1108/978-1-83797-524-220241012

This chapter clarifies how digital fashion based on the Metaverse assists business environmental sustainability, users, and acts as a resource to improve approaches.

Keywords: Metaverse; reshaping; fashion industry; virtual environment; eco-friendly practices; innovative technology

1. Introduction

> I cannot wait to show the world what has developed since the last time we showcased the fashion revolution in the Metaverse on a grand stage. Within one year, we have shown the world one of the strongest and most obvious use cases for the Metaverse yet – digital fashion. (Dr Giovanna Graziosi Casimiro, Source: T. Waite, "Can the metaverse reshape the future of fashion in 2023?," Dazed, January 06, 2023)

The retail sector has experienced a significant upheaval in recent years, with physical storefronts becoming digitized (Jiang et al., 2021). Customers' behavior and spending were further impacted by the COVID-19 pandemic, which made merchants and enterprises rethink their strategies and increase their online presence (Jiang et al., 2021). Furthermore, technological advancements and digitalization continue to drive the world toward digitalization (Shankar et al., 2020). A growing number of customers are switching from traditional brick-and-mortar establishments to internet retailers these days. Consumers can enjoy a more convenient and customized purchasing experience with the aid of cutting-edge technologies (Shankar et al., 2020).

Consumer behavior has fundamentally changed as a result of new digital solutions, with an increasing number of people choosing to communicate with businesses online via tailored platforms and other digital channels (Barrera & Shah, 2023). The fashion business was one that was badly hit by the pandemic (Alexander & Kent, 2021). The industry was negatively impacted by growing online fashion sales and restricted access to physical stores. The global fashion sector was predicted to contract by 25–30% in 2020 as a result of the setbacks (Alexander & Kent, 2021). Retailers are currently searching for technologically advanced and new ways to update the sector in order to prevent being outdated. A new idea known as "digital fashion" has turned up as an outcome of the fashion industry's growing acceptance for combining digital and smart technologies (Baek et al., 2022).

The phrase was initially used in relation to the commencement of the 21st century saw the rise of e-commerce, when wearable computers were the standard word for digital fashion products. But as 3D and augmented reality (AR) have grown, the title "digital fashion" describes the concepts for clothing that use state-of-the-art technology like virtual design, body scanning, and 3D printing (Baek et al., 2022). With an increasing number of fashion companies exploring with AI,

AR, and Metaverse membership, digital fashion has gone even farther and grown more complicated than before (Fig. 1) (Baek et al., 2022). Retailers can adapt to technology by getting into the virtual world early on, and when it takes off, they can establish themselves as major figures in the Metaverse fashion industry (McKinsey, 2022).

1.1. The Rise of the Metaverse

Neal Stephenson launched Metaverse in 1992. He was a writer who foresaw the development of the online Metaverse in his book *Snow Crash*. *Snow Crash* served as inspiration for software engineers in 2003 when they launched the online "Second Life," an application that sanctioned users to generate cartoon icon and liaise with one another in a variety of digital environments (Hollensen et al., 2022). The failure of Metaverse to gain traction could be attributed to a number of problems, including technology and the constraints of devices and networks unable to handle 3D graphics (Lee & Kim, 2022). These days, Metaverse is frequently connected to popular business Meta. In 2021, the company's founder, Mark Zuckerburg, renamed it Meta to emphasize its intention to shape the Metaverse's future (Zuckerberg, 2021). Nowadays, there are numerous virtual Metaverse platforms due to the quick growth of innovation.

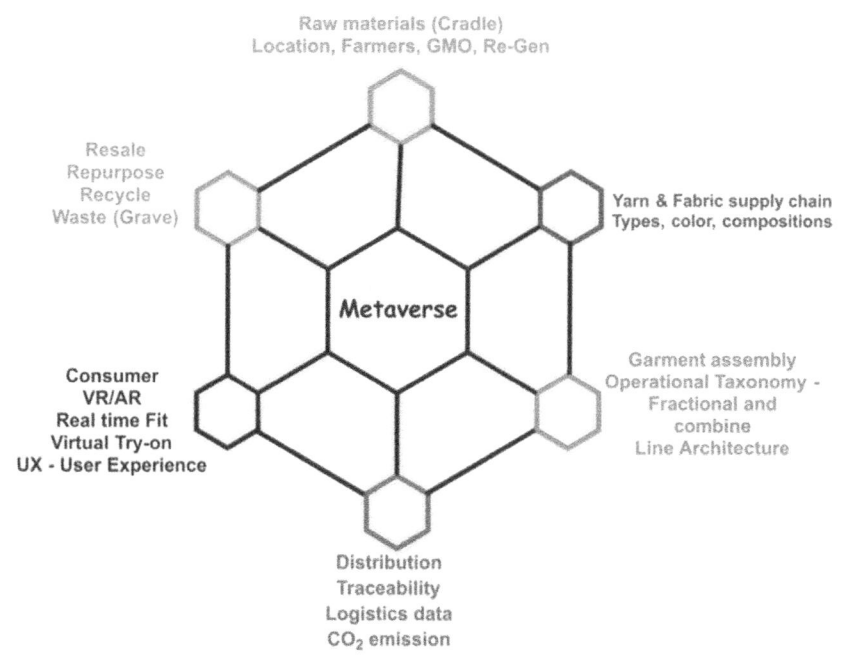

Fig. 1. Fashion Supply Chain Synchronization and Metaverse Transparency. *Source*: Periyasamy and Periyasami (2023).

Case Study 1: Roblox has 58.8 million daily active users worldwide and combines social networking, gaming, and e-commerce. Users can play games, interact with others, and exchange virtual currency in this ultimate virtual world. Roblox is used by a number of retailers in the sector, including Gucci and Nike (Reddit, 2019). Nike revealed in end of 2021 that "Nikeland," their own branded digital environment, would be arriving on Roblox. Fans can interact with numerous brand experiences, meet up, wear virtual Nike items, and play pre-made or customized games in the virtual world Nikeland (Hollensen et al., 2022). Whenever it concerns brands proving that a "sell the lifestyle" frame of mind functions just as well online just the same as offline, Nike is undoubtedly setting the standard (Marr, 2022). Moreover, the Nike-Roblox instance demonstrates that virtual platforms, content, services, resources, and customer and company behavior are the primary "visible" building blocks in fostering awareness of the company and involvement among prospective Nikeland customers and users (Hollensen et al., 2022).

Case Study 2: Early in the spring of 2021, Gucci held their inaugural Metaverse event on the Roblox Metaverse, called Guccis Garden. Over 20 million people visited the effort, demonstrating its success. Gucci Town is currently available on Roblox. A center garden links three unique zones, including a dining venue, an arcade region, and where visitors may buy Gucci products for their Roblox character. Commerce in Metaverse is a completely new and uncharted area of consumption.

The industry is shifting due to the rise of the Metaverse, and this phenomenon will also alter how people interact, produce value, and build civilizations (Lee & Kim, 2022). Big tech businesses are embracing Metaverse platforms to establish business models. Despite being at the cutting edge of Web 3.0's progress, the Metaverse is the subject of relatively little research (Lee & Kim, 2022).

1.2. Definition of Metaverse

Metaverse is defined as "a digital reality that combines aspects of social media, online gaming, AR, virtual reality (VR), and cryptocurrencies to allow users to interact virtually" (Belk et al., 2022).

McKinsey (2022) stated Metaverse as "an emerging 3D-enabled digital space that uses VR, AR, and other advanced internet and semiconductor technology to allow people to have lifelike personal and business experiences online".

Stephenson (2003) stated that "a world where humans as avatars interact with each other and with software agents in 3D space that reflects the real world."

Kim et al. (2012) stated Metaverse as "a collective online space created by combining some physical reality enhanced by a 3D virtu al world and a physically permanent virtual space."

Lee and Kim (2022) stated Metaverse as "the permanent, immersive, mixed reality world where people and people and objects can synchronously interact, collaborate, and live over the limitation of time and space, using avatars and immersion-supporting devices, platforms, and infrastructures."

While the focus and breadth of definitions vary, the term "Metaverse" is generally understood to refer to an online setting in which individuals can engage in virtual and AR interactions through semiconductor technologies and advanced internet. In summary, Metaverse refers to a 3D digital environment that integrates elements of social media, VR, AR, and cryptocurrency to enable individuals to engage in realistic online personal and professional interactions. The advent of Metaverse and its potential for further expansion are contingent upon the supporting factors of AI, AR, Web 3, blockchain, and hardware, as noted by McKinsey (2022).

1.3. Augmented and Virtual Reality

Technology known as AR blends virtual features put on top of real-world settings (Javornik, 2016; Watson et al., 2018; Wedel et al., 2020). According to Javornik (2016), AR adds images, videos, texts, and other virtual objects via digital devices, creating an illusion of space among the user and their physical surroundings. Although there are twelve different definitions of AR, scholars concur that its physical realms, location specificity, mobility, virtuality, synchronization of the digital and interactivity are its most prevalent features (Javornik, 2016).

According to Wedel et al. (2020), AR offers contextual data that enhances usability, appearance, and enjoyment, all of which contribute to a more engaging and dynamic experience.

VR creates an image of reality which is solely based upon virtual information, whereas AR enhances the impression of the physical world with additional data generated by computers (Wedel et al., 2020). Technology advancements in digital displays, computer vision, and computing and motion sensors are the main reasons why the technologies have begun to be used for marketing purposes (Wedel et al., 2020).

Moreover, it is expected that AR and VR will significantly alter the customer experience (Wedel et al., 2020).

Nowadays, companies are testing and utilizing AR technologies in a variety of scenarios. For example, with scanning a good's logo, customers can access digital content or examine a virtual product that has been placed in the surroundings (Javornik, 2016). Using AR in the manner of virtual try-ons and mirrors, wherein a display projects an imitation of the user's face or body with digital accessories like clothing and makeup, is a specific feature which has grown in demand in the fashion and cosmetic industries (Javornik, 2016). It has been demonstrated that using these technologies will boost revenues and purchasing intentions (Wedel et al., 2020). Virtuality can take on various forms (Javornik, 2016). Either the entire globe or just certain virtual elements, like virtual try-ons or avatars, might be seen on the screen. A virtual product simulation, as opposed to a standard website, can offer a greater sense of firsthand experience, which enhances customer engagement.

1.4. Web 3.0

Web 3.0 is the current replay of the World Wide Web (Belk et al., 2022). Web 3.0, according to Stackpole (2022), is an expansion of bitcoin that uses blockchain in novel ways to achieve novel goals. The "permissionless" blockchains that underpin Web 3.0 and cryptocurrencies have no central authority and do not demand knowledge from people about or could put your faith in others who choose to conduct commerce. When someone uses the term "blockchain," they mean this. Owners of Web 3.0 are its developers and consumers.

Furthermore, Web 3.0 is defined by Marr (2022) as a segregated internet that is based on disseminates innovations, i.e., blockchain and autonomous segregated entities (organization) (DAO) as opposed to being centralized on servers that are owned by people or businesses. In continuation Web 3.0, such as blockchain, cryptocurrencies powered by blockchains, i.e., NFT, Ethereum and Bitcoin has a significant impact on how we will utilize the Metaverse's digital realms for work, play, socializing, and education. The main reason that Web 3.0 and the Metaverse are related is that cryptocurrencies may serve as the Metaverse's monetary and economic frameworks.

Furthermore, according to Belk et al. (2022), major technological revolution could be Web 3.0 that allows for the decentralized and democratization of ownership, opening the door for new kinds of ownership. In conclusion, Solis (2022) noted that Web 3.0 is only the beginning and will open the door to greater growth, benefit, and availability.

1.5. Blockchain's Function in the Metaverse and Methods of Payment

A dataset which is accessible by every node in a computer network is what is known as blockchain. A blockchain is an electronic data storage system that works like a digital database. Blockchains are most commonly used in cryptocurrency systems such as Bitcoin, where they are indispensable to maintain a secure and decentralized ledger of transactions. Metaverse world without Blockchain would also be incomplete owing to the various drawbacks of centralized data storage; for these reasons, a major factor in the creation of the Metaverse is blockchain and offers security advantages.

For instance, users can purchase and sell virtual products and clothing in the Metaverse using blockchain-based cryptocurrency instead of relying on 14 conventional payment methods like PayPal or credit cards. In addition to lowering transaction costs, this can improve user security and privacy. There is a debate regarding currency in Metaverse, even though Blockchain was instrumental in creating the Metaverse. Hollensen et al. (2022) stated that bitcoins and electronic currencies are being in use more and more for in-game currency and initial user payments, as well as in games via non-fungible tokens and blockchain-based studios. So, in the grand scheme of things, it might also represent a fair installment of payment in the Metaverse. At the moment, a variety of payment options are accepted in Metaverse, including cryptocurrencies like Bitcoin, Ethereum, and other tokens based on blockchain technology, as well as more conventional options like PayPal and credit cards. For instance, on the Roblox gaming platform, users swap "Robux," or virtual currency, for real money like US dollars when buying and selling products (Roblox, 2023). But if the Metaverse develops further, it's possible that new creative and decentralized payment methods will show up, utilizing blockchain technology to build a virtual economy that is safer and more streamlined (Roblox, 2023).

2. Innovation Within Fashion Retail Industry

2.1. Fashion Industry

According to Noris et al. (2021), studying the fundamental consequences of digital transformation in the fashion sector is an exciting environment. The industry's role in the industrial revolutions and the importance of fashion in mass production today are the reasons behind this (Noris et al., 2021). Furthermore, Pedersen et al. (2018) clarify that the sector has developed into a worldwide enterprise with operations across several nations, regions, continents, and divisions. Fashion firms are beginning to address the negative effects of overconsumption, extensive resource use, and shorter lifespans of goods by strengthening their supply chain management (Pedersen et al., 2018). In addition, an increasing number of firms have incorporated sustainability measures as a means of offsetting disposable waste and pollution. Globalization and new communication technologies have made fashion faster and less expensive. As a result, fashion companies must adapt quickly in order to stay in business (Pedersen et al., 2018). Fast fashion is defined as clothing that is mass-produced and standardized. In their definition, Pederson et al. (2018) include the terms "cheap" and "low quality" (Todeschini et al., 2017). Kong et al. (2020), on the other hand, characterize luxury clothes as elegant, pleasurable, flimsy, and pretentious. According to Kong et al. (2020), despite the fact that many luxury firms engage in sustainability initiatives, consumer opinions toward sustainability in high-end clothing are contradictory. Noris et al. (2021) draw attention to the positive effects of fashion in addition to its negative effects, pointing out that it advances relationships between individuals as well as commercial endeavors and artistic, literary, and musical endeavors. Additionally, fashion connects many fields from disparate backgrounds by assisting people in communicating (Noris et al., 2021).

2.2. Fashion Retail

Most significant changes affecting retail industry nowadays are digitalization (Fig. 2) (Pantano & Vannucci, 2019). Retailers have adopted a variety of strategies in recent years to stay ahead of the digital transition, including interactive storefront windows, contactless payments, etc. Shankar et al. (2020) claim that COVID-19 epidemic had a significant influence on advancements in retail technology. The development of channels and touchpoints between businesses and customers has been pushed by technological advancements, changing the shopping know-how (Alexander & Kent, 2021). Moreover, Shankar et al. (2020) claim that artificial intelligence (AI), which is defined as machines, systems, algorithms,

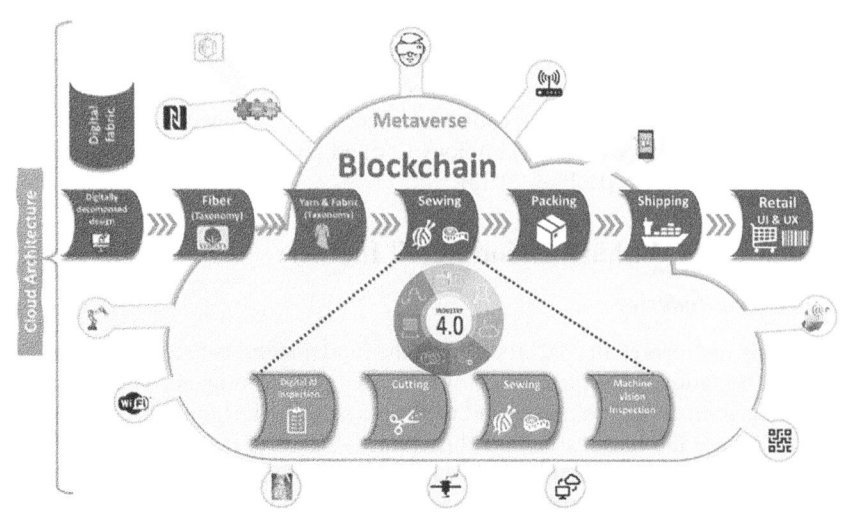

Fig. 2. Effects of the Metaverse that Are Projected on the Textile Manufacturing Sector. *Source*: Periyasamy and Periyasami (2023).

or programs that display intelligence, is responsible for the creation of many of these new technologies. Businesses can use AI to create more personalized recommendation systems, improve customer service, and manage relationships (Shankar et al., 2020). One instance is the business 17 Clinique, which used software to recognize and evaluate customers' skin types and send them customized email recommendations (Pantano & Vannucci, 2019). According to Alexander and Kent (2021), in order to meet consumer expectations for great service, personalization, and convenience, effective physical businesses must be both functional and innovative. As a result, the authors claim that in-store technologies can help satisfy these new requirements (Alexander & Kent, 2021). To ensure business profitability and competitiveness, Pantano and Vannucci (2019) add to this remark by adding that it is essential to continuously monitor and stay up with more complicated technologies. A number of writers have begun to draw attention to the growing online presence, which may eventually take the place of certain actual retail locations (Baek et al., 2022; Joy et al., 2022; Wedel et al., 2020).

2.3. Digital Fashion

The adoption of undifferentiated digital technologies, including wearables, biomaterials, AI, 3D printing and body scanning, AR, and VR, is causing a significant makeover in fashion sector (Fig. 3) (Baek et al., 2022). A new notion of "digital fashion" has emerged from the combination of fashion and information communication technologies (Baek et al., 2022; Noris et al., 2020). According to Baek et al. (2022), the definition that follows is: The definition of "digital fashion" comprises six pertinent themes: printing, supply, body, consumer, virtual, and design. It is virtual development, manufacturing, and representation of an individual's identity through CAD. The digital change that affects how firms

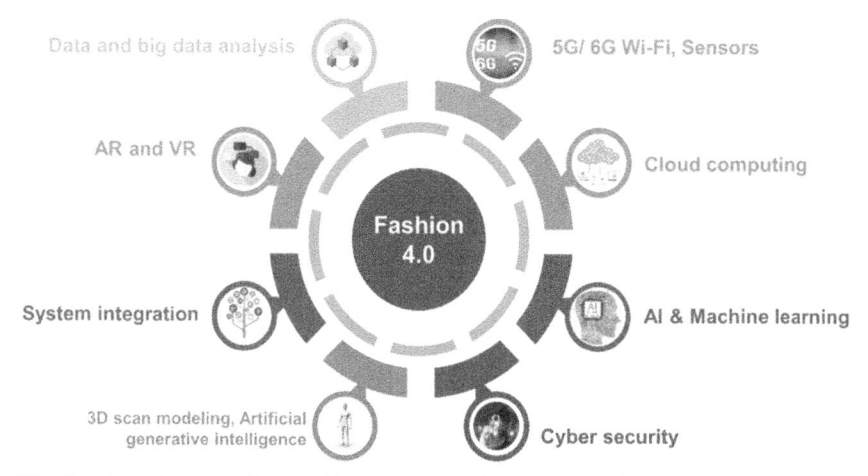

Metaverse: A Game Changer for Reshaping the Fashion Industry 213

Fig. 3. Fashion 4.0. *Source*: Periyasamy and Periyasami (2023).

design, create, and deliver fashion items is encompassed by all six topics (Baek et al., 2022). For instance, 3D body scanning and printing enables designers to use fewer samples, which lowers production and environmental expenses. Additionally, tangible fashion objects can be transformed into intangibles that customers can modify and print using technologies like AR and VR, making for a creative and engaging shopping experience. Baek et al. (2022) go on to say that smart technologies have a big impact on the user experience. A few fashion brands have advanced the customer experience by offering virtual avatar experiences that let users express themselves online in a virtual setting. Digital fashion and e-commerce platforms that offer fashion goods have historically been strongly associated (Baek et al., 2022). However, the idea has become more sophisticated due to the advancement of virtual and 3D technologies. Fashion firms are under pressure to innovate in response to current trends and technology, and an increasing number of them have begun experimenting with Metaverse (Baek et al., 2022; Joy et al., 2022). Joy et al. (2022) report that an increasing number of individuals are prepared to reimburse for digital fashion products (NFTs), allowing them to live twice in the Metaverse. Due to the growing amount of time that younger, tech-savvy consumers spend in virtual places, a number of fashion 19 businesses have begun to actively participate in these platforms. According to Joy et al. (2022), digital fashion will be essential in keeping customers interested as it will enable them to try on several appearances derived from digital clothing. Furthermore, with the aid of digital fashion, fashion firms hope to accomplish an integrated engagement and experience (Joy et al., 2022).

2.4. Role of AI in Metaverse and Fashion Marketing

We need to be aware of the fluid and infinite character of the Metaverse before we can investigate how AI might help with fashion marketing there. For every user, Metaverse helps to create experiences that are deeply individualized and captivating. We have a new, formidable model for fashion advertising when we combine these talents with AI's transformational potential. Few important possibilities are described below (Akram et al., 2022).

2.4.1. Visual Merchandizing Driven by AI

The conventional laws of both time and space are not relevant in the Metaverse, providing countless chances for marketers to showcase their goods. AI has the power to improve this by producing dynamic virtual presentations that are based on user choices, activities, and previous exchanges. Marketing can become more streamlined and individualized with the use of AI algorithms, which could present fashion goods that may catch the eye of a buyer.

2.4.2. AI Styling and Virtual Try-Ons

Through utilizing AI and AR, virtual try-ons have the potential to become a mainstay in the Metaverse. Customers may see how shoes, accessories, and clothing would seem on their virtual avatars, making the purchasing experience realistic.

Additionally, AI-powered styling helpers can expedite the decision-making process by giving outfit suggestions based on the user's body type, preferred styles, and even current fashion trends.

2.4.3. AI-Powered Content Production

By integrating AI, content marketing can take on an entirely novel role in the Metaverse. AI may be used by brands to create highly tailored promotional content that corresponds with the preferences and actions of consumers. AI can also be used to examine data on which marketing campaigns are most effective, creating campaigns that are more focused and effective.

2.4.4. Customized User Experiences

Within the Metaverse, AI may create personalized user experiences by monitoring interactions and responses in actual time and modifying the encounter accordingly. This makes it possible for a company to provide a customized purchasing experience, which improves customer engagement and, in turn, strengthens their bond with the brand.

Using AI to make fashion marketing in the Metaverse as immersive and individualized as possible is the main goal in each scenario. AI's role will surely grow as more firms invest in their Metaverse existence and consumers progressively embrace this new digital edge. Eventually, AI will play a crucial part in creative, inventive, and compelling fashion marketing in the Metaverse.

2.5. Examining the Way AI Is Actually Transforming Fashion Marketing

Fashion marketing is a prime example of how AI a rapidly developing technical breakthrough, is changing the dynamics of numerous industries. Fashion retailers are looking for ways to give more modified experiences, properly forecast trends, simplify distribution networks, and establish proficient procedures. All of these tasks are being revolutionized by AI. This is because they feel pressure to innovate continually and stay forefront of the curve.

Retailers may outperform their rivals in the marketing game by using AI-powered solutions that prioritize the needs of their customers. Fundamentally, today's fashion marketing is anticipating consumer preferences before they are even aware of them. AI maintains this through the use of predictive analytics. It makes use of enormous amounts of data to anticipate customer behavior, preferences, and purchasing patterns. This enables merchants to create effective marketing campaigns that connect shoppers on a human level. In fashion marketing, AI-enabled chatbots and virtual assistants are radically changing the nature of consumer engagement. In addition to offering clients individualized styling advice, product recommendations, and query responses, they are made to mimic human contact. The seamless purchasing experience provided by this real-time interaction greatly boosts consumer happiness and loyalty to the brand.

Many thanks to technologies like AI-based virtual try-on technology and automatic image identification, consumers can now use photos to search for apparel or virtually try on items before making a purchase. This leads to increased customer engagement by making shopping more engaging and participatory. The effect of AI on supply chain optimization and inventory management is equally important to notice. AI helps avoid surplus or shortages situations, minimize waste, and increase business margins by precisely forecasting demand.

Furthermore, AI's capacity to perform sentiment study by combing all the way through social media trends and conversations has proven crucial in swiftly spotting new fashion trends and modifying marketing plans to successfully incorporate them. Furthermore, the fashion industry's environmental initiatives have benefited greatly from AI. Fashion manufacturers are using machine learning algorithms to reduce waste and make more ecologically friendly manufacturing decisions. They display these efforts as part of their marketing campaigns to draw in eco-aware consumers.

3. AI-Driven Brand Innovation and Consumer Engagement

Within fashion marketing, AI has become a key factor in driving consumer engagement. It is being used in a variety of ways that call for investigation and evaluation.

Personalization: When it comes to their interactions with brands, consumers now want more individualized experiences. This is made possible by AI, which examines user behavior, behaviors related to purchases, social networking interactions, and surfing patterns. Brands can increase consumer engagement by utilizing AI to create hyper-personalized experiences. Customers find shopping more relevant and interesting when they receive product recommendation, for example, based on previous purchases/browsing patterns.

Chatbots and Virtual Assistants: With the potential to significantly impact customer engagement, AI-powered chatbots and virtual assistants are quickly emerging as a crucial customer care tool. These solutions offer individualized interactions and smooth, round-the-clock client service. They can exhibit products, respond to questions, and even complete purchases, greatly improving the clientele's experience.

Shopping Experiences: Brands may design immersive and engaging shopping experiences with the use of AI. Take virtual changing rooms as an illustration. Consumer involvement and happiness have increased significantly when they can try on clothing without having to leave their homes. Additionally, it aids in lowering the rate for item profits, boosting sales effectiveness.

Predictive analysis is the ability of AI technology to examine past data and forecast future patterns or consumer behavior. Because of this predictive research, personalized advertising tactics are developed that have a greater impact on consumers and increase engagement charge.

Response Analysis: AI may examine social media sites and other digital exchanges to determine how the general public feels about particular goods, services, or fashions. Gaining insight into consumer attitudes can assist fashion firms in modifying their approaches, such as communication plans, marketing tactics, and product designs, in order to improve customer involvement.

Voice Commerce: The growing trend of AI-powered voice-activated purchasing that offers customers even more convenience and encourages interaction.

3.1. Case Studies of Creative AI-Powered Marketing Initiatives in the Fashion Sector

Fashion brands are using AI-driven marketing campaigns to hold consumers and set themselves apart in a very cutthroat market. These initiatives are becoming more and more creative and inventive. After examining a few noteworthy examples are as follows (Source: digital nexa blog):

> **Case Study 1:** AI-Powered Personal Styling and Stitch Fix: To tailor clothing to each individual consumer, Stitch Fix, personal styling online service, primarily depends on machine learning and AI. The business analyzes customer preferences, responses using AI algorithms and past purchases. Their stylists use the data as a guide to make each client a unique wardrobe, which boosts customer engagement and the effectiveness of marketing campaigns.

> **Case Study 2:** Tommy Hilfiger, in association with **IBM** and The Fashion Institute of Technology (FIT), developed "Reimagine Retail," an AI-powered initiative with the goal of identifying innovative approaches to enhance comprehension of consumer preferences. The AI examines a variety of data sources, including as runway photos and customer evaluations, to assist designers in spotting market trends and ultimately promote brand innovation.

> **Case Study 3:** The AI-driven Virtual Models of Balmain: The French luxury company Balmain shocked the fashion industry by releasing Margot, Shudu, and Zhi, three AI-created digital supermodels.

These remarkably convincing virtual models garnered a lot of attention when they appeared in Balmain's advertisements. Additionally, tech-savvy younger audiences that are more receptive to digital experiences were reached and engaged by this innovation. Burberry's Use of AI in Social Media: Burberry creatively employed AI to announce the arrival of its spring/summer collection, on well-known channels like Facebook and Instagram. They employed a chatbot which offered consumers modified recommendations depending on what questions are being asked and in what series. Through this campaign an effective increase of customer involvement was noticed, almost every consumer shared their personal experiences online.

> **Case Study 4:** Adidas's Snapchat ad: Adidas collaborated with Snapchat to create an AR ad that featured users wearing their new sneakers, which was a novel method for the company to employ AI. Using AI, the campaign projected an online representation of Adidas's newest product on users' feet within Snapchat, creating a unique and incredibly captivating user experience.

4. Challenges and Opportunities

Technological Issues: Because of the complexity of technology, the high cost of AI systems, and the quick evolution of technology standards, creating and sustaining a higher technology ecosystem which combines AI, fashion marketing, and the Metaverse can be difficult (Al-Emran & Griffy-Brown, 2023).

Data Security and Privacy: Because AI systems frequently depend on enormous volumes of data to operate efficiently, data security and privacy concerns are important. Maintaining a careful balance between properly using consumer data and protecting their privacy is a challenge.

Digital Literacy and User Interface: AI and the Metaverse are novel ideas that may be unsettling to conventional users. Creating user-friendly interfaces and bridging this digital divide will be ongoing challenges.

Legal and Regulatory Restraints: As technology advances quickly, legal and regulatory frameworks find it difficult to keep up. In the context of the Metaverse, this creates uncertainty over ownership rights and intellectual property.

User Experience and Realism: It may be difficult to guarantee users a smooth and realistic virtual experience, especially in Metaverse fashion marketplaces. It might not be easy to create digital representations of apparel, texture, and fit that are accurate to life.

4.1. Adoption Barriers for Cutting-Edge Technology in Retail and the Metaverse

Shankar et al. (2020) stated that using new technologies in retail presents a number of difficulties for suppliers, retailers, and customers. The delay between uptake and business reward is one barrier to new technology adoption for enterprises. Certain technologies can be expensive to implement and need supplementary resources, which may discourage shops from using them. Moreover, Shankar et al. (2020)

note that merchants' willingness to embrace new technologies is significantly influenced by regulatory changes. The emergence of AI-powered devices has given birth to a number of ethical dilemmas because of functions like location tracking and facial recognition. Laurell et al.'s (2019) investigation of adoption hurdles for VR technologies was another goal. VR has drawn attention because of its high cost and potential to produce novel client experiences. But according to Laurell et al. (2019), there are a number of possible reasons why VR technology has not been widely adopted, including its technological limitations and lack of network impacts. The application of Metaverse may present some obstacles, which have been the subject of some studies (Dwivedi et al., 2022; Koohang et al., 2023).

Koohang et al. (2023) claim that the Metaverse is developing into an extremely troublesome prospect that allows businesses to communicate with customers on a completely new level. However, because it is growing via the prism of significant Big-tech platforms, it presents several issues in terms of governance, public acceptance, and trust. Ethics, the protection of personal data, and efficient regulation are among the issues that are receiving more attention. Likewise, Dwivedi et al. (2022) draw attention to the number of users has reported inappropriate and offensive conduct. Although Metaverse could advance shared interests and social equality, it must overcome growing ethical and legal obstacles.

5. Imaginary Case Studies Derived from Recent Research and Trends

Let us consider two hypothetical case studies in which fashion firms, designated as Brand A and Brand B, employ AI for their Metaverse marketing.

Case Study 1
Customized Shopping Experience with Brand A

Leading luxury clothing brand A made the decision to use AI to develop a distinctive Metaverse shopping experience. They developed an AI-driven virtual store where each user's preferences are taken into account for the design, atmosphere, and even background music.

The AI customized each display based on the user's social media interests, wardrobe preferences, and past online purchases. Additionally, it provided in-the-moment style guidance during virtual try-ons, greatly enhancing client pleasure. Furthermore, Brand A installed a system that leveraged machine learning algorithms to make recommendations for products based on customers' past purchases and in-store interactions. As a result, each consumer spent a notably longer amount of time in the store, which in turn increased revenue and client retention.

Case Study 2
Brand B's Content Generation by AI and in the Metaverse Influencers

Streetwear brand B, well-liked by Gen Z and millennials, made the bold decision to enter the Metaverse using a strong marketing plan. The brand employed AI algorithms to generate a digital avatar known as a Metaverse influencer, who consistently wore apparel and accessories from its most recent collections, in an attempt to appeal to a younger demographic.

In order to create the avatar's relations as realistic and interesting, AI algorithms examined the conversational patterns, dialects, and current lingo that were popular among their target populations. The avatar took part in online gatherings, parties, and competitions in the Metaverse, consistently making an impression with the stylish merchandise from the firm.

Additionally, they employed AI to determine which kinds of advertisements and social media posts connected best with their target market. The company used this information to produce dynamic, tailored, and interesting content for its social media accounts and Metaverse store, which greatly increased their brand awareness and revenue.

Above case studies are based on present developments and available AI capabilities, notwithstanding their speculation. We might anticipate seeing more and more situations like this as companies investigate the possibilities of AI in the Metaverse.

6. Conclusion

It appears that the Metaverse, a revolutionary disruption, is just around the corner. The Metaverse, the next horizon of the human condition, will necessitate a completely new way of looking at every aspect of human endeavor. In order to design appropriately, businesses, governments, and society at large must comprehend the consequences and effects for stakeholders. The thought of "digital fashion" had become a significant development in fashion business in recent years. The fashion industry places great emphasis on the application of Metaverse technology, which supports sustainability initiatives over a product's whole lifecycle. The fashion business is still in the early phases of integrating sustainability and the Metaverse.

In addition to supporting sustainable production methods, this study presents innovative business tactics that efficiently manage and alleviate challenges of excess inventory and irregular market demand through personalized design. The problems of uneven demand and oversupply beset the traditional fashion business model. This issue occurs when more things are produced without a thorough understanding of what the customers anticipate. Customers can participate in creating their own clothing with the help of the Metaverse platform, which reduces inventory through specialized production and service. As a result, there will be a change in the fashion sector toward increased sustainability. The sewing and production processes are now easier because to the development of digital infrastructure, which eliminates the need for the conventional linear arrangement of different equipment. To achieve adaptability, sustainability, and flexibility, an engineering system must be designed and implemented with diligence.

Furthermore, the application of blockchain and Metaverse technologies has improved supply chain transparency. Consequently, buyers may now obtain extensive details about the product, including the fibers utilized, the final clothing, the possibility of recycling, and rental information. This allows customers to choose the right style, color, fit, and pricing with knowledge. Consequently, the business has a smaller stock of unsold items, all of which are in line with ecological sustainability standards. According to the Metaverse's tenets, efficiency in longevity can be attained through the application of cleaner production practices. From a technological standpoint, the field of baby digital fashion still has room for improvement. In order to tackle these technological obstacles, more money must be set aside for research and development.

References

Alexander, B., & Kent, A. (2021). Tracking technology diffusion in-store: A fashion retail perspective. *International Journal of Retail & Distribution Management, 49*(10), 1369–1390. https://doi.org/10.1108/IJRDM-05-2020-0191

Akram, S. V., Malik, P.K., Singh, R., Gehlot, A., Juyal, A., Ghafoor, K. Z., & Shrestha, S. (2022). Implementation of digitalized technologies for fashion industry 4.0: Opportunities and challenges. *Scientific Programming, 2022*, 1–17. https://doi.org/10.1155/2022/7523246

Al-Emran, M., & Griffy-Brown, C. (2023). The role of technology adoption in sustainable development: Overview, opportunities, challenges, and future research agendas. *Technology in Society, 73*, 102240. https://doi.org/10.1016/j.techsoc.2023.102240

Baek, E., Haines, S., Fares, O., Huang, Z., Hong, Y., & Lee, S. (2022). Defining digital fashion: Reshaping the field via a systematic review. *Computers in Human Behavior, 137*(107407). 10.1016/j.chb.2022.107407.

Barrera, G. K. & Shah, D. (2023). Marketing in the Metaverse: Conceptual understanding, framework, and research agenda. *Journal of Business Research, 155*, 113420. 10.1016/j.jbusres.2022.113420.

Belk, R., Humayun, M., & Brouard, M. (2022). Money, possessions, and ownership in the Metaverse: NFTs, cryptocurrencies, Web3 and Wild Markets. *Journal of Business Research, 153*, 198–205. 10.1016/j.jbusres.2022.08.031.

Dwivedi, Y. K., Hughes, L., Baabdullah, A. M., Ribeiro-Navarrete, S., Giannakis, M., AlDebei, M. M., Dennehy, D., Metri, B., Buhalis, D., Cheung, C. M. K., Conboy, K., Doyle, R., Dubey, R., Dutot, V., Felix, R., Goyal, D. P., Gustafsson, A., Hinsch, C., Jebabli, I., & Janssen, M. (2022). Metaverse beyond the hype: Multidisciplinary perspectives on emerging challenges, opportunities, and agenda for research, practice and policy. *International Journal of Information Management, 66*(66), 102542. https://doi.org/10.1016/j.ijinfomgt.2022.102542

Dwivedi, Y. K., Hughes, L., Wang, Y., Alalwan, A. A., Ahn, S. J. (Grace), Balakrishnan, J., Barta, S., Belk, R., Buhalis, D., Dutot, V., Felix, R., Filieri, R., Flavián, C., Gustafsson, A., Hinsch, C., Hollensen, S., Jain, V., Kim, J., Krishen, A. S., & Lartey, J. O. (2022). Metaverse marketing: How the Metaverse will shape the future of consumer research and practice. *Psychology & Marketing, 40*, 750–776. https://doi.org/10.1002/mar.21767

Javornik, A. (2016). Augmented reality: Research agenda for studying the impact of its media characteristics on consumer behavior. *Journal of Retailing and Consumer Services, 30*, 252–261. https://doi.org/10.1016/j.jretconser.2016.02.004

Jiang, Y., Wang, X., & Yuen, K. F. (2021). Augmented reality shopping application usage: The influence of attitude, value, and characteristics of innovation. *Journal of Retailing and Consumer Services, 63*, 102720. https://doi.org/10.1016/j.jretconser.2021.102720

Joy, A., Zhu, Y., Peña, C., & Brouard, M. (2022). Digital future of luxury brands: Metaverse, digital fashion, and non-fungible tokens. *Strategic Change, 31*(3), 337–343. https://doi.org/10.1002/jsc.2502

Kim, C., Lee, S.-G., & Kang, M. (2012). I became an attractive person in the virtual world: Users' identification with virtual communities and avatars. *Computers in Human Behavior, 28*(5), 1663–1669. https://doi.org/10.1016/j.chb.2012.04.004

Kong, H. M., Witmaier, A., & Ko, E. (2020). Sustainability and social media communication: How consumers respond to marketing efforts of luxury and non-luxury fashion brands. *Journal of Business Research*, *131*, 0148–2963. https://doi.org/10.1016/j.jbusres.2020.08.021

Laurell, C., Sandström, C., Berthold, A., & Larsson, D. (2019). Exploring barriers to adoption of virtual reality through social media analytics and machine learning – An assessment of technology, network, price and trialability. *Journal of Business Research*, 100, 10.1016/j.jbusres.2019.01.017.

Lee, U.-K., & Kim, H. (2022). UTAUT in Metaverse: An "Ifland" Case. *Journal of Theoretical and Applied Electronic Commerce Research*, *17*(2), 613–635. https://doi.org/10.3390/jtaer17020032

Marr, B. (2022, June 1). The amazing ways Nike is using the metaverse, Web3 and NFTs. *Forbes*. https://www.forbes.com/sites/bernardmarr/2022/06/01/the-amazing-way-snike-is-using-the-Metaverse-web3-and-nfts/?sh=3b5af8c856e9

McKinsey. (2022, August 17). What is the metaverse and where will it lead next? *McKinsey*. https://www.mckinsey.com/featuredinsights/mckinsey-explainers/what-is-the-Metaverse

Noris, A., Nobile, T. H., Kalbaska, N., & Cantoni, L. (2021). Digital fashion: A systematic literature review. A perspective on marketing and communication. *Journal of Global Fashion Marketing*, *12*, 32–46. https://doi.org/10.1080/20932685.2020.1835522

Pantano, E. & Vannucci, V. (2019). Who is innovating? An exploratory research of digital technologies diffusion in retail industry. *Journal of Retailing and Consumer Services*, *49*, 297–304. 10.1016/j.jretconser.2019.01.019.

Pedersen, E., Gwozdz, W., & Kant Hvass, K. (2018). Exploring the relationship between business model innovation, corporate sustainability, and organisational values within the fashion industry. *Journal of Business Ethics*, 149, 10.1007/s10551-016-3044-7.

Periyasamy, A. P., & Periyasami, S. (2023). Rise of digital fashion and metaverse: Influence on sustainability. *DESD*, *1*, 16. https://doi.org/10.1007/s44265-023-00016-z

Reddit. (2019). Reddit. https://www.reddit.com/Roblox Corporation

Roblox. (2023). Roblox. https://www.roblox.com/

Shankar, A., Jebarajakirthy, C., & Ashaduzzaman, Md. (2020). How do electronic word of mouth practices contribute to mobile banking adoption? *Journal of Retailing and Consumer Services*, *52*(101920). ISSN 0969-6989.

Stephenson, N. (2003). *Snow Crash: A novel*. Spectra.

Waite, T. (2023). Can the metaverse reshape the future of fashion in 2023? *Dazed*, 06, 2023. https://www.dazeddigital.com/fashion/article/57850/1/can-the-metaverse-reshape-the-future-of-fashion-in-2023-vr-ar-meta-decentraland.

Watson, A., Alexander, B., & Salavati, L. (2018). The impact of experiential augmented reality applications on fashion purchase intention. *International Journal of Retail & Distribution Management*, *48*(5). https://doi.org/10.1108/ijrdm-06-2017-0117

Wedel, M., Bigné, E., & Zhang, J. (2020). Virtual and augmented reality: Advancing research in consumer marketing. *International Journal of Research in Marketing*, *37*(3), 443–465. https://doi.org/10.1016/j.ijresmar.2020.04.004

Zuckerberg, M. (2021, October 28). Founder's letter, 2021. *Meta*. https://about.fb.com/news/2021/10/founders-letter/

Review/Discussion Questions:

RQ1. In what ways will the Metaverse develop and change business environments?
RQ2. Are authorities equipped to handle the Metaverse?
RQ3. How will encounters based around humans be reframed by the Metaverse?
RQ4. What fresh avenues for sustainability can the Metaverse offer?
RQ5. How will the Metaverse's implementations evolve globally?
RQ6. What are the main reasons why people are reluctant to embrace the Metaverse?

RQ7. Do you believe that elder generations will be drawn to Metaverse?
RQ8. In your opinion, what will the fashion industry's biggest obstacles be in the Metaverse?
RQ9. Who do you consider to be the Metaverse's enablers?
RQ10. Did you observe any shifts in consumer behavior in the fashion industry in the past few years?
RQ11. How do you think consumers currently feel about Metaverse? Have you seen any comments about the Metaverse, either favorable or negative?
RQ12. In your opinion, what would entice people to visit stores in the Metaverse over all others?
RQ13. What are the main obstacles to businesses and consumers embracing the Metaverse?
RQ14. How does the finished output of digital fashion fit within the existing notion of digital fashion?
RQ15. Regarding digital fashion as a final product, what could be the research gaps and potential avenues for future investigation?

Key Takeaways:

- It confirmed that businesses are beginning to penetrate the Metaverse, an immersive virtual world, which offers a recently emerging frontier in fashion marketing.
- By leveraging AI to comprehend customer behavior, improve engagement, and spur brand innovation, these Metaverse marketing initiatives have produced greater results.

Chapter 13

Metaverse in Education: Pioneering Virtual World for Cutting Edge Hybrid Learning Experiences

Seema Garg, Namrata Pancholi, Anamica Singh and Anchal Luthra

AIBS, Amity University, Noida, India

Abstract

Metaverse is one of the technologies that has the most promise for the future. However, there is less discussion about teaching using the metaverse. It is possible that most of the educators are ignorant of the metaverse's features and its potential uses. The objective of this chapter is to define the metaverse precisely and discusses the various applications, characteristics, and challenges of metaverse in Education. This chapter explores the pioneering efforts in leveraging the metaverse for educational purposes, highlighting key examples and their impact on the learning experience. The possible applications of metaverse and research encounters in context to education are further reviewed and then explained and included the Artificial Intelligence (AI) functions in the world of metaverse along with learning based on metaverse. Researchers in the domains of educational technology and computer science shall advance an inclusive insight of the metaverse and its potential applications in education using various metaverse techniques like gamified learning, virtual learning, etc. Also, the metaverse role in education starting from the perception of AI has been covered.

Keywords: Metaverse; virtual; education; hybrid; technology; learning

1. Introduction

As the Middle Ages progressed, monasteries formed and cathedral schooling became the most active factor in the preservation of information, and knowledge and in educating clergy. Between the 14th and 18th centuries, the Renaissance was reborn in its best form. There was a sense of the break with the old school and laying of the fundamental principles of humanism in the form of the quest for values and discovery of personal potential and secular education. The enlightenment popularized the defiant prescription of rationality, empirical research, and the process of change. The skill of being able to read and write only being reserved for a select few earlier but with the help of printing presses this has been changed. During the years 1700 to mid-1800, the lives of people transformed the living standards of mankind due to the Industrial Revolution. The revolution brought about changes among societies as well as later on imposed strategies for the moral and economic sectors. Education legislation and the ending of inequality brought on community development and the spread of public-school systems. The requirement to be on schedule, discipline, and high level of needed education for the position. Following it, the literature spiked in the 19th to early 20th century (Krishnan et al., 2023). At the turn of the 20th century, amid the growing influence of the progressive educational movement in the child-centered model, learning-by-doing approach, education of a whole child has begun. Along with the termination of World War II in the mid-20th century, it also yielded a series of positive and negative effects on both parts of the world experienced higher educational rates together with the growth and emergence of post-secondary institutes, e.g., dropping, integration of tech in education.

The ages from the late 20th century to the present are: the one which solves complicated mathematical problems, the one which connects students from all around the globe, and the one which takes away the classrooms and the school walls. Cyber revolutionary education mixed online, individualized courses and world collaboration. Online platforms, dynamic content and interactive tools, credible sources, the power of gamification, etc. have become increasingly prevalent. Thus, the aspect of fast-growing technology and globalization leads us to a bright future. Critical thought and creativity go together with the 21st-century skills, of pressing importance, collaboration, and digital literacy. There is a growing concern about the importance of the age-integrated model of the economy. Teachers must acquire skills in class management, mandate adherence, and teaching to different learning disabilities and cultural backgrounds.

1.1. The Metaverse: A New Frontier for Education

With the immersive and interactive nature of the metaverse, it offers unprecedented opportunities to transform education, making learning more engaging, accessible, and effective. Metaverse in education represents a futuristic approach to education, utilizing interactive and immersive virtual worlds to improve the learning process. With advanced Artificial Intelligence (AI) and machine learning algorithms, the metaverse can tailor not only the content in the educational field but can converge the needs of an individual and the learning styles of each student. The metaverse is reshaping education, providing new opportunities for immersive learning experiences.

The future generation internet, known as Metaverse, is predicted to completely transform society (Hwang & Chien, 2022). The literature that has already been written has not often examined the metaverse in an educational setting, preferring to concentrate on specific technologies that are connected to the metaverse in edification, despite the probable applications of the metaverse in teaching. As a result, many educational scholars may be ignorant of the metaverse, its spheres, and its function in the domain of innovative education. Metaverse is considered to be an important concept to be designed and implemented for a hybrid mode of education. Metaverse use can be made for special instructive purposes like virtual visits to the classrooms of the university (Tarouco et al., 2013) libraries, etc. (Ando et al., 2013). Metaverse creates a learning environment in education by integrating both worlds of augmented and virtual reality (VR) technologies constructing engaging and dynamic learning environments for students which provides new experiences and high immersion through virtualization. Beyond traditional classrooms, metaverse provides a more engaging and dynamic learning experience.

1.2. Gamified Learning Environments

Metaverse is used to bridge the gap between gaming and learning, and it has the potential to be very beneficial for students. It provides an interesting way to conceptualize game-based learning, and it can be used to promote this concept in the online education sector. This technological advancement is contributing to a new concept of gaining knowledge by playing games, which is much more exciting than traditional methods (Faiella & Ricciardi, 2015). This concept not only promotes a betterment of knowledge but also encourages students to explore new possibilities and gain skills through gaming. Eight game components are identified by Apostol et al. (2013) as being utilized in the gamification of education. These features include policies, objectives, outcomes, opinions and incentives, solving problems, narrative, player(s), careful setting, and sense of proficiency. However, the query of what kinds and numbers of game features should be employed to gamify education is still up for discussion. The fusion of gaming with learning via Metaverse has a small but strong significance in the way that students learn. AI can also be incorporated into this method, making it easier for students to learn while having fun at the same time. In the metaverse, students can immerse themselves in realistic or fantastical environments that simulate real-world scenarios or historical events (Garg et al., 2023). Because the metaverse is gamified and immersive, students are guaranteed to be satisfied with the entire learning experience, which boosts motivation and involvement even more. It is impossible to overstate the significance of gamification components in the educational field. It is anticipated that the global market for game-based learning will reach $32.6 billion by 2027, which means that there are still a lot of cutting-edge gamification tactics and strategies that instructors and students may take advantage of.

1.3. Virtual Classrooms: Redefining Learning Spaces

Virtual classrooms in the metaverse are redefining traditional learning spaces. These environments enable educators to create immersive experiences which promote to diverse learning styles. Students can interact with their peer group and with virtual objects, enhancing their understanding of complex concepts. Virtual learning environments in the metaverse can accommodate students with diverse and advanced learning needs and disabilities. Higher education has long been a focus of the use of virtual worlds (Díaz, 2020), which allow teachers and students to research new methods to the process of teaching and learning. ICTs and emerging technologies (Kalina & Powell, 2009) play a major part in the learning environment, keeping interaction and involvement as its fundamental goals. Professionals can attend virtual conferences, workshops, and training sessions from anywhere in the world, keeping their skills updated and relevant. In metaverse, students have the freedom to express themselves creatively and experiment with new ideas without constraints. Virtual art studios, design workshops, and music composition tools empower students to explore their creativity and foster innovation.

1.4. The Philosophy of Inclusive Education Using Metaverse

The term "inclusive education" refers to a teaching-learning environment that is inclusive of all students, regardless of their learning preferences, skill levels, or disabilities. It is promoted by the metaverse. The fact that the technology gives every student, an equal chance to participate in the process of learning is undoubtedly the best parts concerning to education in metaverse. Immersive settings, often known as the metaverse, are both a reality and a promise for the future. Thus, it can be viewed as a process that is still being developed. Therefore, it is more important to establish areas for this new notion to be appropriately and inclusively utilized in education rather than just looking for ready-made purposes or applications. It provides special needs children the opportunity to learn alongside typical students and engage in comfortable interactions. Also, current VR technology is being developed to accommodate the requirements of students with disabilities, enabling them to seamlessly interact and navigate the metaverse environment.

1.5. Hybrid Mode in Education in Metaverse

The concept of a hybrid mode in the metaverse refers to a blend of virtual and physical experiences, where users seamlessly transition between the digital realm and the real world. Students can attend classes in virtual classrooms that mirror real-world environments, such as lecture halls or laboratories. Immersive environments of metaverse, are both a thing of the present and a promise of the future. As such, it can be seen as an ongoing process of development. Hence, rather than merely searching for pre-made uses or applications, it is more crucial to define domains in which this novel idea might be suitably and inclusively applied in education.

This hybrid approach allows for greater flexibility and accessibility, accommodating diverse learning styles and preferences. It aims to integrate elements of augmented reality (AR), VR along with mixed reality (MR) to establish captivating experiences that bridge the gap between digital and physical environments and helps to collaborate with others and experience the world around us.

Through mesh between digital and the physical world, users can intermingle with the digital objects and cardinal content of the hybrid metaverse appareled on the environment through VR like smart glasses or smartphone cameras. With the help of the latest technologies of spatial mapping the, metaverse would be able to trace the real-time physical environments. The simulated content is arranged used like the ones used in the video games. This allows for the involvement of the players and the necessary immersion that they need to place in a changing physical environment. The hybrid mode represents a way, by which users can switch directly from physical to digital interactions becoming one, without other diversions. For example, users could sit in on virtual meetings and events while also being able to stay observed of their concrete environments and tend to actions in copy with the actual objects. The mixed metaverse creates a platform for collaboration not only between people previously we thought so, but also between multiple realities. It does not matter if you join a virtual meeting or work on a project that people can work on together. For example, it can be used to facilitate other ways of the users to perceive digital content or participate in a virtual experience. As well it brings correspondent relationship via virtual and real-world. Creating ergonomic interfaces and experiences which will make the success of the hybrid metaverse possible is inevitably the key.

1.6 Virtual Experiment Learning to Acquire Practical Experience

Students can experience things that would be risky or difficult in the real world first-hand in a safe setting by using the metaverse. Using collaborative technologies to support multi-modal and hybrid education methods has quickly become standard procedure. The need for simultaneous training in classroom settings for individuals who are in person and those who are remote has caused a notable change in the way that colleges, institutions, and schools approach course creation. For example, without endangering oneself or others, one might practice transport management techniques or carry out intricate chemical experiments in the metaverse. One benefit of virtual simulation is that it is available to students around the clock, which increases accessibility and lets them arrange their studies without the strict timetable of traditional practical lessons.

2. Challenges of Metaverse

While the metaverse holds immense potential and applications in education, there are also challenges to consider, for example, access to technology, internet connectivity, device usage, hardware devices, technological literacy, privacy concerns, security breaches, identity theft, cyberbullying, surveillance, and physical and mental health for all students. Greater initial outlay: Creating metaverse platforms and acquiring hardware are two major upfront costs associated with operating in the metaverse. The main barrier to widespread commercial adoption is the low maturity of the necessary hardware and technologies.

Long hours in the metaverse can be taxing for workers, who may get tired and lose their sense of reality. Employees are also concerned about digital security and privacy. Also, graphic limitations are one other challenge, the current state of metaverse technology only allows for cartoonish avatars that lack realism and human emotion, thus restricting the ability to effectively convey ideas and non-verbal messages. There is a need to address these challenges proactively to realize the full benefits of the metaverse in imparting knowledge. Excessive usage of immersive virtual environments in the metaverse may lead to addiction, social isolation, and mental health issues, particularly among vulnerable populations such as children and adolescents. There are also certain technological challenges like Building and maintaining complex virtual worlds with realistic graphics, physics, and interactions entail substantial computational possessions, that impose scalability, latency, and hardware requirements challenges.

3. Opportunities of Metaverse

The metaverse advances experience through majestic and interactional methods that transcend traditional forms of media, enabling users to explore virtual worlds, interact with digital objects, and engage with others in meaningful ways. Virtual collaboration platforms within the metaverse facilitate remote teamwork, co-creation, and knowledge sharing across geographical boundaries, enhancing productivity and creativity in various industries. Organizations will be able to further disperse their workforce globally as metaverse adoption rises. With the help of innovative virtual tools found in the metaverse, team-based tasks like planning, strategizing, and design work that are challenging to complete in standard virtual modes can be completed more successfully. More distinctions exist between work and life. The main issues that remote workers worry about include feeling alone, interacting with co-workers less frequently, and not having clear boundaries between work and personal time. Metaverse can help in simulations, and an environment for virtual training which grants prospects for experiential learning, skill development, and personalized education tailored to individual learning styles. VR applications within the metaverse have the prospect to transmute healthcare delivery, enabling distant consultations, therapeutic interventions, and medical training in immersive virtual environments (Garg & Pancholi, 2023). Virtual meetings, events, and experiences in the metaverse have the power to moderate the necessity for instinctive travel and infrastructure, leading to lower carbon emissions and environmental impact compared to traditional modes of interaction. Several ICT and AI tools were incorporated into the metaverse design, encouraging both individual and group learning (Hwang & Chien, 2022). Ultimately, an assessment was conducted to determine how much a group of students valued their interactions with the metaverse, confirming its applicability both within and outside of the classroom. Unfortunately, its application in education is infrequently explored, potentially leaving educators uninformed about its capabilities and applications.

4. Literature Review

A completely new viewpoint on educational technology will be made possible by the existence of the metaverse (Díaz et al., 2020; Rospigliosi, 2022). It gives students access to fresh training opportunities and environments. It is crucial to recognize that the Metaverse concept is in a state of continuous evolution. More features are likely to develop as technology progresses and fresh ideas come to the forefront. Various companies and projects may adopt distinct technologies and approaches to implement the Metaverse, resulting in differences in its features and capabilities. It has been discussed that the metaverse can be used to conduct various training programs for attaining objectives that were thought to be impossible in the existing world (Siyaev & Jo, 2021). Some of the obstacles that people face in this new world – like space, time, and even threats combated through the learning process can be mounted to enable people to acquire certain materials or skills (Jeong et al., 2022; Wang et al., 2022). More significantly, strong training programs with efficient learning supports can be offered thanks to the metaverse's features. It is anticipated that, over the next ten years, the total application numbers related to the usage of the metaverse in the education sector will rise at a speedy pace. Subsequently, a multitude of significant technology domains such as machine learning, natural language processing (NLP), networks, deep learning, neural network, and blockchain, along with an wide-ranging range of application domains such as manufacturing, healthcare, smart cities, DeFi, and gaming are being examined. The metaverse can prove to be a real game changing technology for the educators in education sector environment, delivering a bunch of substantial benefits, the most owing can be immersive, interactive learning experiences, greater speed of learning in an inclusive environment, and its ability to acquire real world experience (Shalender et al., 2023). Zhang et al. (2022) of prospective research topics regarding the metaverse in education is covered for the purpose of expanding future research. A number of literature reviews were also done on the Metaverse as a whole, such as Narin (2021) and Zhao et al. (2022); consumer behavior in Metaverse and virtual commerce from application design (Shen et al., 2021); digital twins technology (Cimino et al., 2019; Jones et al., 2020; Liu et al., 2021); and three-dimensional virtual worlds (Dionisio et al., 2013). It has been explored enough to learn more about it but no significantly relevant literature review is compiled for the results of the research on the usage of the metaverse in learning and offer suggestions for the future. As a result, a number of questions remain unanswered, such as what kind of Metaverse is utilized in education, as stated in the 2006 roadmap Metaverse, or what forms of learning in education scenarios while assessing the metaverse techniques that are employed. Egliston and Carter (2021) discussed a new category of spatial computing technology known as VR, which depends on the collection and processing of information of the user as physical attributes of them and how they interact with hardware or immediate surroundings. They investigated the Facebook's Oculus case of VR, a VR technology that leads the market and is essential to their aspirations for a metaverse. We do this by using critical data studies. Within the said case, they contend that VR as a statistics-exhaustive technology is not without drawbacks, but rather is rife with power inequality, with the potential to exacerbate wealth disparities, impose algorithmic bias, etc. (Rospigliosi, 2022). The computer-generated universe known as the Metaverse could prove to be the turning point in the acceptance of VR as the entryway to the metaverse (Pancholi et al., 2023). The world's greatest social network online, Facebook, rebranded its online network as Meta. This change reflects a trend that is already evident in the generation currently attending college and university and is quickening in those who will be learning in the future. This shift toward the virtual is probably going to have a big impact on what we think of as interactive learning environments. The adoption of VR offers fresh, incredibly adaptable possibilities for learning settings and experiences that reflect shifts in our social and professional lives. This comprehensive theoretical framework consolidates and discusses several ideas, offering firms a clear plan to successfully implement the metaverse in education for a better and growing education industry.

5. Challenges of Hybrid Learning

Metaverse changes are likely with the upgrade in technology and user expectations. Hence, there will be challenges of new technology and pedagogy when implemented in a virtual world. There is a need for a dedicated server and an administrator for managing interaction between students and teachers as well as digital resources. The administrator creates space for digital resources like LMS, YouTube, Websites, etc., and links them with faculty and students. This should enable both teachers and students to share subject-related matters. Software and Hardware control: A robust internet connectivity along with durable and technologically upgraded hardware is essential for creating a virtual/hybrid educational system. Technology is used to keep the system active even when users are not logged in.

A virtual/hybrid teaching mode is essentially student-centric. It is the responsibility of the faculty to keep student's motivation high and continuously involve them in the learning process. This requires teachers to design engaging digital resources such as multimedia and hyperlinks. Virtual worlds facilitate the integration of diverse digital learning materials in multiple formats, including text, graphics, videos, and web platforms. When it comes to managing and interacting with information and communication technology (ICT) and developing technologies, educators must modify their roles. AI tools can also be used to enhance the teaching-learning process.

In the virtual world, evaluation procedures are similar to hybrid learning procedures. Instructors can use other digital materials that are incorporated into the virtual world or develop examinations directly on the virtual platform. Teachers can design activities that also use mobile phone applications to keep the virtual interaction live within the designed hybrid education model. There were also some privacy concerns which were resolved using encryption and anonymization of personal data. The AI-driven tools resulted in improved learning outcomes. AI helped to tailor the needs according to users' needs leading to better comprehension and retention.

5.1. Example

VirBELA is a virtual world platform for both teachers and students, where they can work collaboratively in real-time experiencing the same in a 3D environment while making use of the virtual world platform VirBELA. It encourages worldwide collaborative learning and connections using interactive tools, audio communication, and customizable virtual avatars. The Virbela platform is used by universities and educational institutions. It also provides immersive 3D environments for teaching, learning, and collaboration. It provides innovative and engaging learning experiences that transcend the limitations of traditional classrooms. There is an excited, resolute crew of instructional creators, brains of developers, 3D sketchers, intense game creators, and psychologists. It lets consumers to invent their customized avatars and also helps them to communicate with others in actual real-time, much like in a physical classroom or campus setting. Stanford and Harvard universities have used Virbela to establish simulated classrooms where young students attend their lectures and also participate in conversations, and virtually collaborate for projects. It has been used to host virtual career fairs, education fairs and networking events, allowing students to connect with the team of employers and professionals from around the world.

Professional Development in future using this platform can be assessed as the Educators could use Virbela for professional development, attending virtual workshops, conferences, and training sessions to enhance their teaching skills. As recent developments in technologies linger to evolve over time, it can be expected to view more thrilling applications that transform the future of education. Some other examples of metaverse in education are virtual field trips in Google Expeditions. With Google Expeditions, students may take advantage of immersive VR experiences to learn about museums, historical places, and natural wonders. With over 900 VR and AR tours available, this platform improves learning by allowing students to have direct experiences without having to leave the classroom. Through interactive dialogues and cultural encounters, VR language learning software by Mondly entails an engaging environment for students in real-world situations alongside innate speakers, improving language acquisition.

6. Metaverse's Future in Education

The metaverse holds immense potential in education and imparts uncountable benefits, particularly for kids, making it a useful educational tool. Nevertheless, there are certain drawbacks to utilizing the metaverse as a platform or tool for learning, such as the expense of the hardware required to enable the metaverse. Because of the lack of deployable infrastructure, apps, and processing power needed for a highly immersive metaverse experience, widespread adoption of metaverse platforms is probably going to take several years. It presents an alluring value proposition that warrants careful observation. It will require further research as a new educational platform before being completely integrated into the educational system.

As of right now, just a few educational courses use the metaverse, which calls for a powerful computer, sufficient bandwidth, and a server. The future of education could lie in the metaverse, given how swiftly technology is evolving.

Metaverse is supposed to be a breakthrough that holds the power to amend the way of delivering education, improving accessibility, engagement, and flexibility to meet the demands of students in the digital age. Future research should look at how well the Metaverse facilitates personalized and adaptable learning, letting students work at their own pace and engage in more relevant and meaningful learning activities. They ought to look into issues with interoperability and standardization as well.

7. Conclusion

It is noteworthy that Metaverse is evolving and has soon become a necessity. Its characteristics may continue to develop as technology advances and new ideas emerge. Because of its engaging, fascinating, and humorous qualities, the Metaverse environment will make a substantial contribution to simulation educational, social environments of learning, regulated, untraced, and distant processes of learning. In a Metaverse framework where corporal blocks have been eradicated, this has opened fresh options that can be used for impartial educational offerings to differently abled students along with the ones facing distress in retrieving various learning sources. All parties involved in education, which includes students, instructors, supervisors, and school authorities, must embrace the technical foundation of Metaverse because it is a whole new technological entity. The reception of sound Metaverse technology will be influenced by social conventions, psychological criteria, and cultural differences. Furthermore, educators could use the metaverse to create virtual replicas of historical sites, scientific laboratories, and cultural landmarks, allowing students to explore these places first-hand without leaving their homes.

References

Apostol, S., Zaharescu, L., & Alexe, I. (2013). Gamification of learning and educational games. *Elearning & Software For Education*, (2).

Ando, Y., Thawonmas, R., & Rinaldo, F. (2013). *Inference of viewed exhibits in a metaverse museum* [Conference session]. International Conference on Culture and Computing, Kyoto (pp. 218–219). https://doi.org/10.1109/culturecomputing.2013.73

Cimino, C., Negri, E., & Fumagalli, L. (2019). Review of digital twin applications in manufacturing. *Computers in Industry*, *113*, 103130.

Díaz, J., Saldaña, C., & Avila, C. (2020). Virtual world as a resource for hybrid education. *International Journal of Emerging Technologies in Learning (iJET)*, *15*(15), 94–109.

Dionisio, J. D. N., Burns, W. G. III., & Gilbert, R. (2013). 3D virtual worlds and the metaverse: Current status and future possibilities. *ACM Computing Surveys (CSUR)*, *45*(3), 1–38.

Egliston, B., & Carter, M. (2021). Critical questions for Facebook's virtual reality: Data, power and the metaverse. *Internet Policy Review*, *10*(4).

Faiella, F., & Ricciardi, M. (2015). Gamification and learning: A review of issues and research. *Journal of E-learning and Knowledge Society*, *11*(3).

Garg, S., Mahajan, N., & Ghosh, J. (2023). Artificial intelligence and its impacts on industry 4.0. *Industry 4.0 and the Digital Transformation of International Business*, *2023*, 123–133.

Garg, S., & Pancholi, N. (2023). *IoT-driven sustainable development and future trends in industries, promoting sustainable management through technological innovation* (pp. 1–11). IGI Global.

Hwang, G.-J., & Chien, S.-Y. (2022), Definition, roles, and potential research issues of the metaverse in education: An artificial intelligence perspective, *Computers and Education: Artificial Intelligence*, *3*, 100082. ISSN 2666-920X.

Jones, D., Snider, C., Nassehi, A., Yon, J., & Hicks, B. (2020). Characterising the digital twin: A systematic literature review. *CIRP Journal of Manufacturing Science and Technology*, *29*, 36–52.

Jeong, H., Yi, Y., & Kim, D. (2022). An innovative e-commerce platform incorporating metaverse to live commerce. *International Journal of Innovative Computing, Information and Control*, *18*(1), 221–229.

Kalina, C., & Powell, K. C. (2009). Cognitive and social constructivism: Developing tools for an effective classroom. *Education*, *130*(2), 241–250.

Krishnan, C., Thapliyal, K., & Singh, G. (Eds.). (2023). *Global higher education and the COVID-19 pandemic: Perspectives, challenges, and new opportunities*. CRC Press.

Liu, M., Fang, S., Dong, H., & Xu, C. (2021). Review of digital twin about concepts, technologies, and industrial applications. *Journal of Manufacturing Systems*, *58*, 346–361.

Narin, N. G. (2021). A content analysis of the metaverse articles. *Journal of Metaverse*, *1*(1), 17–24.

Pancholi, N., Chaudhary, M., & Garg, S. (2023). *Innovation, sustainability, and business models, promoting sustainable management through technological innovation* (pp. 34–47). IGI Global.

Rospigliosi, P. A. (2022). Metaverse or Simulacra? Roblox, Minecraft, Meta and the turn to virtual reality for education, socialisation and work. *Interactive Learning Environments*, *30*(1), 1–3.

Shalender, K., Singla, B., & Sharma, S. (2023). Emerging technologies and their game-changing potential: Lessons from corporate world. *Contemporary Studies of Risks in Emerging Technology, Part A*, *2023*, 61–70.

Shen, B., Tan, W., Guo, J., Zhao, L., & Qin, P. (2021). How to promote user purchase in metaverse? A systematic literature review on consumer behavior research and virtual commerce application design. *Applied Sciences*, *11*(23), 11087.

Siyaev, A., & Jo, G. S. (2021). Neuro-symbolic speech understanding in aircraft maintenance metaverse. *IEEE Access*, *9*, 154484–154499.

Tarouco, L., Gorziza, B., Corrêa, Y., Amaral, É. M., & Müller, T. (2013). *Virtual laboratory for teaching calculus: An immersive experience* [Conference session]. IEEE Global Engineering Education Conference (EDUCON), Berlin (pp. 774–781).

Wang, F. Y., Qin, R., Wang, X., & Hu, B. (2022). Metasocieties in metaverse: Metaeconomics and metamanagement for metaenterprises and metacities. *IEEE Transactions on Computational Social Systems*, *9*(1), 2–7.

Zhang, X., Chen, Y., Hu, L., & Wang, Y. (2022). The metaverse in education: Definition, framework, features, potential applications, challenges, and future research topics. *Frontiers in Psychology*, *13*, 6063.

Zhao, Y., Jiang, J., Chen, Y., Liu, R., Yang, Y., Xue, X., & Chen, S. (2022). Metaverse: Perspectives from graphics, interactions and visualization. *Visual Informatics*, *6*(1), 56–67.

Chapter 14

Creative Synergy: Unleashing the Potential of Artificial Intelligence and the Metaverse

Jasmine Mariappan[a], Supriya Lamba Sahdev[b], Chitra Krishnan[c], Firdous Ahmad Malik[d] and Astha Gupta[e]

[a]*University of Technology and Applied Sciences, Ibra, Oman*
[b]*Alliance University, Bengaluru, Karnataka, India*
[c]*Symbiosis Center for Management Studies, Noida, Symbiosis International Deemed University, Pune, India.*
[d]*University of People, Pasadena, CA 91101, USA*
[e]*AIBS, Amity University, Noida, India*

Abstract

This chapter introduces the era of Artificial Intelligence (AI) and the Metaverse, delving into their integration and profound impact on community, creativity, collaboration, and societal change. It begins by exploring the emergence of the Metaverse and its fusion with AI technologies, highlighting how AI ensures consistency in depicting virtual worlds with diverse laws of physics and economies, thereby enhancing their realism and dynamism through advanced world-building techniques. The chapter further examines AI's role in artistic creation, emphasizing its contributions to art, music, and storytelling across different levels. It also explores collaborative intelligence, focusing on human-AI partnerships in crafting virtual environments and developing virtual collaborators or creative assistants. Additionally, it discusses the democratization of creativity and innovation within the AI-metaverse ecosystem, emphasizing participatory storytelling and community engagement modules. Ethical and societal considerations such as algorithm bias and digital property rights are carefully addressed throughout the discussion. The chapter concludes by summarizing the opportunities and imperatives in AI-Metaverse collaboration, highlighting achievements and

---

The Metaverse Dilemma: Challenges and Opportunities for Business and Society, 235–248
Copyright © 2025 by Jasmine Mariappan, Supriya Lamba Sahdev, Chitra Krishnan, Firdous Ahmad Malik and Astha Gupta
Published under exclusive licence by Emerald Publishing Limited
doi:10.1108/978-1-83797-524-220241014

insights that promote openness, accountability, and inclusivity. In conclusion, this chapter underscores ongoing technological advancements in AI and the Metaverse, poised to revolutionize human interaction, creativity, and self-expression. It advocates for responsible and pragmatic development to achieve positive outcomes for all stakeholders.

Keywords: Artificial Intelligence (AI); Metaverse; creativity; collaboration; ethical considerations; transformative impact

1. Introduction: The Convergence of AI and the Metaverse

The implication of Artificial Intelligence (AI) and a metaverse marks a new stage in the development of modern digital technologies. Science-fiction invented the term "metaverse," long before it became a reference to virtual platforms like Second Life. Nowadays, the real promising metaverse is in the making. Moreover, AI solutions have developed powerful algorithms on pattern recognition, natural language processing (NLP), and machine learning as well as others, thus creating the possibility for intelligent interaction and good decision-making. The term "metaverse," the blending of "meta" and "universe," stands for a collectively virtual space involving a 3D virtual environment that is interconnected and, as well, in which people can engage with each other and the digital objects in real-time (Park & Kim, 2022). The metaverse that was formerly a part of fiction literature is already becoming real due to technological advancements resulting in improved communication and immersive technologies. Different stages for the metaverse birth are the digitization of our reality such as virtual worlds of Second Life, the latest events where key players in tech such as Facebook/Meta have been involved as in the example of the name change of the parent company to Meta (Castell, 2023). These projects had been capable of quickening the creation of virtualized 3D spaces with interactive and collaborative attributes that set a solid groundwork for AI integration with the metaverse.

The metaverse containing AI technologies has now been able to do wonders for the ultimate engagement and intelligence to interrelate. AI algorithms advance the realness as well as the interactivity of the virtual world by facilitating features like procedural generation, natural language understanding, and predictive models. Consequently, the users can participate in virtual worlds more naturally and even play with them, designing their experiences more intensely through their choices and behavior. Integration of AI's cognitive abilities and Metaverse's virtual reality (VR) could redefine industries and certainly reshape interactions among humans. With the help of AI algorithms, which already have advanced machine learning and NLP capabilities, a more vivid and realistic virtual world can be created that includes personalized experiences, intelligent assistance, and dynamic content generation (Pagani & Champion, 2023).

Also, both AI and Metaverse look to bring innovations from multiple domains (Lampropoulos et al., 2022). In addition to entertainment and gaming, the sky is the limit between education and healthcare (Elor et al., 2021). In AI-driven virtual tutoring, for instance, students receive personalized learning experiences while viewing AI-integrated digital art in virtual galleries. Nevertheless, we need to address the problems and ethical issues that could arise like protecting the privacy of users and avoiding biases (Al Kuwaiti et al., 2023). Creative processes spanning different industries in AI are focused more on collaboration and the potential of the metaverse. The AI-driven systems and platforms act as facilitators for individuals to have their inner creative forces explored and expressed, by the way of art, music, storytelling, or design. Via AI authorship techniques, users can invent new concepts, examine different artistic trends, and conduct a variety of virtual experiments with creative content.

As well, AI supports creative intelligence, the type of AI-human collaboration that arises from virtual spaces. Such virtual collaborators and creative companions, powered by AI algorithms, assist users with their ideation, problem-solving, and content creation, and thus creating a fruitful human and machine relationship. Through this co-working mode, creativity and innovation get a boost, and that way there is improvement in VR technology and the digital materials inside the metaverses.

In this chapter, we will explore the dynamic intersection of AI and the metaverse, examining the transformative impact of their convergence on creativity, collaboration, and societal dynamics. Key themes and topics to be explored include:

- How the use of AI algorithms enhances artistic expressions in different fields of art, from cutting-edge projects to AI-powered platforms, and justifying the use of AI for creative purposes.
- Discuss AI applications in VR to come up with scenes with procedural generation and machine learning which will continuously generate dynamic and interactive worlds in the metaverse.
- Shed light on the emergence and working, of virtual collaborators and creative companions in shaping human-AI co-creation in virtual realms to facilitate collaborative creativity and innovation.
- Examine the ethical dimension of AI-metaverse convergence, including subjects such as algorithmic bias, ownership of digital goods, and privacy. Besides that, how we can ensure transparency, accountability, and inclusion in AI-metaverse collaboration will also be covered.

By exploring these themes and topics, we aim to provide a comprehensive overview of the transformative potential of AI and the metaverse, while advocating for responsible and ethical development practices to ensure positive outcomes for all stakeholders.

2. AI-Powered Creativity: From Algorithms to Artistry

AI has been increasingly used to boost creativity so far, which has ignited a paradigm shift, that reshaped traditional methods of all creative disciplines. AI takes the role of a better tool for artists, musicians, and tellers of stories, creating a new avenue for them to explore artistic expressions by using advanced algorithms, as well as, machine learning techniques (Chung, 2022).

2.1. Evolution of AI in Creative Processes

Art: AI algorithms are no longer just data analyzers, but also part of the process of producing visual art. Methods such as Generative Adversarial Networks (GANs) generate novel and visually appealing visuals uniquely. Artificial neural networks can mimic artistic styles and thus generate works that challenge the frontier between human and machine creativity (Elgammal et al., 2017).

Music: In the art of music, online platforms like Amper Music and Jukedeck equipped with AI enable composers and musicians to generate unique music pieces crafted to suit the requirements of a particular need. By processing big data of musical patterns and styles such as melodies, harmonies, and rhythms, the algorithms can compose something to inspire artists and hopefully give them more creative potential.

Storytelling: AI algorithms, especially the ones based on NLP, have brought significant changes to the area of storytelling. Platforms including OpenAI's GPT series can produce sensible text that fits into the input context in response to the provided prompts. Writers and tellers of stories often employ such schemes to, among other things: overcome writer's block, search for possibilities, and create immersive worlds with elaborate characters and exciting plots.

2.2. Impact on Creative Industries

Enhanced Creativity: AI boosts human creativity using new suggestions, alternative options or the simplification of the overall process. Artists, in this case, can play around with new and different processes, methods, and media, thus creating unexpected, thought-provoking, or ground-breaking works of art.

Efficiency and Productivity: AI-equipped tools allow an individual to work smarter and be more efficient as it automates tasks and recommends intelligent suggestions. The freedom to experiment minimizes the distractions associated with material constraints and beneficially affects the conceptualization and refinement process which helps the artists to arrive at more novel concepts and to achieve artistic excellence.

Accessibility and Inclusivity: AI serves to level the user of creative tools and assets making the arts available to people of different backgrounds and proficiency. AI has brought about an environment that allows more people to actively participate thereby creating an inclusive and diverse entertainment community. The voices and the viewpoints that were overlooked are now zoomed in by this factor.

2.3. Challenges and Considerations

Ethical Implications: The use of AI in creative processes raises ethical concerns related to authorship, ownership, and cultural appropriation. Creators must navigate issues of attribution, copyright, and fair use to ensure ethical and responsible use of AI-generated content.

Algorithmic Bias: AI algorithms are susceptible to biases present in training data, which can perpetuate stereotypes and inequalities in creative outputs. Creators must critically evaluate and mitigate bias in AI systems to promote fairness, diversity, and inclusivity in their work

Human-Machine Collaboration: While AI offers powerful tools for creativity, it is essential to maintain a balance between human intuition and machine automation. Collaborative partnerships between artists and AI systems can unlock new creative possibilities while preserving the integrity and authenticity of the artistic process.

In a nutshell, AI-assisted creativity brings a revolutionary change to how art is conceived, produced, and perceived. Through the combination of algorithms and artists' basements, creators unlock the energy of imagination, move beyond the limits of innovation, and redefine the expression of human beings in the era of digitalization. AI is not only immensely impacting, but also reshaping the sectors which include art, graphics, music as well as storytelling. This is using Intelligence and coding with learning to create content that sometimes blurs the line between human creation and computer program-created content.

3. The Metaverse as Canvas: Building Worlds with AI

AI is extremely vital for making wonderful new online places in the constantly changing Metaverse. The people who build-related things there use AI to imagine up all kinds of great fun spots think fake lands, structures, and spots that are like nature but even more excellent than anything we did before.

3.1. AI Technologies Utilized in the Creation of Metaverses

Procedural Generation: Procedural generation is about using computer plans or patterns which we call algorithms to create related things automatically; this means we can make massive and different virtual places. When we use AI, which is computer brainpower, for procedural generation, it can make all kinds of things on its own: mountains, valleys, and buildings; this way, you can see new and different things all the time without getting bored. Because AI does so much of the work, game makers do not have to do everything by hand, which means they can make vast online worlds for us to play in with a large variety (Huynh-The et al., 2023).

Machine Learning: So, in machine learning, we have got these computer programs that figure things out by noticing patterns and thinking through mountains of data; this helps them to guess what is going to happen or decide the right thing to do, which is pretty helpful in building this wonderful online space everyone's into, called the Metaverse. With a boost from AI, the machine learning "brains" can get a sense of what people by watching what they do, what choices they make, and the tenor they give off, all so they can make the virtual world better on the fly; these AI mechanisms are so slick that they can change how bright, textured, and interactive everything is correct as you experiment with it, which makes the whole experience even more engaging and keeps users stoked.

Computer simulations create complex events and actions in online worlds, making the Metaverse more realistic and detailed. AI helps mimic real-related things, such as weather, how things move, and nature's setups, making everything feel more lifelike online. By copying real natural settings, game builders make wonderful digital places that change when players do things, making games or stories inside these places more interesting and fun.

3.2. Examples of AI-Powered World-Building

The *Unreal Engine's MetaHuman Creator* is an innovative AI-driven tool that revolutionizes the process of creating lifelike human characters for video games and virtual worlds. Developed by Epic Games, this cutting-edge software leverages advanced AI algorithms to generate highly realistic human models with precise facial expressions and movements. One of the most remarkable features of MetaHuman Creator is its utilization of sophisticated AI techniques, including machine learning and neural networks, to generate lifelike faces. By employing complex mathematical computations, the tool can produce human characters that exhibit a remarkable level of realism, capturing subtle nuances in facial expressions and gestures (Freedman, 2022).

The essence of the MetaHuman Creator is that it helps in both the democratization of characters as well as their creation at large across the virtual world of storytelling and game development. The traditional way of creating real characters was identified by the intensive use of 3D modeling and animation. The knowledge of those remained only in a hand of professionals, who can either afford it or the ones who studied it in special courses. Nevertheless, this technology will allow the prototyping of characters to be done by the artist, even at varying proficiency levels and the result will also be outstanding. With this democratization of character creation, new and innovative ideas are coming forth at a great speed which also helps in creating a diverse and inclusive arena in the virtual environments. Several users, including designers, story-tellers, and artistic directors, can with the benefit of MetaHuman Creator, populate their scenarios with a very wide variety of people, closely mirroring humanity in real life, looking real and admissible, with various ages, ethnicities, and identities.

Intentionally, MetaHuman Creator enables makers to design adventures and scenes from the Metaverse. This extends the realism of the Metaverse to make it even more appealing to the users. The ease of use and simple interface of the software, along with streamlined workflows, allow creators to attend to storytelling and world-building and not to the technicalities. These interactive creation capacities of the creators widen the storytelling pull and heighten their ability to offer more immersive and captivating experiences to their audiences of the viewers. Finally, it must be noted that MetaHuman Creator by Unreal Engine represents the great change that AI makes to digital content production. With the clever addition of AI technologies, the tool allows creators to express their creativity. They use the powerful immersive Metaverse environments which are created to enhance the overall experience.

The *Minecraft AI World Generator* is an excellent tool that uses knowledgeable AI-related things to make different worlds based on what players say; the AI World Generator looks at what players do to figure out how to put together unique and exciting places to play. Each time you start a new game, it feels fresh and new because the AI helps mix up the land features, areas, and buildings to keep things tailored for you (Salli, 2023).

The ***Urban Planning Simulator of CityEngine*** is an AI-focused program that makes city landscapes and wonderful building designs inside the Metaverse. It uses knowledgeable, automatic ways to make replica cities, roads, and blocks of buildings that look the real deal; this means that people who build these virtual cities get to see and figure out different city layouts well; the Urban Planning Simulator copies several things, how cars move through streets, how people walk around, and how the city affects nature, all so that the people who design these online cities can make them environmentally friendly and strong for the future in the Metaverse.

AI things are changing how virtual worlds are made up for the Metaverse; the knowledgeable technology and programs let people build wonderful and interesting digital places with fancy automatic creation-related things, learning machines, and pretend practices. By looking at real examples where AI was used to build digital landscapes, we get to see the new and exciting things AI can do in making the Metaverse. A thing could spark new ideas in this fast-moving area.

4. Collaborative Intelligence: Human-AI Co-Creation in Virtual Realms

In the world of the Metaverse that's always updating, people are teaming up with computers that think (AI) to mix their creative ideas and fresh inventions smoothly (Rezwana, 2023). By adding AI helpers and virtual creative friends into the way they work together, users can easily share ideas and create wonderful new things without sweat, pushing how far we can go with creative things in virtual places.

4.1. New Trends in Collaboration

Team Efforts in the Digital Space: In the virtual world of the Metaverse, people and AI team up and use their combined energies to make and improve related things, patterns, and thoughts right as they happen. Knowledgeable AI helpers use complex computer math to look at what users suggest and what they do, coming up with new thoughts – providing advice, and helping out when its time to make choices. By adding AI to the way, they work together, people can mix their ideas with the strong thinking and extremely fast analytics of AI; this makes them get work done smarter and come up with fresh, original creations.

Virtual collaborators are AI-driven entities that engage with users in virtual worlds, helping, guidance, and companionship. These virtual creatures can assume diverse manifestations, ranging from chatbots and avatars to digital assistants and creative collaborators. Virtual collaborators utilize NLP and dialogue creation algorithms to interact with users, discuss, provide suggestions, and facilitate collaborative ideation sessions. Virtual collaborators enable users to generate ideas, problem-solve, and explore novel creative paths within virtual environments, erasing human and machine intelligence distinctions.

Creative Companions are knowledgeable computer programs that help people get better at wonderful related things like painting, making music, or coming up with stories; these technology-savvy buddies look at what you are into and what you want to do to give you tips, tell you what is working, and spark new, excellent ideas; the virtual art pals suggest things like color mixes, layout designs, and all different kinds of artistic tenor based on what you like. Music knowledgeable programs go another route, pumping out tunes with the right sounds and rhythm for the mood you are after or the type of music you love. By teaming up with these advanced helpers, people can dive into artsy endeavors they have never tried before, play around with all sorts of ways to create, and supercharge their creativity in a made-up digital world.

4.2. Examples of Interdisciplinary Projects

Collaborative Art Creation with AI: Artists and AI researchers work together to produce interactive art installations that combine human creativity with AI algorithms. Google's "Deep Dream" tool, powered by AI algorithms, generates wonderful and abstract images, for the artists to use in their projects. Artists go beyond the limits of traditional artistic expression and doubt accepted views of authorship and originality when they employ human intuition together with AI tools.

A collaboration between the filmmakers and the engineers who develop AI produces immersive storytelling experiences within the VR environments. AI and digital tools and platforms allow the filmmakers to track the users' interactions and preferences to make the narrative part, behaviors of the character, and plot twists fit in real-time. AI usage enables filmmakers to generate interactive and more engaging fictions which augment to each viewer needs producing stronger immersion and interest in virtual environments.

The integration of AI-based game Development is characterized by a cooperation between game designers and AI experts geared toward the creation of intelligent characters, stunning environments and immersive gameplay within the virtual world. Real-time computation with machine learning algorithms lets game developers create NPCs (non-player characters) that can learn from past battles, acquire knowledge and develop over time in response to each player's behavior. The game makers can use AI-driven technologies to create and develop a game space that is virulent, dynamic, and always challenging players to rise on the level of their skills, imagination, and tactical thinking in virtual organs.

When people team up with AI in digital worlds, they imagine new things easier and freer than before; throwing AI helpers and creative sidekicks into the mixing pot with how we usually get things done, allows everyone to supercharge their brainpower with both smarts-out-of-a-book and calculated moves from a computer brain; they go for the sky to shoot up how amazing and intellectual the ideas can be in the Metaverse. Hanging in techy projects side by side with AI, we humans put together these wonderful and engaging things that pull others in, make them have absolute fun, and change the way we all play in these high-technology spaces.

5. From Consumption to Participation: Empowering Users in the AI-Metaverse Ecosystem

In the world where AI and the Metaverse mingle, more people want everyone to get a chance to be creative and make wonderful things; they are saying that it is important for people to have a say in making and looking after all the related things we see and do there; the stories that grow in the Metaverse are getting shaped by what everyone who uses it thinks and imagines thanks to things they make themselves, ideas that everyone can pitch in on, and stories that everyone gets to help tell.

5.1. The Democratization of Creativity and Innovation

DIY-related things on the Internet: It is where people get to make and share their very own things, drawings, designs, fantastic activities, and games on the computer. Places such as Roblox, Second Life, and Minecraft let people put together whatever they dream up for their online world; look you find online; this whole scene is big on letting all kinds of people show what they have got in a fun way. Plus, it ensures everyone gets a fair shake at being creative and picking out the best on the internet without playing favorites.

Crowdsourced design contests are about getting several people to work together on outstanding design projects, compete, and hang in the AI-Metaverse world; these contests give people a chance to show off how creative they are, how well they can solve a tricky problem, and share the fresh ideas appearing in their heads. Online places Hackathons, Game Jams, and Design Comps make it easy for coders, artists, and all sorts of interested people to team up and make new related things, digital buildings, virtual fashion, interactive stories, or video games; the AI-Metaverse community uses everyone's brainpower and artistic flair to tackle design challenges in this way; this game plan really sparks innovation and breaks down barriers to what we may think is possible in the digital world.

Participatory storytelling involves users actively collaborating and influencing the narrative of the Metaverse through interactive storytelling experiences, role-playing games (RPGs), and collaborative narratives. Platforms such as RPGs, Alternate Reality Games (ARGs), and Interactive Fiction (IF) enable users to engage with virtual worlds, characters, and storylines deeply. Users can shape the story's outcome by making choices and acting. Participatory storytelling in the AI-Metaverse ecosystem involves including users as active participants in the storytelling process. This approach creates a sense of agency, immersion, and community, blurring the traditional distinctions between audience, author, creator, and consumer.

5.2. Community Engagement Initiatives

Get-togethers, online hangouts, significant meet-and-greet events, and beautiful celebrations are excellent for connecting with others, joining forces on art-related things, and throwing out ideas you cooked up to people who dig the AI-Metaverse world; things this brings everyone into one big group where friends help each other out and throw around knowledgeable talk. AltspaceVR, Sansar, and VRChat are a few of the spots where you could find these things going on, with places where artists can show what they have been working on, bands can play jams live, experts yak about intellectual topics, and people share how to do a portion of this excellent thing themselves; these get-togethers create a pumped-up and welcoming tenor where people can show their skills and be, really connecting with others (Franks, 2020).

Skill Development Programs: These are things you can find a lot of, including classes online, workshops at school or computers, and lessons you get through the web; they let you pick up new tricks about how to do wonderful planning in this AI world contained within computer universes called the AI-Metaverse; the perks are that pretty much anyone can jump in, no matter if they are newbies or closer to pro, without emptying their pockets. Schools or programs ensure learning never hits a dead end and everybody gets smarter.

Places Unity Learn, Unreal Engine Academy; and websites such as Coursera have many lessons for building your own video game worlds, making up games, or telling stories that you build around the viewer. With these kinds of learning spots, anyone can spark up their imagination and help keep rolling out the story of what the Metaverse is turning into.

Knowledge-sharing systems, such as forums, social media groups, and online communities, enable individuals to collaborate, provide feedback, and share resources with each other inside the AI-Metaverse ecosystem. These platforms offer users a nurturing and cooperative setting to share ideas, seek guidance, and display their creative endeavors. Reddit, Discord, and DeviantArt are platforms that facilitate the existence of active communities consisting of producers, enthusiasts, and specialists. These communities contribute to developing a culture centered around collaborative creation and collective intelligence inside the AI-Metaverse ecosystem.

5.3. Meta-Formation: Crafting Creativity in the AI-Virtual Tapestry

Making it so that everyone can be creative and come up with new ideas in this AI-Metaverse world means that people get to make their own related things and control what goes on in these virtual spaces; the AI-Metaverse uses things that people using it create. It has got things for many people to do together, like design contests and making up stories with others, which taps into the smarts and creativity of everyone who is there; this makes it so that people who come there can make a mark and help each other making new and wonderful related things; the AI-Metaverse is focused on people forming groups, learning new skills, and passing on what they know. It gives everyone a chance to team up and show off how creative they are, and it plays a part in shaping what these computer-made places might be.

6. Ethical and Societal Considerations: Navigating the Complexities of AI-Metaverse Collaboration

Intellectual property rights, or IPR, become complex when we consider the combination of AI and the online world. We are not only discussing physical objects but also digital items such as internet art, virtual real estate, and collectibles in video games. Honestly, it is quite similar to how we deal with tangible items. Debates arise about who owns the creative work they have developed or acquired online – if you purchase a piece of virtual property in a location Decentraland or build a home there, you are left with a major question: Who truly has the ownership rights? Essentially, it is the online equivalent of disputes we see in everyday life about who owns what – but the twist is that digital items are harder to keep track of since anyone can replicate digital content quickly.

When AI programs used in the Metaverse learn from dodgy data, they start carrying the same unfair points of view, which might end up being pretty hurtful or making existing unfairness even worse; take, for instance, if a tool in the AI that builds characters mainly shows facial features common to ethnic or racial groups, it could unintentionally make people from other groups feel left out. We have seen this bias in AI before – those facial recognition systems that goof up more when scanning people with darker skin. If people are not paying good attention, these unfair components in the algorithm inside the Metaverse might make the unfair gaps we have become even more comprehensive.

6.1. Transparency, Accountability, and Inclusivity

Transparency: Transparency in AI-powered virtual experiences can be achieved by revealing how algorithms operate, the data they rely on, and the possible biases or limitations present in their design. As an example, VR social platforms, such as VRChat and AltspaceVR, could enlighten their users on how the AI moderation systems enforce community guidelines and how they manage user-generated content. Transparency increases trust and, as a result, helps users to make knowledgeable decisions about their participation in virtual spaces.

Accountability: There is a need for developers and platform owners to be accountable for the ethical implications of their AI-powered creations in the Metaverse. This includes recognized features for detecting cases of algorithmic bias and possible unintended consequences that may affect users or perpetuate discrimination. For example, companies such as Facebook (now Meta) have been blamed for the fact that their recommendation algorithms have been used to spread harmful content and fake news on social media platforms. The development of accountability mechanisms like independent audits or oversight boards will help to control these risks and ensure that the responsible people are held to account.

Inclusivity: Creating AI-powered virtual experiences involving inclusiveness implies considering not only the diverse needs but also the varying perspectives of users who come from diverse backgrounds. This includes the accessibility features for users with disabilities, representation of diverse identities within virtual avatars and environments, and antiquing harassment or discrimination in online communication. Likewise, Rec Room has adopted personalized avatars and moderation tools to help create a more welcoming and inclusive community environment. Priority on inclusivity improves the ease and pleasure of virtual experiences for all attendees.

6.2. Frameworks for Responsible Innovation and Ethical Design

Knowing How to Innovate Right: When we think about innovating responsibly with AI and the Metaverse, we need rules about focusing on people's health and happiness, being fair, and making sure things are clear. For instance, there is an enormous group that is focused on creating ethical technology, the IEEE Global Initiative on Ethics of Autonomous and Intelligent Systems, and they have made Ethically Aligned Design; these rules are pretty serious about making sure technology pays attention to what is important to humans, mixing in the right-and-wrong things while building AI, and they want to make sure that there are ways to keep things in check and down-to-earth (Chatila & Havens, 2019).

Fair Design Ways: In the world of AI and the metaverse, an excellent way to make things is to think a lot about what matters to people and to work closely with everyone who has a stake in it. If you want your AI things to care about what various people value, you would put those values into how you build it. The same goes for creating shared virtual things with users; this lets the people who will use it have a say and ensure it works for them. Bringing people into the building process helps makers think about any moral things that might arise and makes everyone feel part of the whole thing.

Sustainability in creating computer-knowledgeable virtual things means we want to use less power, cut out useless digital junk, and be careful about how our online world affects the real, natural world. So, let us say we make those VR games use less electricity by getting more competent at how they are built and using particular kinds of technology that are not so tough on the environment for things like computer collectibles. We should also teach everyone how to be more innovative with their digital gear, so they cause less harm to nature. Solving the tough questions about right and wrong as AI meets this vast virtual universe called the Metaverse means thinking deeply about topics, examining who owns ideas, how those AI judgment calls might be unfair sometimes, and who gets control over many of these digital objects or ideas. We must be open about how things get made, who gets to play, and ensuring everyone is invited. By picking guidelines about inventing new technology responsibly and with good morals, the people making these online spaces can be sure to think of everyone's happiness and health, including many different kinds of people, and keep nature as a priority.

7. Future Horizons: Envisioning the Next Frontier of Creative Synergy

The future scenario is when AI and Meta are becoming one, virtual environments turning into lifelike and interactive ones. Imagine living in a virtual environment where AI companions surround you with warmth and give you what you need depending on your preferences. Also, these companions will predict your emotions and tailor the virtual space based on that. The result will be a personalized experience in limitless virtual environments. The inter-related domains comprise many landscapes including futuristic cities as well as pristine natural environments and therefore promote ongoing exploration and creative collaboration, without any boundary.

In addition, with the rapid development of AI, it evolves from a useful tool to a partner who is working together with human beings in bringing forth great artworks, stories and music compositions that explore the spectrum of creativity and originality. Within the metaverse, storytelling goes through transformational changes, whereby the audience becomes an integral part of the narrative as they interact and influence the narrative outcome through decisions they make. In turn, it fosters curiosity, creativity, and collaboration.

Nevertheless, in the robotic revolution, there are the ethical issues like ownership, attribution, and representation among the AI-produced content, besides the technological challenges, such as development of more human-like AI interactions and the guarantee of data confidentiality and safety. However, admitting these difficulties and setting up an atmosphere that supports diversity and group orientation, we can utilize all the advantages of AI and Metaverse, therefore becoming virtual community with unlimited ideas and inventions.

8. Conclusion

To sum up, this chapter considers how AI and Metaverse might be combined to create virtual spaces of joint construction, which serve as interactive environments conducive to breakthrough progress and exploration. AI integration will allow the use of advanced technologies which make the Metaverse experience of each user unique and immersive. Metaverse will be a place where boundaries between the physical and virtual world are blurred. Swapping roles to consider scenarios – for instance, simulated storytelling apps and collective creating museums – we have established the unexplored territory of human creativity and artistic expression in virtual worlds. On the one hand, as we accompany the coming era in this field, not less serious are ethical aspects and risks that AI leads to the distribution of virtual zones. Our goal also strives for inclusivity, fairness, and privacy of all participants. In the end of these lines, we call readers to interact and participate in the creation of the future cooperative creative processes in virtual environments thus, strengthening the culture of innovation, imagination, and collaboration in digital times (virtual era). The epoch brought by AI technology and the Metaverse is an exciting time full of myriad opportunities for us to discover the superpowers that lie within us and bring to life our limitless imagination.

References

Al Kuwaiti, A., Nazer, K., Al-Reedy, A., Al-Shehri, S., Al-Muhanna, A., Subbarayalu, A. V., Al Muhanna, D & Al-Muhanna, F. A. (2023). A review of the role of artificial intelligence in healthcare. *Journal of Personalized Medicine, 13*(6), 951.

Castell, M. (2023). Facebook is now Meta. *Meta's corporate sociotechnical imaginary and the discursive construction of the Metaverse as the social platform of the future (Master's thesis)*. University of Gottenburg.

Chatila, R., & Havens, J. C. (2019). The IEEE global initiative on ethics of autonomous and intelligent systems. In *Robotics and well-being* (pp. 11–16). Springer.

Chung, J. J. Y. (2022, October). *Artistic user expressions in AI-powered creativity support tools* [Conference session]. Adjunct Proceedings of the 35th Annual ACM Symposium on User Interface Software and Technology (pp. 1–4).

Elgammal, A., Liu, B., Elhoseiny, M., & Mazzone, M. (2017). *Can: Creative adversarial networks, generating "art" by learning about styles and deviating from style norms.* preprint arXiv:1706.07068.

Elor, A., Powell, M., Mahmoodi, E., Teodorescu, M., & Kurniawan, S. (2021). Gaming beyond the novelty effect of immersive virtual reality for physical rehabilitation. *IEEE Transactions on Games, 14*(1), 107–115.

Franks, P. C. (2020, June). *Work-in-progress – Developing criteria for virtual reality courses based on virtual world experiences* [Conference session]. 2020 6th International Conference of the Immersive Learning Research Network (iLRN) (pp. 369–372). IEEE.

Freedman, E. (2022). *Non-binary binaries and unreal MetaHumans.* MIT.

Huynh-The, T., Pham, Q. V., Pham, X. Q., Nguyen, T. T., Han, Z., & Kim, D. S. (2023). Artificial intelligence for the metaverse: A survey. *Engineering Applications of Artificial Intelligence, 117*, 105581.

Lampropoulos, G., Keramopoulos, E., Diamantaras, K., & Evangelidis, G. (2022). Augmented reality and gamification in education: A systematic literature review of research, applications, and empirical studies. *Applied Sciences, 12*(13), 6809.

Pagani, M., & Champion, R. (Eds.). (2023). *Artificial intelligence for business creativity.* Taylor & Francis.

Park, S. M., & Kim, Y. G. (2022). A metaverse: Taxonomy, components, applications, and open challenges. *IEEE Access, 10*, 4209–4251.

Rezwana, J. (2023). *Towards designing engaging and ethical human-centered AI partners for human-AI co-creativity.* [Doctoral dissertation. The University of North Carolina at Charlotte].

Salli, M. (2023). *3D game character animations in unreal engine 5: Creation and implementation.* Packt Publishers.

Chapter 15

Good Governance and Implementation

Gaurav Duggal[a], Manoj Garg[a] and Achint Nigam[b]

[a]SVP, Jio Platforms Limited, Hyderabad, Telangana, India
[b]Birla Institute of Technology and Science, Pilani, Rajasthan, India

Abstract

In this chapter, we describe the importance of good governance in the metaverse. It offers unlimited opportunities and presents unique governance challenges. First, we describe the concept of good governance and its relevance to the metaverse. We emphasize that the speed of metaverse adoption depends upon the presence or absence of effective governance. Recognizing the metaverse as the next iteration of the internet, we present significant governance issues. Some issues such as interoperability, security, safety, privacy, law, and digital inequality are critical governance issues in the metaverse. Next, we explore the diverse governance frameworks to ensure the implementation of policies and regulations. These frameworks include decentralized governance, cross-sector collaboration, and standards-based governance. We also describe the best practices which are essential for good governance. To materialize the concepts and principles discussed, we present a compelling case study centered on Decentraland. This insightful exploration dissects a decentralized autonomous organization (DAO)-based governance structure, offering valuable insights into the intricacies and stages of governance proposals. We acknowledge both the merits and potential drawbacks inherent to this approach. This chapter aims to offer an all-encompassing view of metaverse governance, essentially serving as a comprehensive roadmap for traversing the multifaceted landscape of this digital frontier.

Keywords: Metaverse; governance; Decentraland; interoperability; decentralized autonomous organizations; blockchain; decentralized governance

1. Introduction

Metaverse (Wang et al., 2022), the next iteration of the internet creates tremendous opportunities (Wang et al., 2022) in various industries such as healthcare, travel, education, online gaming, entertainment, and agriculture. It also presents significant governance challenges (Fernandez & Hui, 2022). As we engage on this new technology, it becomes crucial to establish good governance principles and ensure effective implementation. According to Wikipedia, governance is the process of decision-making and how the decisions are implemented. Good governance should have transparency, accountability, participation, and the rule of law. Good governance in the metaverse plays an important role in encouraging innovation, growing trust, protecting user rights, and growth of the metaverse. It also plays a vital role in the functioning of institutions and organizations. It ensures that decisions are made with efficiency, integrity, and the best interests of all stakeholders in mind.

Transparency is the core principle of good governance (Fernandez & Hui, 2022). Transparency means the decisions are taken according to the rules and regulations (Parigi et al., 2004). It also means that information is freely available for the taken decisions. Anyone can access that information. It allows the decision-makers accountable for their decisions. We are living in an era where information is easily available and scrutinized, and transparency enables responsible governance. Involving stakeholders in the decision-making process ensures that decisions are informed and balanced. Involving employees in corporate decisions and engaging citizens in governmental policy making results in better governance. In the metaverse, decentralization enables users involved in framing rules and regulations that judge their digital experiences. This type of involvement not only improves the quality of decisions but also creates a feeling of ownership and engagement.

Rule of law is another core principle in good governance. This principle ensures that decisions are made according to designed rules and regulations. It prevents random decisions and reduction of corruption. Ethical behavior (Fernandez & Hui, 2022) is also important in good governance by which credibility and trust are built. Following ethical standards results in maintaining safe and respectful environment in the metaverse. It also results in having the environment free from cyberbullying (Upadhyay et al., 2023), harassment (Qasem et al., 2022), and other forms of misconduct.

Efficiency in resource management is a crucial element of good governance. Resource optimization is essential in different aspects such as the allocation of public funds in government or the utilization of corporate resources in businesses. Resource efficiency is particularly relevant in digital spaces, where computing power and energy consumption can impact both the environment and the user experience. A strategic vision provides the guiding light for decisions and actions within the scope of good governance. It outlines long-term goals, values, and aspirations, which in turn influence short-term decisions. A well-defined vision not only ensures consistency in decision-making but also helps organizations navigate uncertainties and challenges by providing a clear sense of direction.

Conflict resolution mechanisms are essential in good governance. Disagreements are unavoidable, but how they are managed can significantly impact the harmony of an environment. Effective conflict resolution enables collaboration and prevents escalation. Adaptability is also essential in effective governance in the metaverse. The ability to adapt to new technological advancements and meet community expectations is crucial for maintaining relevance and effectiveness. Governance models should adapt to rapid technological changes and emerging user behaviors. Sustainability is an essential consideration within the realm of good governance. Sustainable governance considers the long-term well-being of stakeholders, future generations, and the environment. In the metaverse, sustainable governance could involve addressing two aspects. One aspect is to address the digital divide to ensure equal access to virtual experiences. Another one is to minimize the environmental impact of digital infrastructure.

The metaverse, often termed as the next iteration of the Internet, necessitates a thoughtful approach to governance. The rate of metaverse adoption will heavily depend on the presence or absence of effective governance structures. The rest of the book chapter is organized as follows: governance issues in metaverse are described in Section 2 whereas governance frameworks are explored in Section 3. Section 4 discusses the best practices for good governance. Metaverse governance is studied through a case study on Decentraland in Section 5. We conclude the book chapter in Section 6.

2. Governance Issues

Addressing critical governance issues is essential for the metaverse's long-term success. These issues include interoperability, security and safety, privacy, law, incentives, competition, and digital inequality. Now, we describe these issues below.

2.1. Interoperability

In metaverse, interoperability (Ghirmai et al., 2022) indicates that the ability to visit different virtual environments smoothly and move their data to preferred locations or metaverse service providers (MSP). A non-interoperable metaverse environment might limit the user's avatar, identity, and data to a specific MSP. If interoperability standards are established then users can traverse various virtual worlds seamlessly ensuring an interconnected digital experience. Establishing interoperability in the metaverse is essential for several reasons. It enables connecting a vast number of individuals and having shared experiences. As different virtual worlds become interconnected, users from diverse backgrounds can interact and collaborate with each other. As a result, it creates a global community.

Users get more enjoyment when users from different virtual worlds interact and share their experiences. For example, if shopping in one virtual world and attending live music in another virtual world become seamless, users feel more convenient. This results in more people engaging in metaverse platforms. For new users also, this seamless traveling from one virtual space to another virtual space enables excitement and enjoyment. The ability to traverse different virtual platforms encourages innovation among creators. As interoperability becomes standard, creators need to spend extra time to retain their users. This results in the development of new technologies and improved content quality. Users can enjoy multiple choices on different metaverse platforms.

2.2. Security and Safety

Ensuring the security and safety (Chen et al., 2022) of users is another essential concern in the metaverse. Strong security measures such as encryption, secure authentication, and secure communication channels must be implemented. Also, addressing cyberbullying, harassment, and assaults is crucial to maintaining a safe virtual environment for all users. Cyberbullying and harassment affect the mental and emotional health of individuals. In VRChat, there are incidents of cyberbullying and harassment. virtual rapes on female avatars. It can damage the mental balance of the victim.

2.3. Privacy

Protecting user privacy (Chen et al., 2022; Lee et al., 2023) is a critical aspect of metaverse governance. Policies should be implemented to protect the user privacy. Clear data sharing guidelines and informed consent must be established to have user trust and safeguard personal information. Encryption, digital twin avatar, and secure authentication are few techniques which can be employed to protect the privacy. Also, a private replica of virtual world (parallel metaverse) can be created to protect the privacy of individuals who are actively engaging in metaverse platforms.

2.4. Law

Legal frameworks are essential to govern the metaverse activities (Qin et al., 2022; Sia, 2023). There may be legal challenges when different virtual platforms work together regarding ownership, control, and handling of data generated in the metaverse. There is a need to establish new laws for new categories of virtual crimes, such as offenses and abuses committed by the avatars. There are some important issues to address such as ownership, property rights, and copyright for virtual assets. For example, if someone buys virtual land, how should existing laws can be applied in the metaverse scenario. Are the same laws applied or new laws to be established? Laws need to be established to address the dominance of single company in the metaverse and limiting users over their experiences.

2.5. Digital Inequality

Metaverse access is not available to all countries due to various factors, and it leads to digital inequality (Göknur et al., 2023). These factors include economic differences, geographic location, digital and technological infrastructure, and digital literacy. To ensure the metaverse provides equal opportunities for all, efforts must be made to bridge the digital divide. Otherwise, some segments of people could not experience the metaverse and the opportunities it provides. Some countries cannot afford metaverse technologies. Solutions should be established to handle these issues so that metaverse opportunities can be availed by all the people and feel an immersive experience. Three suggestions are provided to reduce digital inequality in a recent study (Natalie Lacey, 2023). One suggestion is to speak about opportunities to participate in the metaverse platform like experiencing a new city or location. Another one is to explain how people can participate in the metaverse without significant investment in the device. The last one is to build the awareness that the metaverse is "for people like me" by showing some experiences.

3. Governance Frameworks

In this section, we describe different governance frameworks for effective governance in the metaverse. These frameworks include decentralized governance, cross-sector collaboration, and theoretical standards-based metaverse governance. Now, we describe these governance frameworks below.

3.1. Decentralized Governance

Decentralization in metaverse refers to the power and control are distributed among the users, and it is not held by a single entity or authority. Decentralized governance framework uses the concept of decentralization in metaverse. All the individuals and stake holders have the power in decision-making process. Blockchain technology uses decentralization concept. It is a decentralized ledger that can store information and transactions in secure and transparent manner without the need of intermediate entities. Now, we describe the components of decentralized governance framework.

3.1.1. Blockchain Technology

Blockchain technology (Gadekallu et al., 2022) is the core entity of decentralized governance in the metaverse. This technology can store all governance related activities in a transparent and secure way. Users can verify the governance activities because of its transparent nature. This technology enables confidence in the governance process ensuring that decisions are transparent and resistant against attacks.

3.1.2. Decentralized Autonomous Organizations (DAOs)

DAOs (Goldberg & Schär, 2023) establishment is central pillar of this governance framework. A DAO is a digital management structure controlled by smart contracts with decisions stored on a blockchain. Smart contract executes actions based on predefined rules and outcomes. DAOs play a significant role in metaverse allowing users to make decisions collectively that can impact the virtual environments. Voting mechanisms can be employed by DAOs for the decision-making processes.

3.1.3. Token-Based Voting

Token-based voting mechanisms are utilized by many metaverse governance systems (Goldberg & Schär, 2023). These tokens are in the form of non-fungible tokens (NFT) (David & Won, 2022) or cryptocurrencies. Participants get granting power based on number of tokens or cryptocurrencies they own. For example, users who have many tokens have a greater influence on governance decisions and users who have less tokens have a lesser influence. These tokens represent the ownership in the metaverse, such as virtual land or digital assets. Users can buy land, virtual assets, in-game items using these tokens. Different virtual worlds have different cryptocurrencies for doing transactions. For example, MANA is the currency in Decentraland whereas Linden dollar is the currency in Second Life, a virtual metaverse platform. This token-based approach provides a concrete connection between ownership and decision-making power.

3.1.4. Proposal and Voting Mechanisms

Users in metaverse create new proposals which can impact the current virtual platform. These proposals cover a wide range of topics such as revising virtual platform rules, and implementing new features that advance the metaverse in technical perspective. Once a proposal is created then opinions about the proposal must be gathered by the members of the community. These opinions can be gathered through voting mechanisms. Token holders cast their votes on the created proposals. Blockchain technology is used in the voting mechanism to ensure security and transparency.

3.1.5. Transparent Decision Records

Blockchain technology is used to record all governance decisions. This technology ensures that decision records are stored in a transparent manner. Transparency ensures accountability and responsible governance. It assures that corruption is reduced and opinions of minorities are taken into account. Transparency means sharing the information and acting in an open way. It ensures that sufficient information is provided in an easy and understandable manner.

3.1.6. Incentive Mechanisms

Tokens are provided to the users as a reward for their active participation in governance related decisions in metaverse. The tokens are in the form of NFTs and cryptocurrencies. These type of incentive mechanisms help in getting active participation among the community members in metaverse.

3.1.7. Community Engagement

Active participation from the user community is the primary aspect to the success of decentralized governance (Rathore, 2018). Several communication channels are established to allow robust decisions and collaboration among participants in the community. These channels include online forums, custom governance user interfaces, and social media platforms. Discussions in these communication channels enable users to voice their opinions and actively engage in decision-making process.

3.1.8. Dispute Resolution

The virtual worlds are no more immune to disputes than the physical world. Trading in virtual real estate, NFTs, and cryptocurrencies can trigger conflicts between users and MSP or between the users themselves. To solve these types of conflicts, effective dispute resolution frameworks are established (AlLouzi & Alomari, 2023). Conflicts may arise in the metaverse environment for a variety of reasons. For example, a metaverse operator might decrease or increase the number of available virtual properties, increase the price of the properties, a user might fail to transfer an NFT, or a platform operator might cancel the user's account. Strong dispute resolution mechanisms are established to handle dispute related issues. These frameworks enable mediation and resolution which ensures that conflicts are addressed constructively.

3.1.9. Evolving Governance Structures

Governance structures can change over time because of the changing needs of the metaverse's technological advancement. Governance frameworks should adapt to these types of changes. The user community iteratively refines the rules to guide the metaverse's development. This type of approach ensures that the metaverse's governance remains dynamic and adaptive.

Decentralized governance plays a vital role in metaverse growth. It allows users to actively participate in governance decisions. As the metaverse continues to evolve, governance frameworks must change accordingly.

3.2. Cross-Sector Collaboration

Cross-sector collaboration framework is another governance framework in metaverse. This governance framework involves collaboration between governments, technology companies, regulators, and user communities (Lin et al., 2022). It is a structured approach. Establishing consortiums, multi-stakeholder platforms, and industry bodies can promote dialogue, encourage sharing of information, and assist the development of effective governance frameworks. This framework aims to create a responsible virtual environment. It allows for innovation while safeguarding the interests of all participants in the community. The key components in this framework include identifying stakeholders, creating communication channels, defining interoperability standards, educating users, promoting innovation, handling disputes, emphasizing transparency, and allowing for scalability.

3.3. Theoretical Standard-Based Metaverse Governance (TS-MG)

The metaverse is a digital world that combines virtual and real elements, offering immersive experiences. To build the metaverse, technical standards are crucial (Yang, 2023). These standards guide how the metaverse works and is experienced. They cover various aspects like extended reality tech for immersion, digital twin tech for real-world imagery, and blockchain for the economic system. The virtual and real worlds merge in the metaverse's economic, social, and identity systems. Users can create and modify content. Standards also drive commercial applications. Technology is a driving force, guided by governments or market players. Standards come from government bodies or industry groups. Unlike traditional industries, metaverse standards are established early due to rapid growth. Thus, setting standards early is crucial to manage the metaverse later. There are three components in this framework such as formulation of standards, compatibility of standards, and security of standards (Yang, 2023, pp. 3–5).

3.3.1. Formulation of Standards

Three elements guide the early establishment of metaverse standards:

- Accumulating technical expertise in advance helps cut down the construction costs of the sub-universe in the metaverse. Technical standards and protocols simplify data coding. The metaverse accommodates users with diverse requirements, creating a realistic virtual world that continually expands its boundaries. These metaverse technical standards are open source and known for their creative capabilities. They represent the best current practices, providing a standard path for the development of the sub-universe.
- Creating artificial scarcity and diverse resources in the metaverse for enhanced user experiences. The transition from mobile internet to metaverse offers new digital opportunities, benefiting those who establish standards and secure scarce resources.
- Controlling metaverse rule-making for investment benefits. Early entrants like Facebook and Tencent sought advantages through technical rules. Improved governance and influence of standard-setters help early adopters gain tech dividends in the less-regulated metaverse.

3.3.2. Compatibility of Standards

Technical standards' compatibility is vital. The metaverse depends on connectivity; isolated parts cannot form a true metaverse. Compatibility ensures different sub-universes can connect and interact. It's like ensuring websites can work together on the internet. A metaverse needs various technical standards for rendering, AI, asset formats, etc., to interact seamlessly. Compatibility fosters innovation and integration between the digital and physical worlds.

3.3.3. Security of Standards

Metaverse security involves data, networks, and AI risks. Standards must address data breaches, hacking, and misuse. Governments can safeguard metaverse security by setting secure technical standards, especially for data protection.

International cooperation is needed due to data crossing borders. Countries need unified standards for data protection to ensure consistent security.

3.3.4. Phased Governance Countermeasures

Metaverse development has stages: early, growth, and maturity. In the early stage, standards have low compatibility but high security. Sub-universes cannot connect seamlessly. In the growth stage, compatibility improves but trade-offs with security are made. Some sub-universes connect well, some do not. This can lead to cellular or hierarchical governance. In the mature stage, all sub-universes have high compatibility and security, forming a complete metaverse. Governments play a role in steering the metaverse through these stages. They need to balance compatibility and security, ensuring a safe and interconnected metaverse.

3.3.5. Policy Suggestions for Metaverse Technical Standardization and Governance

The following are the three main policy suggestions for the TS-MG framework (Yang, 2023, p. 8).

Development Strategies:

- Set development goals for metaverse standards.
- Establish mandatory and voluntary standards for safety and transparency.
- Develop security standards and promote blockchain technology.

Cooperation:

- Encourage global cooperation through trade and technology agreements.
- Ensure joint planning and transparent processes to avoid conflicts.
- Foster international dialogue and cooperation in metaverse standards.

Industry-Level Focus:

- Manage standardization strategies of platforms to prevent monopoly.
- Support industry alliances and rapid responses to specific technical needs.
- Issue metaverse standards to support regulations and policies.

4. Best Practices for Good Governance

Best practices should be followed for good and effective governance. These practices include establishing standards (technical, economic, ethical, regulatory, and user experience), laws and regulations, policies and incentives, and good infrastructure. Now, we describe these practices below.

4.1. Standards

Standards in the metaverse play a crucial role in ensuring good governance and responsible management within this evolving digital frontier. These standards encompass a wide range of aspects, from technical and interoperability standards to ethical and behavioral guidelines.

4.1.1. Technical Standards

4.1.1.1. Interoperability. One of the primary technical standards in the metaverse is interoperability (Bennett, 2022). This involves creating protocols and technical specifications that allow different virtual worlds, platforms, and digital assets to interact seamlessly. Interoperability ensures that users and assets can move freely between different metaverse spaces, promoting inclusivity and open access.

4.1.1.2. Data and Security. Cybersecurity risks are increasing and poses significant challenges in the metaverse. Some of the risks include identity theft, virtual property theft, and hacking of digital twin operations. Users interact with other users through avatars. These interactions could leak personal data of the users and their preferences. So, standards related to data protection, encryption, and identity protection should be established (Yang, 2023). These standards help in maintaining the integrity of user information and build trust in the metaverse.

4.1.1.3. Scalability. Scalability in the metaverse refers to the capacity of the metaverse to increase in size as the user base increases without affecting the user experience. Scalable metaverse should remain efficient in all scenarios. Some scenarios include increase in concurrent users, increase in scene complexity, and mode of user interactions. It is estimated the user base in metaverse can tremendously increase by 2025. As active users increase every day, scalability is a major concern in metaverse. Standards for scalability are crucial due to dynamic and rapidly growing nature of the metaverse. These scalability standards ensure that the metaverse infrastructure can support growing number of users without compromising the performance.

4.1.2. Economic and Financial Standards

4.1.2.1. Virtual Currency. Virtual currencies are used to perform any financial transaction in Metaverse (Park & Kim, 2022). For example, users can buy virtual land, digital asset, and in-game items using virtual currencies. Some virtual currencies in metaverse include SAND in Sandbox, MANA in Decentraland, Linden dollar in Second Life, Robux in Roblox, etc. Standards for the creation, use, and exchange of virtual currencies must be established. This helps prevent fraud and ensure financial transparency within virtual economies.

4.1.2.2. Digital Property Rights. Establishing standards for digital property rights in the metaverse is essential. It ensures that user's ownership of digital assets, such as land and virtual real estate is legally recognized and protected (Dong & Wang, 2023).

4.1.3. Content and Ethical Standards

4.1.3.1. Content Moderation. Content moderation refers to the process of monitoring and managing user-generated content in metaverse platforms (Hine, 2023). This content moderation ensures that users are following standards and guidelines set by the virtual platforms. The content includes text, image, audio, and video. It is a challenging task in metaverse due to its nuanced 3D nature and the way users immerse themselves in this new virtual world. Effective content moderation is crucial for safe virtual environment. Combination of AI-driven content analysis methods and human interpretation can be applied for content moderation in metaverse platforms. Standards should be established for content moderation in metaverse to define what is acceptable and unacceptable in terms of user-generated content. These standards help in maintaining a safe environment free from harassment, hate speech, cyberbullying, harmful content, and other forms of misconduct. Meta established an independent institution named Oversight Board (OB) (Wong & Floridi, 2023) to review Facebook's and Instagram's content moderation decisions.

4.1.3.2. Digital Identity. Individuals in metaverse interact through avatars. Identity theft is one of the major concerns in metaverse. Apart from mimicking digital identity through the avatars, it is also possible mimic voice. There are advanced AI algorithms for voice cloning to mimic the voice. So, users should be careful regarding these concerns as it damages them personally and financially. Standards regarding identity representation and verification can help in preventing identity theft (Wu & Zhang, 2023).

4.1.4. Governance and Regulatory Standards

4.1.4.1. Decentralized Governance. Standards for decentralized governance frameworks like DAOs ensure that decision-making processes are transparent and accountable (Goldberg & Schär, 2023). For example, Decentraland is following decentralized governance framework.

4.1.4.2. Regulatory Compliance. In the metaverse, collaboration with regulatory bodies and adherence to legal standards is vital. This helps to navigate legal complexities and protect user rights (Hutson et al., 2023). Issues such as taxation, intellectual property, and consumer protection are addressed by regulatory compliance standards.

4.1.4.3. Transparency and Accountability. Transparency standards ensure that metaverse platforms disclose relevant information about their operations and financial activities. Metaverse platform providers that are transparent about they use the data and benefits the customers overtake their competitors. Standards for accountability hold entities responsible for their actions, creating trust among users (Wang et al., 2022). Blockchain technology is used in metaverse to maintain transparency and accountability.

4.1.5. User Experience and Accessibility Standard

4.1.5.1. User Interface (UI) and User Experience (UX). Immersive UI design is the key to navigate the complex virtual world. UI designers should prioritize the immersion, personalization, and inclusivity. This can help in shaping the metaverse that not only meet the technological expectations but also encourages meaningful conversations in the virtual world. UI designers play a crucial role in designing UI that defines user digital experiences across the vast expanse of metaverse. Standards for UIs and experiences provide a user-friendly metaverse (Far & Rad, 2022). These standards promote usability and accessibility for all users, including those with disabilities.

4.1.5.2. Accessibility. How metaverse will work for people with visual disabilities and impairments? For people with visual disabilities, we can use screen reading capabilities along with audio description. For people with visual impairments, there should be choices to increase the contrast and turn on a color blind mode. For deaf or hearing impairment users there are several solutions. For deaf, text to speech technology can be used. In this approach, people write words and audio is generated through their avatar using AI algorithms. For hearing impairment users, sign language interpretation service can be used, which can be useful to carryout verbal conversations. Standards for accessibility should be established. These standards ensure that the metaverse is accessible to users with disabilities, including those who use assistive technologies.

Standards in the metaverse are critical for good governance. They comprise technical, economic, ethical, regulatory, and user-centric aspects. These standards serve as a foundation for a well-governed metaverse. This ensures that it remains secure, transparent, and sustainable as it continues to evolve. As the metaverse continues to grow, ongoing collaboration among stakeholders will be crucial to refining and implementing these standards effectively.

4.2. Laws and Regulations

To ensure the good governance in metaverse, laws and regulations must be established (Turdialiev, 2023). These laws define how virtual platforms operate and protect the user rights. Digital property laws should be implemented in metaverse. The rules related to virtual ownership of different items such as land, in-game items are defined by these laws. Data privacy regulations (Chen et al., 2022) should be established. These regulations define the rules such as how the user data is collected and stored in virtual environments. These rules also help in protecting the user information from hackers. Content moderation laws are equally important (Hine, 2023). The laws related to what type of content can be posted and what is acceptable, what is not acceptable are defined here. These laws help in reducing the harmful and abusive content in the virtual environment. A key consideration is the one which require international cooperation, i.e., how to handle national boundaries has no clear understanding in metaverse.

Regulation for virtual currencies and transactions is also essential. They help in preventing fraudulent transactions and keep the transactions safe and secure. Intellectual property laws also should be implemented. These rules ensure that users' innovations are safeguarded and recognized. Laws related to taxation must be established. These laws help to pay the tax thereby contributing to the growth of the economy. Child safety laws are important in virtual environments (Phippen, 2022). Children can be protected from seeing inappropriate content. The goal behind these rules and regulations is to have a balance between innovation and user protection. They form the foundation of good governance in the metaverse.

4.3. Policy and Incentives

Creating effective policies and incentives is essential for good governance in the metaverse. Policies provide a structured framework. They create the rules and establish boundaries to protect users and their digital assets. Such policies comprise areas like data privacy, content moderation, and digital property rights. These policy guidelines act as a roadmap for metaverse platforms and communities. Governments should support the development and adoption of the metaverse. Recently, World Economic Forum identified that Seoul, Dubai, and Santa Monica are the leading cities in the growing metaverse sector as reported by ABI research (Shashwat Sankranti, 2023). The report predicted that around 700 cities worldwide will adopt metaverse technology. Seoul is committing to USD180 million to develop a national metaverse ecosystem. Metaverse plays a significant role in Dubai's economic growth. In Santa Monica, the metaverse is adapted through a social media app called FlickPlay. The global metaverse market is expected to reach $936.6 billion by 2030 according to Statista (Shashwat Sankranti, 2023).

Incentives, on the other hand, are another essential aspect of good governance. These incentives may help in positive behavior and community engagement in the platform. For example, metaverse platform providers give incentives to content creators and developers to give quality experiences in the metaverse. Similarly, users are given incentives for reporting harmful, abusive, and hate content and actively participating in governance decisions. Policies and incentives should adapt to any new technological changes in the metaverse. This adaptability ensures the metaverse platform is ready to accommodate the evolving needs of diverse users in the community

4.4. Infrastructure

Infrastructure is the digital backbone for good governance (Dwivedi et al., 2022). The infrastructure can be in terms of technical, social, and organizational level. Strong technical infrastructure enables the metaverse operates smoothly without any issues. It involves in the development and maintenance of secure and scalable systems. A local high bandwidth and low latency infrastructure is required. It requires development in gigabit speeds, milliseconds latency with local and cloud computing capability. Governments should support the organizations that are building the infrastructure required for metaverse in the form of tax incentives, subsidies, and encouragement of collaboration.

5. Exploring Metaverse Governance: A Case Study of Decentraland

In this section, we explore the metaverse governance through a case study focused on Decentraland.

5.1. Decentraland

Decentraland is a metaverse platform built on Etherum blockchain technology (Guidi & Michienzi, 2022). Users can buy virtual land through the MANA cryptocurrency. These virtual plots bought in the form of NFTs. Decentralized governance system is employed through DAOs in Decentraland platform. With MANA currency users engage in financial transactions and governance decisions. It is committed to have cross-platform compatibility and offers monetization opportunities. Due to these reasons, it is positioned as an exciting player in landscape of virtual worlds.

5.2. Decentralized Governance in Decentraland

Decentraland employed a decentralized governance model in their platform. Decision-making capability is not concentrated in a single entity but spread across its community members (Goldberg & Schär, 2023). This makes the virtual platform robust. It can easily adapt to new technological advancements using this governance model. Each member has the opportunity to frame the platform's rules and regulations. They cast the votes for different proposals, rules, and decisions through voting mechanisms. So, the community members play a significant role in taking the virtual platform to new heights. Transparency is also existing in this platform. Anyone can have access to rules and regulations. The users can easily understand the rationale behind the decisions made in the digital platform. This type of governance structure safeguards against the concentration of power.

5.2.1. DAO-Based Governance

Decentraland's architecture focuses on decentralizing the power among its users through the management of assets on blockchain and platform servers which are managed by the DAO (Goldberg & Schär, 2023). The DAO can change the rules of the virtual environment. Rules and actions are predefined in smart contracts and all transactions are recorded. All interested individuals can engage and participate according to the rules provided in the smart contracts. There is no single authority but decision-making power is distributed among the users of the platform. The users can participate in decision-making through a voting mechanism. All the actions or activities within the DAO are available to the public and transparency is ensured. Any individual member can see the activities and can question the organization decisions. Decisions related to resource allocation and proposals can be taken through voting by the DAO members.

5.2.2. Working of DAO

The DAO in Decentraland uses a combination of two approaches for the decision-making process. In the first approach, community members in the DAO can participate in decision-making through a voting mechanism without any fees for voting. This enables the individuals holding MANA, NAMES, or LAND can participate in the DAO's activities. MANA is a Decentraland's fungible cryptocurrency token,

LAND is a non-fungible digital asset that represents the parcels of virtual land, and NAMES is a NFT. Multi-signature (multi-sig) wallet is used by DAO to implement the off-chain decisions on the blockchain. This multi-sig wallet is controlled by a committee known as the "DAO Committee." The off-chain decision execution is the responsibility of the DAO Committee. Security of operations is guaranteed by using the multi-sig wallet. The DAO includes an additional layer of protection through a second multi-sig wallet which is owned by the SAB (Smart Assets Bureaucracy). This secondary multi-sig wallet enhances the security measures implemented by the DAO Committee further bolstering the overall security of the DAO's operations.

The DAO consists of an intricate framework composed of various layers, entities, and platforms, which are shown in Table 1.

Table 1. DAO Entities and Their Descriptions.

Platform or Entity	Description
Governance dApp	The main interface is located at governance.decentraland.org. In this portal users login, generate proposals, and participate in voting.
Snapshot	Store proposals, votes and outcomes securely and in a decentralized manner. Users can delegate their voting power.
Aragon	Secure platform to manage and create collection of smart contracts to run a DAO. Backend of Decentraland's DAO is constructed using Aragon.
DAO Committee	Group of three individuals chosen by the community members. This committee is responsible for executing binding actions that have been approved through votes.
Security Advisory Board (SAB)	Oversees the DAO Committee and promptly addressing vulnerability and bug reports. Plays a vital role in ensuring the security of Decentraland's smart contracts.
The Forum	It is the communication hub for DAO. It is a space for voters to engage in discussions concerning the potential impacts and concerns associated with a proposal.
Discord Servers	DAO operates on two discord servers. One is related to general announcements, discussions, and inquiries related to the DAO. Another server is related to monthly Town Hall meetings and specific channels for working groups focusing on more complex matters.

5.2.3. Stages of Governance Proposal

There are three stages in governance proposal such as pre-proposal poll, draft proposal, and governance proposal. These stages are shown in Table 2.

5.2.4. Drawbacks of DAO

The Decentraland DAO has its shortcomings as a method of governance. It has limited options as it is almost automated. The binding proposals listed in the Governance Decentraland app can be used to approach the functions of smart contracts. But these functions are limited in number. Even appending and altering these functions or other governance procedures is way too tricky. The community members will have to follow a rigorous three-stage process to advance toward a binding governance proposal. In this kind of platform, bringing about changes is a time-consuming procedure.

When all members actively participate in every decision-making process within an organization, it can result in slow progress and hindered development. It may take a significant amount of time for members to comprehend and make decisions regarding project changes and advancements. For instance, if the DAO intends to purchase a NFT, it might need to explain the concept of NFTs to certain members. In some cases, other members may struggle to grasp the concept, and those explaining it may face difficulties in ensuring understanding among everyone. This situation creates bottlenecks that could potentially lead to the loss of the NFT to another interested buyer who can act swiftly.

Automated systems lack the interpretation or logic of votes which is observed in traditional voting processes involving humans. There is also an argument that automation may eliminate critical thinking. This is critical for significant organizational changes. Voting power and token distribution disparities may lead to decision-making concentration of few people only. This is not good for a decentrailzed governance framework.

Table 2. Stages of Governance Proposal in Decentraland. VP: Voting Power.

Stage	Proposal	Submission threshold	Passage threshold	Voting period	Goal
1	Pre-proposal poll	100 VP	500K VP	5 days	Introduce a governance issue
2	Draft proposal	1000 VP	1M VP	1 week	Present a potential policy
3	Governance proposal	2,500 VP	6M VP	2 weeks	Formalize the past draft into a binding governance outcome

6. Conclusion

In this chapter, we discussed the importance of good governance in the metaverse and its implementation. We explored several governance issues in the metaverse. These include interoperability, security, safety, digital inequality, etc. Governance models should address these issues for the effective working of virtual reality environments. We examined different governance frameworks in this chapter. We observed that decentralized governance plays a crucial role in the metaverse. For example, Decentraland uses a decentralized governance framework in its virtual world platform. We also described the best practices for good governance. We discussed the governance framework through a case study on Decentraland. We explained the DAO-based governance structure in Decentraland. The DAO-based governance has some limitations like a rigorous three-stage process for governance proposal. The principles and insights presented in this chapter will serve as guidelines for the metaverse in the future also.

References

AlLouzi, A., & Alomari, K. (2023). Adequate legal rules in settling metaverse disputes: Hybrid legal framework for metaverse dispute resolution (HLFMDR). *International Journal of Data and Network Science*, 7(4), 1627–1642. http://dx.doi.org/10.5267/j.ijdns.2023.8.001

Bennett, D. (2022). Remote workforce, virtual team tasks, and employee engagement tools in a real-time interoperable decentralized metaverse. *Psychosociological Issues in Human Resource Management*, 10(1), 78–91. http://dx.doi.org/10.22381/pihrm10120226

Chen, Z., Wu, J., Gan, W., & Qi, Z. (2022, December). *Metaverse security and privacy: An overview* [Conference session]. In 2022 IEEE International Conference on Big Data (Big Data) (pp. 2950–2959). IEEE. http://dx.doi.org/10.1109/BigData55660.2022.10021112

David, L. E. E., & Won, L. S. (2022). Nft of Nft: Is our imagination the only limitation of the metaverse? *The Journal of The British Blockchain Association*.

Dong, Y., & Wang, C. (2023). Copyright protection on NFT digital works in the Metaverse. *Security and Safety*, 2, 2023013.

Dwivedi, Y. K., Hughes, L., Baabdullah, A. M., Ribeiro-Navarrete, S., Giannakis, M., Al-Debei, M. M., ... Wamba, S. F. (2022). Metaverse beyond the hype: Multidisciplinary perspectives on emerging challenges, opportunities, and agenda for research, practice and policy. *International Journal of Information Management*, 66, 102542.

Far, S. B., & Rad, A. I. (2022). Applying digital twins in metaverse: User interface, security and privacy challenges. *Journal of Metaverse*, 2(1), 8–15.

Fernandez, C. B., & Hui, P. (2022, July). *Life, the metaverse and everything: An overview of privacy, ethics, and governance in metaverse* [Conference session]. 2022 IEEE 42nd International Conference on Distributed Computing Systems Workshops (ICDCSW) (pp. 272–277). IEEE.

Gadekallu, T. R., Huynh-The, T., Wang, W., Yenduri, G., Ranaweera, P., Pham, Q. V., ... Liyanage, M. (2022). Blockchain for the metaverse: A review. *arXiv preprint arXiv:2203.09738*.

Ghirmai, S., Mebrahtom, D., Aloqaily, M., Guizani, M., & Debbah, M. (2022, December). *Self- sovereign identity for trust and interoperability in the metaverse* [Conference session]. 2022 IEEE Smartworld, Ubiquitous Intelligence & Computing, Scalable Computing & Communications, Digital Twin, Privacy Computing, Metaverse, Autonomous & Trusted Vehicles (SmartWorld/UIC/ScalCom/DigitalTwin/PriComp/Meta) (pp. 2468–2475). IEEE.

Göknur, E. G. E., Youssouf, M. M., & Darnadji, D. (2023). Digital divide and Africa in the upcoming metaverse era: A study on the examples of Chad and Djibouti. Prof. Dursun KOSE, Ph. D. thesis, p. 388.

Goldberg, M., & Schär, F. (2023). Metaverse governance: An empirical analysis of voting within Decentralized Autonomous Organizations. *Journal of Business Research*, *160*, 113764.

Guidi, B., & Michienzi, A. (2022, July). *Social games and Blockchain: exploring the Metaverse of Decentraland* [Conference session]. 2022 IEEE 42nd International Conference on Distributed Computing Systems Workshops (ICDCSW) (pp. 199–204). IEEE.

Hine, E. (2023). Content moderation in the metaverse could be a new frontier to attack freedom of expression. *Philosophy & Technology*, *36*(3), 43.

Hutson, J., Banerjee, G., Kshetri, N., Odenwald, K., & Ratican, J. (2023). Architecting the metaverse: Blockchain and the financial and legal regulatory challenges of virtual real estate. *Journal of Intelligent Learning Systems and Applications*, *15*.

Lee, L. H., Bermejo, C., & Hui, P. (2023). The metaverse with life and everything: An overview of privacy, ethics, and governance. *Metaverse Communication and Computing Networks: Applications, Technologies, and Approaches*, 293–310.

Lin, Z., Xiangli, P., Li, Z., Liang, F., & Li, A. (2022, March). *Towards metaverse manufacturing: a blockchain-based trusted collaborative governance system* [Conference session]. The 2022 4th International Conference on Blockchain Technology (pp. 171–177).

Natalie Lacey. (2023). Are immersive experiences creating a new digital divide? https://www.weforum.org/agenda/2023/01/davos23-immersive-experiences-close-digital-divide/

Parigi, V., Leader, W., Geeta, P., & Kailasam, R. (2004). Ushering in Transparency for Good Governance, Centre for Good Governance, Hyderabad, 30 December 2012. http://www.cgg.gov.in/workingpapers/Ushering_in_Transparency.pdf

Park, S. M., & Kim, Y. G. (2022). A metaverse: Taxonomy, components, applications, and open challenges. *IEEE Access*, *10*, 4209–4251.

Phippen, A. (2022). Protecting children in the metaverse: it's easy to blame big tech, but we all have a role to play. *Parenting for a Digital Future* https://eprints.lse.ac.uk/114781/1/parenting4digitalfuture_2022_03_23.pdf.

Qasem, Z., Hmoud, H. Y., Hajawi, D. A., & Al Zoubi, J. Z. (2022, June). *The effect of technostress on cyberbullying in Metaverse social platforms* [Conference session]. International Working Conference on Transfer and Diffusion of IT (pp. 291–296). Springer International Publishing.

Qin, H. X., Wang, Y., & Hui, P. (2022). Identity, crimes, and law enforcement in the metaverse. arXiv preprint arXiv:2210.06134.

Rathore, B. (2018). Metaverse marketing: Novel challenges, opportunities, and strategic approaches. *Eduzone: International Peer Reviewed/Refereed Multidisciplinary Journal*, *7*(2), 72–82.

Sia, C. C. (2023). The role of legal governance framework in the metaverse world. In *Strategies and opportunities for technology in the metaverse world* (pp. 321–330). IGI Global.

Shashwat Sankranti. (2023). *Global Metaverse Leaders Emerge: Seoul, Dubai, and Santa Monica spearhead WEF report's list*. https://www.wionews.com/business-economy/global-metaverse-leaders-emerge-seoul-dubai-and-santa-monica-spearhead-wef-reports-list-664998

Turdialiev, M. (2023). Legal discussion of metaverse law. *International Journal of Cyber Law*, *1*(3).
Upadhyay, U., Kumar, A., Sharma, G., Gupta, B. B., Alhalabi, W. A., Arya, V., & Chui, K. T. (2023). Cyberbullying in the metaverse: A prescriptive perception on global information systems for user protection. *Journal of Global Information Management (JGIM)*, *31*(1), 1–25.
Wang, Y., Su, Z., Zhang, N., Xing, R., Liu, D., Luan, T. H., & Shen, X. (2022). A survey on metaverse: Fundamentals, security, and privacy. *IEEE Communications Surveys & Tutorials*, *25*(1), 319–352.
Wong, D., & Floridi, L. (2023). Meta's oversight board: A review and critical assessment. *Minds and Machines*, *33*(2), 261–284.
Wu, H., & Zhang, W. (2023). Digital identity, privacy security, and their legal safeguards in the Metaverse. *Security and Safety*, *2*, 2023011.
Yang, L. (2023). Recommendations for metaverse governance based on technical standards. *Humanities and Social Sciences Communications*, *10*(1), 1–10. https://doi.org/10.1057/s41599-023-01750-7

Chapter 16

Dark Side of the Metaverse and User Protection

Gaurav Duggal[a], Manoj Garg[a] and Achint Nigam[b]

[a]Jio Platforms Limited, Hyderabad, Telangana, India
[b]Birla Institute of Technology and Science, Pilani, Rajasthan, India

Abstract

In this chapter, we explore the dark side of the metaverse and the need for user protection. While the metaverse offers multiple opportunities it also poses significant risks for users, such as privacy concerns, addiction, harassment, and cyberbullying. First, we discuss the various threats that users may encounter such as online harassment, assaults, cyberbullying, hate speech, identity theft, and virtual property theft. As per the Center for Countering Digital Hate, an incident of violation occurs every seven minutes within VRChat, a popular virtual reality game. The level of misconduct in the metaverse can surpass the extent of internet harassment. Virtual reality gaming has been associated with various health issues like sleep deprivation, and insomnia as well as mental health concerns such as depression, anger, and anxiety. We examine how these issues may impact user's physical and mental health. The sensors and devices used in the metaverse collect a vast amount of user biometric data and spatial data. Interactions between users and metaverse could be leaked. We examine different methods that improve user protection, including everyone from enhanced security protocols via the application of privacy-enhanced technology to several avatars, two-factor authentication, and user educational and awareness programs. Moreover, we explore how the newest technologies, like blockchain and artificial intelligence, play a role in making user safety more important. We finished the course with the study of the case of Second Life, the virtual reality gaming platform, and pointing out some of the problems that exist within it.

Keywords: Metaverse; darkside; user protection; Second Life; blockchain; hate speech

1. Introduction

The Metaverse, an immersive virtual world, brought a new dimension to the way we engage with digital platforms and offered users a highly immersive and perceptible experience (Ning et al., 2023). Ultimately any word can be traced back to its origin which in this case is the book Snow Crash by Neal Stephenson published in 1992 (Stephenson, 1992). Stephenson shows the metaverse concept as a virtual world existing along with the physical world, where users interact with one another through some digital representations known as avatars. Facebook rebranded as Meta, which was revealed by Mark Zuckerberg in October 2021. After this name change, metaverse gets significant attention among diverse communities including academia and industry. It has unlimited opportunities in different domains such as entertainment (Niu & Feng, 2022), education, healthcare, travel, household, and commerce (Jeong et al., 2022). Users can get a good immersive experience and engagement in all these industries. Although the metaverse has significant advantages it also has a dark side (Frenkel & Browning, 2021). As per the Center for Countering Digital Hate (CCDH, 2021), a violation incident happens every seven minutes in the VRChat application, a widely popular virtual reality game.

In this chapter, we focus on the risks, challenges, and ethical issues of the metaverse. By showing readers the potential negative effects of the metaverse, we aim to make them see the multi-layered of this new tech and the path for the responsible usage and development of the metaverse. As users involved in the metaverse platform, there is a possibility to encounter privacy and security concerns (Wang et al., 2022). The interconnected nature of this virtual environment enables data collection and potential security breaches (Rickli & Mantellassi, 2022). Users' details, virtual identities, and activities become vulnerable to cyberattacks (Di Pietro & Cresci, 2021). Protecting user privacy and creating strong security measures in the metaverse is important to ensure a safe and trustworthy environment. Moreover, the metaverse attracts some challenges regarding addiction and excessive usage of this new technology (Dwivedi et al., 2022). As users get more interest and excitement in using the metaverse, they may neglect their relationships and real-world responsibilities. Understanding the reasons for users' excessive engagement and addiction within this metaverse and designing techniques to reduce its negative effects are needed for healthy and balanced metaverse usage.

Although the metaverse provides opportunities for social connectivity and interactions, it also attracts challenges regarding social and psychological impact. Heavy dependence on virtual interactions in the metaverse can lead to detachment from the real world. As users more concentrated on virtual interactions, some real-world skills such as face-to-face communication skills, and emotions may be compromised. So, it is essential to develop strategies that promote healthy interactions in the metaverse. The rest of the book chapter is organized as follows. Section 2 explores the dark side of the metaverse, Section 3 discusses the concept of user protection and corresponding strategies. A case study on Second Life, a metaverse platform, is discussed in Section 4, and finally, the conclusion of the book chapter is given in Section 5.

2. Exploring the Darkside of Metaverse

In this section, we describe the dark side of the metaverse usage. As the metaverse gets significant attention and popularity, it has some challenges that we face in the real world. Some concerns like online harassment, assaults, cyberbullying, hate speech, identity theft, etc., are increasing within the metaverse (Access Now, 2021). Now, we discuss these issues below.

2.1. Online Harassment

Online harassment (Frenkel & Browning, 2021; Molano & Grillio, 2023) in the metaverse is a significant threat. Harassment is possible in the metaverse like in the real world. Some users engage in harmful behavior with other fellow users in terms of cyberbullying, stalking, and the spread of false information. These types of behaviors can cause emotional depression, and damage the mental well-being of the affected individual. For a safer environment, it is crucial to establish strong mechanisms to address these issues.

2.2. Assaults

Assaults in the metaverse are a serious concern (Frenkel & Browning, 2021). These may lead to issues such as distress and trauma. Addressing these issues is very important to have a safe environment in the metaverse. Some solutions like reporting mechanisms should be implemented so that users can feel safe and actively participate in the metaverse.

2.3. Cyberbullying

Cyberbullying has become a significant issue (Qasem et al., 2022) in the metaverse. Reporting tools need to be developed by the metaverse service provider to report instances of cyberbullying. Yıldız and Tanyıldızı (2023) conducted a study analyzing the news containing the cyberbullying in metaverse. A total of six articles were identified about cyberbullying in the metaverse which are published in Turkish national press. The discourse analysis method is used to analyze these stories. Teodorov (2023) investigates solutions for preventing cybercrimes in the metaverse. This study also explores challenges in addressing cybercrimes in metaverse. Technology solutions such as blockchain and AI can be established apart from framing new laws for addressing cybercrimes. Stavola and Choi (2023) proposed a new framework to identify deepfakes in the metaverse. The data for the study include expert interviews from South Korea, online sources. This study utilizes routine activities theory and Eysenck's theory of criminality to design a framework to identify deepfakes in the metaverse.

2.4. Hate Speech

Hate speech exists in virtual communities in the metaverse (Shariff et al., 2023). Hate speech can be expressed in several forms, including images (Yang et al., 2019), text (Fortuna & Nunes, 2018), audio (Ibañez et al., 2021), video (Wu & Bhandary, 2020), memes (Kiela et al., 2020), cartoons (Bleich, 2012), symbols (Waseem & Hovy, 2016), and gestures (Gutiérrez, 2022). Users target other individuals based on their religion, race, and other characteristics in the metaverse. This disturbs the mental health and overall well-being of the victim and leads to leaving the virtual reality environment. Governments should frame laws to handle hate speech to have a healthier environment (George, 2015). To mitigate hate speech, various AI-based models can be implemented (Del Vigna et al., 2017).

Sanghvi et al. (2023) proposed a novel approach called "MetaHate" that uses artificial intelligence (AI) and blockchain (BC) to detect hate speech in a metaverse environment. Several machine learning models are used to analyze Hindi-English code-mixed datasets. The authors showed that combining AI and BC technologies effectively handles hate speech in the metaverse through their approach "MetaHate."

2.5. Identity Theft

Identity theft is a critical issue that needs to be dealt with in the metaverse to achieve a safe and secure experience. Users in the Metaverse platform employ avatars in their communications with others (Cheong, 2022). Hackers can also be after the IDs. Attacks such as cryptocurrency theft and privacy data theft can have devastating effects since both the financial and emotional well-being is being affected. Consequently, solid authentication processes and powerful algorithms need to be used to protect users against such types of theft.

George et al. (2019) explore the third dimension of verification in movement between the immersive virtual reality and real world. The presenters suggest a technique where the users have to recognize a set of 3D objects in a room to complete the authentication process. For assessing the factors that have an impact on interaction and security by phone entering IVR and real-world settings, a prototype was developed which was a 3D replica of a real room. On their conclusions, the authors obtained that 3D passwords are secure against shoulder surfing attacks.

2.6. Health Concerns

While the metaverse provides good immersive and engaging experiences, it also has negative effects on users' health (Huang et al., 2023). Users should balance in spending the time for virtual world and real world to maintain a healthy life. Sleep deprivation and insomnia are different health concerns related to metaverse. Now we describe these health issues below.

2.6.1. Sleep Deprivation

Users often spend excessive amounts of time in a metaverse environment which can lead to sleep deprivation. Excessive usage of the metaverse platform can impact regular sleep patterns. As a result, it negatively affects the health condition. Also, it leads to an increased risk of mental and physical health disorders. Maintaining sufficient rest is essential to have good health.

2.6.2. Insomnia

Insomnia is a sleep disorder characterized by difficulty falling asleep. Excessive spending time in the metaverse can affect the natural sleep-wake patterns which can lead to insomnia. To reduce the risk of insomnia, healthy sleeping habits should be established.

2.7. Mental Health Issues

The metaverse can have a serious impact on mental health in addition to health and threat issues (Adnan Kayyali., 2022). So, it is important to understand how metaverse affects the mental health to get a healthy metaverse experience. Depression, anger, and anxiety are various mental health issues associated with metaverse. Now we describe these mental health issues below.

2.7.1. Depression

Although, the metaverse provides good virtual interactions and connections, it can also lead to isolation and loneliness (Usmani et al., 2022). Excessive usage of metaverse environment can have depression symptoms. There should be a balance between real-world connections and virtual world connects to have a healthier life. To reduce the risk of depression in the metaverse, there is a need to give more importance to real world relationships and get counseling if needed.

2.7.2. Anger

Several factors like virtual conflicts, ability to hide behind anonymity can lead to anger in metaverse. Anger should be avoided or controlled to create healthy surroundings in metaverse. It is essential to establish conflict resolution strategies in the metaverse environment to handle anger issues.

2.7.3. Anxiety

Metaverse can have huge number of opportunities and experiences, which can trigger anxiety (Usmani et al., 2022). Some factors like fear of missing out (FOMO) and the pressure to keep updating with the latest technologies can lead to high levels of anxiety. To reduce the anxiety related symptoms, one should give importance to self-care, and have realistic boundaries.

Addressing these issues in the metaverse lead to safer and healthier virtual environment for all users.

3. User Protection

As more users interact with virtual environments, it is essential to have robust user protection mechanisms (Zhao, 2022). Companies that operate in the metaverse must give priority to user and data protection (Jamia Kanan, 2023). If the companies operating in the metaverse do not have strong mechanisms for user protection, it is difficult for them to survive in the long run. This is because users may lose trust in the corresponding metaverse platform and may leave that platform. Transparency should be maintained while collecting user data. While maintaining transparency, security measures should be built to protect user information. Balancing data privacy with user convenience is challenging. For example, Meta is taking steps to give importance to data protection and privacy through age verification procedures, privacy-enhancing technologies, and information transfer tools (Hadi Michel, 2021).

In this section, we discuss the measures to improve user protection in the metaverse. These security measures include advanced security protocols (Xu et al., 2022), privacy-enhanced technologies (Fiege et al., 1987), blockchain (Gadekallu et al., 2022), AI (Pham et al., 2022), and user education (Sebastian, 2022). Now, we describe these measures below.

3.1. Advanced Security Protocols

Users create virtual avatars and engage in various activities in the metaverse. These interactions are keep increasing. During these interactions there is a possibility that user data could be leaked and compromised. So, safeguarding user data is a critical aspect. Advanced security protocols (Falchuk et al., 2018; Park & Kim, 2022; Yfantis & Ntaliani, 2022) should be implemented to protect the sensitive information from attackers. These security protocols include strong authentication mechanisms (Kürtünlüoğlu et al., 2022) to prevent unauthorized access, secure communication channels (Lin et al., 2023) for safe data transmission, and robust encryption techniques (Xu et al., 2022) to protect the user data. For example, multi-factor authentication (MFA) (Sethuraman et al., 2022) can be employed to protect users from unauthorized access. Secure communication channels like HTTPs can be utilized to protect the data transmission between metaverse platform servers and users. End-to-end encryption can be employed between the user's device and metaverse servers. By implementing strong security measures, we can build confidence in user.

Avatar's two factors ought be deployed and the sending out service suppliers should protect information (Park & Kim, 2022). Falchuk et al. (2018) suggested that there are two approaches to ensuring privacy security. The first method pointed "cloud of clones." At this stage, the aim is to create a rather intricate situation where the user is not able to determine the exact location, stances, and habits with any degree of accuracy. The program produces such a number of avatars that resemble your morning face. The second scheme stands for my keeping of a private memorabilia. The user can make it out for the piece of virtual world and may request the private copy may be created. For instance, if the consumer wants to have the shopping experience in private then the service provider can provide the sample of the virtual store just for the consumer. The online store's virtual items will include some of the things that the user wants to buy without the others being exposed to such things. Virtually the technique that is presented by Yfantis and Ntalianis (2022) constitutes the same digital twin avatars that will reside in the parallel metaverse as well. The digital twin avatar is a similar avatar created for an individual as well as the current metaverse where a parallel virtual world is created which is the other element of Park and Kim (2022) work. The authors develop an enhanced measure by creating intended behavior for avatars and the same virtual world. If a user wants to be there instead of his digital twin avatar in the parallel metaverse that is made of a combination of the other metaverse he may be invisible in the basic virtual world and appear in the other parallel metaverse. On the contrary, the absence of the possibility to follow the path of the user's movements and the activities of the user is the disadvantage of this option. Another is his digital twin avatar can be in the actual metaverse and his twin avatar in the parallel metaverse. At the same time, the anonymity of users poses a challenge in carrying out tracking of their activities.

AES (Advanced Encryption Standard) algorithm (Abur et al., 2022) can be applied to obscure names of people in the online world of services. CryptoImg was introduced by Ziad et al. (2016) to tackle the stream of security concerns of the current cloud services. CryptoImg is a public domain, programming toolkit. This is the place where the users do the necessary operations on the ciphered photos using homomorphic encryption algorithms. According to the study by Yang et al. (2023), they designed a reliable authentication framework for individual avatars' traceability in the metaverse. Rather than using singular-identity avatars, the authors introduced detail-oriented double check for the avatar's context.

3.2. Privacy-Enhanced Technologies

User privacy is an essential aspect of user protection in the metaverse. One way to protect the user is to anonymize the user. Privacy-enhanced technologies (PET) are used to preserve the user anonymity. Zero-knowledge proofs is one of the techniques that belongs to privacy-enhanced technology. These zero-knowledge proofs enables users to prove the authenticity of information without revealing the actual information itself. Various types of data such as biometric and spatial information are captured by extended reality (XR) devices to provide an immersive experience to the users (Fernandez & Hui, 2022). This could lead to compromising of users' data. Sensors in XR devices collect sensitive information by scanning surroundings. Head-mounted displays (HMDs) can gather other information such as eye tracking which may reveal some personal preferences. PET is used to protect sensitive data before sharing it with cloud services.

Nyyssönen et al. (2023) proposed a method for anonymous collaboration in the metaverse. The authors performed experiments in a custom-made metaverse. They observed the anonymous users' interactions in a custom-made metaverse. The study found that sound modulation can be applied to anonymize the users to protect the user's privacy to some extent. Nair et al. (2023) present an approach based on incognito mode in virtual reality. The authors use epsilon-differential privacy to protect the sensitive data attributes. They also developed a universal Unity VR plugin called "MetaGaurd." This plugin is compatible with many VR applications.

3.3. Blockchain Technology

The blockchain as a system allows for numerous benefits for the users of the virtual reality space. These are largely attributable to the peer-to-peer, autonomous and verifiable aspects of blockchain tech (Gadekallu et al., 2022). This astounding ability of the Blockchain technology to keep the records of the user interaction unalterable is the main point of discussion. Scammers can process payments securely and quickly because all transactions are to be validated and confirmed by users. Smart contracts have the ability to denominate and secure the digital assets. Building trust in the communication and commerce between the different parts of the Metaverse ecosystem is made possible by blockchain technology. It is leading into virtual services, thus, offering users additional ways of using more activities in the metaverse. Decentraland, a metaverse mode, employs blockchain technology for the purchase and sale of virtual land.

The blockchain feature of the smart card platform ensures secure mutual authentication (Ryu et al., 2022). The proposed method for this will involve the usage of biometric technology and Elliptic Curve Cryptography (ECC) in a way that ensures secure communication between the individuals and the platform servers. Yadav et al. (2023) offer a solution to blockchain authentication method in metaverse. This proof mechanism lays the foundation for zero knowledge. The security is BAN maintained, it is further made certain through Scyther tool and another tool called AVISPA which they use to test protocols and applications of internet. The outcomes show that the proposed the techniques are suitable to diminish the various threats of the researchers presented their solution on the market and demonstrated that their method beats current protocols.

Shen et al. (2020) described blockchain-driven security system for the cross-domain situation of the industrial IoT. The authentication process has an identity-based signature which is used in the next step. The privacy protection mechanism as a primary function of the identity management mechanism designedly prevents devices from being disclosed. As illustrated by Kim et al. (2023), blockchain has a unique capability to deliver a secure and privacy-preserving authentication. The authentication method performs which enables the SHAI skeptics to log in and use the XING services without notifying the details. The suggested model keeps up with privacy issues and also offers several advantages for security purposes compared to other available options of credential accesses.

3.4. AI-Powered Security Solutions

AI techniques (Meurisch & Mühlhäuser, 2021; Pham et al., 2022; Pooyandeh et al., 2022) discover that AI is the main component for the safety of the users in the metaverse. The threats which might be unauthorized access, the phishing attacks, the malware attacks can be done through the AI security processes. The metaverse employs AI such as transformers, RNNs, CNNs, random forest, and many others, to prevent attackers accessing user data. The research is now focused on more advanced AI algorithms such as generative adversarial networks (GAN) in the search for the deep fake detectors.

Analyzing the user behavior patterns and anomalies with AI models is one possible algorithmic approach. To illustrate this, let me give you the following example: if a particular IP address has an unusually high number of failed sign-ins, an AI-equipped system will be able to block that IP address. It is mainly due to the fact that the intruder may go further, targeting the system through advanced techniques. The network might add some extra video verification after asking the customer to give the identity. Through the tremendous data analysis, AI can capture and learn fast the new intrusions and thus always stay up-to-date with innovative attacks. This enables the real-time identification of threats and sets in proactive counter measures to avert security breaches therefore providing the safety of the metaverse users.

3.5. User Education and Awareness Programs

User education and awareness programs play an important role in user protection in the metaverse (Sebastian, 2022). Online safety awareness programs should be conducted by metaverse platform providers to create awareness among the users. These programs include educating users regarding creating unique and strong passwords, being cautious when sharing personal information, and avoiding clicking suspicious links. If the users click suspicious links unknowingly there is a possibility of gaining the personal and financial information by hackers. So, users should be very careful while clicking the suspicious links. They should observe the links for its originality before clicking. By creating awareness and providing users with the required information, they can make informed decisions to protect their security. As a result, we can build a safe and secure environment for all users.

4. Case Study: Second Life

Besides that, we will expose the problems of the metaverse in relation to Second Life. Second Life is a virtual reality gaming platform designed by Linden Lab and officially launched in 2003. Avatars are created and customized by users who interact with other users and engage in different activities in the virtual universe. We performed the analysis of the articles which were on the ongoing events in the Second Life and the probable impact of Second Life on users. This case study explores some issues such as addiction, privacy concerns, harassment, and their impact on mental and physical health. While Second Life offers a platform for creativity, socialization, and commerce, there is also a dark side of it that affects the individuals' real lives.

4.1. Addiction and Excessive Engagement

Although Second Life provides opportunities for creativity, social interaction, and communication, it also has risks related to addiction and excessive engagement. Users may become addicted due to its metaverse experience. There are several factors such as virtual achievements, desire for social interaction, and escaping the real-world problems that can lead to addiction in Second Life. Excessive engagement in Second Life can lead to negative effects for users. It affects mental and emotional health, as users may become isolated from real life. According to an advisor on the second life community page (Angelikiinha, 2019), excessive engagement in Second Life (SL) and neglecting real-life duties might have serious implications. Addicting to SL "Skill Games" and losing money might have financial effects. It is necessary to understand all the risks associated with SL and maintain a healthy life.

4.2. Impact on Real Life

Addiction to Second Life can have negative consequences. Excessive engagement with the Second Life often leads to neglect of real-life responsibilities, such as work, relationships, and personal well-being. Users may experience degrading mental health, broken relationships, and social isolation. These virtual worlds attract such that it may not be possible for users to disconnect completely from them.

4.3. Impact on Relationships

According to a Reddit user (Estoric Engima, 2010), online gaming can impact real-life relationships, as evident in a case where a person's girlfriend is engrossed in the game Second Life. There are two problems causing distress: her excessive gaming and her virtual relationship within the game. She spends all day playing, making it difficult to spend time together. Additionally, she has a virtual husband, leading to feelings of neglect and potential infidelity. The partner's concerns are valid as emotions can develop within virtual relationships. It is crucial to have open communication and find a balance between gaming interests and real-life connections. Compromises and professional help may be necessary to resolve these issues and foster a healthy relationship.

According to an article on The Guardian.com (Morris, 2018), a British couple is getting divorced after the wife discovers her husband's online affair in the virtual world of Second Life. In this virtual reality game, players create avatars and interact with others. The husband's avatar had a relationship with another player's character, leading to real-life consequences. This incident highlights the impact of virtual relationships on real-life marriages.

4.4. Obsolete Software and an Emphasis on Sexual Activities

Another dark side of Second Life is its obsolete software as well as the platform's emphasis on sexual activities. Some users on this platform claim that the Second Life software is not updated to the latest technologies and missing the user expectations. This resulted in dissatisfaction for users who want to have a wide range of virtual world experiences. There are some issues with sexual content and activities in Second Life. Some critics claim that Linden Labs prioritized the adult entertainment business, keeping aside the other potential uses of the platform. This emphasis led to disappointment among Second Life users who joined for non-sexual reasons. An article (Homayoun, 2017) from The New York Times explored how some users become heavily invested in their virtual identities, leading to a sense of disconnect from their actual selves. According to a review by a parent, In Second Life there is a significant problem with explicit content and sexualization. Avatars often engage in graphic activities, even in areas that are supposed to be suitable for all audiences. This raises concerns about the platform's content moderation procedures.

4.5. Privacy and Security Concerns

Second Life raises concerns regarding privacy and security. Instances of virtual harassment, stalking, and even real-life identity theft have been reported. In 2018, The Independent newspaper reported on a case where a Second Life user's personal information was stolen and used to harass them offline. Privacy and security concerns in Second Life pose significant risks to users. According to an article on techcrunch.com (Techcrunch, 2006), a recent security breach of Second Life, a high-profile virtual reality game, has raised serious concerns about the protection of user data within the platform. This breach, the first of its kind since Second Life's inception in 2003, compromised a database containing unencrypted user information, including names, addresses, encrypted passwords, and encrypted payment details

According to a review by a child, Second Life provides no customer support (Beth1226, 2022). They take your money and then close your account without any assistance or resolution. They seem to ignore complaints, especially regarding sexual predators on the platform. If you try to speak up, they will close your account and block you, preventing you from making any complaints. She has come across many similar experiences where Second Life fails to provide customer support and keeps all the items you have paid for when they close your account. In her opinion, this is an awful game, and she strongly advises against playing Second Life to avoid becoming a victim of their practices. In a recent review by a person called Callan (123KAL, 2016), he mentioned how Second Life allows for great creativity and customization but lacks safety measures. There are no moderators, and new users are often targeted by older ones. Stalking is ignored, and there's no way to contact Linden Labs for help. Reports are filed but no feedback is given, and there's no direct support for dealing with abuse. Predators prey on unsuspecting new users, and there is no warning about the safety issues in Second Life. Even long-time users and those who have invested a lot in the platform receive no assistance when facing harassment or stalking. Second Life lacks a proper moderation mechanism and handles safety poorly. It's disappointing that such a creative and popular virtual world neglects to address these important issues.

Linden Lab is sued by its ex-employee on the basis of different claims (Paris Martineau, 2019). The Linden Lab Corporation is the mother company of Second Life. Such problems involve hacking of systems for cyber security reasons, breach of anti-money laundering regulations, data misuse, and child abuse. Allegedly, she encountered negativity when she raised these questions to the top managers of the company.

5. Conclusion

In this chapter, we have addressed the issues related to the dark side of the metaverse. These issues include cyberbullying, assaults, mental and emotional health issues, etc. We described user protection and explored the different technologies like blockchain, AI, and privacy-enhanced technologies to safeguard the users. Next, we have examined the negative implications of the metaverse through a case study on Second Life.

We observed that there are different negative concerns associated with Second Life. These concerns include mental health problems, relationships, privacy, and overall well-being. The case study is done through an in-depth review of real-life examples and articles. Addiction and excessive engagement are two major concerns in Second Life. Real-life relationships may be in trouble because of excessive engagement. Few users are satisfied with the platform's concentration on sexual activities. User education, responsible usage, increased safety standards, and privacy protection are important steps toward mitigating the negative impact and establishing a healthy virtual environment

References

Abur, M., Junaidu, S., & Obiniyi, A. (2022). Personal identifiable information privacy model for securing of users' attributes transmitted to a federated cloud environment. *International Journal of Information Technology, 14*(1), 421–435.

Access Now. (2021, December 10). *Virtual worlds, real people: Human rights in the metaverse*. https://www.accessnow.org/human-rights-metaverse-virtual-augmented-reality/

Adnan Kayyali. (2022). *The dark side of the metaverse*. https://insidetelecom.com/the-dark-side-of-the-metaverse/

Angelikiinha. (2019, August 23). *Is bad design ruining SL?* https://community.secondlife.com/forums/topic/441970-is-bad-design-ruining-sl/

Beth1226. (2022). *Parent and kid reviews on second life – crooks*. https://www.commonsensemedia.org/website-reviews/second-life/user-reviews/adult

Bleich, E. (2012). Free speech or hate speech? The Danish cartoon controversy in the European legal context. In K. R. Khory (Ed.), *Global migration: Challenges in the twenty-first century* (pp. 113–128). Palgrave Macmillan US. Springer.

CCDH. (2021). *New research shows metaverse is not safe for kids*. https://counterhate.com/blog/new-research-shows-metaverse-is-not-safe-for-kids/

Cheong, B. C. (2022). Avatars in the metaverse: Potential legal issues and remedies. *International Cybersecurity Law Review*, 1–28.

Del Vigna, F., Cimino, A., Dell'Orletta, F., Petrocchi, M., & Tesconi, M. (2017, January). *Hate me, hate me not: Hate speech detection on Facebook* [Conference session]. Proceedings of the first Italian conference on cybersecurity (ITASEC17) (pp. 86–95).

Di Pietro, R., & Cresci, S. (2021, December). *Metaverse: Security and privacy issues* [Conference session]. 2021 Third IEEE International Conference on Trust, Privacy and Security in Intelligent Systems and Applications (TPS-ISA) (pp. 281–288). IEEE.

Dwivedi, Y. K., Hughes, L., Baabdullah, A. M., Ribeiro-Navarrete, S., Giannakis, M., Al-Debei, M. M., Dennehy, D., Metri, B., Buhalis, D., Cheung, C. M. K., Conboy, K., Doyle, R., Dubey, R., Dutot, V., Felix, R., Goyal, D.P., Gustafsson, A., Hinsch, C., Jebabli, I., ... Wamba, S.F. (2022). Metaverse beyond the hype: Multidisciplinary perspectives on emerging challenges, opportunities, and agenda for research, practice and policy. *International Journal of Information Management*, 66, 102542.

Estoric Engima. (2010). *Secondlife is ruining my relationship and I want the opinions of some gamers about my situation*. https://www.reddit.com/r/gaming/comments/emkic/secondlife_is_ruining_my_relationship_and_i_want/?rdt=63965

Falchuk, B., Loeb, S., & Neff, R. (2018). The social metaverse: Battle for privacy. *IEEE Technology and Society Magazine*, 37(2), 52–61.

Fernandez, C. B., & Hui, P. (2022, July). *Life, the Metaverse and everything: An overview of privacy, ethics, and governance in Metaverse* [Conference session]. 2022 IEEE 42nd International Conference on Distributed Computing Systems Workshops (ICDCSW) (pp. 272–277). IEEE.

Fiege, U., Fiat, A., & Shamir, A. (1987, January). *Zero knowledge proofs of identity* [Conference session]. Proceedings of the nineteenth annual ACM symposium on Theory of computing (pp. 210–217).

Fortuna, P., & Nunes, S. (2018). A survey on automatic detection of hate speech in text. *ACM Computing Surveys (CSUR)*, 51(4), 1–30.

Frenkel, S., & Browning, K. (2021). The Metaverse's dark side: Here come harassment and assaults. *The New York Times*. https://www.nytimes.com/2021/12/30/technology/metaverseharassment-assaults.html

Gadekallu, T. R., Huynh-The, T., Wang, W., Yenduri, G., Ranaweera, P., Pham, Q. V., Costa, D. B. D., & Liyanage, M. (2022). Blockchain for the metaverse: A review. *arXiv preprint arXiv:2203.09738*.

George, C. (2015). Hate speech law and policy. *The International Encyclopedia of Digital Communication and Society*, 1–10.

George, C., Khamis, M., Buschek, D., & Hussmann, H. (2019, March). *Investigating the third dimension for authentication in immersive virtual reality and in the real world* [Conference session]. 2019 IEEE conference on virtual reality and 3d user interfaces (vr) (pp. 277–285). IEEE.

Gutiérrez, Á. L. (2022). Non-verbal communication in hate and sexist speeches: Hate and sexist discourses without words. Visual review. *International Visual Culture Review/Revista Internacional de Cultura Visual*, 12(1), 1–20.

Hadi Michel. (2021). *Improving user experience in our transfer your information tool*. Retrieved December 1, 2023 from https://about.fb.com/news/2021/08/improving-user-experience-in-our-transfer-your-information-tool/

Homayoun, A. (2017). The Secret Social Media Lives of Teenagers. *The New York Times*. https://www.nytimes.com/2017/06/07/well/family/the-secret-social-media-lives-of-teenagers.html

Huang, Y., Li, Y. J., & Cai, Z. (2023). Security and privacy in metaverse: A comprehensive survey. *Big Data Mining and Analytics*, 6(2), 234–247.

Ibañez, M., Sapinit, R., Reyes, L. A., Hussien, M., Imperial, J. M., & Rodriguez, R. (2021, December). *Audio-based hate speech classification from online short-form videos* [Conference session]. 2021 International Conference on Asian Language Processing (IALP) (pp. 72–77). IEEE.

Jamia Kanan. (2023). *Metaverse Dangers: How to protect brands from the dark side*. https://sproutsocial.com/insights/metaverse-dangers/

Jeong, H., Yi, Y., & Kim, D. (2022). An innovative e-commerce platform incorporating metaverse to live commerce. *International Journal of Innovative Computing, Information and Control*, 18(1), 221–229.

Kiela, D., Firooz, H., Mohan, A., Goswami, V., Singh, A., Ringshia, P., & Testuggine, D. (2020). The hateful memes challenge: Detecting hate speech in multimodal memes. *Advances in Neural Information Processing Systems*, *33*, 2611–2624.

Kim, M., Oh, J., Son, S., Park, Y., Kim, J., & Park, Y. (2023). Secure and privacy-preserving authentication scheme using decentralized identifier in metaverse environment. *Electronics*, *12*(19), 4073.

Kürtünlüoğlu, P., Akdik, B., & Karaarslan, E. (2022). Security of virtual reality authentication methods in metaverse: An overview. *arXiv preprint arXiv:2209.06447*.

Lin, Y., Du, H., Niyato, D., Nie, J., Zhang, J., Cheng, Y., & Yang, Z. (2023). Blockchain-aided secure semantic communication for AI-generated content in metaverse. *IEEE Open Journal of the Computer Society*, *4*, 72–83.

Meurisch, C., & Mühlhäuser, M. (2021). Data protection in AI services: A survey. *ACM Computing Surveys (CSUR)*, *54*(2), 1–38.

Molano, J. C., & Grillo, M. (2023). Metaverse and virtual reality: Is it possible to be sexually harassed in a non-physical space? In R. Hassan & K. Patel (Eds.), *Digital media & pandemic: experience & ameliorations* (p. 103), The International Institute of Knowledge Management (TIIKM).

Morris, S. (2018). Second Life affair leads to real life divorce. *The Guardian*. https://www.theguardian.com/technology/2008/nov/13/second-life-divorce

Nair, V. C., Munilla-Garrido, G., & Song, D. (2023, October). *Going incognito in the metaverse: Achieving theoretically optimal privacy-usability tradeoffs in VR* [Conference session]. Proceedings of the 36th Annual ACM Symposium on User Interface Software and Technology (pp. 1–16).

Ning, H., Wang, H., Lin, Y., Wang, W., Dhelim, S., Farha, F., Ding, J., & Daneshmand, M. (2023). A survey on the metaverse: The state-of-the-art, technologies, applications, and challenges. *IEEE Internet of Things Journal*, *10*(16), 14671–14688.

Niu, X., & Feng, W. (2022, June). *Immersive entertainment environments-from theme parks to metaverse* [Conference session]. Distributed, Ambient and Pervasive Interactions. Smart Environments, Ecosystems, and Cities: 10th International Conference, DAPI 2022, Held as Part of the 24th HCI International Conference, HCII 2022, Virtual Event, June 26–July 1, 2022, Proceedings, Part I (pp. 392–403). Springer International Publishing.

Nyyssönen, T., Heimo, O. I., Helle, S., Lehtonen, T., Mäkilä, T., & Jauhiainen, J. S. (2023). Anonymous collaboration in metaverse. *Human-Centered Metaverse and Digital Environments*, *99*(99).

Paris Martineau. (2019, August 16). *A former infosec director at Linden Lab alleges the company mishandled user data and turned a blind eye to simulated sex acts involving children*. https://tinyurl.com/linden-lab

Park, S. M., & Kim, Y. G. (2022). A metaverse: Taxonomy, components, applications, and open challenges. *IEEE Access*, *10*, 4209–4251.

Pham, Q. V., Pham, X. Q., Nguyen, T. T., Han, Z., & Kim, D. S. (2022). Artificial intelligence in the metaverse: A survey. *arXiv e-prints*, arXiv-2202.

Pooyandeh, M., Han, K. J., & Sohn, I. (2022). Cybersecurity in the AI-based metaverse: A survey. *Applied Sciences*, *12*(24), 12993.

Qasem, Z., Hmoud, H. Y., Hajawi, D. A., & Al Zoubi, J. Z. (2022, October). *The effect of technostress on cyberbullying in metaverse social platforms* [Conference session]. Co-creating for Context in the Transfer and Diffusion of IT: IFIP WG 8.6 International Working Conference on Transfer and Diffusion of IT, TDIT 2022, Maynooth, Ireland, June 15–16, 2022, Proceedings (pp. 291–296). Springer International Publishing.

Rickli, J. M., & Mantellassi, F. (2022). *Our digital future: The security implications of Metaverses*. Geneva, GCSP Strategic Security Analysis.

Ryu, J., Son, S., Lee, J., Park, Y., & Park, Y. (2022). Design of secure mutual authentication scheme for metaverse environments using blockchain. *IEEE Access*, *10*, 9894498958.

Sanghvi, H., Bhavsar, R., Hundlani, V., Gohil, L., Vyas, T., Nair, A., Desai, S., Jadav, N. K., Tanwar, S., Sharma, R., & Yamsani, N. (2023). MetaHate: AI-based hate speech detection for secured online gaming in metaverse using blockchain. *Security and Privacy*, 7(2), e343.

Sebastian, G. (2022). A study on metaverse awareness, cyber risks, and steps for increased adoption. *International Journal of Security and Privacy in Pervasive Computing (IJSPPC)*, 14(1), 1–11.

Sethuraman, S. C., Mitra, A., Galada, G., Ghosh, A., & Anitha, S. (2022, December). *Metakey: A novel and seamless passwordless multifactor authentication for metaverse*. 2022 IEEE International Symposium on Smart Electronic Systems (iSES) (pp. 662–664). IEEE.

Shariff, S., Dietzel, C., Macaulay, K., & Sanabria, S. (2023). Misogyny in the metaverse: Leveraging policy and education to address technology-facilitated violence. In *Cyberbullying and online harms* (pp. 103–116). Routledge.

Shen, M., Liu, H., Zhu, L., Xu, K., Yu, H., Du, X., & Guizani, M. (2020). Blockchain-assisted secure device authentication for cross-domain industrial IoT. *IEEE Journal on Selected Areas in Communications*, 38(5), 942–954

Stavola, J., & Choi, K. S. (2023). Victimization by deepfake in the metaverse: Building a practical management framework. *International Journal of Cybersecurity Intelligence & Cybercrime*, 6(2), 2.

Stephenson, N. (1992). *Snow crash*. Bantam Books.

Techcrunch. (2006, September 9). *Metaverse breached: Second Life customer database hacked*. https://techcrunch.com/2006/09/08/metaverse-breached-second-life-customer-database-hacked/

Teodorov, A. V. (2023, May). *Cybercrimes in the metaverse: Challenges and solutions* [Conference session]. Proceedings of the International Conference on Cybersecurity and Cybercrime-2023 (pp. 209–215). Asociatia Romana pentru Asigurarea Securitatii Informatiei.

Usmani, S. S., Sharath, M., & Mehendale, M. (2022). Future of mental health in the metaverse. *General Psychiatry*, 35(4), e100825.

Wang, Y., Su, Z., Zhang, N., Xing, R., Liu, D., Luan, T. H., & Shen, X. (2022). A survey on metaverse: Fundamentals, security, and privacy. *IEEE Communications Surveys & Tutorials*, 25, 319.

Waseem, Z., & Hovy, D. (2016, June). *Hateful symbols or hateful people? predictive features for hate speech detection on Twitter*. Proceedings of the NAACL student research workshop (pp. 88–93).

Wu, C. S., & Bhandary, U. (2020, December). *Detection of hate speech in videos using machine learning* [Conference Session]. 2020 International Conference on Computational Science and Computational Intelligence (CSCI) (pp. 585–590). IEEE.

Xu, H., Li, Z., Li, Z., Zhang, X., Sun, Y., & Zhang, L. (2022, May). *Metaverse native communication: A blockchain and spectrum prospective* [Conference session]. 2022 IEEE International Conference on Communications Workshops (ICC Workshops) (pp. 7–12). IEEE.

Yadav, A. K., Braeken, A., Ylianttila, M., & Liyanage, M. (2023, June). *A blockchain-based authentication protocol for metaverse environments using a zero knowledge proof* [Conference session]. 2023 IEEE International Conference on Metaverse Computing, Networking and Applications (MetaCom) (pp. 242–249). IEEE.

Yang, F., Peng, X., Ghosh, G., Shilon, R., Ma, H., Moore, E., & Predovic, G. (2019, August). *Exploring deep multimodal fusion of text and photo for hate speech classification* [Conference session]. Proceedings of the third workshop on abusive language online (pp. 11–18).

Yang, K., Zhang, Z., Tian, Y., & Ma, J. (2023). A secure authentication framework to guarantee the traceability of avatars in metaverse. *IEEE Transactions on Information Forensics and Security*. 18, 3817–3832.

Yıldız, İ., & Tanyıldızı, N. İ. (2023). An analysis of news containing cyberbullying in the metaverse. In G. Sarı (Ed.), *Handbook of research on bullying in media and beyond* (pp. 196–214). IGI Global.

Yfantis, V., & Ntalianis, K. (2022). *Exploring privacy measures in the community metaverse.* IEEE Technology Policy and Ethics. IEEE.

Zhao, R., Zhang, Y., Zhu, Y., Lan, R., & Hua, Z. (2022). Metaverse: Security and privacy concerns. *arXiv preprint arXiv:2203.03854*.

Ziad, M. T. I., Alanwar, A., Alzantot, M., & Srivastava, M. (2016, October). *Cryptoimg: Privacy preserving processing over encrypted images* [Conference session]. *2016 IEEE Conference on Communications and Network Security (CNS)* (pp. 570–575). IEEE.

123KAL. (2016, May 13). *Second life – Most helpful*. https://www.metacritic.com/game/pc/second-life/user-reviews

Printed and bound by CPI Group (UK) Ltd, Croydon, CR0 4YY
21/11/2024